PLENTY OF BLAME TO GO AROUND

Jeb Stuart's Controversial Ride to Gettysburg

Eric J. Wittenberg & J. David Petruzzi

SB

Savas Beatie

New York and California

Cataloging-in-Publication Data is available from the Library of Congress.

ISBN 1-932714-20-0

05 04 03 02 01 5 4 3 2 1
First edition, first printing

SB

Published by
Savas Beatie LLC
521 Fifth Avenue, Suite 3400
New York, NY 10175
(E-mail) editorial@savasbeatie.com

Savas Beatie titles are available at special discounts for bulk purchases in the United States by corporations, institutions, and other organizations. For more details, please contact Special Sales, P.O. Box 4527, El Dorado Hills, CA 95762, or you may e-mail us at sales@savasbeatie.com, or visit our website at www.savasbeatie.com for additional information.

Cover Art: "The Shelling of Carlisle — July 1-2, 1863," by Ron Lesser. © 2003 Ron Lesser. All rights reserved.

The original oil painting was commissioned by F&M Trust of Chambersburg, Pennsylvania, for the 2003 Commemoration of the 140th Anniversary of J.E.B. Stuart's Shelling of Carlisle in July 1863. The painting (41"x27") is in the permanent collection of the Cumberland County Historical Society in Carlisle. Limited Edition prints are available at the society or through the Chambersburg Heritage Center, Chambersburg, Pennsylvania. For more information on the artist, please go to www.ronlesser.com.

This book is dedicated to the memory of the men
of both sides who followed the guidon.

It is also respectfully dedicated to the memory of Brian C. Pohanka,
historian, mentor, preservationist, and friend.
Your wise counsel will be missed.

Major General James Ewell Brown (JEB) Stuart, General Lee's
cavalry chief and commander of the expedition.

Contents

Contents (continued)

Maps and illustrations have been placed throughout
the text for the convenience of the reader.

Preface

The Gettysburg Campaign has had more than its share of controversies, many of which began before the guns fell silent. From the time the confident and stalwart Jeb Stuart was surprised by Alfred Pleasonton's Union troopers at Beverly Ford in the predawn of June 9, 1863, near Brandy Station, Virginia, until after Stuart's arrival on the Gettysburg battlefield late on the afternoon of July 2, the Southern cavalry chieftain was the subject of much chatter among the Confederate upper crust. Not much of it was complimentary. Southern newspapers lambasted Stuart for allowing himself to be surprised by the Federals at his own headquarters on Fleetwood Hill, and tongues wagged among the infantry that perhaps Stuart was not up to his former game.

Debate over the merits and results of Stuart's ride to Pennsylvania was, and still is, a virtual cottage industry. Not long after the war, as Gettysburg evolved into "the battle that lost the war" (whether justified or not), arguments raged among veterans in newspapers, magazines, articles, books, and face-to-face. Non-veteran commentators of all types got in on the act.

Any serious treatment of the Gettysburg Campaign must, out of sheer necessity, mention in some form the impact Stuart's ride had on the outcome of the three-day conflagration in Pennsylvania. Today, an increasingly educated reading public demands it. To do otherwise is to leave a gap so large that the work itself will collapse into it, leaving the reader feeling somehow unfulfilled. Discussions about Stuart and his proud horsemen—the "eyes and ears" of Robert E. Lee's army—and their detachment from it during the ride north have become an integral thread in the fabric known as the Gettysburg Campaign.

In fact, entire books have been devoted to this subject. In the middle of the postwar controversy among the veterans came John Singleton Mosby's *Stuart's Cavalry in the Gettysburg Campaign* (1908). An icon of the Confederacy and southern pluck—and one of Stuart's most stalwart supporters—Mosby argued for Stuart's case as well as any lawyer could hope. As would be expected, the appearance of the book stirred up the hornet's nest anew and left surviving veterans (notably officers who had served under Lee and Stuart) and anyone else with an opinion, freshly invigorated to debate the issues in public speeches and a new round of newspaper articles.

More recently, Mark Nesbitt, in *Saber and Scapegoat: J.E.B. Stuart and the Gettysburg Controversy* (1994) took up Stuart's defense with fresh perspectives on the tactics of Stuart's ride and the ensuing debates between the cavalier's supporters and detractors. In many ways Nesbitt's book updated Mosby's work but missed out on many primary sources that have surfaced in the years since the publication of the partisan's tome in 1908. Because of this, we concluded there was more work yet to be done in order to tell this story as fully and as completely as it deserves.

We did not set out to write a book that dealt so heavily in the controversy itself. Our initial intention was to produce a detailed tactical treatment of the battles and skirmishes that Stuart's brigades fought along the way to Gettysburg, with but a cursory discussion of the controversy in a final chapter. Although several good articles and books have recently appeared dealing with Stuart's scraps with Federal cavalry during his ride, we were aware of many untapped resources in manuscript collections, historical repositories, and veterans' memoirs and letters that were not fully utilized, if utilized at all. We have been collecting these sources jointly and separately over a combined thirty years of studying these actions. Even George Rummel's wonderful and indispensable book *Cavalry on the Roads to Gettysburg: Kilpatrick at Hanover and Hunterstown* (2000) doesn't take advantage of many of these resources. Precious little has been written about the fight at Westminster or the shelling of Carlisle. Nothing at all has been written about the critical skirmish at Fairfax Court House, which occurred even before Stuart crossed the Potomac River. And so we set out to write a detailed study of the entirety of Stuart's advance to Pennsylvania using every reliable resource—the more obscure the better—we could find, and leave much of the controversy for perhaps another book.

About halfway into the project, however, we quickly realized that the magic and mystery of those days drew us in like a spider's web; we were joyfully stuck in its grasp with no hope of escaping. As we found more and more sources (many of which began to change and enhance our opinions), and delved deeper into the tactics and mechanics of the ride, we discovered we could not separate the tactical treatment from the controversy and do either one of them justice. We therefore determined to take this book to the level at which we now present it to you.

We think we have prepared the most detailed tactical discussion of these events ever attempted, and draw upon a myriad of published and unpublished primary and secondary sources to do so. Those sources helped us flesh out these events and bring them to life. We have also tackled the controversy that has evolved over the years—much more deeply than we had originally intended. After much discussion, we decided to include the words of the various commentators who have addressed the raid verbatim, so that our readers can determine the merits of their arguments for themselves. Three full chapters are devoted to the controversy. The first deals with early critics, the second with early supporters, and the third with how modern historians and writers interpret these events. We conclude with our own analysis of these events, all of which taken together give rise to the title of this book. We have amply illustrated the book with photos of participants, important locations, and contemporary illustrations. A number of detailed maps have been included to help readers better understand the narrative.

Acknowledgements

The interpretations set forth herein are our own, and we accept full responsibility for them as such. If there are errors in the telling of this story, they are our errors, and we hope we can be forgiven for them.

As with any project of this nature, we have a considerable number of people to thank for their support, and we hope that we haven't missed anyone. In case we have missed you, please overlook our oversight and know that we appreciate your assistance. We confess that, without exception, this work would have been far less than what it is without your generous and gracious assistance.

Gettysburg Campaign historian and author Tom Ryan read several early drafts of the manuscript and offered numerous suggestions that proved very helpful. Tom is also responsible for pointing out the groundbreaking entry in the John B. Jones diary that proves once and for all that Stuart did send word to his superiors of the northward movement of Joe Hooker's Army of the Potomac, which directly contradicts some of the claims of his detractors. We believe every other historian has overlooked this gem.

Scott Mingus, Sr. of nearby York knows the backroads of Central Pennsylvania like the back of his hand, and helped us pin down Stuart's route of march and also provided us with useful primary source material that has never been used in other treatments of these events. We are very grateful to Scott for his efforts on our behalf. Dave and Carol Moore of Gettysburg freely allowed us to use their lovely home on Herr's Ridge as our local base of operations, and Dave, always eager to go battlefield stomping, accompanied us on our reconnaissance of Stuart's route.

After reading a draft of our manuscript, author and cavalry aficionado Al Ovies alerted us to primary sources that disproved the generally accepted notion that George Custer and most of his Michigan Brigade accompanied Judson Kilpatrick on the latter's march from Littlestown to Hanover, Pennsylvania, on the fateful morning of June 30. As with the Jones diary entry, we thank Al for his alertness and for assisting us in finally setting the record straight. Many other pieces of the puzzle now fit, and the development of the Hanover fight makes a great deal more sense.

Our close friend and cavalry devotee, Michael Nugent, read the manuscript and gave us the benefit of his insight, as did James Cameron. No one recognizes silliness better than Jim, and he pointed out several blatant errors we happily corrected, all of which motivated us to think through our conclusions more fully. Horace Mewborn also provided us with good insight and with important suggestions as to sources to employ to make our work stronger. Tom Perry, who is an authority on Stuart's life and career, read our manuscript and offered very useful comments. David Arthur's keen editorial skills and good eye for detail were put to good use on an early draft of this manuscript. David was also the person to suggest we expand the scope of our study to include the controversy, and we are grateful to him for doing so.

Robert J. Trout, the leading authority on the Confederate horse artillery, willingly gave us his time and effort by reviewing and commenting on an early version of our manuscript. His comments improved the quality of this book, and we are grateful.

John Heiser, a historian at the Gettysburg National Military Park, drew the maps that bring the words on these pages to life. John has retired from mapmaking to allow time for other responsibilities, so we were especially honored when he consented to do the maps for this book. He also graciously opened the Park's research library to us on several occasions and pointed out material crucial to our work. Gary Kross, a Gettysburg Licensed Battlefield Guide, took us on a tour of Stuart's ride from Westminster to Gettysburg, offering keen insights and observations along the way. Without his help, the driving tour in Appendix D would not be as detailed or accurate as it is. Allen Aimone at the archives of the U.S. Military Academy at West Point, New York, has long been a willing assistant in providing source material on academy graduates. Mark Grimsley read the manuscript and graciously penned the Foreword, for which we are grateful. We must also thank the staff at the U.S. Military History Institute, Carlisle Barracks, Pennsylvania, for the years of expertly assisted research and study in their massive collections. Bryce A. Suderow of Washington, D.C. assisted us in gathering many important primary sources for use in this study—some of it at the last possible moment.

We are especially grateful to our publisher Theodore P. Savas, the director of Savas Beatie LLC. Ted demonstrated a great deal of faith in us by accepting this manuscript for publication, and did a fine job editing it and offering suggestions that made it stronger. He also exhibited a great deal of patience when we flooded him with new primary source material at the last moment. We know we placed a burden on him and his staff by doing so. Thanks again, Ted, and also to Sarah Stephan (copyediting), Lee Merideth (indexing), and the rest of the staff at Savas Beatie.

Finally, we express our appreciation and devotion to our wives, Susan Skilken Wittenberg and Karen Lynn Petruzzi. They invest as much in our research and writing as we do—including too much lost time with our families while we visit libraries and archives, drive endlessly over dusty wartime road traces, clutter our homes with mountains of papers and books, talk for hours on the phone as we flesh out our ideas, and spend our evenings and weekends locked in front of a computer. But along the way they give us supportive pats on the shoulder and allow us time to think, write, and think some more. We owe them the most of all.

Eric J. Wittenberg and J. David Petruzzi

Foreword

On the evening of May 12, 1864, Major General James Ewell Brown Stuart succumbed to a gunshot wound received the previous day in a sharp cavalry fight at Yellow Tavern, a few miles outside the Confederate capital of Richmond, Virginia. Although barely thirty-one years old at the time of his death, Stuart was one of the South's paladins, a living legend. More to the point, in a month in which Union armies seemed to pressure Virginia on every side, he was one of General Robert E. Lee's most prized subordinates. Lee received a dispatch bearing news of Stuart's injury while struggling to stave off a determined enemy attack at Spotsylvania Court House. A nearby captain watched as the Confederate chieftain folded the paper and said slowly, "General Stuart has been mortally wounded: a most valuable and able officer." He paused a moment, added, *"He never brought me a piece of false information"*—and turned away so that those around him could not read the depth of his emotions. The captain thought no higher praise "could fall from the lips of the commanding general touching his Chief of Cavalry."[1]

What no one could decently say in such an hour, but which few in the Army of Northern Virginia ever forgot, was that the previous summer the "valuable and able" Stuart had left Lee bereft of any information, false or otherwise, as the army had moved toward its great collision with the Union Army of the Potomac at Gettysburg. Many blamed Stuart for the

---

1. W. Gordon McCabe, in Robert E. Lee, *Recollections and Letters of General Robert E. Lee* (New York, Doubleday, Page & Company, 1904), 125.

bitter defeat that ensued. Lee's aide, Col. Charles Marshall, went so far as to suggest that Stuart should have been court-martialed, even shot. Others, notably Maj. John S. Mosby, the famed partisan leader, defended Stuart with equal passion. In the decades that followed, every Confederate who lived through those days joined Stuart in death, but the argument went on. It persists to this day.

Eric Wittenberg and J. David Petruzzi have given us a welcome new account of Stuart's fateful ride during the 1863 Pennsylvania campaign. It is, to begin with, a highly detailed narrative of what occurred, from the ride's origin as a fairly straightforward assignment to screen the Army of Northern Virginia's advancing right flank, to the series of misfortunes that created a gap of seven days from the time that Stuart's troopers left Lee's army to the time they rejoined it on the evening of the second day of the fight at Gettysburg. It is also a thorough study of the controversy sparked by the ride, a wrangle that in many ways was the Confederate counterpart of the clash between Gens. George G. Meade and Daniel Sickles over who really deserved credit for the Union victory at Gettysburg.[2]

The authors have done heroic labor among the wealth of primary sources bearing on Stuart's activities between June 25, when with three brigades he embarked on a ride around the supposedly quiescent Army of the Potomac; and July 2, when his battered column belatedly completed its circumnavigation of the Union army. Even more importantly, Wittenberg and Petruzzi are thoroughly versed in Civil War cavalry operations, including the oft-overlooked realities of feeding and caring for thousands of horses under combat conditions. America in the 1860s had about one horse for every fourth man, woman, and child. Virtually everyone knew firsthand the paradoxically vulnerable nature of such large, powerful animals. Nowadays, Americans outnumber horses by forty-two to one, and real equestrian knowledge is confined to out-of-the-way pockets of modern society. Few buffs who thrill to tales of Civil War cavalry raids are aware that a horse must be re-shod after no more than a hundred miles of travel (Stuart's ride covered at least twice that distance). Confederate cavalrymen waged pitched battles with their

---

2. See Richard A. Sauers, *Gettysburg: The Meade-Sickles Controversy* (Washington: Brassey's, 2003).

Union counterparts at Westminster, Hanover, and elsewhere, but Confederate farriers and blacksmiths waged a no less vital campaign to keep their mounts fit for operations. The authors keep this sort of critical detail constantly before the reader's eye.

They also portray, in highly specific terms, the men on both sides who fought and shaped Stuart's controversial ride: their pre-war backgrounds, their combat records, their passions, strengths, and foibles. At the center is Jeb Stuart himself. Was he guilty of "a useless, showy parade," as one Confederate staff officer sneered, or was he a conscientious officer who made the best choices he could among an option of difficulties?[3]

It would be impossible to narrate the ride without at least hinting at the answers to these questions, but the authors are so complete and even-handed in their approach that the case is never cut and dry. They devote three whole chapters to a fascinating account of the various arguments and counter-arguments used to condemn or rehabilitate Stuart before finally offering a compelling assessment of their own. The book's title—*Plenty of Blame to Go Around*—suggests the direction of their conclusions. It also indicates the authors have chosen what John Keegan has termed the "accusatorial" approach to military history. Historians who employ this method, writes Keegan, "implicitly put someone or something—a general or an army—in the dock, charge him or it with a crime—defeat if a friend, victory if an enemy—and marshal the evidence to show his or its responsibility."[4]

In his classic work *The Face of Battle*, Keegan makes the case for a different, "inquisitorial" approach that "would allow the historian . . . to discuss battles not necessarily as conflicts for a decision, but as value-free events—for it is as events that they appear to many participants and to most non-combatant spectators—and if one began from their unpartisan stance one might well hit on a clearer view of what real significance it was that a battle held."[5] It sounds quite enlightened. Yet in much of his subsequent work, Keegan himself adheres to the "accusatorial" approach, which suggests both its value to the military historian and the difficulty of

---

3. G. Moxley Sorrel, quoted *infra*, p. 228.

4. John Keegan, *The Face of Battle: A Study of Agincourt, Waterloo, and the Somme* (New York: Viking Press, 1976), p. 74.

5. *Ibid.*

avoiding it. In any event, controversy drenches Stuart's ride so thoroughly that to eschew the accusatorial approach would be to miss much of the operation's significance.

What is needed, then (to adjust Keegan's metaphor a bit), is something akin to an investigative commission, one that seeks to apportion responsibility but which does so judiciously. Wittenberg and Petruzzi know their subject so well, and are so sensitive to the complexities of waging a Civil War operation, that while unafraid to judge, they do so with an impressive degree of deliberation. And their eventual apportionment of "blame" is anything but a scattershot, plague-on-all-your-houses affair. It is measured, fair-minded, and insightful.

Plenty of Blame to Go Around is unabashedly traditional in its approach to military history. That is no bad thing. Certainly it is indispensable for military historians (whether professionals like myself or gifted amateurs like Wittenberg and Petruzzi) to integrate their chosen subject matter into general history, to avoid insularity, and to place themselves fully in conversation with other fields. But this involves a broadening of military history, not a dilution of it. We lose rather than gain if we lose sight of the field's traditional concerns. Victorian ideas of manliness, to take a case at random, undoubtedly played a significant role in shaping Stuart's ride. They enhanced or detracted from command relationships according to how well officers affirmed or impeached the masculinity of their peers. They affected combat motivation: soldiers fought in no small measure so as to preserve their reputation as a man among men. But the participants in Stuart's ride did not consciously think in these terms, and to focus on such considerations to the exclusion of what they *did* think about—time-space calculations, the water level at crucial fords, the availability of food and forage, the maintenance of horses, the dangers of combat, the care of the wounded, the disposal of the dead—would be to distort an event one is supposedly trying to understand.

Here, then, is Stuart's ride as the troopers on both sides would recognize it—well researched, vividly written, and shrewdly argued. It is, in short, as good an account of the ride as we are likely to get.

Mark Grimsley
The Ohio State University

Introduction

A s the sun went down on the evening of June 21, 1863, Maj. Gen. Jeb Stuart faced something new to him. His vaunted mounted forces had that day been soundly beaten on the field of battle. Major General Alfred Pleasonton's Yankee horsemen, in an effort to reach Ashby's Gap, a critical gateway to the rich Shenandoah Valley, defeated Stuart's troopers in a day-long engagement at Upperville. The plumed cavalier had a close shave. "The 1st Dragoons tried very hard to kill me the other day," he reported to his wife Flora. "Four officers fired deliberately at me with their pistols while I was putting a Regiment at them which routed them."[1] Stuart's favorite staff officer, the Prussian mercenary Maj. Heros von Borcke, had been badly wounded in the neck—mortally, it was thought—and Stuart was terribly distressed at the loss of his comrade. If Pleasonton's troopers pushed through Ashby's Gap they would find what they were seeking: the location of the main body of the Army of Northern Virginia, which was passing north on its way toward Pennsylvania. Although Upperville was Stuart's first clear-cut battlefield defeat, his troopers still managed to prevent the Federal horse soldiers from pushing through Ashby's Gap.[2]

"The affair is considered quite discreditable to General Stuart . . . his officers [are] discouraged and mortified, and his men bordering on a state of demoralization," declared *The Charleston Mercury*. "Officers under Stuart declare that the effort to give him a large command and maintain him in his position is working great mischief to the cavalry service."[3] The correspondent slammed the performance of the Confederate chief. "You may be sure it gives me no pleasure to indict such a soldier as [Stuart], but the heavy force now under his command is too large for him, in that it requires a head that can conceive and combine as well as execute the orders of others."[4]

The past few weeks had not gone well for Stuart. When Lt. Gen. Thomas J. "Stonewall" Jackson was mortally wounded at the end of the second day at Chancellorsville, Stuart assumed command of Jackson's Second Corps and performed superbly under extremely adverse circumstances. Led by Stuart, the Southern infantry drove the Federal Third Corps from Hazel Grove and hammered the Army of the Potomac back into its final line of defense. The Second Corps bore the brunt of the fighting at Chancellorsville, and Stuart—who had never commanded infantry—played a major part in its success.[5]

In June 1863, Virginia-born James Ewell Brown Stuart was 30 years old. He was an 1854 graduate of West Point, where the commandant, Col. Robert E. Lee, befriended the young man. Stuart always wanted to be a cavalryman. While a cadet he wrote, "Had you not rather see your Cousin or even your brother a Bold Dragoon than a petty-fogger lawyer?"[6] He earned the unflattering nickname "Beauty" during his cadet years, but was popular with his fellow cadets. When he graduated Stuart served with the 1st Cavalry on the Kansas frontier. He married Flora Cooke, the daughter of legendary cavalry commander Col. Philip St. George Cooke. In October 1859, Stuart served as a volunteer aide to Lee in the capture of John Brown at Harpers Ferry. When Virginia seceded in 1861, Stuart resigned his commission and became colonel of the 1st Virginia Cavalry. He became famous almost immediately; the charge of the 1st Virginia helped shatter Union lines at Manassas in July 1861.

Stuart was promoted to brigadier general in September 1861 and gained immortality for his so-called "Ride Around McClellan" during the 1862 Peninsula Campaign. A promotion to major general followed on July 25, 1862, and he assumed command of the cavalry division of the Army of Northern Virginia, a post he held for the rest of his short life (with the exception of his brief stint in command of Jackson's Corps at Chancellorsville). "He proved himself a premier intelligence officer, combining the highest skill and intrepidity," noted one biographer. Robert E. Lee often referred to Stuart as "the eyes and ears of the army," and he came to depend heavily on Stuart's accurate and timely intelligence reports.[7]

Stuart wanted—but did not receive—permanent command of Jackson's Corps. Instead, Lee reorganized the Army of Northern

Virginia from two infantry corps to three and promoted Richard S. Ewell and A. P. Hill to lieutenant general and assigned them to command the Second and Third corps, respectively. Stuart returned to command Lee's cavalry. Some historians have speculated that Stuart was desperate for his own promotion to lieutenant general, and that he felt slighted by being passed over for promotion and corps command.[8] "It is rumored," reported Confederate Maj. Gen. William Dorsey Pender in a letter to his wife, "that Stuart has tendered his resignation because they will not give him this corps, but I cannot think him so foolish."[9] Pender was right—the rumor was false. Stuart remained in command of the cavalry, but many speculated he was sulking about being passed over for permanent command of Jackson's infantry.

On June 9, 1863, Alfred Pleasonton's people got the drop on Stuart at Brandy Station. The Union horsemen nearly defeated their Southern counterparts in a brutal day of fighting that still stands as the largest cavalry battle in American history. The Richmond newspapers excoriated Stuart for being surprised at Brandy Station, a charge that rankled Stuart. "*The Richmond Examiner* of the 12th lies from beginning to end," he indignantly declared to Flora.[10] "Maybe by mid-June of 1863 Stuart had reason to wonder about his capacity to live up to his legend," declared biographer Emory N. Thomas.[11] Some historians speculate that the aggressive criticism leveled at Stuart after Brandy Station forced him to find a way to redeem his now-tainted reputation and regain his role as the darling of the Southern newspapers. They claim Stuart wanted to do something spectacular in order to regain the limelight that he had lost in the wake of the nearly disastrous June 9 battle.

Stuart redeemed himself by actively and diligently screening the Army of Northern Virginia's passage down the Shenandoah Valley as it moved northward toward the Potomac River. He fended off Pleasonton's many attempts to punch through the Confederate cavalry screen and find the main body of Lee's army. Scouting, screening, and reconnaissance were the traditional roles of cavalry, and Stuart excelled in this role—particularly during the fighting in Loudoun Valley during the second half of June. Winning battles was not his primary task during these actions, however; keeping the active and diligent Union cavalry away from Lee's infantry was his goal. Even though the Southern cavalry fought stubbornly and lost the fight at Upperville, Stuart still managed to keep

Pleasonton's horsemen from locating Lee's army as it tramped northward through the Shenandoah Valley.

As the Army of Northern Virginia moved north, Lee assembled Stuart's seven brigades of cavalry. Those seven brigades were commanded by Brig. Gens. Fitzhugh Lee, Wade Hampton, William E. "Grumble" Jones, Beverly H. Robertson, Albert G. Jenkins, John D. Imboden, and Col. John R. Chambliss, Jr. (temporarily commanding the brigade of the wounded Brig. Gen. W. H. F. "Rooney" Lee). This was the largest mounted force cobbled together by the Confederacy to date, and had thus far served well in the nascent campaign. However, Stuart's defeat at Upperville triggered the beginning of a new chapter in the history of the army's cavalry, one that has been the subject of untold pages of written argument and acerbic assertions.

Ever restless, Stuart began searching for other ways to make his command useful. "Although Stuart had been roughly handled in the fights in Loudoun with the mixed command of Pleasonton's cavalry and infantry, he was buoyant, and as full of pluck and fight as ever," recalled Col. Thomas L. Rosser, commander of the 5th Virginia Cavalry.[12] Stuart established his headquarters at Rector's Crossroads on June 22, eager to contribute to Lee's invasion of the Northern states. That morning, Stuart wrote to Lt. Gen. James Longstreet, commander of the Army of Northern Virginia's First Corps, and Lee's senior subordinate, looking for suggestions as to how best to contribute to the campaign. "The enemy retained one army corps (Fifth) at Aldie, and kept his cavalry near enough to make attack upon the latter productive of no solid benefits, and I began to look for some other point at which to direct an effective blow," he wrote. "I submitted to the commanding general the plan of leaving a brigade or so in my present front, and passing through Hopewell or some other gap in Bull Run Mountains, attain the enemy's rear, passing between his main body and Washington, and cross into Maryland, joining our army north of the Potomac."[13]

Perhaps Stuart wanted to recapture the glory of two prior rides around the Army of the Potomac. "Stuart made to Lee a very unwise proposition, which Lee more unwisely entertained," keenly observed Col. Edward Porter Alexander, the acting chief of artillery for the Army of Northern Virginia's First Corps.[14] Lee approved the idea. "Upon the suggestion of [General Stuart] that he could damage the enemy and delay his passage of the river by getting in his rear, he was authorized to do so," was how Lee would one day phrase the matter in his report of the Gettysburg Campaign.[15]

One modern historian suggests Stuart actually presented this plan in a meeting with Lee and Longstreet at Paris, Virginia, on June 18. "At this meeting he apparently introduced the thought of riding around Hooker as one of the options," postulated Stephen W. Sears.[16] Regardless of when Stuart introduced his idea, it is clear that Lee not only knew of the plan but approved it. Lee said as much in his campaign report.

Anticipating his ride, Stuart had already assigned one of his primary scouts, Frank Stringfellow of the 4th Virginia Cavalry, the task of reconnoitering the Potomac River fords for the best place to cross. Stringfellow was ordered to rendezvous with Stuart's command at Salem (now known as Marshall), Virginia, on or about June 20 and report his findings. The scout found that Rowser's Ford was relatively unguarded and passable, but he had to make his way back to Stuart to report his findings. Unfortunately, Stringfellow was unable to get to Salem until June 26, well after Stuart had already kicked off his ride. Stringfellow tried to find the Confederate cavalry column, but instead was captured by a Federal cavalry patrol when he was thrown from his horse and knocked unconscious. Before too much longer he was in Washington, D.C.'s Capitol Prison.[17] Stuart would have to do without his best scout's services in choosing a route north.

The day after his defeat at Upperville, Stuart received his new mission from Robert E. Lee. On June 22, Lee's personal secretary, Col. Charles Marshall wrote the following:

> General: I have just received your note of 7:45 this morning to General Longstreet. I judge the efforts of the enemy yesterday were to arrest our progress and ascertain our whereabouts. Perhaps he is satisfied. Do you know where he is and what he is doing? I fear he will steal a march on us, and get across the Potomac before we are aware. If you find that he is moving northward, and that two brigades can guard the Blue Ridge and take care of your rear, you can move with the other three into Maryland, and take position on [Lt. Gen. Richard S.] Ewell's right, place yourself in communication with him, guard his flank, keep him informed of the enemy's movements, and collect all the supplies you can for the use of the army. One column of General Ewell's army will probably move toward the Susquehanna by the Emmitsburg route; another by Chambersburg. Accounts from him last night state that there was no enemy west of

Frederick. A cavalry force (about 100) guarded the Monocacy Bridge, which was barricaded. You will, of course, take charge of Jenkins' brigade, and give him necessary instructions. All supplies taken in Maryland must be by authorized staff officers for their respective departments–by no one else. They will be paid for, or receipts for the same given to the owners. I will send you a General order on this subject, which I wish to see strictly complied with.[18]

After this order was written, Lee directed Marshall to repeat it. "I remember saying to the general that it could hardly be necessary to repeat the order, as General Stuart had had the matter fully explained to himself verbally and my letter had been very full and explicit," Marshall explained in his postwar memoirs. "I had retained a copy of my letter in General Lee's confidential letter book. General Lee said that he felt anxious about the matter and desired to guard against the possibility of error, and desired me to repeat it, which I did, and dispatched the second letter." The second set of orders followed the next day.[19]

General Longstreet wrote two important missives, one to Lee and the second to Stuart. To Lee he penned the following: "General: yours of 4 o'clock this afternoon is received. I have forwarded your letter to General Stuart with suggestion that he pass by the enemy's rear if he thinks that he may get through. We have nothing of the enemy to-day."[20] Longstreet's note to Stuart reads as follows: "I think that you can move across the Potomac without disclosing our plans. He speaks of your leaving, via Hopewell gap, and passing by the rear of the enemy. If you can get through by that route, I think that you will be less likely to indicate what our plans are than if you should cross by passing to our rear."[21]

Lee informed Lt. Gen. Richard Ewell, the new commander of Jackson's former Second Corps, that Stuart and part of his command would be departing soon to rendezvous with him and his infantry. "I also directed General Stuart, should the enemy have so far retired from his front as to permit of the departure of a portion of the cavalry, to march with three brigades across the Potomac, and place himself on your right and in communication with you, keep you advised of the movements of the enemy, and assist in collecting supplies for the army," he ordered. Lee's directive put Ewell on notice to keep an eye out for Stuart's cavalry.[22]

The second set of orders penned by Marshall was delivered to Stuart on June 23. These orders read as follows:

If General (Joseph] Hooker's army remains inactive, you can leave two brigades to watch him, and withdraw with the three others, but should he not appear to be moving northward, I think you had better withdraw this side of the mountain to-morrow night, cross at Shepherdstown next day, and move over to Fredericktown.

You will, however, be able to judge whether you can pass around their army without hinderance, doing them all the damage you can, and cross the river east of the mountains. In either case, after crossing the river, you must move on and feel the right of Ewell's troops, collecting information, provisions, &c.

Give instructions to the commander of the brigades left behind, to watch the flank and rear of the army, and (in the event of the enemy leaving their front) retire *from* the mountains west of the Shenandoah, leaving sufficient pickets to guard the passes, and bringing everything clean along the Valley, closing upon the rear of the army.

As regards the movements of the two brigades of the enemy moving toward Warrenton, the commander of the brigades to be left in the mountains must do what he can to counteract them, but I think the sooner you cross into Maryland, after to-morrow, the better.

The movements of Ewell's corps are as stated in my former letter. Hill's first division will reach the Potomac to-day, and Longstreet will follow to-morrow. Be watchful and circumspect in all your movements.[23]

It rained heavily on the night of June 23. Instead of sleeping in a nearby house, Stuart camped beneath a tree. Major Henry B. McClellan, his adjutant, tried to dissuade Stuart from assuming his soggy bivouac. "No!" exclaimed Stuart. "My men are exposed to this rain, and I will not fare any better than they." With that, Stuart lay down on his oilcloth and went to sleep, doing his best to ignore the downpour. Late that night a courier arrived from Lee carrying an envelope marked "confidential." McClellan opened the letter and realized it contained written instructions from the commanding general. "The letter discussed at considerable length the plan of passing around the enemy's rear," he recalled. "It informed General Stuart that General Early would move upon York, Pa., and that it was desired to place his cavalry as speedily as possible with that, the advance division of Lee's right wing." Although no copy of this third letter has ever been found, McClellan claims to have recalled its contents clearly:

> The letter suggested that, as the roads leading northward from Shepherdstown and Williamsport were already encumbered by the infantry, the artillery, and the transportation of the army, the delay which would necessarily occur in passing by these would, perhaps, be greater than would ensue if General Stuart passed around the enemy's rear. The letter further informed him that, if he chose the latter route, General Early would receive instructions to look out for him and endeavor to communicate with him; and York, Pa., was designated as the point in the vicinity of which he was to expect to hear from Early, and as the possible (if not probable) point of concentration of the army. The whole tenor of the letter gave evidence that the commanding general approved the proposed movement, and thought that it might be productive of the best results, while the responsibility of the decision was placed on General Stuart himself.

After reading such an important communication, McClellan decided to awaken the slumbering cavalier.[24] Stuart read the orders, cautioned his adjutant about not opening and reading confidential dispatches, and went back to his soggy bed.[25] The general was pleased. Another ride around and behind enemy lines was in the offing. "Raiding was Stuart's hobby," noted staff officer Theodore S. Garnett, "and one which he *rode* with never failing persistence."[26]

These orders clearly gave Stuart discretion to ride around the Army of the Potomac and to try to wreak havoc on the enemy's rear. These orders impressed on Stuart the need to join Ewell and screen his right flank, and to do so quickly. Stuart ordered the veteran brigades of Brig. Gens. Fitzhugh Lee, Wade Hampton, and Col. John R. Chambliss to rendezvous at Salem on June 24. The stage was now set for one of the great controversies of the Civil War.

In Stringfellow's absence, Stuart depended on the scouting skills of Maj. John S. Mosby, who had already established a sterling reputation as a guerrilla. Mosby had the task of trying to find out the dispositions of Joe Hooker's Union army. Mosby left with two men on June 22, and was nearly captured by a squad of troopers of the 5th New York Cavalry, but safely completed his mission, returning on June 24 to report the results of his expedition. "Stuart was anxiously waiting to hear what Hooker was doing," recounted Mosby. "He must then have received General Lee's order of 5 p.m., of the 23d, to start the next day and put himself on Ewell's right on the Susquehanna. It gave him the choice of routes—through the Valley by Shepherdstown, or by Hooker's rear. The news I brought of the situation in Hooker's army determined him to take the latter route." Mosby reported that Hooker's army was quiet, waiting to see what Lee's intentions were, and that there was no evidence of movement by the Army of the Potomac.[27]

Mosby reported the positions of the Army of the Potomac's scattered corps to Stuart, noting, "they were so widely separated that it was easy for a column of cavalry to pass between them. No corps was nearer than ten miles to another corps. On all the roads were wagon-trains hauling supplies," recalled Mosby. "I pointed out to Stuart the opportunity to strike a damaging blow, and suggested to him to cross the Bull Run Mountains and pass through the middle of Hooker's army into Maryland. There was no force to oppose him at Seneca Ford about twenty miles above Washington—where I had recently crossed."[28]

Mosby preferred to use Hopewell Gap in the Bull Run Mountains, which would enable him to pass between Maj. Gen. Winfield Scott Hancock's Second Corps at Thoroughfare Gap, and Pleasonton's cavalry at Aldie. This route would avoid the heavily traveled Warrenton Turnpike by passing to the north of it. Stuart, however, preferred crossing at Glasscock's Gap on the other side of Hancock's position. Stuart's chosen route would have unforeseen but significant consequences for his expedition.

"The contemplated enterprise, if it had not been defeated by a cause that Stuart could not control, was far less difficult and involved far less hazard than the ride around McClellan on the Chickahominy," observed Mosby. The next day, June 25, Mosby planned to take twenty to thirty men and meet the head of Stuart's column ten or twelve miles south of Aldie along the Little River Turnpike, and from that point lead the way toward Seneca Ford.[29] Mosby and his detachment spent the night of June 24 on the western side of the Bull Run Mountains before moving out early the next morning. For unforeseen reasons they never linked up with Stuart's column, a failure that had far-reaching consequences for an expedition that had not yet even begun.[30]

Stuart based his plan for the ride on Mosby's scouting report. The cavalry general spent the 24th preparing and issuing detailed orders to Beverly Robertson, who outranked Grumble Jones:

> GENERAL: Your own and General Jones' brigades will cover the front of Ashby's and Snicker's Gaps, yourself, as senior officer, being in command.
>
> Your object will be to watch the enemy; deceive him as to our designs, and harass his rear if you find he is retiring. Be always on the alert; let nothing escape your observation, and miss no opportunity which offers to damage the enemy.
>
> After the enemy has moved beyond your reach, leave sufficient pickets in the mountains, withdraw to the west side of the Shenandoah, place a strong and reliable picket to watch the enemy at Harper's Ferry, cross the Potomac, and follow the army, keeping on its right and rear.
>
> As long as the enemy remains in your front in force, unless otherwise ordered by General R. E. Lee, Lieutenant-General Longstreet, or myself, hold the Gaps with a line of pickets reaching across the Shenandoah by Charlestown to the Potomac.
>
> If, in the contingency mentioned, you withdraw, sweep the Valley clear of what pertains to the army, and cross the Potomac at the different points crossed by it.
>
> You will instruct General Jones from time to time as the movements progress, or events may require, and report anything of importance to Lieutenant-General Longstreet, with whose position you will communicate by relays through Charlestown.
>
> I send instructions for General Jones, which please read. Avail yourself of every means in your power to increase the efficiency of your command, and keep it up to the highest number possible. Particular attention will be paid to shoeing horses, and to marching off of the turnpike.
>
> In case of an advance of the enemy, you will offer such resistance as will be justifiable to check him and discover his intentions and, if possible, you will prevent him from gaining possession of the Gaps.

In case of a move by the enemy upon Warrenton, you will counteract it as much as you can, compatible with previous instructions.

You will have with the two brigades two batteries of horse artillery.[31]

*   *   *

Much remained to be done before the ride could begin. "Three days' rations were prepared, and, on the night of the 24th, the following brigades, Hampton's, Fitz. Lee's, and W. H. F. Lee's, rendezvoused secretly near Salem Depot," recounted Stuart in his after-action report. "We had no wagons or vehicles excepting six pieces of artillery and caissons and ambulances. Robertson's and Jones' brigades, under command of the former, were left in observation of the enemy on the usual front, with full instructions as to following up the enemy in case of withdrawal, and rejoining our main army." Brigadier General Fitzhugh Lee's Brigade had to ride from north of Snicker's Gap to the place of rendezvous. Fitz Lee, Stuart's protégé and favorite subordinate, was back in the saddle for the first time in weeks. "This brigade was now for the first time for a month under the command of its noble brigadier, who, writhing under a painful attack of inflammatory rheumatism, nevertheless kept with his command until now."[32]

The Confederate cavalrymen spent the night camped in a field near Salem, uncertain as to what was about to take place. They kept their horses saddled so that they were ready to move out on a moment's notice, and spent the evening cooking three days' rations, unaware of their destination or plans.[33] It would be eight days before they would have the luxury of unsaddling their horses again; for many, it would be many days before they again enjoyed a decent meal. They slept the sleep of men unaware of what fate had in store for them.[34] "We were now about to start on an expedition which for audacious boldness equaled if it did not exceed any of our dashing leader's exploits," later observed Capt. William W. Blackford, Stuart's engineering officer.[35]

That night, Stuart sent for sixteen-year-old Pvt. John W. Peake of the 6th Virginia Cavalry. The youngster served as one of the cavalry chief's couriers, and Stuart sent him off to carry a message to Robert E. Lee: "You will find me near Berryville, west of the Blue Ridge." Peake made a thirty-mile ride and found Lee's headquarters. "I shall never forget it," recalled Peake. Lee rose to meet the teenaged courier, who dismounted, saluted, and handed over the large envelope he had carried through the night. Lee held it in his hand and said, "You have been riding your mare hard."

Peake replied, "Yes, General; I did not know how important it was." Peake hesitated before asking, "General, can I get a feed of corn for my horse?"

Lee pointed and answered, "We have no corn for our horses; there is some good grass. Take your saddle off, lie down, and take a sleep. I want you to go back to General Stuart tonight." After his brief rest Peake mounted and rode off to find Stuart's headquarters. He arrived about midnight. The command was ready to march in the morning.[36]

Stuart was taking with him his three best brigades, along with his favorite subordinates. They had no way of knowing their expedition would turn into one of the most virulent of all of the controversies associated with the Gettysburg Campaign.

This is their story.

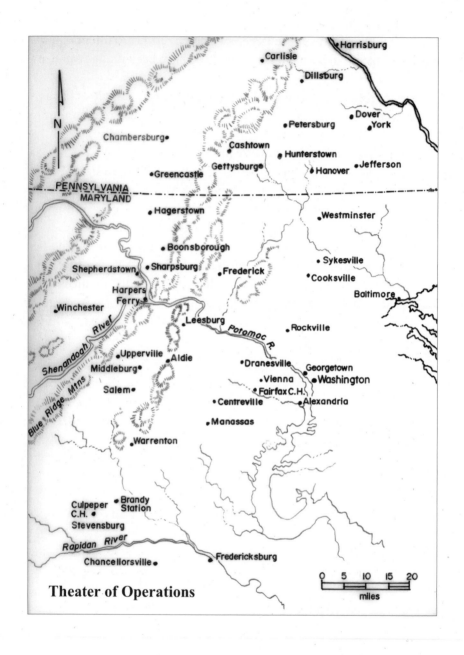

Theater of Operations

Chapter 1

The Ride Begins

"This was the commencement of a march which lasted
almost without halt for two weeks."

— Capt. Theodore S. Garnett, Stuart's staff

About 1:00 a.m. on June 25, 1863, James Ewell Brown ("Jeb")
Stuart, accompanied by his staff and escort, mounted and silently
rode from Rector's Crossroads in the direction of Upperville.
"The next thing I remember, we were riding along the Upperville-
Middleburg road with two or three brigades of cavalry following us,"
recalled Stuart's junior engineering officer, Capt. Frank S. Robertson.[1]

The horsemen rode as quietly as possible because Union troops still
held the Bull Run Mountains, which commanded a view of every
movement of consequence in the region, and Maj. Gen. Winfield S.
Hancock's Second Corps occupied Thoroughfare Gap.[2]

The long column of Confederate cavalry presented quite a sight.
Captain William Willis Blackford, Stuart's thirty-two-year-old
engineering officer, looked them over with pride. "No one could ride
along the lines of this splendid body of men and not be struck with the
spirit which animated them," he noted with pride.[3] Some, including
members of Wade Hampton's Brigade, had lost their horses in the June
21 Battle of Upperville, and rode doubled up on mounts in the hope of
finding new horses along the way.[4]

One of five distinguished brothers in the Confederate service,
Blackford loved being a soldier. Born in Fredericksburg, William was
educated in a private school funded by his father and worked as a civil
engineer to put himself through the University of Virginia.[5] In 1856,

Captain William W. Blackford,
Stuart's chief engineering
officer, in a postwar view.

Robert Trout

Blackford married the eldest
daughter of Governor Wyndham
Robertson. He and Mary settled
in Buena Vista, where Blackford
became Robertson's partner in
plaster mining.[6] Though opposed
to secession, Blackford could not
abide Lincoln's early-war call
for Virginia troops. He left his
wife and four children to join a cavalry company he had earlier raised in
Washington County. Captain William E. "Grumble" Jones, a former
U.S. Dragoon officer, commanded the company, which numbered
among its privates John Singleton Mosby.[7]

First Lieutenant Blackford and his company drilled at Ashland
before joining Lt. Col. Jeb Stuart's 1st Virginia Cavalry. Stuart was so
impressed by the lieutenant that he appointed Blackford adjutant of the
regiment. A promotion to captain of Engineers arrived in May 1862.
After serving a few weeks in the Engineer Corps Blackford rejoined
Stuart's divisional staff at the cavalier's request.[8]

By the time Stuart's column got moving on June 25, Blackford was
well aware of the influence his commander held over the troops. "They
knew they were starting on some bold enterprise, but their confidence in
their leader was so unbounded that they were as gay and lively as it was
possible for them to be, for up to that time no reverse had crossed their
path, and they believed themselves and their leader invincible."[9]

Just before the winding column of Confederate cavalry reached the
arched stone bridge over Goose Creek, Stuart jumped his horse over a
fence on the left side of the road and ordered a courier to turn the head of
the column at that point. His staff realized that instead of heading toward
the Shenandoah Valley, Stuart was setting out after Joe Hooker's army.[10]

Captain Theodore Garnett, aide-de-camp and clerk to JEB Stuart.

Robert Trout

"Little did we dream that this was the commencement of a march which lasted almost without halt for two weeks," observed Theodore S. Garnett, a member of Stuart's staff.[11] The Confederates drove a small detachment of pickets from the mouth of Glasscock's Gap and continued through the mountain pass in the hope of cutting off any Federal infantry that might be lingering inside Thoroughfare Gap. "Moving to the right, we passed through Glasscock's Gap without serious difficulty, and marched for Hay Market," reported Stuart.[12]

The column moved through the night, silently riding on. With the coming of dawn, the gray clad horsemen found themselves near Buckland on the eastern slope of the Bull Run Mountains. "Across the plain, to our left, were the white tops of an immense wagon train, which, at the distance of two or three miles, presented the appearance of a huge flock of sheep," recalled Garnett. "Here then, though, was the object of our silent march over the mountains. All that remained to be done was to 'charge the camp.'" The Confederate cavalrymen did not realize that they had spotted the rear of Hancock's Federal infantry column. The riders cautiously continued on toward the train until they were close enough to attack. They were preparing for the assault when, to their surprise, they discovered at least a division of infantry guarded the train. Hancock's entire corps was passing through Haymarket heading north toward Gum Springs, his infantry distributed through his trains. "They had taken the alarm and were hurrying off as fast as whip and spur would carry them—the infantry marching on the flank," concluded Garnett.[13]

Stuart chose a good position and opened with artillery on Hancock's passing column with effect, "scattering men, wagons, and horses in wild confusion; disabled one of the enemy's caissons, which he abandoned, and compelled him to advance in order of battle to compel us to desist," recounted the general. The first shot hit a caisson. "This 'good shot' highly delighted the general, who turned round laughing, and called attention to the accuracy of the fire," reported thirty-two-year-old John Esten Cooke, a cousin of Jeb's wife Flora Stuart, and who served on Stuart's staff as a scribe. "The individual addressed laughed in response, but replied, 'Look out, though; they are going to enfilade you from that hill on the right, General.'"

"Oh! I reckon not," Stuart responded confidently.

A puff of white smoke rose from the wooded knoll and a shot screamed by, grazing the top of one of the Southern caissons. "This was followed by another and another; the enemy were seen hastily forming line, and advancing sharpshooters; whereupon Stuart ordered back his guns, and dismounted cavalry to meet them."[14] One of the Southern horse artillerists later recounted, "Breathed's battery was ordered into position, raking Hancock's column until they sent a heavy body of infantry against the battery, and not until they came uncomfortably close did we limber up and leave. Stuart, not wishing to disclose his force, withdrew after capturing some prisoners."[15]

Some of the first shots fired by Stuart's artillery fell among the men of the 1st Minnesota Infantry. Private Isaac Lyman Taylor noted in his diary, "At 12 m., as we approach Haymarket some cavalry appear on a bluff south of us & while the boys are

Captain James Breathed commanded horse artillery that rode with Stuart's expedition.

National Archives

earnestly arguing the question 'Are they our men?', a white puff of smoke and the unearthly screech of a shell closes the debate & a unanimous decision is rendered in the Neg[ative]."[16] Lieutenant William Lochren, also of the 1st Minnesota observed, "There were several casualties, and Colonel [William] Colville's horse was killed under him."[17] The exploding shells "put to flight and into great panic a crowd of sutlers, negroes, and other camp followers that were lingering in the rear of Gibbon's Division," noted another Minnesotan, "and it is said that there were some ludicrous scenes."[18]

One exploding shell hit and killed Pvt. Israel D. Jones of the 19th Maine Infantry, the first man in his regiment to be killed in action. "In less than ten minutes from the time that Mr. Jones was chatting cheerfully with the man marching at his side, he was buried by the roadside," recounted his regiment's historian. Colonel Francis E. Heath called on his regimental musicians to play a tune, ordered the flags unfurled, and had his men double-time out of range, carrying Jones's body with them. This moment of defiance was short-lived, however. The Maine men unceremoniously buried Jones's bloody corpse in a shallow grave along the side of the pike. The makeshift burial haunted Heath for the rest of his life. Of all his Civil War actions, Heath most regretted not having made time for a proper Christian burial for Jones.[19] "The forming of Harrow's brigade and the advance of Webb's [brigade] caused [Stuart's men] to leave the field," observed a Minnesotan.[20]

A running fight broke out, with the Federals holding their flank. "Soon the line had passed on and disappeared," recalled Cooke.[21] The 72nd Pennsylvania Infantry brought up the rear of Hancock's column. Some of the Pennsylvanians were sent out as flankers, separating them from the rest of Hancock's corps. "Knowing the enemy to be ahead in our front, also on our flank and in our rear," recounted Maj. Samuel Roberts, "I felt the prospect of the 72nd rejoining the division somewhat doubtful and I can only attribute our good fortune in not being attacked to an absence of knowledge upon the part of the Confederates, that a regiment was in rear of the division."[22]

Stuart made "their exit as unpleasant as possible," recalled Theodore Garnett, by killing a few Union draft horses, exploding a caisson, and taking a handful of men prisoner.[23] "We shelled them a little and they soon retreated," recalled an officer of the Jeff Davis Legion Cavalry, Wade Hampton's Brigade.[24] "We moved against Thoroughfare Gap, and

Major General Alfred Pleasonton, commander of the Army of the Potomac's Cavalry Corps. Pleasonton was an inefficient publicity hound who missed at least one opportunity to devastate Stuart prior to Gettysburg.

crossing the rugged mountains, attacked a wagon train, but did nothing more than throw some shells in among them," wrote an officer of the 9th Virginia Cavalry of John R. Chambliss's Brigade.[25] "As we approached Haymarket we passed a disabled caisson left behind, which showed the accurate firing of the rebel artillery," noted an admiring Major Roberts.[26]

Although Stuart did not realize it, his command was interposed between portions of Hancock's command. Brigadier General Samuel K. Zook's brigade was at Gainesville. Couriers dispatched to reach Zook were captured, including Captain Riley Johnson of the 6th New York Cavalry, the commander of the Second Corps' cavalry escort.[27] General Hancock immediately reported the encounter with Stuart to army headquarters: "a force, estimated by observers who can be relied on, as from four regiments to 6,000 men, with one battery of artillery. They have driven in my cavalry, but nothing further as yet."[28]

General Hooker responded by instructing his cavalry commander, Alfred Pleasonton, to send a brigade of cavalry to join Hancock's column.[29] One of Brig. Gen. David M. Gregg's brigades marched at once, but by the time it arrived Stuart's column had moved on and the Union horse soldiers did not search aggressively for the enemy. Instead, they escorted the Union infantry, permitting Stuart to escape unmolested.[30] Once it became clear the following day that the threat from Stuart's column had passed, Pleasonton asked that these horsemen be returned.[31] The encounter was the first instance of good fortune to mark Stuart's journey to Pennsylvania.

Stuart would have to wait for most of the morning until the Union infantry passed. Because Stuart knew Hancock was the extreme left of Hooker's army, he realized the entire Army of the Potomac was moving north toward the Potomac River.[32] "As Hancock had the right of way on my road, I sent Fitz. Lee's brigade to Gainesville to reconnoiter, and devoted the remainder of the day to grazing our horses, the only forage procurable in the country," he later reported.[33]

Stuart was surprised to find Hancock's infantry blocking his path. According to John Mosby's intelligence report, the enemy infantry was still at Centreville, Union Mills, and Wolf Run Shoals. "Stuart did not hear from me because Hooker's troops were marching on all roads between us," explained Mosby. "As the artillery firing had ceased in the morning, I concluded that he had gone back and I did the same."[34] The decision deprived Stuart of Mosby's latest intelligence reports. He would

Major Henry B. McClellan,
Stuart's competent adjutant, in
a prewar image.

Williams College

soon be forced to make a difficult
choice without any recent
intelligence to rely upon.

Before withdrawing to
Buckland in an effort to deceive
the Federals as to his true
intentions, Stuart dashed off a
report concerning Hancock's movement to Gen. Robert E. Lee,
commanding officer of the Army of Northern Virginia. "It is plain from
General Lee's report that this messenger did not reach him, and
unfortunately the dispatch was not duplicated," observed Stuart's
adjutant, Maj. Henry Brainerd McClellan. "Had it reached General Lee
the movement of Hancock's corps would, of itself, have gone far to
disclose to him the intentions of the enemy as to the place where a
passage of the Potomac was about to be effected."[35] However, this
message did reach the Confederate War Department in Richmond, where
a clerk filed it away but did not pass it on to Lee, perhaps assuming Lee
had also received it.

Although born and raised in Philadelphia, twenty-two-year-old
Henry McClellan was of blue-blooded New England stock. He trained
for the ministry and graduated from Williams College in 1858, but
relocated to Cumberland County, Virginia and took a position as a
teacher instead of following the cross. The transplanted Southerner
joined the 3rd Virginia Cavalry at Ashland as a private in Co. G (The
Cumberland Light Dragoons) in June of 1861.[36]

By throwing his lot with the South, McClellan turned his back on his
Yankee roots. Four of his brothers served with the Union Army, and a
first cousin, Maj. Gen. George B. McClellan, was twice commander of
the Army of the Potomac. Despite Henry's ties to the North and lack of
military training, Stuart favored him early in the war. Stuart plucked

McClellan from the 3rd Virginia (where he had been serving as adjutant with the rank of captain), promoted him to major, and named him assistant adjutant general. McClellan replaced the young and popular Channing Price, who had been mortally wounded at Chancellorsville in early May 1863.[37]

Although a staff officer, McClellan proved his mettle as a combat leader at Brandy Station on June 9, when the young adjutant took command of horsemen and artillery on Fleetwood Hill as Federal cavalry seemed to be attacking from all sides. His admirable management of the crisis prompted Stuart to lavish praise upon his loyal staff officer, who "displayed the same zeal, gallantry, and efficiency which has on every battlefield, in the camp or on the march so distinguished him."[38]

The presence of Hancock's infantry made it impossible for Stuart to follow the route originally selected. He now had to choose between retracing his steps and crossing the Potomac at Shepherdstown, or continuing on and carrying out the letter and the spirit of Lee's orders. "To carry out my original design of passing west of Centreville, would have involved so much detention, on account of the presence of the enemy," Stuart explained, "that I determined to cross Bull Run lower down, and strike through Fairfax for the Potomac the next day. The sequel shows this to have been the only practicable course."[39]

If Stuart elected to retrace his steps and cross the Potomac River at either Shepherdstown or Williamsport, he faced at least sixty miles of mountainous road, and he could not have hoped to reach Shepherdstown for two days, or June 27. After crossing the Potomac, he would still have had another sixty miles to ride just to reach York, and would have to cross South Mountain along the way, deep in enemy territory. "It should not therefore be wondered at if this consideration alone decided Stuart to persist in the movement already begun," observed his staffer McClellan, "especially when there was also the hope of damaging the enemy in his rear and thus delaying his movements. Moreover he had a right to expect that the information he had forwarded concerning the movement of Hancock's corps would cause [Beverly] Robertson and [William E.] Jones to be active on their front, and would put General Lee himself on the alert in the same direction."[40]

The timetable for Stuart's ride was thrown off during its opening hours that morning of June 25. He had no way of knowing it would never get back on schedule.

*   *   *

When darkness fell the heavens opened wide, making men and horses miserable. "That night was rainy and disagreeable, and we spent it without shelters or fires," glumly reported Lt. George W. Beale of the 9th Virginia Cavalry.[41] Unlike the men in the ranks who enjoyed no such luxuries, Stuart and his staff were invited to spend a warm night in a handsome mansion near Bucklands, "where all slept under cover but Stuart." Per his usual practice, the general spread his blankets out under a tree and slept in the rain, although not before enjoying a sumptuous dinner. "That supper is one of the pleasant memories the present writer has of the late war," fondly recalled Cooke:

> How the good companions laughed and devoured the viands of the
> hospitable host! How the beautiful girls of the family stood with
> mock submission, servant-wise, behind the chairs, and waited on
> the guests with their sweetest smiles, until that reversal of all the
> laws of the universe became a perfect comedy, and ended in an éclat
> of laughter! General and staff waited in turn on the waiters; and
> when the tired troopers fell asleep on the floor of the portico, it is
> certain that a number of bright eyes shone in their dreams. Such is
> the occasional comedy that which lights up the tragedy of war.[42]

Instead of riding on, Stuart and his command dawdled at Buckland Mills for ten hours waiting for Mosby to return. The scout made a weak effort to reconnect with Stuart's column but never did make contact again. Thus, the ten hours of lost time at Buckland Mills—for no good reason—set Stuart's schedule irretrievably behind. This was one of several questionable tactical decisions made by Stuart along the way, and it would cost his command dearly.

Stuart broke bivouac early on the morning of June 26 and rode through Brentsville to the vicinity of Wolf Run Shoals, a strongly fortified place on the Occoquan Creek. They had to halt again in order to graze their horses, which were fast breaking down as a consequence of hard marching without grain.[43] However, the opportunities for grazing were not good. "Had very poor grazing for horses, this being a miserably poor country & the armies having entirely consumed it," noted an officer of the 3rd Virginia Cavalry.[44] Fortunately, "no enemy disturbed our march and the only attack we made was upon some cherry trees which were along the road, bending beneath the rich, ripe fruit."[45] The horsemen bivouacked for the night somewhere between Brentsville and Wolf Run Shoals.

Stuart's column was in the saddle again early on the morning of June 27. "Having ascertained that on the night previous the enemy had disappeared entirely from Wolf Run Shoals, a strongly fortified position on the Occoquan, I marched to that point, and thence directly for Fairfax Station," reported Stuart, "sending General Fitz. Lee to the right, to cross by Burke's Station and effect a junction at Fairfax Court-House, or farther on, according to circumstances."[46] The Confederates crossed Occoquan Creek and pushed on to Fairfax Station, where they found a small supply of welcome grain for their horses.

Majors Andrew Reid Venable and Henry B. McClellan, and Capt. John Esten Cooke, along with a single courier, rode off to find a blacksmith whose services were sorely needed. They found a local smithy about one-half mile east of Fairfax Station. While the blacksmith went to work on the horses, his wife served the weary soldiers a sumptuous breakfast of fresh butter, sweet meats, real coffee, and cherry pies, "which caused the wandering staff officers to break forth into exclamations of rapture." The famished Confederates attacked the pies with vigor, enjoying the rare treat.

A sudden commotion in the yard was all that was needed for the Southern riders to leave their cherished cherry pies behind and dash outside to see what was causing all the fuss. They quickly found out: several mounted Yankees were heading for the house. "Look out!" exclaimed Major Venable. "There are the Yankees!"

"They are running by—they won't stop," observed Cooke. "What are you going to do?"

"I am going to put the bridle on my horse," declared Venable, who did as he said, saddled his horse, and mounted.

"Well, I am going to have to wait to have the shoes put on mine," said the more practical Cooke, who watched as Venable (on his right) and McClellan (on the left) accompanied by the courier, scattered. Another party of blue clad horsemen was approaching at a full gallop. A shot rang out. Cooke had just enough time to mount and pass across the front of this party at full speed, additional shots and jeers ringing in his ears. "We plunged through a swamp, jumped fences and fallen trees, and reached the forest-cover, penetrated a thicket, and stopped to listen," recalled

Cooke. "The shouts died away; no sound of hoofs came, and doubling back, we came once again to the station to find the meaning of everything."[47]

The Confederate horse soldiers were resting and quietly feeding their mounts when the advance guard of about twenty men, who had gone to scout in the direction of Fairfax Court House, began firing in the woods not far from the main body. "One after another of the advance guard emerged from the woods, halting occasionally to fire back," recalled Theodore Garnett, "at what we could not tell; but it sounded unpleasantly to say the least of it."[48] This was now their second unpleasant surprise in two days, and the threat had to be dealt with.

Stuart, together with his staff and escort, were resting with their horses unbridled, "not dreaming of an enemy nearer than the Court-House, some two miles distant, nothing between us but some fifteen or twenty men, and these retreating toward us," remembered Garnett. When they reported the probable capture of Venable, McClellan, Cooke, and the courier, Stuart snorted. "Oh! They are too intelligent to be caught." When the scouting party related the abandonment of the cherry pies, Stuart laughed.[49] His amusement was short-lived, however, for serious business remained to be done. When the bulk of the Confederate column reached the outskirts of town, "The First North Carolina Cavalry, of Hampton's brigade, was seen coming over the hill near the station, and General Stuart sent word to General Hampton to bring it up on a gallop."[50] The fight was on.

"In a few minutes Hampton came dashing up, and close behind him Major [John H.] Whitaker, leading the First North Carolina Cavalry. Stuart pointed to the woods and told Hampton to push ahead, as his horse was unbridled, and see what the firing meant." The Tar Heels thundered into the woods at a furious gallop. "Presently a blue-coat was seen galloping off ahead of us and we raised a yell which must have made the retreating vidette shake to his very spurs. On we dashed, more in the spirit of a fox chase than a cavalry charge." The 1st North Carolina spotted a squadron of the 11th New York Cavalry, also known as Scott's Nine Hundred, in a wood lot about one hundred yards away, "in beautiful order, sabers flashing and uniforms glittering in the bright sunlight, under the full headway of a gallant and well-ordered charge." The New Yorkers, who were part of the cavalry forces assigned to the defenses of Washington, D. C., were on their way to Centreville on a reconnaissance

Lieutenant George A. Dagwell, Co. C, 11th New York Cavalry, poses in a faded wartime image. Dagwell was wounded and taken prisoner at Fairfax Court House on June 27, 1863.

History of Scott's 900

when they ran into Stuart's column. The men of the 11th New York did not realize they had found Stuart's main body; instead, they were convinced the Southerners in their front were Mosby's guerrillas on a horse rustling expedition. A rude surprise awaited them.[51]

Lieutenant George A. Dagwell of the 11th New York held the advance. The lieutenant reported to Maj. S. Pierre Remington, the Federal commander, that they would all be gobbled up if they did not get to the rear.

"What?" answered a stunned Remington, who was described by an acquaintance as "a brave, dashy soldier, and a loyal comrade all through our term of service."

Dagwell answered, "Turn back, turn the other way and run, there is a whole rebel brigade under the hill!"

Remington countered, "Front into line—march!"

"That settled it, the gallant old boy had blood in his eye, and was always in for a fight whenever and wherever the opportunity presented itself, and say d—n the conditions," remembered Dagwell. "I shall always believe the major thought at this point of the fight that we were still fighting Mosby."[52]

On they came, looking determined to ride right through the advancing Confederates. Major Remington foolishly gave the order to draw sabers and charge. "With a mighty yell that had been pent up for

"Fairfax: Fight with Gen. Wade Hampton's Brigade Rebel Cavalry."

History of Scott's 900

five or six minutes, and which seemed an hour, we went for them: down our side and up their side of the ravine, but they did not wait for us," recalled a New York lieutenant.[53] An Irish private named Malone took off after one of the rebels. "Surrender, ye divil, or I'll shoot the top ave the head ave ye!" he hollered, brandishing his saber all the while.[54] The charge, observed a local newspaper, was made "with so much impetuosity that half of the Confederates were captured before recovering from their surprise."[55]

"Major Remington charged upon the enemy with drawn sabers, and succeeded in capturing about one-half of the enemy," reported Col. James B. Swain, the regiment's commander. "Before, however, he could succeed in rallying his small force, the rebels recovered their presence of mind, and Companies B and C were forced to cut their way through, abandoning prisoners and all." Soon, chaos reigned as each man tried to slash his way to freedom.[56]

"Our squadron in advance, which was commanded by one of our most gallant officers, had just reached the Court House when they were attacked with drawn sabers by a squadron of Federal cavalry mounted on magnificent gray horses, which chased them from the Court House, driving them pell-mell back upon the main body," recounted a Southern officer.[57]

"The suddenness and impetuosity of this charge was the occasion of serious disorder in the ranks of the leading squadron of the First North Carolina. They were close upon us before the command to draw sabers was given, but seeing our numbers increasing as the column closed up, they halted and delivered a volley, which mortally wounded Major Whitaker, who was trying to rally his men." The Yankee volley also wounded a few of Whitaker's men.[58]

The loss of their commander briefly demoralized the Tar Heels, prompting Hampton to cry out, "stand fast" and telling the next squadron to "come ahead." The New Yorkers veered off their course and headed for the woods, as if they intended to attack Hampton's rear. Hampton spotted the movement and sent a squadron to pounce upon them from the flank while he pressed on from the front. "This movement virtually surrounded the Federals, and as soon as they saw their predicament, they broke and fled incontinently. The most exciting chase then took place, and when the men were recalled there was not a foe to be seen or heard of, save some thirty or forty prisoners and a few dead and wounded."[59]

Remington's horse was shot in the breast in two places during the melee. Captain Alexander G. Campbell, commander of Company B, was last seen

Major S. Pierre Remington led the contingent of the 11th New York Cavalry at Fairfax Court House on June 27, 1863.

History of Scott's 900

charging the Confederates after killing an enemy officer with his revolver. Lieutenant Augustus B. Hazelton, also of Company B, was twice fired at but safely led part of his command out of the chaos. Sergeant Henry O. Morris was not wounded, but shot the officer who assaulted Remington.[60] Lieutenant Dagwell charged at the head of about ten men, each of whom was desperately trying to cut his way to freedom.[61] Major Remington and eighteen of his men escaped.[62] Others straggled in for several days after the fighting ended.[63] When he reported to his commanding officer, Remington said, "We found the rebs, and here are all that are left of us."[64] The Confederates killed, wounded, or captured "the greater portion, among them several officers; also horses, arms, and equipments," Stuart noted. "The First North Carolina Cavalry lost its major in the first onset—Major Whitaker—an officer of distinction and great value to us."[65] Stuart bagged nearly 80 of the New Yorkers, meaning that he now had prisoners of war to contend with.[66]

"I think that without exception the most gallant charge, and the most desperate resistance that we ever met from the Federal cavalry, was at Fairfax, June [27] 1863, when Stuart made a raid around the Union army just before the battle of Gettysburg," recalled a Confederate officer. "The Federals, though outnumbered ten to one, fought until every man of them was ridden down, shot down, or cut down; none escaped. We ever afterwards spoke of this affair as the 'charge of the Gray Devils.'"[67]

The New Yorkers realized that they had stirred up a beehive. "Had we known that we were attacking the advance of Gen. J. E. B. Stuart's division of cavalry and artillery, it is doubtful if even the dashing major would have ordered a charge," recalled one of them.[68]

The New Yorkers did indeed suffer frightful losses in their heroic but foolhardy charge. None of them escaped. Of the 82 men who went into battle, four were killed, one officer and 20 men were seriously wounded and captured, and 57 others, including three officers, were taken prisoner. All 57 had their horses fall or shot from under them, and many were badly injured when Southern horses trampled them. In spite of it all, Colonel William B. Swain, the commander of the 11th New York Cavalry, praised Remington's valor. "He went out supposing that he was to go and recover and return Government property, in charge of a guard," noted Swain. "He found himself and his handful of men precipitated upon a regiment of rebel cavalry. Whatever valor, coolness, and determination could perform was accomplished by Major Remington and his command." Swain concluded, "I am agreeably surprised to see even the remnant he brings into camp."[69] However gallant his actions, Major Remington's courage cost his command dearly; it also further delayed Stuart's advance by nearly half a day.[70]

Stuart interrogated one of the prisoners. How many men had made the charge? he inquired. The prisoner told him that there was only a single squadron. "But where are the rest?" asked Stuart. "Are you not the advance of Pleasonton?" The prisoner claimed he knew nothing of Federal Cavalry Corps commander Alfred Pleasonton or his command. "And you charged my command with eighty-two men? Give me five hundred such men and I will charge through the Army of the Potomac with them," declared Stuart in response.[71] The general had no way of knowing that a similar scene would play out just three days later, and that it would slow down his ride nearly an entire day.

Stuart's tone took on a hard edge. He approached Lieutenant Dagwell, the senior officer among the prisoners, and asked whether there was an officer by the name of Campbell in their party. Dagwell replied in the affirmative.

"Is he a prisoner?" asked Stuart.

"No, sir."

"What are the names of the other officers among the prisoners?"

"Lieuts. Holmes and Hazelton," responded Dagwell.

Stuart told Dagwell that one of his men had reported that a Captain Campbell of the Federal squadron had ordered his men to kill any Confederate prisoners. He declared that if he ever caught Campbell, he would hang him as high as highness.[72] Stuart ordered Dagwell to go into the guard lot, where the prisoners were being held, and gather all of the prisoners from the 11th New York Cavalry as they were about to be paroled. Not long afterward Major McClellan, Stuart's adjutant, paroled the prisoners, who rode off for Washington. Soon after departing, they found elements of Col. Charles Russell Lowell's 2nd Massachusetts Cavalry out scouting for Stuart's command.[73]

After brushing aside the stubborn New Yorkers, the Confederates continued on to Fairfax Court House, where Stuart received a message from Fitz Lee at Annandale. While advancing on Annandale, Lee had captured a sutler's train and its small cavalry escort. A local businessman named Moses Sweitzer, described as an army purveyor, was also riding with the train, as were a few sutlers.[74]

Colonel Charles Russell Lowell, the commander of the 2nd Massachusetts Cavalry. His regiment should have been picketing the Potomac River crossings on June 28, 1863.

USAMHI

"The sutlers' wagons were preparing to move toward Alexandria when they heard the most unearthly yells and a shower of balls whizzed all around them," reported a Washington newspaper. "In a moment the whole body of rebel cavalry were upon them."[75] Fitz sent a large portion of his command into the town to seize every suspicious person while the rest of his brigade plundered the sutlers' wagons, helping themselves to all sorts of wondrous treats with a value of $4,000.00. "The Confederates after taking them had not the politeness to give him a receipt for them, or even a promise to pay an equivalent 'ten years after the recognition of the Confederate States by the U. S. Government,'" grumbled a local writer of the *Alexandria Gazette*.[76] The small Federal cavalry escort was taken prisoner and marched off to a stay at Richmond's notorious Libby Prison. After clearing out the town, Lee's Brigade, now loaded down by their booty, marched toward Fairfax Court House, where it arrived during the afternoon.[77]

When Fitz Lee's men found $400 worth of liquor in a house, Lee posted guards in front of the residence; only officers were permitted to enter. The officers, however, freely availed themselves of the alcohol each time it was offered. They also took all of the horses and forage from the house of a local man named J. B. Heath. According to a newspaper the Confederate troopers were polite and well-dressed. However, "Lee himself was very boastful, and asserted that the crisis had at last come."[78]

As the dragnet widened, Moses Sweitzer hid in a nearby house while his clerk secreted himself in the barn. The former was discovered by Fitz

Lee's men. Sweitzer's wife pleaded with Fitz Lee not to take her husband, claiming his lame leg left him unable to do any harm to the Confederate government. A local minister joined her entreaties, describing how Sweitzer had vigorously defended a local woman who had been accused of being a Union spy. Faced with this evidence, Fitz Lee finally gave in to their pleas, grabbed a pen, and made out a pass. "This is to certify that Moses Sweitzer is turned loose to go home and behave himself," he wrote, his tongue planted firmly in his cheek. "It is done on account of his defense of a harmless lady."[79]

After burning some of the wagons and an ambulance containing medicines they could not use, the Confederates loaded the remaining wagons with plunder and marched off to rejoin Stuart's column at Fairfax Court House. As soon as they withdrew, Sweitzer's clerk emerged from his hiding place with $3,500.00 of Sweitzer's money he had the foresight to save. He joined Sweitzer and a Mr. Lee of Alexandria, the only commissary clerk to escape the raiding Confederates. The three gradually made their way to Alexandria, where they arrived on the morning of June 28.[80]

Fitz Lee and Stuart inspected the town of Fairfax Court House and its environs. Both found evidence of recent occupation by Union soldiers, "but the information was conclusive that the enemy had left this front entirely, the mobilized army having the day previous moved over toward Leesburg, while the local had retired to the fortifications near Washington." Although Stuart had not heard back from Mosby, all indications were that Stuart would be able to pass in the rear of the Army of the Potomac. Hooker had maintained his headquarters at Fairfax Court House before heading north in pursuit of the Army of Northern Virginia, so there was an ample bounty of supplies and other prizes to be had there. Stuart halted his column for a few hours to rest and refresh men and horses, enjoying the supplies left behind by the enemy.

Stuart's progress had been badly impeded by the frequent need to stop and graze his horses, "as we had no wagons with us, having to depend on the country for forage for both men and horses," recounted one of his horse artillerists. "The country that we passed through was desolate in the extreme, having been the camping ground for both Confederates and Federals for nearly three years."[81] The men appreciated the opportunity to rest and feed their mounts, for which much hard work still remained.

Armed with the important results of his reconnaissance and the interrogation of the prisoners, Stuart sent a courier to General Lee with the information, along with a duplicate to the War Department in Richmond. "I took possession of Fairfax C.H. this morning at nine o-clock, together with a large quantity of stores," he wrote. "The main body of Hooker's army has gone toward Leesburg, except the garrison of Alexandria and Washington, which has retreated within the fortifications."[82] This message was proof positive Stuart had performed the vital role of passing on critical intelligence to both Lee and the War Department. Unfortunately, neither the courier nor the intelligence ever reached the army commander, a failure that set the stage for decades of controversy that continues to this day.[83]

Moses Sweitzer, who had narrowly escaped from Fitz Lee at Annandale, also owned a store in Fairfax Court House. He was "perhaps, as well known as General Hooker himself, and certainly 'kept a better hotel,' though he reckoned without his host on this particular occasion." Sweitzer maintained two large warehouses brimming with "the good things of the world," including "such luxuries as pickled oysters, sardines and crackers, canned fruits, ginger-cakes by the barrel, shoes, socks, hats, gloves and clothing of every kind," recalled Garnett. "Imagine two brigades of Confederate cavalry turned in on such pasture. The houses were crowded with scores of laughing, yelling, singing, squeezing, pushing, and hungry troopers who rapidly placed this 'stock' where it would do the most good."[84] An officer with the Jeff Davis Legion agreed: "We had a gay time eating cheese, butter, molasses, etc."[85]

When they moved out again, "every man had on a white straw hat, and a pair of snowy white cotton gloves. Every trooper carried before him upon the pommel of his saddle a bale of smoking tobacco, or a drum of figs; every hand grasped a pile of ginger-cakes, which were rapidly disappearing." When McClellan, Venable, and Cooke made their way back from their encounter with the Yankee troopers, the razzing of their comrades greeted them. Their comrades had a good laugh at the sorry plight of the three veterans of the cherry pie episode before handing the staff officers their fair share of the bounty.[86]

Stuart also partook of the windfall. He sat on his horse in the middle of the street, chuckling as he watched the scene unfold. One member of his staff handed him a new pair of white cotton gloves, which he put on, and offered Stuart a box of cigars, which the non-smoking cavalier declined. Stuart enjoyed a box of dried figs and drank some lemonade prepared for him by some nearby troopers.[87] This was precisely the sort of folly Stuart most enjoyed, and he indulged heartily while the opportunity lasted. Still, plenty of serious work remained to be done.

For some horses, the rest at Fairfax came too late. The animals were beginning to break down all along the road, and many of Stuart's troopers found themselves dismounted. Those whose horses were finished were sent to the rear because of a lack of fit mounts. "A considerable squad turned to the rear at Fairfax," noted an officer of the 2nd North Carolina Cavalry.[88] Major Thomas Waller of the 9th Virginia Cavalry and several other officers of his regiment were given leaves of absence, and a number of enlisted men were furloughed because their horses were unfit for further service.[89] What began as a trickle of broken-down horses grew into a steady stream as the ride continued, slowly bleeding away Stuart's effective strength.

After a respite of several hours, the column mounted up again and headed for Dranesville. They arrived late in the afternoon, where they found the campfires of Maj. Gen. John Sedgwick's Federal Sixth Corps burning west of town. Chambliss's Brigade prepared for a fight but the enemy did not appear.[90] Several of Sedgwick's stragglers were captured. They indicated that the blueclad infantry had moved out that morning, heading for the Potomac River fords.[91]

A difficult choice faced the Confederate commander, explained John Esten Cooke. "What would Stuart do—what route would he now follow? There were few persons, if any, in the entire command, who could reply to that question. Cross at Leesburg? To merely follow up Hooker while Hooker followed up Lee, was very unlike Stuart. Strike across for the Blue Ridge, and cross at Shepherdstown? That would lose an immense amount of invaluable time and horse-flesh. Cross below Leesburg? That seemed impossible with the artillery, and difficult even for cavalry. The river was broad, deep, with a rocky and uneven bed; and so confident were the enemy of the impossibility of our crossing there, that not a picket watched the stream."[92]

The stage was set for the second instance where good luck graced Stuart's expedition. His advance on Rockville had sent tremors of panic throughout the Federal forces assigned to the defenses of Washington, D.C. Federal cavalry forces assigned to the defenses of the national capital had been stationed throughout Maryland, picketing the Potomac

River at various locations. However, Col. Charles Russell Lowell's 2nd Massachusetts Cavalry had been ordered to ride to Knoxville, Maryland, on June 26. Twenty-five miles later, Lowell received contradictory orders recalling him. Hooker wanted Lowell to report to Maj. Gen. William H. French's command. However, Maj. Gen. Samuel P. Heintzelman, in charge of the defenses ringing Washington, countermanded Hooker's order. As a result, on June 28 Lowell obeyed Heintzelman's directive and returned to the mouth of the Monocacy River near Frederick.[93]

When he reached the Monocacy, Lowell learned Stuart's command had already crossed the Potomac "at the very ford I was especially to watch; that there had been no picket there at all, and no notice had gone either to Washington or to Hooker till nearly twelve hours after the crossing," as Lowell later recounted. Lowell immediately set off in pursuit of Stuart and caught up, urging his advance guard to tail Stuart at a distance of less than one mile, which his men did, capturing a lieutenant and four privates along the way. "I have been after them for eighteen hours," Lowell reported on June 29, "but presume that I shall not harm them much."

The squabbling over whether Hooker or Heintzelman had authority to give Lowell orders meant that the critical crossing at Rowser's Ford was left unguarded and available for Stuart's use.[94]

Chapter 2

Across the Potomac

"The wagons were brand new, the mules fat and sleek, and the harness in use for the first time. Such a train we had never seen before and did not see again."

— Col. Richard L. T. Beale, 9th Virginia Cavalry

C rossing the Potomac River was a major milestone for the Confederate horsemen, and the failure to picket one of the fords was a Federal mistake Jeb Stuart willingly exploited. The Southern leader ordered his lead brigade under Brig. Gen. Wade Hampton to move directly for Rowser's Ford below Leesburg. As it did so, the troopers of the 2nd North Carolina "came in sight of Hancock's rear near Leesburg," recounted one of the Tar Heels. "Placing pickets we halted until after sunset, and then coming back several miles turned through a pine thicket without a road and having to use our hands to keep from losing our hats went into the road that leads to the Potomac river at Rowser's Ford."[1]

The general who led his men to Rowser's Ford was a steel-eyed South Carolinian built like a bull with a fighting spirit to match. Reputedly one of the richest men in the antebellum South, Wade Hampton's veins coursed with the blood of martial history. His grandfather, Wade Hampton I, was a revered Revolutionary War officer in Col. William Washington's cavalry.[2] His father, Wade Hampton II, served as a dragoon officer during the War of 1812.[3] Although he had no formal military training, Wade Hampton III left his vast plantations at the age of 43 when the war broke out, personally financed "Hampton's Legion," a contingent of South Carolina infantry, cavalry, and artillery, and set out to defeat the Yankees.[4]

National Archives

Brigadier General Wade Hampton

After commanding infantry early in the war, Hampton accepted Gen. Robert E. Lee's offer to command a brigade of horsemen in Stuart's cavalry division in July 1862. A superb horseman and a born leader, Hampton quickly demonstrated a natural grasp of mounted tactics. One Confederate, who observed him leading a mounted charge at Upperville just one week before Stuart set out north, called Hampton "a veritable god of war." Unlike so many officers with formal training, the former gentleman planter had an innate genius for mounted warfare.[5]

While Hampton prepared his men to cross the Potomac River, Chambliss's Brigade remained at Dranesville until Fitz Lee's Brigade came up. As Hampton approached the river, a local civilian who had just forded the wide waterway greeted him. He had good news. There were no pickets posted on the far side, and the river—though two feet higher than normal—was still fordable. With that, the South Carolinian guided his riders to the northern bank early in the night. He sent back word to Stuart, however, that crossing artillery at Rowser's Ford was impossible.[6]

Captain Richard B. Kennon, one of Stuart's staff officers, examined another ford lower down the river to see if the artillery could cross there.[7] His investigation found the passage impractical because of quicksand, rocks, and rugged banks.[8] Kennon, the grandson of Revolutionary War hero Gen. Richard Kennon, was born on November 10, 1835, in Norfolk, Virginia. He married Louisiana Barraud Cocke, daughter of future Confederate general Phillip St. George Cocke, in 1860. War interrupted his training as a physician in the spring of 1861. Kennon enlisted in the 4th Virginia Cavalry and was quickly appointed first lieutenant. He resigned his commission in November 1861 for a commission as first lieutenant and adjutant in the Provisional Army of the Confederate States of America. Kennon reported to the 8th Virginia Cavalry and was assigned to Stuart's staff in April 1863.[9]

"The Potomac was about a mile wide, the water deep, and the current strong," recalled Kennon. "I made the plunge in early night. The horse swam magnificently. When tired I would get off on a boulder, holding the bridle to let him rest.

Captain Richard B. Kennon, the first of Stuart's troopers to cross the Potomac River at Rowser's Ford.

Robert Trout

I reached the Maryland side. The night was calm, but no moon. However, as soon as the breathing of [the horse] came back to normal I sprung into the saddle and we took the plunge to return." A figure emerged from the woods when Kennon reached the Virginia side. He could not make out who it was in the darkness. The man placed his hand on Kennon's bridle and the captain dismounted to a bear hug from Stuart himself, who declared, "God be praised. I never expected to see you again."

Kennon saluted. "Where did you come from General?"

"I have been here all the time," responded the cavalry chief. "Can we make it?" Kennon told him of the current and other disadvantages of crossing at Rowser's Ford.[10] Stuart was determined not to give this ford up without at least trying it. "The ford was wide and deep and might well have daunted a less determined man than our indomitable General, for the water swept over the pommels of our saddles," recalled engineering officer Blackford.[11]

Six Federal prisoners captured that morning of the 27th near Fairfax were among the first forced to try the ford. The unfortunates were "quartermaster and commissary clerks, just out from Washington, and had spent the night in the city," recounted William J. Campbell, clerk of the 9th Virginia Cavalry's adjutant staff. "When captured they were starting out to join their respective commands." Campbell recalled their dandy attire as consisting of broadcloth, beaver hats, kid gloves, and "boiled" shirts. The nattily clad prisoners balked at the order to wade the river. "One of the prisoners protested against wading, as he did not want to spoil his fine clothes. About this time Gen. Stuart rode up and inquired the cause of the delay. On being told he promptly ordered them to enter the water, and he watched them plunge with evident amusement."[12]

The brief episode of gaiety over, the serious business of crossing began. "The spectacle was an impressive one as we forded the river," recalled a veteran of the 13th Virginia Cavalry. "The moon was shining beautifully, and a solemn silence seemed to pervade the troops, unbroken save by the splash of the horses' feet in the water as we passed from Virginia's soil."[13] The 3rd Virginia Cavalry was the first to cross in the perfect darkness. "You could hardly see your horse's ears," recalled a horse artillerist. "Each man as he rode past the battery was given a shell or cartridge to carry over. They did not relish the idea of handling the ammunition and growled very much at this duty imposed upon them. This had to be done, as the water reached the backs of an ordinary size

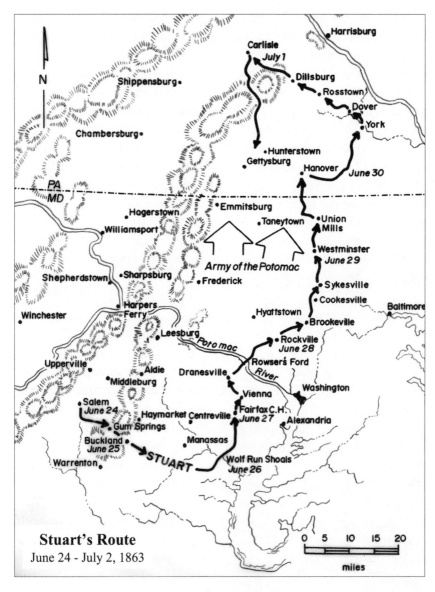

Stuart's Route
June 24 - July 2, 1863

horse, and of course was over the limber chests and caissons," he continued. "Gen. Stuart knew that if his ammunition got wet his artillery would be useless and would hamper his movements very much. His artillery was his right arm and saved him from defeat on many a battle field."[14]

Once on the other side, the shell-bearers deposited their precious cargo on the shore, leaving it to be re-loaded into the caissons. "The guns and caissons, although entirely submerged during nearly the whole crossing, were safely dragged through the river and up the steep and slippery bank, and by three o'clock on the morning of the 28th, the rear-guard had crossed and the whole command was established upon Maryland soil," recalled Maj. Henry McClellan. "No more difficult achievement was accomplished by the cavalry during the war." The night was quiet and moonlit, and the sight of horse after horse making its way across the nearly mile-wide Potomac in water that covered the saddles of the riders presented quite a spectacle. McClellan left a detailed account of the ordeal of the crossing:

> Where the current was strong the line would unconsciously be borne down the river, sometimes so far as to cause danger of missing the ford, when some bold rider would advance from the opposite shore and correct the alignment. Energy, endurance, and skill were taxed to the utmost; but the crossing was effected, and so silently the nearest neighbors were not aware of it until daylight.[15]

"Before 12 o'clock that night, in spite of the difficulties, to all appearances insuperable, indomitable energy and resolute determination

triumphed," Stuart declared. "Every piece was brought safely over, and the entire command in bivouac on Maryland soil. In this success the horse artillery displayed the same untiring zeal in their laborious toil through mud and water which has

Colonel Williams C. Wickham, commander of the 4th Virginia Cavalry. The 4th Virginia served as Stuart's rearguard once across the Potomac River.

Library of Congress

distinguished its members in battle."[16] The men noticed an immediate difference. "Oh, what a change!" declared Blackford. "From the hoof-trodden, war-wasted lands of old Virginia to a country fresh and plentiful. The march for three days had been through a country naturally poor at its best, but stripped by war of all the little it once had."[17]

Once on the far side, Confederate horsemen took possession of the C & O Canal, which constituted one of the major lines of supply for Hooker's army. Colonel Williams C. Wickham of the 4th Virginia Cavalry, Fitz Lee's Brigade, commanded Stuart's rear guard. His men captured a number of canal boats, some containing troops and contraband blacks.[18] "One, a splendidly rigged craft, with the stars and stripes flying profusely over it, and freighted with a live cargo, in the shape of Yankee officers and officials, was anchored and taken in, to their great surprise and mortification," recalled one of Hampton's South Carolinians. "The others were richly laden."[19]

Stuart explained his idea for putting the canal out of commission while saving the boats. "I propose to turn all of them crosswise in the canal and then cut the sluice gate to the river," he said. "That will tear out such a big opening that it will leave them high and dry for sixty to ninety days."[20] They did just that, stranding the canal boats. "We took the mules, 24 in number, on with us," recalled 2nd Virginia cavalryman Pvt. Rufus Peck. "We helped the women and children from the boats and took their furniture out, as we didn't want to destroy private property. It was hard to do then, with them all crying like they did, but such is war."[21] Stuart interrogated his prisoners and ascertained the Army of the Potomac had been at Poolesville the previous day and was now in motion for Frederick. He also learned a more stunning bit of news: Major General George G. Meade had replaced Joe Hooker in command of the army.[22]

Although Stuart's ride north was already behind schedule, his men and horses were exhausted from the ordeal of their crossing. The long hours in the saddle without rest were taking their toll on troopers and animals alike. Captain Blackford, his engineering officer, brought two horses with him on the expedition, his favorite mare Magic and a stallion named Manassas. "Not a mouthful of grain had I been able to beg, borrow, or steal for my horses," he lamented, "and where I could not find it, there was apt to be none to be found." Magic looked so gaunt that Blackford was afraid to ride her, so she was led behind Manassas. "The necessity for stopping to graze the horses on this march had delayed us a great deal, both in the time it took and the weakening of the animals from such light diet."[23] Blackford expected to go into battle at some point during the expedition, and he wanted to save Magic for combat. Manassas was also not at full strength, for he had been wounded during the June 25 attacks against part of General Hancock's corps. Stuart knew his command was in a weakened condition and that his horses needed a few hours rest. In spite of the additional delays added to his already behind schedule journey, he ordered a few hours of rest for his men and animals.[24]

His men were not in much better condition. Lieutenant Francis H. Wigfall, a member of Capt. James Breathed's battery of horse artillery, left a vivid description of his own appearance the next day. "My boots were utterly worn out, my pantaloons were all one big hole as the Irishman would say, my coat was like a beggar's and my hat was actually falling to pieces in addition to lacking its crown which has allowed my hair, not cut since some time before leaving Culpeper to protrude and gave a highly picturesque finish to my appearance." Fortunately for the dilapidated lieutenant, he found some new pants and a new hat on June 29. His tatterdemalion condition was representative of Stuart's column as a whole.[25]

The men enjoyed their respite on the morning of June 28. "Had an excellent feed for horses and men," remembered an officer of the 3rd Virginia Cavalry.[26] The men scattered in the fields, unsaddled their horses, and turned them out to graze. "It was refreshing to watch the canal boats come gliding innocently and unexpectedly into these sleepy Rebs," recalled Capt. Frank Robertson, a member of Stuart's staff. A descendant of Pocahontas, Robertson could trace his ancestry back to the beginnings of Virginia's history. Born in Richmond in 1841, he was the son of a former governor of Virginia. Frank was a student at the University of Virginia when war came in the spring of 1861. He was commissioned a lieutenant in the Virginia service and spent two months drilling at the Virginia Military Institute before joining the 48th Virginia Infantry. Health problems, however, kept him from serving with his regiment. When he was well enough to return to duty in March 1863, Robertson joined Stuart's staff as an engineering officer.[27]

"I was lying only a few steps from the canal when one packet, well loaded with Yankee officers and many ladies, came trotting in," continued Robertson. "The astonishment, if nothing more, of the passengers when they saw hundreds of Rebs filling the landscape was intensely interesting. They stared blankly at us as they passed on to where we had a committee at work giving paroles and burning freight boats. We were in no condition to accept prisoners, so the passengers proceeded joyously to Washington, the gorgeously uniformed officers with paroles in their pockets." The other boats, including two loaded with whiskey, were burned.[28]

Stuart established his headquarters in a nearby home. The ladies of the house prepared an excellent breakfast for the Virginian and his staff. "The sun was rising and everybody was preparing to move off," recalled Theodore Garnett. "The ladies expressed an earnest desire to see our command, so they walked with me to the gate and I pointed out about two brigades in the meadow below the house, which could scarcely be seen through the thick fog. But soon the mist cleared away and they looked long and eagerly at the first Confederate troops they had ever seen, expressing their great astonishment at what seemed to them, such an immense multitude."[29]

"I realized the importance of joining our army in Pennsylvania, and resumed the march northward early on the 28th," wrote Stuart. Hampton was sent to Rockville via Darnestown while the remaining two brigades took the direct route to Rockville. "On the advance we took the most obscure road through the country, evading the pikes," noted an officer of the 5th Virginia Cavalry. "It was a long and tedious march, with little of interest except an occasional skirmish with home guards."[30] Along the way Hampton encountered small parties of the enemy which, with a number of wagons and teams, he captured. The efficient South Carolinian reached Rockville in advance of the main body. Chambliss's Brigade, led by the 9th Virginia Cavalry, had a running fight with the 2nd New York Cavalry, but "a dashing charge made by one squadron of the Ninth Virginia cleared the road effectively," as Garnett recalled the clash. "I remember seeing several prisoners pass me going to the rear with bloody heads, showing that the saber had been at work."[31] Sabers or not, the fresher horses of the New Yorkers easily outpaced the tired Confederate mounts, which prevented the Southerners from taking many prisoners during this skirmishing.[32]

When he arrived at Rockville, Hampton encountered what he believed to be a large force of the enemy. He reported this to Stuart, who brought up Chambliss's Brigade to reinforce Hampton. "It was past noon when Stuart entered Rockville," recalled Major McClellan, but the enemy had already disappeared, retreating in the direction of Great Falls. One of Hampton's South Carolinians colorfully claimed that he and his comrades pounced on "several officials of the Baboon dynasty on pleasure excursions in the vicinity—causing the trembling-kneed tyrant to barricade the streets with barrels, boxes, etc., etc., against a *coup de main* of this energetic 'rebel.'"[34]

The Confederates speedily took possession of the important town, which was situated on the direct wagon road from Washington, D. C. to the Army of the Potomac. In other words, Stuart's command sat firmly astride the Union army's lines of communication with the War Department. The horsemen enjoyed tearing down miles of telegraph lines, rendering that mode of communication inoperable.[35]

Not long after taking possession of the town, a sight that stunned even the veterans of Stuart's command rolled into the view of Stuart's advance scouts: a Union wagon train eight miles long. The snake-like dusty white canvas-topped wagons were approaching Rockville from the direction of Washington. Union quartermaster officer Capt. Henry Page commanded the train, which had only half a dozen or so cavalry escorts for support.[36] The teamsters manning the train were largely unarmed. "There was not a musket, carbine, or pistol among this whole company of teamsters," a Washington newspaper later reported. The train consisted of 140 brand-new wagons and mule teams. Most of the wagons carried at least one bale of hay and one bag of high-quality grain. As this ponderous column heading for the Army of the Potomac approached Rockville, a local clergyman galloped to the head of the train to report that the advance of a large force of Confederate cavalry had captured another train of 28 wagons, and that the enemy was in possession of the town.[37]

Panic gripped the Federal teamsters when they spotted the Confederate cavalry. With only a few options, none of them good, the teamsters up front attempted to turn their wagons around to escape. "Seeing the necessity of prompt action if we captured this train," recalled clerk William J. Campbell of Col. Richard Beale's 9th Virginia, "we sent a man back to Col. Beale . . . for a squadron to charge the train, but before the squadron reached us Gen. Stuart arrived and asked for volunteers to join us in the charge we had offered to lead, and several promptly volunteered."[38] "Stuart's face flushed at the thought of capturing this splendid prize," observed Captain Cooke, "and shouted to a squadron to follow him, and the main column to push on, he went at a swift gallop on the track of the fleeing wagons."[39] Stuart sent Chambliss's Brigade in pursuit, with orders to push ahead at a gallop, and not to draw rein until they had overhauled the leading wagon of the train.[40] "A circus was on that I have never seen paralleled," recounted Captain Robertson.[41]

Troopers from the 9th Virginia Cavalry, Chambliss's Brigade, set their spurs and pursued the wagons. As they passed a nearby home, the woman of the house ran out, clapping her hands in excitement. "Push on!" she yelled. "You have nearly caught them!" After riding a mile or so, the Virginians spotted a small party of enemy cavalry drawn up in line across the road in what would prove to be a vain attempt to protect the wagons. The troopers with the fastest horses were ordered forward to reinforce the men leading the pursuit, but before they got within two hundred yards the Federal horsemen ineffectively fired a volley, wheeled, and fled as fast as their horses would carry them.[42] "They fired at us and ran," clerk Campbell reminisced, "but we held our fire for closer game."[43]

Captain Page was in the middle of the train when the Confederates made their dash. He hastily jumped his horse over a fence and headed for the woods, dodging a hail of bullets as he abandoned his charges to the tender mercies of Jeb Stuart and his Southern cavalrymen. Page eventually made his way back to Washington, having lost both his wagon train and his dignity.[44] So did an artist working for *Harper's Weekly*. He, too, had been traveling with the wagon train. When the shouting and shooting began he joined a few others lucky enough to be mounted on fleet horses and escaped Stuart's dragnet.[45]

Another lucky soul was the driver of a mail wagon, who had left Baltimore that morning. According to a newspaper account, he was not far from the wagon train when he spotted flames leaping into the sky. When he spotted Southern horsemen dashing across a field toward him, the driver whipped his horse back across a small drawbridge, drew it up after him, and saved his mail and himself from capture. Prudently, he headed back toward Baltimore, picking up some of the escaped teamsters along the way.

Lieutenant Thomas Lee and a handful of men from the 2nd South Carolina Cavalry of Hampton's Brigade led the chase, with Captain Blackford riding along with them.[46] "After them we flew, popping away with our pistols at such drivers as did not pull up, but the more we popped the faster those in front plied the whip," recalled Blackford, "finally, coming to a sharp turn in the road, one upset and a dozen or two others piled up on top of it, until you could see nothing but the long ears and kicking legs of the mules sticking above bags of oats emptied from the wagons upon them." The pile-up forced the rest of the column to halt, ending the chase.[47] "In several places I saw as many as four wagons, with their teams, gully with the poor mules stretched upon the ground beneath the wagons, struggling in vain against the heavy burden and strong harness that held them, sufferers, in their places," recounted Lieutenant Beale, whose squadron helped lead the pursuit.[48]

When he spotted this spectacle, Stuart burst into laughter, turned toward a fellow officer, and exclaimed, "Did you ever see anything like that in all your life!"[49] The farthest wagon was within only three or four miles of Washington. "The dome of the capital was distinctly visible from the spot at which this wagon was halted," remembered Garnett.[50] "When we neared the end [of the train] we were in sight of the steeples of Georgetown," recounted Campbell.[51] One of Hampton's men left a more colorful description: "Jeb contented himself with a naked-eye view of the steeples and spires of this modern Sodom."[52]

"This was certainly a very bold move, and it is to be hoped that they will not be allowed to escape with them," observed a correspondent writing for a New York newspaper.[53] A Washington newspaper sounded a similar note. "This was a pretty bold dash, almost within range of the guns of some of the city forts," declared the reporter. "We had no idea that any rebel troops were so near us."[54]

"Some of the wagons immediately faced to the rear, executing the movement so nicely that it would have brought the blush of shame to the face of any old teamster on the plains," noted one of Breathed's horse artillerists. "I have often heard it said by old teamsters that I have met out west on the plains that they could turn a six mule wagon on a tin plate, but the movements of those demoralized and stampeded teamsters came nearer executing that movement than anything I had ever seen."[55] Some of the panicked Union teamsters tried to cut their teams loose in a desperate effort to escape. Others jogged along leisurely, resigned to being captured, while still others set their wagons ablaze to prevent them from being taken by Stuart's men.[56] "Not one [wagon] escaped, though many were upset and broken, so as to require their being burned," Stuart reported. "More than one hundred and twenty-five best United States model wagons and splendid teams with gay caparisons were secured and driven off. The mules and harness of the broken wagons were also secured."[57]

As the Southern troopers soon discovered, most of the wagons contained oats intended for the animals of the Army of the Potomac. "Here was a godsend for our poor horses," remembered a relieved Blackford. "It did one's heart good to see the way the poor brutes got on the outside of those oats."[58] The rest of the wagons were carrying bread, hardtack, bottles of whiskey, sugar, hams, knives, forks, and other useful items. "The bacon and crackers, as well as the whiskey, proved to our jaded and hungry troopers most acceptable," explained Col. Richard L. T. Beale, commander of the 9th Virginia Cavalry.[59]

Richard Beale was born on May 22, 1819 at Hickory Hill, in Westmoreland County, Virginia. The graduate of Dickinson College and the University of Virginia was admitted to the bar in 1839. He was practicing near his birthplace when he was elected to a single term of Congress in 1846. Beale was also a delegate to the state constitutional convention in 1851 and a member of the Virginia House of Burgesses from 1858 to 1860. Beale enlisted as a first lieutenant of cavalry in a company called Lee's Light Horse, which later became a company of the 9th Virginia Cavalry. He was successively promoted captain, major, lieutenant colonel, and finally colonel of the regiment and served credibly in every campaign in which Stuart's cavalry was engaged. Although untrained as a soldier, Beale was both competent and reliable. Stuart would need his steady advice and competence during the Gettysburg Campaign.[60]

General Lee's operating orders for the expedition specifically instructed Stuart to do what he could to obtain supplies for the use of the army. Here were 125 fully loaded wagons, a glittering prize Stuart was loath to give up. "The wagons were brand new, the mules fat and sleek, and the harness in use for the first time," observed Colonel Beale. "Such a train we had never seen before and did not see again."[61]

The treasure trove also posed a serious logistical dilemma. Stuart now had more than 600 mules to feed on top of his own command's horses, the wagons would slow down his column—which was already well behind schedule—and he had hundreds of prisoners who needed to be guarded. Whether Stuart gave serious consideration to destroying the train is not known. What we do know for certain is that he made up his

Colonel John R. Chambliss, Jr., temporary commander of Stuart's third brigade.

Library of Congress

mind to take the 125 wagons with him into Pennsylvania. The decision triggered a controversy that has raged for more than 140 years.

The victory created other headaches for Stuart. The pursuit and capture of the train scattered Chambliss's Brigade across the Maryland countryside. The Virginians would have to be reorganized before they could continue on their journey. The man responsible for leading them was Col. John R. Chambliss, Jr., a thirty-year-old former member of the West Point Class of 1853, where his best friend was Union Brig. Gen. David M. Gregg. Chambliss resigned his commission the next year to become a Virginia planter, an occupation he enjoyed until 1861. He served in the militia and as an aide-de-camp to the governor of Virginia until the state troops were taken over by the Confederacy. Chambliss was commissioned as colonel of the 41st Virginia Infantry and then as colonel of the 13th Virginia Cavalry in July 1861. After service south of the James River and on the line of the Rappahannock River during the Maryland Campaign, the 13th Virginia was assigned to Brig. Gen. William H. F. Lee's Brigade in November 1862. When "Rooney" Lee was wounded on June 9 at Brandy Station, Chambliss, as Lee's senior colonel, assumed temporary command of the brigade. His regiments had fought hard in the Loudoun Valley fighting, and Chambliss had already proven himself to be an experienced and dependable cavalryman.[62]

The serendipitous meeting with the wagons increased Southern morale and turned Confederate eyes toward the enemy capital, which offered a tempting target for the ambitious Stuart. However, it did not take the general long to realize that Fitz Lee's Brigade would not be able to reach the outer defenses of the enemy capital at Washington before darkness set in, and the Federals would have plenty of time to move sufficient troops to defend the road leading into the capital. "I firmly believe we could have captured Washington that day," was Captain Robertson's optimistic but mistaken recollection.[63]

Determined to at least investigate the opportunity, Stuart and Garnett rode out to reconnoiter. They rode for a while along the length of the train until they stopped in front of a farmhouse to ask how far they were from Georgetown. "Six miles," responded the frightened farmer. Garnett remembers watching Stuart closely. "As the General rode away I noticed the expression of his countenance. He was evidently balancing in his mind the chances in favor of our entering Washington City, and he was trying to make up his mind to give up the attempt," concluded the staffer.[64]

Stuart soon made up his mind. "To attack at night with cavalry, particularly unless certain of surprise, would have been extremely hazardous; to wait till morning, would have lost much time from my march to join General Lee, without the probability of compensating results," was how he explained his decision to avoid Washington. "I therefore determined, after getting the wagons under way, to proceed directly north, so as to cut the Baltimore and Ohio Railroad (now becoming the enemy's main war artery) that night. I found myself now encumbered by about 400 prisoners, many of whom were officers. I paroled nearly all at Brookeville that night, and the remainder next day at Cooksville. Among the number, were Major [James C.] Duane and Captain [Nathaniel] Michler, Engineers, U.S. Army."[65]

With the wagons making for such a long train, Stuart issued an order designed to close it up. "To make the wagon train shorter, two of the mules [of each four-mule team] were detached from each wagon and placed in a drove," recalled Pvt. J. A. Buxton, one of Stuart's couriers and a trooper with the 2nd North Carolina Cavalry.[66] Most of the wagons were still heavy with provisions, and only two mules were now available to pull each one. Stuart's troopers were now burdened not only with the train, but with a herd of over 200 loose mules that would accompany the column north.

It did not take long for word of the loss of the wagon train to reach the Federal War Department. "The wagon train is still here, burning. The rebel pickets are 2 miles from here. Citizens just in report a force of infantry and cavalry of about 8,000 or 10,000 in Rockville. This is pretty reliable, as I get it from several, among them a man said to be a Union man, who was taken near here, carried to Rockville, and paroled. They took all the horses about here," was how the only partially correct report read. "It was some of Stuart's men that burned the wagon train. Two of the teamsters escaped. The rest were all taken. One of the teamsters is near here, wounded. Wire is in bad condition beyond me, and will be impossible for me to repair, as three poles have been cut down and the wire taken away. The wagons are badly burned; some of them entirely destroyed. They left about one hour ago."[67]

The loss of the wagon train set off a flurry of recriminations among the Union army's quartermaster department. "Last fall I gave orders to prevent the sending of wagon trains from this place to Frederick without escort. The situation repeats itself, and gross carelessness and inattention to military rule has this morning cost us 150 wagons and 900 mules, captured by cavalry between this and Rockville," an angry Quartermaster General Montgomery C. Meigs wrote to Brig. Gen. Rufus Ingalls, the Army of the Potomac's chief quartermaster. "Yesterday morning a detachment of over 400 cavalry moved from this place to join the army. This morning 150 wagons were sent without escort. Had the cavalry been delayed or the wagons hastened, they could have been protected and saved. All the cavalry of the Defenses of Washington was swept off by the army, and we are now insulted by burning wagons 3 miles outside of Tennallytown. Your communications are now in the hands of General Fitzhugh Lee's brigade."[68]

Ingalls replied a few hours later. "The cavalry that left before the wagon train has not been heard of here. Had the train been guarded by any ordinary force, the result would have been the same. Its starting was ill-timed and unfortunate. There is a powerful force of rebel cavalry between here and Rockville. Our own cavalry is in motion, and the army will march in the morning. We must and will fight to the end."[69] The failure to send an escort with the wagon train prompted Meigs to order an investigation of the episode.[70]

Thomas Nelson Conrad of the 3rd Virginia Cavalry was one of Stuart's best-known and most effective scouts. An ordained minister, Conrad was a daring and bold scout who regularly forayed into Washington, D.C. In late June he was operating in the vicinity of the national capital, seeking information on the disposition of the Union armies. Stuart had made a promise to Conrad: the next time the cavalier crossed the Potomac, Stuart would use Conrad as a guide for a hell-for-leather dash into Washington with his whole command with the intent of making the White House his headquarters. Taking Stuart at his word, Conrad mounted his horse and rode through Georgetown, the District of Columbia, and up the Rockville Pike to Tenallytown, where he found the rifle pits and entrenchments manned by War Department clerks and merchants armed with muskets nervously awaiting the enemy's approach.

Alert pickets ordered the minister to halt and explain where he was going and his business once he got there. He was also instructed not to ride beyond the trench lines unless he wished to be captured or killed by the rebels, who were supposedly just over the hill and who would be on the outskirts of the city in a few hours. Amused, Conrad insisted on continuing his ride, explaining that his business in Rockville would suffer by his absence—especially if the rebels were there. After a few minutes of discussion he was permitted to proceed so long as he was willing to take the risk.

Conrad had not ridden far beyond the rifle pits when he spotted Yankee videttes on every hilltop prepared to signal the Confederate advance with their carbines. He continued on until he met a courier from the Army of the Potomac dashing at full speed toward the capital. The courier reined in on seeing Conrad, dismounted, and raised his carbine, calling on Conrad to halt. When the scout complied, the courier ordered him to advance if he was a friend, state who he was, his business, and where he proposed to go. "It was not a very desirable position for [a] chaplain-scout, as you may imagine," recalled Conrad. "The fierce and excited manner of the Yankee soldier, with carbine uplifted and hand on trigger, was not calculated to make me feel comfortable." Conrad nonchalantly answered to the courier's satisfaction, and the Yankee lowered his carbine. He was a courier from the Army of the Potomac, he explained, and he had dispatches for Washington. To Conrad's amazement, the rider explained that Hooker had been relieved of command and Maj. Gen. George G. Meade had taken his place. As he dashed off, the rider yelled back over his shoulder for Conrad to be on the lookout for Stuart's cavalry, which had just passed through Rockville.

Conrad was within five miles of Rockville and wanted to catch up to Stuart's column, so he quickened his pace, hoping to overtake it before the troopers passed out of reach. To his frustration, another Federal courier stopped him with the same questions, slowing his ride to Rockville. By the time Conrad finally reached the town Stuart had been gone for several hours, and was now beyond his reach. The series of delays deprived Stuart of the services of one of his most reliable and most daring scouts.[71]

The proximity of such a large force of Confederate cavalry to the Federal capital engendered panic in Washington. That night, a few of Chambliss's stragglers were captured seven miles from Georgetown. They reported that Stuart's command was en route to attack the Baltimore & Ohio Railroad. This intelligence, combined with the loss of the wagon train, meant "Washington has been in a state of great alarm today, although there has been very little manifestations other than usual upon the streets," reported a newspaper correspondent. "Little knots of men are to be seen everywhere eagerly discussing 'the impending crisis.' No story is too incredulous to find plenty will credit it all. The public, as a general thing, however, know very little of the real condition of affairs."[72]

The presence of so many enemy cavalry operating on the outskirts of the national capital triggered a reaction from the military forces assigned to the city's defenses. "Every available soldier had been given to Meade, and the city was at the mercy of the 'rebel raiders,'" observed Southern scout Conrad. "The clerks from all the departments and the able-bodied men from every quarter were hurried to the entrenchments around the city for its defense. It was even said that a gunboat was detained at the navy yard to receive the cabinet and other high officials, with their most important papers, in the event of the rebel cavalry dashing into the city."[73]

The Federals tried to mount a credible pursuit of Stuart, but they did not have sufficient force available to take on three brigades of Confederate cavalry. Only 300 troopers from Lowell's 2nd Massachusetts Cavalry set out after the Southerners. "You may laugh and think it preposterous for one Battalion, three hundred strong, chasing three Brigades of the renowned cavalry, twelve thousand in number," observed one of the Massachusetts men, "yet such is the fact, and we followed them up so close that at times our advance guard was not more than three quarters of a mile from the rebel column. We arrived at Rockville at 10 P.M. and saw a number of army wagons yet burning, having been set on fire by rebels." The Bay State riders could do little other than follow at a safe distance and helplessly watch the enemy.[74]

Like Fairfax, Rockville offered the gray riders a virtual cornucopia. "We had for several days been marching on small rations, but now our needs were abundantly supplied for the time, by the kind citizens of Rockville, and from the captured wagons, a few of which contained provisions," recalled one of Chambliss's 13th Virginia troopers.[75]

Rockville resident John Higgins described Stuart's occupation of the decidedly pro-Southern town. "Three brigades of rebels in all, about noon captured an incoming Federal wagon train of 170 wagons and swept the whole country clean of horses and servants," he wrote. "During the day they brought in 600 prisoners, men, soldiers, citizens and put them in the court house. Their yells were so terrific at each fresh arrival of prisoners." In spite of the terrifying Rebel yells, the behavior of the occupiers impressed Higgins. "Not withstanding all, they behaved better than I expected, never entered the houses. They vowed they were gentlemen and do not distress women and children and destroy dwellings."[76] Gentlemen they may have been, but the Rockville citizens were not sorry to see the gray horde move on later that day.

*   *   *

Fully cognizant he was far behind schedule and that he had no choice but to keep moving, Stuart left Rockville, his column burdened with 125 wagons and hundreds of mules. The inconvenience of escorting the massive wagon train was immediately obvious to every trooper. "We had scarcely set

Captain John Esten Cooke,
Stuart's cousin and staff
officer.

Library of Congress

out from Rockville before many of us began to regret our capture, foreseeing that the train would impede our movements, and be very difficult to guard in passing through the enemy's country," noted a Virginian.[77]

The long and winding column passed a women's seminary in Rockville. "Flocks of the pretty maidens congregated on the front to greet us, showing strong sympathy for our cause, and cutting off all the buttons they could get hold of from our uniforms as souvenirs," recounted Blackford. "In passing along the street I saw a very duplicate of my little daughter Lizzie. Never have I seen so remarkable a likeness between two people. Frank Robertson was as much struck with it as I was. Twenty years after he met her there, a grown woman."[78]

A pretty girl spotted Capt. John Esten Cooke of Stuart's staff. She rushed from the portico of the seminary building, pirouetted, and clapped her hands with joy at spotting Confederate soldiers. "Oh! Here is one of General Stuart's aides!" she exclaimed. She pulled some hair from the mane of Cooke's horse as a souvenir on the grounds that he was "a Secession horse." Stuart, who was riding a short distance behind Cooke, followed shortly, "gay, laughing, his blue eyes under the black feather full of the joy of the soldier, and a wild welcome greeted him. The scene was one which beggars description," recalled Cooke.[79]

D. C. Keeler, the mail agent for the Army of the Potomac's Twelfth Corps, together with a few members of his staff, was riding toward Frederick from Washington to rejoin the army. Just outside Rockville he encountered a recently discharged Union surgeon who had just come from Great Falls, where some of Stuart's troopers had captured him. The doctor reported that the enemy had burned six canal boats there and did considerable damage to the canal. When the doctor produced discharge papers, Fitz Lee had written out a pass that instructed his men to allow the doctor "through the pickets of the Army of Old Virginia, he being discharged, and glad to get away from the tyranny of the United States Government." As Keeler and his companions rode out of Rockville, a rebel picket stopped them. Because they were wearing civilian clothing, the picket informed him that he would allow them to pass into the town, but not out. Keeler had to wait for the passage of the entire Confederate column before resuming his ride north.[80]

As they rode and rolled along, Stuart's troopers fanned out across Montgomery County, seizing horses wherever they found them, "pouncing with special vim upon the fat animals owned by the Quakers about Sandy Spring," observed a Washington newspaper. "Some of them skirted as near Washington as Silver Spring, on the Seventh Street road, but left again in considerable haste." The reporter speculated that numerous Maryland citizens had joined the Confederate column, "swelling their numbers considerably and making themselves useful as guides from their knowledge of the country and the locality of good stock."[81]

The raiders halted the stagecoach that connected Washington with the B & O at Laurel, Maryland, taking the horses but leaving the driver and the passengers alone to make their way to Laurel on foot, a distance of nearly fourteen miles. The passage of the raiders also panicked local farmers, who headed for the safety of the defenses of the national capital en masse, driving their horses and cattle before them.[82]

The Confederate column enjoyed the pretty countryside. "Passed through a beautiful & highly cultivated, though not very rich, section of country," noted an admirer, "the people having seen but little war in this part of Montgomery County." Played out horses broke down regularly on the march, leaving the troopers with no option but to comb the countryside for replacement mounts. Some of Stuart's troopers entered a saddler's shop in Laurel, helping themselves to fine new saddles and the horses penned outside.[83] They spent the night of June 28 at Brookeville after rumors of nearby enemy soldiers delayed their advance again. Like Rockville, a bevy of beautiful girls greeted the Confederates, hailing them as conquering heroes. They "thronged back and forth with baskets of cakes, and bread, and meat, and huge pitchers of ice-water— penetrating fearlessly the press of trampling hoofs and ministering to the necessities of the rebels with undisguised satisfaction," recalled a Southern staff officer.[84]

The column arrived at Brookeville about 6:00 p.m., much to the surprise of the local populace. Stuart visited the home of Rev. W. Kent Boyle, a Methodist minister, for his headquarters. "They did us no harm, except to eat our meat and bread, which according to Scripture we refused them not," reported Reverend Boyle. "Our house was occupied all night by the Rebels and paroled Government officers, although they confined themselves to one room and the porch." Stuart spent an hour on Reverend Boyle's porch and gave him a written statement that he had used the porch and room for the purpose of paroling prisoners, thus preventing any trouble should Boyle be called to account for their presence in his home. The note stated that Stuart and his troops had commandeered the house for their own purposes. "I never saw a more polite though motley crew, behaving themselves with perfect decorum, save the impressment of horses," continued the Reverend. "Mine, however, escaped. Two of the officers, Major Deane and Captain Mickling, of the United States Engineers, were as perfect gentlemen as I ever saw." A Washington newspaper reporting on Stuart's visit concluded his column "was the same rebel force which passed northwest of this city last evening in the direction of Westminster, doubtlessly aiming to reach their forces at York or Gettysburg, which gave rise to the alarm here last night."[85]

The Confederates soon reached Cookesville, where the advance encountered and scattered a small party of the enemy and took a few prisoners. "Having heard that a party of the enemy were ahead, sent forward two Regiments to surprise & capture them," recorded an officer of the 3rd Virginia Cavalry, "but they had themselves captured one of Gen. Lee's couriers & learning our proximity, fled."[86] Some of the captives claimed they belonged to the "Seven Hundred Loyal Eastern Shoremen."[87] Stuart decided to parole these prisoners, a time-consuming process that Major McClellan described as "a useless task; for the Federal authorities refused to acknowledge the parole, and returned officers and men immediately to duty."[88] Stuart also paroled all of his other prisoners, including Duane, Mickling, and the sutlers taken by Fitz Lee at Annandale.[89]

Stuart mounted his men at 1:00 a.m. on June 29 and rode on. He was so exhausted he fell asleep in the saddle. Tottering from side to side, the general presented a comical appearance. Stuart was not alone in his exhaustion; many of his men sat their horses while sound asleep. "I remember the laughable specter of Major McClellan, sitting grave, erect, and motionless upon his horse in front of a country store by the roadside, to which the animal had made his way and halted," recalled Cooke. "The Major seemed to be waiting—for somebody, or something—meanwhile he was snoring."[90] Many fatigued troopers fell out of the saddle, rudely awakened when their bodies crashed to the ground.

Fitz Lee's Brigade, meanwhile, reached the railroad soon after daylight after riding all night. The Virginians burned the bridge at Sykesville and tore up the track at Hood's Mills after Stuart's main body crossed over it. "Much time was consumed in tearing up the track at Hood's Mill, destroying the bridge at Sykesville and the telegraph lines," noted one of Breathed's gunners. "This was thoroughly done and the last link between Meade and Washington was broken."[91] Once again, this process delayed the advance of the Confederate column and set Stuart's schedule back even further. Although the destruction of the railroad, bridge, and telegraph line had taken some time, explained Stuart, "this work was effectually accomplished, and the last means of communication between General Meade's army and Washington was destroyed."[92] The Confederates overestimated the damage, which was not significant. "The damage done to the road at the two points named can be repaired in two or three hours, and if nothing further is done the travel will not be interrupted," declared a Washington newspaper on June 30.[93] Another correctly observed, "The effect of the raid is to interrupt communication with the Army of the Potomac."[94]

Stuart also established measures to intercept trains on the Baltimore & Ohio Railroad. He knew Hooker had been relieved of command of the Army of the Potomac, and expected the deposed general to return to Washington via the railroad. Although Stuart wanted to capture "Fighting Joe," word reached the Federal authorities that Stuart's command was ahead laying in wait, so the train took the alarm and turned back. Hooker, who had already lost his command, was thus spared the indignity of being captured by the Confederate cavalry.[94] Stuart's men remained in possession of the Baltimore & Ohio Railroad nearly all day and spent the night there.[95]

In addition to Hooker's removal, Stuart had also learned the Federal army was moving northward through Frederick. "It was important for me to reach our column [main army] with as little delay as possible, to acquaint the commanding general with the nature of the enemy's movements, as well as to place with his column my cavalry force," explained Stuart.[96] At 10:30 a.m. on June 29, the cavalrymen were in the saddle again and heading for Westminster, Maryland. Matters were about to take a more serious turn for Stuart's command.

Unpleasant surprises lay ahead.

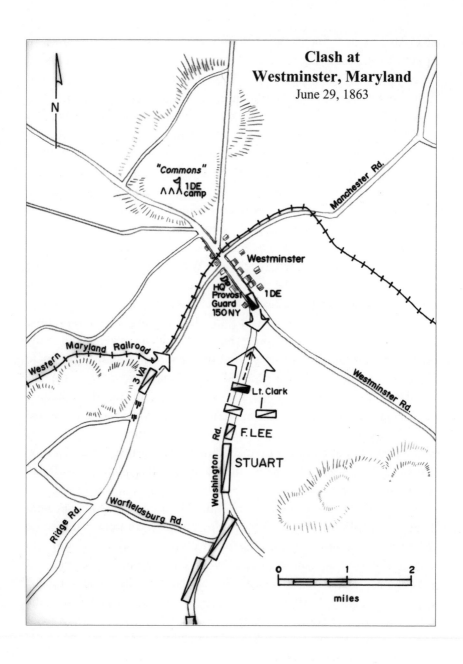

Clash at
Westminster, Maryland
June 29, 1863

N

"Commons"
∧∧∧ 1DE camp

Manchester Rd.

Westminster

HQ
Provost
Guard
150 NY

1DE

Western   Maryland   Railroad

3 VA

Westminster Rd.

Lt. Clark

F. LEE

Washington Rd.

STUART

Ridge Rd.

Warfieldsburg Rd.

0   1   2

miles

Chapter 3

Cavalry Clash at Westminster

"An almost suicidal bravery."

— A. H. Huber, Postmaster, Westminster, Maryland

By the penultimate day of June, Maj. Gen. Jeb Stuart and his horse soldiers had been in the saddle five full days. Everyone was rapidly approaching the limit of human physical endurance. The combination of the detour, the skirmish at Fairfax, and the capture of the wagons had thrown their schedule out the window. There was no possibility of reaching Hanover, Pennsylvania, by the morning of June 28 (as Stuart had originally planned). Instead it was Westminster, Maryland, they rode into on the afternoon of June 29.[1]

In addition to being the seat of Carroll County, Westminster was a critical railhead. The Western Maryland Railroad passed through the town, and the city was about to become a major Union logistics center during the coming battle of Gettysburg. A rail supply terminus, the railroad was an integral part of the so-called Pipe Creek Line, a defensive position scouted by the Army of the Potomac's active and diligent engineering officers. Stuart, however, did not know this, which set the stage for a confrontation in the streets of the town. For several weeks a small detachment of Lt. Pulaski Bowman's 150th New York Infantry had been performing outpost duty and watching for saboteurs in occupied Westminster. Bowman established his headquarters in the Odd Fellows Hall on East Main Street, a central place for the citizens to gather for meetings and entertainment.

Major General Robert Schenck, the commander of the Middle Military District headquartered in Baltimore, had a small cavalry force attached to his command. General Schenck realized the small contingent of New York infantrymen was probably inadequate to hold the town. He also knew Stuart's large cavalry column was operating in Maryland, and that it was probably headed for Westminster on its way into Pennsylvania. On June 27 Schenck ordered Maj. Napoleon Bonaparte Knight, commander of the 1st Delaware Cavalry, to take two companies (about 95 men) and ride toward Westminster to perform outpost and picket duty.[2]

Knight had briefly enlisted in a Confederate regiment at the beginning of the war, deserted, and joined the 1st Delaware Cavalry. Unfortunately for the Union cause, Knight's martial skills did not match the legacy of his impressive name. When the regiment's colonel, George P. Fisher, resigned as a consequence of his failure to recruit an entire regiment, Knight assumed command of the battalion. The major had very little combat experience, and that deficiency was about to play a devastating role in the coming days.

The 1st Delaware Cavalry organized at Wilmington on January 20, 1863, but it was not a full regiment. Instead of the normal complement of ten horse companies, the small state was only able to raise seven understrength companies, which were eventually consolidated into four active companies. The 1st Delaware had served mostly in the defenses of Baltimore, and so had seen very little action. The expedition to Westminster marked their first real foray into the field.

Major Knight selected Companies C and D, commanded by Capt. Charles Corbit and Lt. Caleb Churchman, respectively, to accompany him to Westminster. The Delaware horsemen arrived there without incident about 11:00 a.m. on June 28. The town was quiet, which was to be expected on a Sunday morning with the local citizenry at worship. Knight and his men rode so quietly through the town that many of the locals were not even aware that Delaware cavalry was in their midst.[3]

Their presence did not go unnoticed for long. "The entry of the troops occasioned considerable excitement for though but little news was permitted to be furnished, it was known that the Government anticipated a Confederate advance in the direction of Baltimore," remembered one witness, "and with Longstreet and Hill on the principal thoroughfare 25 miles northwest and Ewell 40 miles east, the sending of a few hundred cavalrymen to Westminster intensified the nervous alarm."[4] Major Knight and his troopers camped on high ground on the northern edge of

A postwar image of
Captain Charles Corbit.

Carroll County Historical Society

town in an area known as The
Commons, adjacent to the
campus of today's McDaniel
College.[5] This high ground,
which had been used as a picnic
area for decades before the war,
commanded not only the town
itself but the main route through
Westminster. It, too, was an
integral part of the Pipe Creek
Line. From The Commons, Knight could see his outpost on the far end of
the town without having to lift his field glasses.[6]

Company C's Capt. Charles Corbit was twenty-five years old in June
1863. He stood nearly six feet tall, was strong, vigorous, broad
shouldered, and deep chested. "He was in every way an ideal volunteer
soldier," recalled Gen. James H. Wilson, a Delaware native who
achieved prominence commanding Union cavalry forces in 1864 and
1865. Corbit's ancestors crossed the Channel to England with William
the Conqueror before immigrating to Pennsylvania with William Penn
many centuries later. "They were from the first serious, self-respecting
people, connected by marriage with the best families of England,
Pennsylvania and Delaware," continued Wilson. The young cavalry
officer organized a company of militia cavalry that became Company C
of the 1st Delaware. As he rode into Westminster on June 28, the captain
counted four officers and 89 enlisted men in his command. Although
Major Knight was nominally in charge of the contingent of Delaware
horsemen, Corbit had tactical command.[7]

Major Knight picketed all of the roads leading into the town and
prepared to hold the crucial railhead. The Delawareans were confident
they had established a sufficient early warning network.[8] Lieutenant
Bowman's detachment of the 150th New York Infantry was guarding the

railroad depot in Westminster. Bowman informed Knight that there was no enemy at either Gettysburg or Hanover. When local citizens confirmed these reports, Knight passed the intelligence along to General Schenck and settled down for the evening, expecting to spend a quiet night in the hospitable Maryland town.[9]

About 9:00 that night the picket post on the Hampstead Road northeast of the town reported Southern cavalry advancing in their direction. "We were immediately in the saddle, and went out to meet them," remembered Major Knight.[10] Within the hour, however, word arrived that the enemy was approaching along a different road. "About ten o'clock or perhaps a little later that night when most people were in bed and I among their number the whole town was alarmed by a cavalry picket whose station was a mile or more out on the Manchester Road, came dashing into town, firing his pistol and keeping on firing through the town until he reached the camp on The Hill," recalled a local physician.[11]

Knight believed the enemy was aware of his presence and was trying to attack his rear and cut off his line of retreat. The inexperienced major wisely fell back to the junction of the two roads and waited for the enemy to arrive. He deployed pickets to cover every road in an effort to ascertain the precise whereabouts of the enemy, whom he presumed was Stuart's cavalry. The pickets, however, failed to find any enemy cavalry. "Supposing that the rebels had retired," Major Knight later reported, "I at once marched back and reoccupied the town, extending my pickets to a greater distance from the town on all the roads."[12]

A local citizen remained unimpressed by the night's activities. He explained why in an account published after the war:

> After awhile the cavalry came back in good order and resumed their camp. It turned out, as we learned the next morning, greatly to the chagrin of the cavalry and their special friends in the town that the picket on the Manchester Road, who had created all the excitement, was under the impression that a large body of Confederates were advancing on the town, and so, rushing into camp, informed the Captain and he, thinking that 'prudence was the better part of valor,' concluded to leave and so they did in pretty lively style. The 'great body of Confederates' who had so alarmed the pickets proved to be a singing school that had just let out and the boys and girls were going home with no thought of blood in their hearts.[13]

Regardless of the cause of the disturbance, the major and his men finally hunkered down for the night and spent a quiet evening enjoying the hospitality of the loyal Marylanders. There was still no sign of the enemy when morning arrived. Because many of the 1st Delaware's horses had been "rendered almost unfit for service by marching over the stony road without shoes," Major Knight ordered the mounts shod on the morning of June 29. The battalion's blacksmiths brought up their wagons and went to work, a process that consumed most of the day.[14]

Jeb Stuart intended to pass through Westminster on his northward ride to Pennsylvania. The cavalier had no precise idea where the main body of General Lee's army was operating, and seems not to have fully appreciated the nature of the danger facing him in the Maryland countryside.[15] Reports that the enemy was moving northward through Frederick reached the general. "It was important for me to reach our column with as little delay as possible to acquaint the commanding general with the nature of the enemy's movements, as well as to place with his column my cavalry force," he explained in his after-action report.[16] Stuart set out to accomplish his objective unaware that Major Knight and his intrepid band of Delawareans were squarely across his proposed line of advance. The head of Stuart's column followed a ridge road and approached Westminster from the east between 4:00 and 5:00 p.m. on June 29. The handful of pickets watching that route were captured before they could spread the alarm.[17]

For the Delaware troopers, the 29th of June dawned bright and clear. The day grew very hot as the sun climbed in the sky. The presence of the Delaware horse soldiers did not disrupt the local citizens, who did their best to go about their normal affairs.[18] Nor did the presence of Westminster's civilians disrupt Major Knight, who spent a pleasant afternoon refreshing himself in the tavern at the Westminster Hotel on Main Street.[19] By the time Stuart's Confederates arrived, the major was so intoxicated he was unable to take the field. His troopers had spent a restful day tending their horses and writing letters—a welcome respite from their usual labors. The idyllic last Monday of June was about to end in a way few imagined.

Five members of the 1st Delaware Cavalry were having their horses shod in Michael Baumann's blacksmith shop on the east end of the town, "a stone's throw from the point on Main Street where it was intersected by the Washington road," when the small advance guard of Fitz Lee's column pounced on them. The assault captured all five men, together with their outstanding horses.[20] The sudden transition from soldier to prisoner deprived the 1st Delaware Cavalry of its early warning system. Major Knight's lackadaisical deployments were about to extract a heavy price from his command.

Luckily for the Union troops, a young lawyer from Westminster named Isaac E. Pearson spurred his well-lathered horse into town to report Stuart's approach along the Washington Road. According to General Wilson, "This news came as a surprise, which was followed by a few minutes of excitement but not much uncertainty." Hearing cries that the enemy was advancing, local merchants quickly locked up their shops and the townsfolk scurried into their basements for safety.[21] Upon hearing the news, Captain Corbit yelled out "to horse!" and formed his small command of about 70 troopers, his squadron having been depleted by the deployment of picket posts on the roads surrounding Westminster and by the poor condition of some of the battalion's horses.

Corbit formed his men on East Main Street, Westminster's main thoroughfare. The green Delawareans moved out toward the intersection of East Main Street and Pennsylvania Avenue to find Stuart's horsemen. The Delawareans rose in their stirrups, waved their sabers, and cried out, "Clear the street!" prompting those curious local citizens who had not yet hidden themselves to scramble indoors.[22] Corbit dispatched Lt. D. W. C. Clark and an advance guard of twelve men to feel the enemy and ascertain his position. After advancing a short distance out the Washington Road, Clark and his men turned about and galloped back with news that a large force of Confederate horsemen was in their immediate front. The lieutenant escaped with a hole in his hat and a saber wound to his arm to prove it.[23]

Corbit paused at the tavern long enough to report the news to Major Knight and to ask for orders. Knight promptly ordered Corbit to move at once against the enemy. However, Major Knight, apparently afraid of being captured and treated as a deserter as a consequence of his brief term of service with the Confederacy, declined to leave the tavern or to take tactical command of the fight, leaving Corbit in command by default.[24]

Fortunately, Charles Corbit was equal to the occasion. Taking the trot to the front, the captain and his little band of inexperienced horsemen spotted the head of Stuart's column approaching the town. "Draw sabers!" cried Corbit. With his bugler sounding the charge and the encouraging cheers of some of the local women ringing in their ears, Corbit led his troopers forward into the astonished vanguard of Stuart's 4,000 horsemen. The Delawareans demonstrated "an almost suicidal bravery" in launching their charge, remembered one witness.[25] The attack struck the massed gray cavalry at the intersection of the Washington Road and East Main Street. The two roads intersected at a sharp angle which, together with the stout rail fencing on all sides, created a natural bottleneck. The sudden attack prompted a member of the Delaware regiment to claim that the charge "was more heroic than Cardigan's Six Hundred at Balaklava."[26] It wasn't just the three score and ten Delaware troops Stuart's men had to deal with. According to a sergeant riding with the 2nd Virginia Cavalry, the citizens "disputed our entrance by firing into our ranks from windows and behind houses."[27]

The shock of the audacious charge drove back Fitz Lee's troopers in some confusion and forced them to reform under difficult circumstances. The Southerners rallied and countercharged, with Fitz's 4th Virginia Cavalry in the lead. "Gen'l Fitz Lee came galloping to the head of our regiment and led us in a charge," recorded a trooper of the 2nd Virginia.[28] Lee sent the 3rd Virginia Cavalry on a flanking maneuver, but the route was so long that the skirmish ended before they could pitch into the affair.[29] Still, the swirling fight was described by one as "short, sharp, and decisive."[30] Corbit's stubborn and vastly outnumbered horsemen obstinately repulsed two or three countercharges in the narrow roadway. The weight of Southern numbers finally told, however, and Corbit and his men were chased back through the town. "A pistol shot killed [Corbit's] horse while it was throwing up its head under pressure of the rein and thus fortunately covering its rider behind." Corbit struggled free from the dead animal and, with pistol in hand, stood to face his enemy. The gallant captain was swept up and captured while standing astride his dead charger.[31]

Fitz Lee's devastating countercharge gobbled up most of Corbit's Company C. "Our boys were crowded out of the Washington pike by an overwhelming force, some escaping . . . and some being taken prisoners," recalled Lt. William W. Lobdell, the 1st Delaware's adjutant. The Confederates forced Lobdell into a barnyard at the intersection of East Main Street and Pennsylvania Avenue on the western edge of town. The adjutant only escaped by running and jumping his thoroughbred to safety down the Baltimore Pike. Once clear of the town's confines he high-tailed it to the safety of Reisterstown. Lieutenant William J. Reedy had two horses shot from under him and only escaped from Fitz Lee's troopers by mounting the animal of a brother soldier who had been shot dead by his side. A pistol ball passed through the rim of Lt. D. W. C. Clark's hat, and his arm was badly bruised by the side stroke of a Virginia saber.[32]

When Lt. Caleb Churchman's Company D, which was deployed on the north end of the town, spotted the plight of their comrades it pitched into the fray. These Delawareans also fought desperately, and a hand-to-hand melee raged in the streets of Westminster. Two troopers of the 1st Delaware were killed during this fighting. A member of the 4th Virginia's Company K recalled that the 1st Delaware Cavalry "fought like Turks, killing a good number of our best men, but strange to say our company, which was in front, lost none. Companies C and D, which came to our relief, lost several good officers and some men."[33]

Lieutenant St. Pierre Gibson was a member of the Little Fork Rangers of Culpeper County, Virginia. The Rangers made up Company D of the 4th Virginia Cavalry. Gibson possessed unusual courage, and could usually be found at the head of his company when it went into battle. As the Rangers formed to charge, Gibson jokingly quipped, "Give me some crackers, boys, I'll do your fighting for you."[34] The daring lieutenant was shot while leading his company's charge. "Lieutenant Gibson, too proud and too brave to yield an inch, maintained his position alone," recounted a citizen who watched the Virginian's duel in the streets. "In an instant, scores of foes were around and about him, sabers flashed right and left above him, and pistols blazed in his face; but his enemies awed by his stern and defiant courage, for a few moments dared not approach within striking distance of his terrible sword-arm." A Delaware sergeant rode straight at Gibson, "a pistol flash, and a bluecoat rolled in the dust dead; another flash, and the gallant Southerner also fell shot through the brain."[35] Ironically, Gibson hit the ground in front of an undertaker's office; his horse ended up in Lee's camp.[36]

Lieutenant John W. Murray, Company C, 4th Virginia Cavalry, also rode at the head of his charging troopers. When he and his men came together with Lieutenant Churchman's Company D, Murray lifted his sword arm and began swinging his saber right and left. "Alas, for the noble brave!" recalled Everett Pearson of Westminster, who watched the fighting raging in the streets. "Just as the first flush of victory had crowned his gallantry he too fell."[37] One of Stuart's staff officers noted that Gibson and Murray were "among the best" officers in the 4th Virginia Cavalry and would be sorely missed.[38] "Gallant and meritorious, they were noble sacrifices to the cause," lamented Stuart.[39]

Joe Stallard, another trooper of the Little Fork Rangers, was chasing a Yankee horseman when the Northerner abandoned his horse and took refuge in a nearby home. The owner of the house refused to turn his new guest over to the Confederates, but when Stallard threatened to burn the house down if the owner did not surrender the refugee horse soldier, the owner reluctantly complied. Few of the men from the 1st Delaware escaped the dragnet cast by Fitz Lee's Virginians.[40]

Major Napoleon Knight, the commander of the decimated 1st Delaware regiment, tried to explain the debacle. "The enemy having been so heavily re-enforced," he reported, "drove the two companies back to the main pike, the men of my command fighting all the time with the greatest bravery and determination, and contending hotly for every inch of ground."[41] A member of the 1st Delaware offered a similar perspective. The regiment, he noted, was "driven through the streets, some of them fighting, some fleeing. Many were cut down from their horses and captured. A few escaped through the aid of Union citizens."[42]

The rookies had fought bravely in the face of overwhelming odds, but had suffered mightily in the process. "I cannot close this report without calling your attention to the bravery and intrepidity of the officers and men of my command," wrote Knight, "whose efficiency and determination of purpose has saved us from utter annihilation."[43]

Knight's claim of credit was disingenuous. Although many members of the 1st Delaware Cavalry claimed he had been too ill to command his troopers that day, in reality the major was too drunk to take the field. Whatever credit deserves to be dolled out for the 1st Delaware Cavalry's remarkable fight belongs to Capt. Charles Corbit, whose courage and willingness to assume command briefly halted Stuart's advance. "One of the survivors of the affair at Westminster was asked today if Corbit fought well," explained General Wilson. "Did he fight well?" was the reply, "Why damn it, he was the fight!"[44] Major Henry B. McClellan, Stuart's able adjutant, later wrote that the resistance of the 1st Delaware Cavalry was "brief but stubborn." He also noted that "this fight was more gallant than judicious on the part of Major Knight."[45]

Soon after the skirmish Knight learned of the Confederate flanking column on Ridge Road advancing on his rear. The news prompted him to fall back via the Reisterstown Road. Knight ordered Lieutenant Churchman and the survivors of his company to cover the retreat. Churchman's company still had plenty of fight left and contested every step. The contest was so brisk the company lost all but seven of its men and Churchman joined Corbit as a prisoner of war.[46]

The fighting left vivid memories with everyone who witnessed it. "First came horses at the top of their speed, that left their riders on the battle ground," recounted one Westminster citizen. "Then, outnumbered many to one, over ground on which they had advanced, came the Union troops. The advance of the victors, cutting and slashing, and the rear guard of the retreat, looking over their shoulders, warding off as well as they could the terrible blows struck with force as if to cleave man and horse."[47]

A single Westminster citizen, Francis Shriver, joined the fighting, a gallant bit of participation that earned him the sobriquet, "the John Burns of Westminster." Shriver was "one of the most decided loyalists to be found in Maryland," explained one who knew him well. Described as an "intrepid old man," Shriver was fifty years old in June 1863, "but as active and vigorous as a man of half that number of years." Shriver lived on the west end of the town near Knight's camp.[48] When Corbit called "boots and saddles" Shriver mounted up and fell in with the Delaware troopers. Armed only with a pistol, he stood and fought with Corbit until the 1st Delaware broke under the weight of Fitz Lee's assault. Shriver "[was] on horseback when the Delaware Cavalry passed through the street, dashed in with the front file, shot the first fire, unhorsing a Lieutenant Randalf," who was taken to the home of a local to recover. Although he was in the midst of the melee, Shriver "fortunately escaped without injury, save a flash of gunpowder in the eye from a pistol shot in the hands of an officer. When retreat was ordered, he got off as fast as his horse 'John' would carry him."[49] Shriver wheeled and escaped by making good use of his intimate knowledge of the town's side streets. He survived the summer combat and lived to the ripe old age of 83. Lee's troopers searched Shriver's house and premises and sent parties out on the road to catch him, but he escaped toward Cockeysville. The Southerners were very "impertinent to his daughters, who, in reply to threats against their father, denounced them as traitors, and expressed the hope that not one of them would ever get back to Virginia."[50]

Two other Westminster natives were involved in the fighting, but they wore Confederate gray and rode into town with Stuart's advance. Francis and Henry Neal, sons of Abner Neal, grew up at their father's home on the North side of Main Street. In September 1862, the brothers enlisted at Darkesville, Maryland, as privates in James Breathed's battery.[51] The Federals were retreating down Main Street in the teeth of Fitz Lee's counter blow when Francis and Henry manned their guns, which dropped trail east of the railroad tracks almost directly in front of their family home. They survived the swirling fight and the war, but their Southern sympathies and service cost them dearly; neither brother ever returned home again.[52]

With only a handful of men remaining, Major Knight and his surviving horse soldiers fell back to Reisterstown while elements of Lee's Brigade followed them. Knight spotted a lieutenant of the 1st Connecticut Cavalry and ordered him to hold the pursuers in check while Knight rallied his little force on the south side of the town. Knight directed Lt. William J. Reedy, now in command of the shattered remnant of Company C, to push on and turn back seven or eight fugitives, who were about a mile in advance. Reedy could not rally the panicked greenhorns, who fled to safety in Baltimore with the lieutenant accompanying them.[53]

"The fugitives were pursued a long distance on the Baltimore road, and I afterward heard created great panic in that city, impressing the authorities that we were just on at their heels," crowed Stuart in his after-action report of the Gettysburg Campaign.[54] Major Knight, whose immediate entourage had been whittled down to Adjutant Lobdell, another lieutenant, and two enlisted men, halted his retreat about one mile from the town. Knight was determined to return to Reisterstown, which they would then occupy. The major was making his dispositions to confront another attack when a courier spurred up with a dispatch from General Schenck. The 1st Delaware was to return to Baltimore forthwith. Knight and his remnants willingly complied with the order, leaving behind 67 men killed, wounded, and missing, including Corbit and Churchman. The 1st Delaware also lost a wagon laden with hospital supplies, camp, and garrison equipment, and all of the regimental books and papers. The Confederates also captured Lt. Pulaski Bowman of the

150th New York Infantry, along with ten of his men, and took them with them when they moved on.[55]

Schenck did not report the 1st Delaware's ordeal to Halleck's headquarters until the next day. "Last evening a superior force of rebel cavalry drove Major Knight, with 95 Delaware cavalry, from Westminster, killing, wounding, or capturing most of his command," the general explained. "A heavy rebel cavalry force was reported last night advancing on Baltimore by the Reisterstown road, and we prepared to receive them, but they did not come." Confusion reigned. There were, continued a befuddled Schenck, "Reports and indications of rebel cavalry in different directions, but I have not the remotest idea where General Meade's cavalry or any portion of his army now is, so that I know not in what direction to look out. Can you give me any information that you think it necessary I should have as to the disposition of the two armies?" General Halleck, who was equally frustrated, responded, "I have had no communication with the Army of the Potomac since the line to Frederick was broken." No one knew with certainty where Stuart was, where he was heading, or whether the main body of the Army of the Potomac could bring him—or the rest of Lee's army—to bay.[56]

The balance of Stuart's command slowly passed through Westminster. "Some of the regiments marched by in silence, others sang familiar ballads as they marched along," recalled a local citizen who watched the spectacle. "A few riotously disposed shrieked, whistled and cheered. The flags were nearly all folded, the bugles made no sound, the orders were few and short, and there was an entire lack of that pomp and pageantry which all expected to see in an army. It was very evident that the men meant 'business' and not play."[57]

A few Southern troopers foraged in the town and paid for their prizes with Confederate money. "The men got hats, boots, shoes & such things as they needed," observed one of Fitz Lee's officers. Stuart's men fanned out through the town, helping themselves to whatever bounty they found. Fitch's dry good store was completely gutted; Bowen & Gehr, commission merchants at the depot, also lost heavily, as did Meixell & Orndorf, which lost about $700 in flour and feed.[58]

When some of Stuart's troopers spotted the Federal flag flying above the cupola of the county courthouse, they ascended the steps and happily tore the banner down. Thirteen local ladies had sewn the oversize flag and had signed their names on its stars, so the loss was particularly devastating for the Westminster civilians.[59] Other troopers destroyed railroad property in an effort to deny this critical resource to the advancing Federals.

"Here, for the first time since leaving Rector's Cross-Roads, we obtained a full supply of forage, but the delay and difficulty of procuring it kept many of the men up all night," Stuart noted. "Several flags and one piece of artillery without a carriage were captured here. The latter was spiked and left behind." The weary Southerners had been marching and fighting for days and welcomed the respite offered by the comfortable camp site a few miles north of Westminster toward Union Mills.[60]

Stuart entered the town in the wake of his weary horsemen. According to local legend, as the cavalier rode along his column on East Main Street, a saucy little girl named Mary Shellman loudly blurted out that the Southern chieftain was a "Johnny Red Coat." Upon hearing the tease, Stuart is said to have stopped his horse and informed the little lady that punishment would be summarily meted out for her brash display of loyalty to the Union—a kiss. Motioning for her to approach, Stuart leaned over and scooped her up. "The kiss delivered, the general moved on," the legend concludes, with Stuart leaving in his wake a slightly embarrassed, if not thoroughly charmed, little Maryland girl.[61]

Stuart's first order of business in Westminster was a call for his commanders to assemble. On the east side of the old City Hotel Stuart, Fitz Lee, John Chambliss, and Wade Hampton huddled to decide their next course of action.[62] After his council of war Stuart stopped to take tea at the home of John C. Frysee, the Southern-sympathizing cashier of the Westminster Bank, enjoying "all the honors" his cheerful host could bestow.[63] A citizen of the town got a good look at the Southern cavalry chieftain. Stuart "seemed to have a heavy load of care on his mind, and whilst at tea it was noticed that, though at times full of spirits, he occasionally grew abstracted and thoughtful."[64]

Stuart told the assembled crowd that he expected the decisive battle of the war to occur soon. His host inquired, "General Stuart, do you have any doubt about the outcome of the battle of which you spoke?"

"None at all," responded the cavalier. "I have the utmost confidence in our men, and I know that if they are given a ghost of a chance they are sure to win."[65]

Stuart also had casualties to care for. Dead and wounded men were in the streets of Westminster where they fell in the heat of combat. The two dead men from Delaware, Cpl. William Vandegrift and Pvt. Daniel Welsh, were buried in temporary graves at the Old Union Church, which also served as a hospital for wounded men of both sides.[66] Late in the afternoon of June 29, local women came to Stuart to ask permission to bury Lieutenants Murray and Gibson. The appreciative general readily agreed, and "the bodies of these young heroes were left in their charge."[67] The ladies carefully tended to the remains and laid them to rest in the graveyard in the Ascension Episcopal Church. Lieutenant Murray was buried under a marked tombstone, while Lieutenant Gibson's body was laid to rest in an unmarked grave next to him. Two years after the end of the Civil War Gibson's body was claimed and removed to Virginia. Murray's body remains in the church graveyard to this day.

The general did not indicate that it was time to leave until almost midnight. By this late hour a large crowd had gathered in the hope of catching a glimpse of the famous cavalryman. The observers gave him three cheers as he mounted his horse. Stuart responded with a deep bow and rode off into the night.[68] According to local lore, after he was informed of the disposition of his column, which was strung along the road to Union Mills, the exhausted Stuart fell asleep "straddling a chair on the sidewalk in front of a house on East Main Street in Westminster until about 7:00 a.m." Sore and tired, Stuart remounted and rode the length of his command until reaching the van, which was encamped at Union Mills seven miles to the north. When they departed Westminster, Stuart's command took with it three Westminster civilians, including G. W. Webster, the local state's attorney (who was shot while attempting to escape), Keener Shriver, son of Augustus Shriver, and Dr. Charles A. Billingsley, who was released at Hanover Junction. However, the Confederates refused to part with his horse, forcing Billingsley to make it home on foot.[69]

The small settlement of Union Mills was founded when two brothers, Andrew and David Shriver, established a gristmill and sawmill near Big Pipe Creek on the main road between Littlestown and Westminster in 1797. The name was intended to celebrate their business partnership. Unbeknownst to the brothers, it would eventually carry with it significant irony.[70] In the 1820s their children divided the property and built a house directly across the road from the family homestead on a hill overlooking the road. Two of Andrew's sons, Andrew K. and William Shriver, lived in the homes. William and his family lived in the new home, a large white house, while Andrew and his family occupied the original property. William ardently supported the Confederate cause, and his four sons served in the Southern army, including one who was a member of Fitz Lee's 1st Virginia Cavalry. William was a Southern sympathizer though he owned not a single slave. Andrew, who was a slave owner, however, remained loyal to the Union. His son served with the 26th Pennsylvania Emergency Militia. Union Mills was no longer united or wholly Union.[71] The tense situation, proximity, and divergent philosophies of the two families strained the relationship nearly to the breaking point. "Our two families lived close together," recorded Andrew's youngest son Louis Shriver, "and although we continued to visit back and forth, social intercourse was always strained and often resulted in unhappy arguments."[72]

At 10:00 p.m., a horseman dressed in gray startled the occupants of William Shriver's home when he knocked loudly on the door. Confederate cavalry, he informed them, was on its way to Union Mills. "In a short time they came, thick as bees," remembered William's daughter Kate. By 2:00 a.m., Mrs. Shriver and the other ladies of the house had fed several hundred famished Southerners. Many of the troopers had grabbed flapjacks off the large kitchen's griddle even before they had completely cooked. Fitz Lee refused a bed in the house, choosing instead to sleep in Andrew Shriver's apple orchard—something that likely rankled the Unionist sibling.[73]

A nephew of Robert E. Lee, Fitz was one of the Confederacy's youngest and most talented cavalry officers. He was also one of Stuart's favorites. A graduate of the West Point Class of 1856, Lee began the Civil War as a staff officer but rose to command the 1st Virginia Cavalry in April 1862.[74] Promoted to brigadier general that July, Fitz took command of Stuart's first brigade in the newly formed cavalry division, as Stuart proclaimed "congratulations for myself and the Country in having such a Brigadier." Fitz Lee was Stuart's protégé, and his quick wit earned him the sobriquet "the laughing cavalier." As Stuart's favorite subordinate, Fitz was a member of Stuart's inner circle.[75]

Stuart, despite Westminster lore that he slept on a porch until 7:00 a.m., likely awoke much earlier and arrived at Union Mills before daylight. Within a short time he, Fitz Lee, and their respective staff officers were crowded into the William Shriver family dining room feasting on fat biscuits. After the hearty meal the group adjourned to the

Brigadier General Fitzhugh "Fitz" Lee, Stuart's favorite subordinate.

family's piano. "I wish you had heard General Stuart sing accompanied by all the rest, 'If you want to be a bully boy, jine the cavalry,'" recalled Kate Shriver. "His eyes sparkled and he kept time with his spirit; and with it all the elegant gentleman. General Lee joined and Major McClellan played and sang some splendid songs. General Stuart promised to come and see us if he ever got within 25 miles." In the interim, a servant handed out bread to the hungry troopers until the supply ran out.[76] Ironically, the Union Twelfth Corps, which was also marching toward its date with destiny at Gettysburg, spent the approaching night camped on Andrew Shriver's farm at Union Mills. Its presence helped restore Andrew's faith in the ultimate victory of the North.

During the night Stuart learned a large body of Union cavalry was camped just seven miles distant at Littlestown, Pennsylvania. The force was Brig. Gen. Elon J. Farnsworth's brigade of the Third Cavalry Division, a newly-created division that had received a new commanding officer only two weeks earlier.[77] With a dangerous enemy in close proximity just across the Mason-Dixon Line, Stuart knew an encounter was likely.[78]

When Stuart mentioned a guide was needed, William's sixteen-year-old son Herbert Shriver, who knew the roads intimately, offered his services. After singing a few more songs in the Shriver parlor, Stuart announced, "Young man, I want to know about the dirt or country roads, up yonder leading to Hanover." He spread a map over the table and asked, "Are the roads wide enough for artillery?"

The boy told the general that wagons could easily fit on the roads, an answer that seemed to satisfy Stuart. The general smiled and told the teenager, "Now listen. I want you to come with me, you aren't afraid; I'm sure, are you? Now take me up to your mother's room, and I will ask her permission, is that okay with you?"[79] Stuart personally asked Mrs. Shriver if he could take the boy along as a guide, promising to keep him safe. He also declared he would send him to the Virginia Military Institute with a paid education and would find a place for the lad on his personal staff once Herbert finished his studies. After setting out a fresh plate of biscuits, rolls, and hot coffee, Mrs. Shriver managed to swallow her maternal concerns and gave Herbert permission to accompany Stuart, though she did manage to ask, "Isn't he too young?"[80] A few minutes later the boy set off on the greatest adventure of his young life, riding at the plumed cavalier's side.[81]

Five miles away was the Mason-Dixon Line and Pennsylvania. Littlestown, where Stuart knew Federal cavalry had spent the night, was just two miles beyond. The Southerners watered their horses in a stream while Stuart sent scouts ahead to reconnoiter. Near Littlestown they spotted a large force of Union troops and reported to Stuart "with raised hands, riding with dangerous speed, reporting with lost breath, almost in panic."[82] After consulting with his officers Stuart decided not to attack. Instead, he detoured toward Hanover on a dirt road. The seemingly insignificant change of plans had far-reaching consequences no one could foresee at the time.[83]

Early that morning Stuart paroled his Delaware prisoners. It was more probable than not that a battle with Union cavalry would be fought soon, and the last thing Stuart needed was to be hampered with captives. Stuart addressed an impromptu conference with his prisoners while Corbit and Churchman listened. After commending their gallantry Stuart added that the Delawareans "ought to be fighting for the Confederacy rather than against it."[84]

The delay engendered by the clash at Westminster had prevented Stuart from crossing into Pennsylvania one day earlier. Although Stuart could not have known it, the gallant stand by Capt. Charles Corbit and the rookies of the 1st Delaware Cavalry had held up Stuart's command just long enough to make possible a much larger and more important combat at Hanover with Brig. Gen. Judson Kilpatrick on June 30—a fight that would consume nearly an entire precious day. As we shall soon discover, when Stuart finally shook himself loose from Kilpatrick and rode toward York, Pennsylvania, Lt. Gen. Richard Ewell's Second Corps was already gone, having been recalled to the Cashtown-Gettysburg concentration area by General Lee. Had Stuart not lost several hours battling the 1st Delaware Cavalry and chasing fugitives, he might have caught up with Ewell's infantry near York. Had that occurred, the entire battle of Gettysburg might have evolved differently.

Stuart also did not realize that the head of Winfield Scott Hancock's Federal Second Corps was only three miles away from Westminster on the night of June 29. Corbit's rash charge nearly permitted the Union infantry to catch up to Stuart's exhausted horsemen. Hancock sent a special messenger to General Meade with this important intelligence in the hope that Brig. Gen. David M. Gregg's Second Cavalry Division would arrive in time to intercept Stuart's column.[85] Fortunately for Stuart, Gregg's men did not interrupt his ride.

Judson Kilpatrick, however, was another matter.

Chapter 4

The Battle of Hanover Begins

"We had apparently waked up a real hornet's nest."

— John Esten Cooke, Stuart's Staff

W hen the 1,600 residents of Hanover, Pennsylvania, began their day on June 30, 1863, they had no way of knowing that the little York County town's moment in the limelight of history had arrived. Momentous events were unfolding all around them, and two of the major players and their commands were about to pay Hanover a visit.[1]

Judson Kilpatrick's division of 3,500 sabers screened the Army of the Potomac's front and center as it trekked north in pursuit of the Army of Northern Virginia. Kilpatrick's specific task was to locate Confederate Lt. Gen. Richard Ewell's Second Corps, which was believed to be moving east from Chambersburg.[2] Kilpatrick did not know that Stuart had camped the previous night at Union Mills, Maryland, just seven miles southeast of his own men at Littlestown. The reason rested with David Gregg and his Second Division. Gregg was operating east of Kilpatrick, but was not advancing as rapidly as the little Celt's command and so did not detect Stuart's presence. John Buford's First Division was riding west of Kilpatrick, heading for the South Mountain's Monterey Pass above Fairfield. Buford's troopers had their own date with destiny the next day on the fields west of a small town called Gettysburg.

A native of New Jersey, Judson Kilpatrick graduated as a member of West Point's May 1861 class. He opened his Civil War career as an infantryman and was the first Federal Regular officer to be wounded. In

USAMHI

Brigadier General Judson Kilpatrick, commander of the Army of the Potomac's Third Cavalry Division, clashed with Jeb Stuart at Hanover and Hunterstown.

December 1861, Kilpatrick became colonel of the 2nd New York Cavalry.[3] When General Pleasonton reorganized the Army of the Potomac's mounted arm in an unprecedented shake-up of its hierarchy, he insisted that Kilpatrick be promoted to brigadier general of volunteers, effective June 14, 1863.[4] The twenty-seven year-old Kilpatrick, dubbed "Kill-Cavalry" by admirers and detractors alike, took command of his newly formed Third Division that same day.[5]

Stuart intended to ride for Littlestown until he learned Federal cavalry occupied the area. With that news in hand, Stuart opted instead for a move to Hanover, hoping to slip by any Yankee horsemen and link up with Ewell's infantry near the Susquehanna. However, what the gray cavalier did not know was that Kilpatrick's command was also making for Hanover.

Colonel John Chambliss took the advance of Stuart's column on the Hanover Road.[7] He sent mounted details along other roads to collect serviceable horses and supplies and watch for the Federals everyone now knew were operating in the vicinity.[8] The six guns of the horse artillery, as well as the captured wagons, followed Chambliss. Behind the wagons marched Wade Hampton's Brigade, which had the odious burden of guarding the cumbersome vehicles.[9] Fitz Lee's Brigade was given the important task of guarding the column's left flank and rear, and would soon be sent farther west to a position between the Littlestown and Hanover roads.[10]

The column advanced fitfully northward. The horsemen, groggy from lack of sleep and with some dozing as they rode, had no idea of their destination. Although they had not yet recovered from twenty-four hour stints in the saddle, unexpected skirmishing, and dangerous patrols in unfamiliar country, they remained steadfast in their resolve. Colonel Beale of the 9th Virginia, in particular, believed he knew why the ride into Pennsylvania was taking place: "The time had come to pay back in some measure the misdeeds of [Northern] men who, with sword and fire, had made our homesteads heaps of ruin."[11] Beale's son, Lt. George W. Beale, Company C, 9th Virginia, described the Southerners' feelings in a more somber tone when he wrote his mother a few days later. "Both men and horses being worn out," he explained, "all of us regarded the prospect of a fight with no little regret and anxiety."

Under young Herbert Shriver's guidance, Stuart covered a few miles on the main road before turning Chambliss's and Hampton's brigades (as well as the wagon train) onto a secondary parallel route running over Conewago Hill and into Hanover. Locals aptly referred to it as the "back road" into town. The road rose and fell with each mile, a virtual roller coaster track up and down several considerable hills. This leg of the journey was particularly grueling for the wagons. Each steep incline brought the heavy-laden wagons nearly to a halt, with curses and shouts heard up and down the train as teamsters whipped and threatened the stubborn mules to press on. Despite the best efforts of man and beast, the gap between the head of the wagons and the rear of Chambliss's Brigade (held by the 13th Virginia Cavalry) grew wider. Chambliss, however, kept a steady pace. Later that morning the troopers in his advance guard reached a small group of buildings along the road known locally as Gitt's Mill, a sleepy rural grist mill named for Josiah W. Gitt.

As the main column rolled and rode northward, Fitz Lee's troopers rode along the Littlestown Road. They followed it northwest for a time before turning east onto a secondary road paralleling Stuart's route. This allowed Lee to screen the vulnerable left flank of the long moving column, the side closest to the suspected location of the enemy. Like Stuart, Lee operated small detached patrols on side roads and farm lanes to keep a sharp eye out for any wandering bluecoats anxious to locate the Confederate horsemen. Early in his march Lee's efforts paid off when one of his patrols discovered important news about Kilpatrick's cavalry—the enemy column was riding right into Stuart's intended path. Lee fired off a dispatch to his chieftain, warning him of the danger ahead:

On March, Nine A.M.

GENERAL—A citizen direct from Littlestown informs me that General Kilpatrick, with four regiments—of which the First Virginia, Fifth *[sic]* Vermont and Fifth New York are three, and six pieces of artillery—left that place this morning for Hanover. The road that I am on strikes the Littlestown and Hanover road at McSherrysville *[sic]* road, not a half mile from Hanover. Very respectfully, your obedient servant,

Fitzhugh Lee,
Brigadier General, Commanding.

Unfortunately for the Southerners, the courier bearing the dispatch was captured and Stuart never received the warning. If he had, he would have realized that Kilpatrick had already left Littlestown and that the opposing columns were about to converge. Stuart's intent to bypass Kilpatrick by taking the alternate route to Hanover was instead carrying him directly toward the enemy.[12]

The Union cavalry was much more dispersed than Stuart's compacted columns. As Capt. James H. Kidd of the 6th Michigan Cavalry put it, "Kilpatrick's command was badly scattered" that morning.[13] From the division's bivouac at the Richfield Estate in Frederick, Maryland, Kilpatrick issued orders early on June 29 that divided his command's ride north. Only the First Brigade of the division, commanded by newly promoted Brig. Gen. Elon J. Farnsworth, was with Kilpatrick in camp at Littlestown that night. The 1st and 7th Michigan regiments of the Second Brigade, led by an equally freshly minted brigadier general named George A. Custer, were dispatched with orders to reach Emmitsburg, Maryland, on the 29th, and then ride northeast across the Mason-Dixon Line to hook up with Kilpatrick the next day.[14] Custer's remaining pair of regiments, the 5th and 6th Michigan, had been performing arduous scouting duty in and around Gettysburg. Kilpatrick ordered these Wolverines to rejoin him at Littlestown no later than daylight on June 30.[15]

The sun had not yet appeared on the horizon when Kilpatrick roused Farnsworth's troopers from their slumber with orders to continue riding in the direction of Hanover. After a hastily prepared and insufficient breakfast, the troopers saddled in the

Brigadier General Elon J. Farnsworth, commander of Kilpatrick's First Brigade. Farnsworth's men opened the fighting with Jeb Stuart at Hanover on June 30.

USMHI

darkness and began forming a column of fours.[16] One of Farnsworth's men fondly remembered "the enthusiasm of the loyal men and women of this little Pennsylvania town, and how with patriotic songs and cheers, they entertained us and fed us as we halted in the main street of the village."[17] Kilpatrick rode at the head of his column, followed by his staff and his headquarters guard, which consisted of one squadron from the 1st Ohio Cavalry.[18]

Tall and handsome, with a thick moustache that reached to his jaw line, twenty-five-year-old Elon Farnsworth donned a borrowed coat that morning. He had only been promoted to brigadier general two days earlier, and so had not yet found the time to secure a proper uniform or insignia. General Pleasonton, the army's cavalry chief, loaned his young protégé one of his old jackets.[19] It was anything but a tailor-made fit, however, for Pleasonton was considerably shorter than the new brigade commander.

A descendant of veterans from the French and Indian War, American Revolution, and War of 1812, Elon Farnsworth had been an incurable prankster in his youth. In his third year at the University of Michigan, Farnsworth was expelled when one student died during a rowdy frolic of drinking. The death triggered serious introspection, and the young man decided to turn his life around. He was working as a civilian forager at the Army's Camp Floyd in Utah when the Civil War broke out in April 1861.[20] When his politician uncle formed the 8th Illinois Cavalry, Farnsworth joined as a quartermaster.[21] He became captain in December 1861 and joined Pleasonton's staff. After assuming command of his regiment at Brandy Station, Farnsworth impressed the cavalry leader so much that Pleasonton tapped the young officer to lead a brigade in Judson Kilpatrick's division.[22]

Farnsworth's brigade consisted of four regiments. Three of them were veteran units. The 1st Vermont, the small 1st West Virginia, and the 5th New York were all recruited during the first year of the war. The 18th Pennsylvania, however, was organized during the summer and fall of 1862. Although the Pennsylvanians had been in a few minor scraps, they had yet to see a real fight.[23] Their commander was Lt. Col. William Penn Brinton, a well-educated man who hailed from a prominent Philadelphia family. Brinton's Keystone troopers assumed the critical position that morning, riding at the rear of Kilpatrick's column. A squad of forty troopers from the 18th Pennsylvania's companies L and M led by Lt.

USAMHI

Brigadier General George A. Custer, flamboyant commander of the Michigan Cavalry Brigade in Judson Kilpatrick's division.

Henry C. Potter served as the column's rearguard. They trailed about one mile behind the main body with orders to "keep a sharp lookout" for any of those Confederates suspected to be somewhere in the countryside.[24] Lieutenant Potter was also instructed to watch for stragglers and encourage them to keep up, but his most important tactical assignment was keeping his little band's eyes peeled for any attempt at a surprise attack against Kilpatrick's rear.

The four guns of Lt. Samuel Elder's Battery E, 4th U. S. Artillery, rolled along in the center of Farnsworth's brigade. The battery's seasoned, reliable, and professional gunners had served in several major battles and numerous skirmishes. Consistent with standard protocol, Elder's guns were interspersed among the troopers to protect them and keep them readily available for action.

George Custer, a former staff officer for cavalry corps commander Alfred Pleasonton, was elevated to brigadier general on June 28 at Pleasonton's request (along with Farnsworth and Wesley Merritt). At the tender age of twenty-three, Custer was on his way to a spectacular career. Although he graduated at the bottom of his West Point class of 1861, Custer's legendary good luck (which would abandon him in a very public way thirteen years later) deposited the ambitious young man in a coveted staff billet with the Army of the Potomac's first commander, Maj. Gen. George B. McClellan. He was later assigned to General Pleasonton's staff, where his boldness and courage caught the cavalry chieftain's eye. Shortly after Pleasonton assumed corps command, he arranged for Custer's promotion from temporary captain to brigadier general of volunteers on June 29, 1863. Tall, brash, handsome, athletic, and a born horseman, the "Boy General with the Golden Locks," as Custer would soon be known, was still an unknown commodity as a field commander.[25]

Custer apparently anticipated his promotion because he had quickly secured a unique custom-made uniform that looked smarter and fit better than any in the corps. Captain Kidd, Company E, Custer's 6th Michigan, recalled elements of his young commander's natty garb: a suit of black velvet trimmed in gold lace, blue navy shirt, crimson necktie, and broad-brimmed black hat turned down rakishly on one side.[26] To most men in the brigade Custer was nothing more than a name. "Who is [Custer], and what is he like?" mused a trooper of the 1st Michigan. "No one knows, only they say he is a young sort of a fop in his looks, with long, golden, curly hair. Some one says he is a quick, nervous boy, and fights the fight before his opponent is ready."[27] On this day his troopers would discover whether the boyish-faced brigadier's moxie matched his outlandish attire.

Custer's new "Michigan Brigade" consisted entirely of Wolverine troopers and was composed of the 1st, 5th, 6th, and 7th Michigan regiments. As ordered, the 5th and 6th Michigan arrived at Littlestown just as Farnsworth began breaking camp.[28] Colonel George Gray's 6th Michigan was ordered to remain at Littlestown to guard Farnsworth's route and scout the area for signs of the enemy. Colonel Russell Alger's

5th Michigan, meanwhile, was ordered to ride south toward Westminster, where the men were to scout for rebel cavalry. Smaller squads of ten men each were detailed from both Farnsworth's brigade and the Michigan regiments to scout the roads flanking the route of advance.[29]

After riding for much of the night, Custer arrived at Littlestown with his 1st and 7th Michigan regiments two hours before daylight. After a quick conference with his commander, Custer rode with his regiments, followed by Lt. Alexander C. M. Pennington's six guns of the 2nd U.S. Artillery's Battery M, from Littlestown toward Hanover. Custer and his regiments had a one-hour head start on Farnsworth's brigade. "He [Custer] passed through Hanover at sunrise, leaving word with the few citizens he passed to look out for a hungry lot of Yanks coming in the rear," recalled one of Kilpatrick's troopers.[30] Pennington's guns had only joined Custer the day before, when the new brigadier assumed command of his brigade.[31] Originally organized for Mexican War service in 1847, the battery had seen heavy work in every major battle in the East since First Bull Run. The lanky Pennington, a graduate of the West Point Class of 1860, assumed the reins of battery command just after Antietam in late September 1862.[32]

Although it had been raining heavily during the past week and lightly that morning, the roads radiating from Littlestown, Union Mills, and Hanover were in surprisingly good condition—at least for those riding near the lead of the column.[33] The passage of thousands of hoofs, however, churned the roads into a muddy gruel through which artillery wheels (and, in the case of Stuart's column, wagon wheels and uncooperative mule teams) cut deep ruts. Troopers farther down the column quickly discovered the glue-like mud made what would have otherwise been a pleasant ride difficult for both man and beast. Although Kilpatrick's route followed flatter terrain than that over which Stuart's men rode, Farnsworth's regiments and Elder's guns were often forced to quicken their pace to keep up as line officers and sergeants called out for the men to "close up!"[34]

The condition of the roads was not the only factor slowing Kilpatrick's pace. For several days his new command had been constantly marching and skirmishing in the mostly hot weather, all without adequate food or rest. The 6th Michigan's Captain Kidd recalled

University of Michigan, Bentley Historical Library

Captain James H. Kidd, 6th Michigan Cavalry.

the work done by the Wolverines in and near Gettysburg the previous day and night:

> All day . . . [we] were scouting south and east of Gettysburg. Nor did the march end with the day. All night we were plodding our weary way along, sleeping in the saddle or, when the column in front would halt, every trooper dismounting, and thrusting his arm through the bridle rein, would lie down directly in front of his horse, in the road, and fall into a profound slumber. The horses too would stand with drooping heads, noses almost touching their riders' faces, eyes closed, nodding, but otherwise giving no sign, and

careful not to step on or injure the motionless figures at their feet. The sound of horses' hoofs moving in front served to arouse the riders when they would successively remount and move on again.[35]

Their loyal horses were fatigued and their backs sore. Many dropped out of Kilpatrick's column, unable to lift another leg. When the most jaded beasts gave out altogether, dozens of troopers gathered their saddles and equipment, slung them over their shoulders, and struggled along on foot in an effort to keep up with the column. Some procured new mounts from the herd of serviceable animals driven along in the column, while others had to walk on their own as best they could.

Just before 8:00 a.m. Kilpatrick and the head of his column entered the tiny crossroads hamlet of Mudtown, an aptly named clump of houses and farm fields one-half mile from Hanover.[36] The troopers continued along the Frederick Road toward Hanover's town square, through which Custer had earlier ridden. Two local boys, Samuel and John Forney, had been plowing since dawn in their family's field adjoining the road. The spectacle of Kilpatrick's column immediately drew their attention. The teenagers tied their horses, jumped up on the fence along the road, and sat down to watch the troopers ride past.

"Near the head of the column and in the center of the turnpike rode the youthful Kilpatrick," Samuel recalled decades later. "On both sides of him were the members of his staff." Kilpatrick eyed the curious young boys, who sat transfixed as if watching a parade. Reining his horse aside, Kilpatrick asked the lads for the location of the home of Jacob Wirt who, Kilpatrick had learned earlier, could provide a map of the area. The boys told the general that the home could be found ahead along the road, just as it intersected the square in Hanover. Satisfied, Kilpatrick thanked the lads and spurred his mount to rejoin the head of his column.

Kilpatrick was not the only one who stopped to converse with the boys. While speaking with one officer, Samuel noticed a soldier approaching him wearing a gray uniform. "Who is he?" asked the boy.

"He is a scout, we captured him up the road and he is our prisoner now," the lieutenant answered. The officer allowed the captured Confederate to approach the boys and speak with them.

"So you are plowing corn," the Confederate said to Samuel. Looking around, the prisoner continued. "I often plowed corn myself down in North Carolina, before I entered the army. I am a soldier now but I wish I were back in my native State, working quietly in the fields like yourselves, for this is a cruel war and I hope it will soon be over."

The boys watched as the Southerner was led away with the column. Another captured scout came riding along shortly thereafter. By the time General Farnsworth and his staff entered Mudtown, the boys were climbing down from the fence. They had ignored their plowing long enough and it was time to go back to work. As they moved "slowly along between the rows of corn" they glanced at the road, watching wistfully while the column walked past.[37] The Southern scouts, two of many sent out by Stuart the previous evening to gather information on the Federals operating in the area, did not betray the location of Stuart's brigades to Kilpatrick.

At the time of its earliest settlement in the 1750s, Hanover was known as "Hickorytown" because of the area's many hickory swamps and dense forests. Most of its original inhabitants were of German descent, and it is believed Richard McAlister, who plotted the town on his land in 1763, named it after the German monarch of Hannover, Germany. McAlister named the new town's four major roads after the cities to which they led: Carlisle, Baltimore, York, and Frederick. The latter route led through Mudtown and was the one along which Kilpatrick's troops were advancing.[38]

As the blue horsemen drew near the town, Kilpatrick sent an order back along the file to unfurl the national colors. The approaching soldiers and their banners were a welcome sight for the loyal citizens who lived so close to the Mason-Dixon Line. "At Hanover, the inhabitants came out in throngs to welcome us, freely giving bread, meats, coffee, pie, cake, etc.," Chaplain Louis N. Beaudrye of the 5th New York Cavalry jotted in his journal.[39] A trooper with the same regiment wrote home that the soldiers "were warmly greeted by the loyal people—especially the ladies, who waved the starry flags and sang patriotic songs, besides distributing refreshments through the ranks. We found it quite different to the treatment we received from the fair sex in Virginia."[40]

Each command, in turn, enjoyed the generosity of the locals, some of which was motivated by Kilpatrick's pleas for food for his men. The 38-year-old Rev. Dr. William K. Zeiber, pastor of the Emmanuel Reformed Church and chairman of the town's Committee of Safety, announced the need for supplies to the gathering crowds.[41] "A most enthusiastic and hearty welcome was given the weary horsemen. . . .

Women and girls crowded the sidewalks, tendering them food. Regiment followed regiment up Frederick street, halting a few minutes on Centre Square . . . [there were] cheers and blessings for the brave men and the flag they followed."[42] This idyllic scene brought a few minutes of peace to the tired Yankee horsemen. "No one seemed to dream of how sadly the scene was to be changed in a few minutes," recalled one of them.[43]

Like Stuart's men, Kilpatrick's troopers wore the weariness of their campaign on their faces. "Dirty, bedraggled and unshaven as they were," recorded one witness, "most cordial and enthusiastic was the welcome they received. Cheers from men, patriotic songs from the girls, greeted them on all sides."[44] Captain Henry C. Parsons of the 1st Vermont Cavalry vividly recalled a similar welcome many years later: "Flags waved everywhere. Bells were ringing. Hundreds of school children stood in the market square singing songs of welcome. . . . Matrons and maidens and children ran with bread and milk, beer and pretzels . . . It was a scene perhaps unsurpassed in all the marches of war."[45]

Unsurpassed or not, the citizens of Hanover had good reason to feel relief at the blue troopers' surprise arrival. News of a "Rebel invasion" had abounded in the area for several weeks, just as it had for much of the war up to that time. The constant fear caused anxiety among the more timid inhabitants. "During the early summer of 1863, all was excitement and turmoil on the Pennsylvania border. The alarm was sounded, 'The Rebels are coming!' almost every day," local citizens recalled. "Rumors of all kinds of battles, of burnings, of robberies and other outrages, rendered the people restless and fearful, and only those with the strongest nerves could get sound sleep at night. No man knew what the next day would bring forth." As an editorial in a Hanover newspaper declared in mid-June, "Our town has been in an intense state of excitement during the last few days. A thousand and one rumors are circulated in the course of the day. . . . From what can be gleaned from the reports it is certain that the rebels are on this side of the Potomac, in some force, variously estimated at from six to twenty thousand."[46] To save their valuables from the clutches of what were feared to be marauding enemy bands, Hanover citizens, as they did several times before, scrambled to take precautions.[47] "Horses and cattle, store goods and valuables were hidden away or hurried for safety from the spoiler to points in the happy land beyond the Susquehanna [River]."[48]

On the morning of June 27, three days before Kilpatrick's arrival, many of the citizens' fears became a reality when a panicked local farmer galloped through the town shouting, "The enemy will soon be here! They are now in McSherrystown!" Only moments after the farmer's warnings a squadron of Lt. Col. Elijah V. "Lige" White's 35th Battalion of Virginia Cavalry trotted smartly into the town square along Carlisle Street. White's troopers had been dispatched by Maj. Gen. Jubal Early to destroy the bridges and telegraph lines at Hanover Junction (twelve miles to the northeast) and to determine if there was a Federal presence in or around Hanover.[49] Haggard, dirty, and weary, the Southerners appeared to the locals more like "ragamuffins . . . than the boasted veterans of Lee's army."[50]

A small group of town leaders mustered up enough courage to gather in the square to meet White when the rebel leader rode to the front of the prominent Central Hotel to address them. White demanded the surrender of the town and assured the gathering that no one would be harmed if they complied. Though many of his men were "roughly dressed," White announced that his men "were gentlemen and were fighting for their belief in a just cause. They did not make war on civilians, and no one would be harmed so long as they did not attack the troops or otherwise cause trouble."[51] White ordered his 150 troopers to dismount and purchase clothing and such from the town's merchants if they wished. Those who made purchases from what little stock was left in the stores did so with the disdained Confederate currency.[52] One local merchant received a Confederate draft for a large purchase. The purchaser told him the document would be honored if the merchant visited the South, to which he replied, "it would not be worth a darn."[53]

White's raiders remained in Hanover until noon. They spent most of their time cutting telegraph wires until a bugle call ordered them to mount up, wheel into column, and set off for Hanover Junction, which they reached about 2:00 p.m.[54] By the time Kilpatrick trotted into town the Hanover civilians had experienced more than the usual panic-laced warnings. What they did not know was that they had thus far only had a small taste of what was to come.

White's unexpected visit convinced many Hanoverians that Kilpatrick's troopers comprised another invasion column. The Confederates had cut all the telegraph wires in the area, explained one local historian, so Hanover had "no telegraphic communication with the outside world" for several days.[55] Kilpatrick's advance guard and the familiar flying colors soon allayed their fears. As the citizens brought out food and drink upon Kilpatrick's arrival, his grateful troopers reached down from their saddles to accept the gifts. Some of the town's officials, who had surrendered the town to Lige White only a few days earlier, were more than happy to gather around Kilpatrick and offer their services. Smiles, exclamations of joy, and outreached hands greeted the sandy-whiskered boy general as he dismounted. Accompanied by staff officers, Kilpatrick entered the 62-year-old Jacob Wirt's home on Frederick Street just off the square. Once inside he listened intently while leading citizens offered up animated accounts of White's visit.[56] When Kilpatrick inquired whether anyone knew of other enemy movements, the town fathers could offer nothing more than that the rebels were "supposed to be quite near."[57]

Happily for Kilpatrick, his information about Wirt owning a large map of the area proved correct. At the general's request, the homeowner proudly led them to a large wall map of York County displayed in the front parlor of his home. Wirt told Kilpatrick and his officers (including Farnsworth, who arrived during the final minutes of the conference) they could take the map with them. The young generals studied the map carefully and asked myriad questions about the county's roads and nearby towns in an effort to glean as much information about the local territory as possible.[58]

Surrounded by his own staff, the dashing Farnsworth stepped out of the Wirt house to rejoin his brigade while Kilpatrick saddled up to ride to the head of the column. Knowing their weakened condition, Farnsworth decided to allow his regiments to rest. He ordered a partial dismounting of the 5th New York, which was "resting in a line extending from Frederick Street, through Center Square, and a short distance down Abbottstown Street. The troopers were being fed by the patriotic citizens."[59]

Within a few minutes, the head of the 18th Pennsylvania's column entered Hanover and "halted in the main street of the town, accepting the hospitalities of the good people of the place," remembered one witness.[60] Quickly recognizing the Pennsylvania coat of arms on the banners of their compatriots, the citizens thronged to the streets so thickly the regiment's forward progress ground to a halt. The lead elements of Farnsworth's brigade, with Kilpatrick riding along, had already passed through the town heading north on the Abbottstown Road. The Pigeon Hills, a range of rolling eminences about three miles north of Hanover, provided Kilpatrick with a clear view of the town and valley behind him. As the tired horses slowly climbed and descended the steep slopes to the north, Farnsworth's 18th Pennsylvania prepared to follow.

Captain Thadeus S. Freeland was in command of the 18th Pennsylvania's Company E, one of the flanking patrols detached from the overnight camp in Littlestown. Colonel Brinton had ordered Freeland's troopers to march parallel to the column. Freeland's men left for their mission once the main body cleared the camps. They took a little-used road to the left of the Hanover Road, which put them on a course west of the main route of march. Lieutenant Henry C. Potter and his rear guard detail allowed the column to advance about one mile up the road before following it. Eventually Freeland's course carried him back onto the Hanover Road, where his detail and Potter's small column rode together for a time before Freeland headed east on another side road to continue scouting the flanks.[61]

While most of Farnsworth's regiments had reached Hanover, Freeland's detail moved on a parallel course covering the right flank. His troopers soon reached the tiny hamlet of Gitt's Mill, only three miles southwest of the Hanover town square. His relatively untested men were riding slowly along the dirt road when someone spotted one of John Chambliss's Confederate scouting parties near a blacksmith shop atop Conewago Hill. One of the sharp-eyed Southerners spotted the Yankees about the same time.

Both sides seemed surprised to find enemy troops moving along the same road. The two opposing parties, each about equal in number, stopped and stared at their opposites for a few moments. Almost as if on cue, Freeland's men raised their shoulder arms and began firing at a range of 200 yards, a considerable distance for their single-shot breech-loading carbines. Although the range was long, one of Freeland's men killed a member of the 13th Virginia Cavalry. The first shots and the first fatality of the Battle of Hanover were written into history near the mill of Josiah Gitt.[62]

Freeland wisely disengaged quickly. His responsibility was not to wage a prolonged engagement of any size; it was to reach his supports as quickly as possible and report the presence of the enemy. The captain spurred his little group north up the road where, he hoped, he would find the main blue column. Instead of Kilpatrick, however, Freeland's men encountered another small mounted patrol riding toward Hanover. The captain and his men reined in their horses in the belief the patrol was another of the many small units dispatched by Kilpatrick that morning. By the time Freeland overtook the party, he realized his mistake. It was too late to avoid what was about to unfold.[63]

The unidentified patrol was a larger body of men from the 13th Virginia Cavalry. They quickly sized up Freeland's small command and surrounded the sweaty bluecoats before the enemy could draw their weapons or set spur to their mounts. Unfortunately for Kilpatrick, the minute or so of fitful shooting at Gitt's Mill was too distant from Hanover to be heard, especially over the clank and clatter of a miles-long file of marching horses, chattering troopers, and rumbling artillery. Without shot or shout Freeland's squad fell into the hands of Confederates riding much closer to Kilpatrick than anyone suspected.[64]

Oblivious to Freeland's fate, Potter and his forty Pennsylvania troopers arrived at Mudtown behind Kilpatrick's main column and stopped to water their horses at a small stream trickling under the road. Potter later recalled that while pausing, "a farmer came from a house close by calling to me, 'The rebs have taken my horses and cows!'" As Potter tells the story,

> I went with him to his barn, where he showed me the empty stalls and pointed out in the distance a small body of troops who had with them one of those old-fashioned

Lieutenant Henry C. Potter, 18th Pennsylvania Cavalry. He led Judson Kilpatrick's rearguard on the ride to Hanover.

History of the 18th Regiment

> Conestoga wagons. These troops had on blue coats. . . . I told the
> farmer I would have his stock returned to him and left, not being
> satisfied in my mind. I sent Corporals [Frank A.] Street and [Isaac
> I.] Dannenhower to see who they were. They came back saying it
> was Freeland. We went on, these troops getting closer and their
> numbers increasing. I was suspicious as their guidon was very red.[65]

Potter had good reason to be suspicious: Freeland's group, as Potter
well knew, consisted of less than a dozen troopers. "When about a mile
from the town the road they were on turned sharply into the one we were
on," continued Potter, "and about sixty of them came out directly in front
of us. They called on us not to shoot, but [to] surrender saying, 'We've
just captured some of you'uns,' and they would not shoot."[66]

Potter, however, was not to be so easily taken. As his men rode
slowly toward the enemy he quietly instructed his comrades to act on his
signal. "When we got very close to them we fired . . . they scattered and
we went through them," Potter reported. "It did not take them long to
recover and they came after us. We ran toward the town and a bend in the
road brought into view the rear of our regiment dismounted."[67]

About the time Potter ran the Southern gauntlet, Kilpatrick
dismounted for a short halt to allow Farnsworth's regiments to close up
on his elevated position beyond the Pigeon Hills north of Hanover near
the York Pike. It was nearly 10:30 a.m. A lone discharge from a field
piece boomed from the hills south of town, its low dull blast
reverberating through the air. The artillery thunder startled both men and
horses. Kilpatrick whipped his head around and looked back in the
direction of the town, with head after head of the miles-long column of
horsemen and artillerymen doing likewise. Some of the troopers of the
1st Vermont, who were leading the march, cast their gaze to the young
general, who by this time was staring intently in the direction of the
village. Was the discharge celebratory or did it portend something more
sinister?

The artillery salvo also startled a trooper of the 5th New York
Cavalry, who was still with his regiment in the town. "Our brigade was
drawn up in a column of fours in the main street, and we were enjoying
ourselves finely, when the report of a cannon and the bursting of a shell in
our rear caused a great commotion," he wrote home a few weeks later.
"The rebels had attacked our rear. It was so unexpected as to almost
create a panic."[68] Another horseman from the same New York outfit

recalled that while he was savoring the Hanoverians' kindness "a gun boomed in our rear, right where we had come from. . . . In about two minutes came another boom, and this time a shell came screeching up the street, and in a few minutes the pot and kettle brigade came dashing through our ranks, yelling that the whole rebel army was right after them."[69]

Lieutenant Stephen A. Clark's Company F, 1st Vermont Cavalry, was riding near the head of the column when the artillery discharge notified everyone an engagement was at hand. "We were having a grand jubilee on loyal soil when all of a sudden, like a clap of thunder from a clear sky, came the report of artillery and small-arms in our rear," recalled Clark. "We quickly gathered up our reins, grasped our carbines and revolvers, and were ready to meet anyone in deadly conflict that had the audacity to disturb our pleasure."[70]

The Forney boys were attending to their plow at Mudtown when they heard "loud yells and shrieks" south down the Littlestown Road. Sprinting as close as they dared, they saw Southern cavalrymen "dashing down the road and just as these mounted men were approaching the rear of Farnsworth's brigade, they fired a volley from their carbines," young Samuel remembered. "In a few minutes, the fields immediately north of the Littlestown road and west of Hanover were filled with mounted soldiers. The Union troops had quickly fallen back through town to the assistance of the rear regiment which had been attacked."[71] Wasting no time, the boys hurriedly unhitched their horses and rode them hard toward McSherrystown for the relative safety of a neighbor's farm.

The second and subsequent rounds of artillery, followed by a scattering of small-arms fire, provided Kilpatrick with his answer: the commotion was no friendly celebration. The general dispatched a courier north to Abbottstown to find Custer and the 1st and 7th Michigan and order them back to Hanover with all haste.[72] Kilpatrick leaped into the saddle of his already jaded mount and spurred it hard back down the pike toward the Pigeon Hills he had just crossed. Private Samuel L. Gillespie, a young bugler in the 1st Ohio Cavalry detachment assigned as the general's bodyguard, recalled that his commander "mounted his horse in haste and rode back to Hanover, it was said, in twenty minutes." Tasked with defending Kilpatrick, the Buckeyes put spurs to their horses in an effort to keep up with him, but several of their horses were injured in the attempt to match his pace.[73]

When Kilpatrick reached the ridgeline he paused to assess what lay below. Troopers and caissons choked the road leading back to town. Realizing he would get bogged down on the Abbottstown Road, he turned his mount's head and galloped into the fields on the right, dashing through the saddle-high wheat and cornfields, jumping each of the many fences in the way. Kilpatrick pushed his horse at breakneck speed with only a single flag-carrying sergeant riding by his side. His staff and escort fell farther behind with every stride. Captain Henry Parsons of the 1st Vermont was still in town when the firing began. He was watching the long column to the north when he spotted a lone officer racing toward Hanover for all he was worth. It did not take him long to realize who the rider was. "[Kilpatrick] rode with a sergeant beside him, carrying his flag, coming at a furious rate, distancing his bodyguard and all his staff," Parsons recalled.[74]

Spotting the rear of the Federal column after his near-disaster with the Southerners at Mudtown, Lieutenant Potter raced his squad of Pennsylvanians ahead to the safety of his regiment. There was a near collision as Potter's wide-eyed troopers galloped into and through the division's wagons, ambulances, horses, and teamsters. The noise of Potter's shots had already caused some panic in the rear of Kilpatrick's column. Major William B. Darlington of the 18th Pennsylvania reported that "some ambulances, which were in the rear, were driven by the

frightened drivers through our ranks, creating so much confusion that we were compelled to retreat through the town."[75] The only officer near the rear of the 18th Pennsylvania's column, 21-year-old 2nd Lt. Samuel H.

Major John Hammond, commander of the 5th New York Cavalry, Judson Kilpatrick's division.

USAMHI

Treasonthick, was so surprised by the proximity of the enemy and outbreak of hostilities that he failed to issue any orders to the scattering Pennsylvanians and teamsters.[76]

One intrepid pair of hospital stewards, however, responded quickly to the pandemonium and valiantly saved their wagon. Privates Augustus Forsyth and Henry Spaulding of the 5th New York Cavalry were in charge of Dr. Lucius P. Woods's valuable medical stores when the Confederates made their presence known. The pair devised a plan to save the supplies. "As the enemy approached," noted a *New York Times* reporter one month later, "they made a vigorous attack upon the covering of the wagon with their swords—cutting a dozen or more holes in the top—when Spaulding, who was sick, suggested to Forsyth, who was driving, that he (Spaulding) should drive, and the other drive off the assailants with a six-shooter one of the party had. This arrangement was carried into effect; the enemy was driven away, and the worthy surgeon's traps were saved to the service."[77]

Not everyone immediately realized what the firing signified. Some troopers from the 5th New York and 1st Vermont were in the square at the time, and for a while believed a welcome salute had been fired in their honor. The screaming whine of the first artillery shell passing overhead and crashing in the town disabused them of this notion.[78]

The commander of the 5th New York was Maj. John Hammond, a New Yorker from a prominent family who was about to play an important role on the Hanover stage. John was a child of privilege born on August 17, 1827, in Crown Point, New York. His family owned the Crown Point Iron Works, which generated a substantial fortune for the Hammonds. After attending the best schools he graduated from Rensselaer Polytechnic Institute and, eager for adventure, journeyed west to try his luck in the California gold rush of 1849. He spent three years on the west coast without much luck and decided to return to Crown Point in 1852. Once back home he married and was working in the family business when war broke out. Determined to play a part in what was shaping up to be the adventure of a lifetime, John joined the 34th New York Volunteer Infantry and fought with the regiment at Bull Run in July 1861. His offer to raise a company of cavalry was accepted, and the troopers became part of the 5th New York Cavalry. Hammond was promoted to captain and later to major in 1863.[79]

Hammond was well liked and respected by his men. "No man is better adapted mentally and physically for this arduous branch of the service than he," declared the regimental chaplain of the 5th New York. "He is strong and cool. He is a great favorite with the men of this command. He *leads* the men, does not *send* them. This they admire."[80] Hammond would need all of his faculties this day. Responding to the sound of the incoming shell, he turned atop his black charger and yelled at the top of his lungs for the now-frozen citizens to "run into their houses, as a fight was on."[81]

As the detachment of the 13th Virginia charged into Potter's men along Frederick Street, "for a moment, all was confusion," recalled Capt. John W. Phillips of the 18th Pennsylvania's Company B. "The impetuous charge of the enemy brought some of their troops in the midst of our men, and hand-to-hand contests were had with the sabre." As the Virginians slashed away at the untested Keystone horsemen, Colonel Chambliss ordered the artillery of McGregor's battery to fall out of column and unlimber on a ridge overlooking the town on either side of the road leading to Westminster. This position on the Samuel Keller and Jesse Rice farms dominated the town from the south, and the Confederate gunners took advantage of their prime perch to rapidly send several shells into the town and the blue mass milling about below them.[82] The Confederate shelling of the town, opined an editorial a few days later in the *Hanover Citizen*, was "an act wholly unworthy of a civilized people and contrary to the usage of civilized warfare."[83]

The 13th Virginia's assault scattered the Pennsylvania ambulances and wagon teams and split their hastily mounting troopers in twain. "The attack was determined and fierce, the main and side streets [of the town] swarmed with rebel cavalry," was how Kilpatrick candidly described the event in his official report. "The Eighteenth Pennsylvania was routed."[84] Part of the regiment fled west toward McSherrystown while another section was driven, as Stuart reported, "pell-mell through the town" up Frederick Street.[85] Captain John Esten Cooke, one of Jeb Stuart's staffers, rode forward to see what the commotion was all about. "Well, General," he reported when he rode back to inform Stuart, "Chambliss has driven them, and is going right in."

"Good!" declared Stuart. "Tell him to push on and occupy the town, but not to pursue them too far."

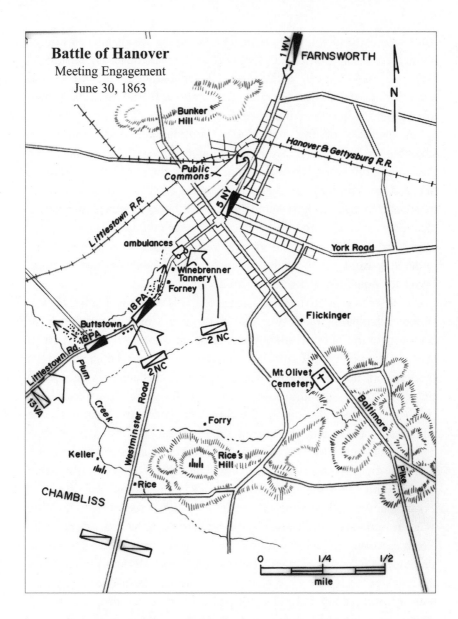

Battle of Hanover
Meeting Engagement
June 30, 1863

Cooke rode off to give Chambliss his orders and found the Virginian advancing rapidly in column of fours to charge the enemy, who was drawn up on the outskirts of town. "Before he could issue the order it was rendered somewhat nugatory by the blue people in front," Cooke later wrote in his memoirs. "We had supposed their force to be small, but it was now seen to be heavy. They swarmed everywhere, right, left, and front; rapidly formed line of battle, and delivering a volley at short range in the faces of the Confederates, made a gallant and headlong charge."[86] The aggressive spirit enthusiastically encouraged by Stuart and demonstrated this day by Chambliss, committed the Southern horsemen to a fight nobody expected or even wanted.

A battalion of the 2nd North Carolina, acting in support of Chambliss's Virginians, raced their mounts across fields to strike the flank of the retreating Pennsylvanians.[87] "Here the [2nd North Carolina] behaved in a most gallant manner, charging a heavy force of Yankees where two Regts., though double the 2nd in numbers, refused to charge," recalled a Tar Heel captain.[88] "It was here . . . the cutting and slashing was done," recalled the 18th Pennsylvania's Lieutenant Potter, "and for a few in the very front it was a hand-to-hand fight."[89] Cooke agreed, writing, "We had apparently waked up a real hornet's nest."[90]

"The 'rebs were in the town," recalled the 18th Pennsylvania's Pvt. J. Wilber Shephard, "[and] we had to drive the men and women [of Hanover] in their homes so they would not be shot."[91] Baltimore Street resident Samuel Althoff quickly returned to his home when he heard the shooting out on Westminster Road. He found his family hiding in the cellar. "Eager to watch the contest, I went to the garret of my house and climbed out the trap door to the roof," he later explained. What he witnessed was something he never forgot. "I saw the mounted soldiers dashing back and forward along the roads and in the fields west of town. In a grain field southwest, I saw Confederate sharpshooters raising from the tall grain and firing at the Union troops in and around the town."[92]

Citizens in and near the square, in the midst of feeding and fawning over the Federals, were caught in the maelstrom of the new attack as the North Carolinians burst through back alleys onto Frederick Street, slamming the Pennsylvania troopers back into the 5th New Yorkers, who were nearer the square. The New Yorkers were caught in a hard place, with a rolling attack behind them and artillery shells dropping across their front. Captain Parsons of the 1st Vermont later recalled the scene: "Suddenly a shell crashed through the buildings; then another, and a third. In a moment the whole scene was changed. The population had vanished into the houses and hiding-places. . . . The rear guard had been driven in, and came thundering down the street." The half of the 18th Pennsylvania still in town fled down Abbottstown Street to the railroad depot. For the moment, at least, Hanover was in the possession of the Southerners.[93]

Some 18th Pennsylvania troopers were easy prey for the Virginians and North Carolinians. As the mounted Confederates dashed across the fields they spotted a small rear guard commanded by Lt. Thomas P. Shields. At the first commotion, Shields galloped his 25 men southeast through an alley to attempt a flanking maneuver against what he mistakenly believed was a small enemy force. When he and his men burst into an open field off Baltimore Street, however, Shields discovered to his surprise that he had inadvertently interjected his men into the middle of a large group of Southerners. Within seconds the Pennsylvanians were nearly surrounded. Although Shields and about six other Pennsylvanians were quickly taken prisoner, the rest managed to turn their horses head-for-tail and escape.[94]

General Farnsworth was riding at the head of his brigade near the tiny hamlet of New Baltimore, about one mile north of Hanover, when the noise of the fight raging behind him reached his ears. The young general promptly directed his 1st West Virginia and 1st Vermont to turn around and ride toward the town and form a line of battle to the southeast.[95] Like all good officers Farnsworth wanted to see things for himself, so he spurred his horse toward the square and ended up in the midst of the confusion along the Abbottstown Road.[96] In response to Farnsworth's orders, Maj. Charles Capehart of the 1st West Virginia Cavalry rallied his men for the task facing them. "Remember, boys," he admonished, "we are on the free soil of old Pennsylvania, with Stars and Stripes unfurled to cheer us on to battle. We will drive the rebels off her soil!"[97]

When the Virginians and North Carolinians thundered into the center of town, they found Major Hammond's 5th New Yorkers spread out in the square, many of whom were dismounted. A local ran up to Hammond and pointed to a vacant field a block away, recommending it as the ideal place to form his regiment.[98] "With his accustomed coolness and bravery, Maj. Hammond . . . quickly withdrew from the street to the open field near the rail road depot, [and] ordered the boys into line," recalled Chaplain Boudrye.[99]

Hastily breaking column and dashing from the square, the New Yorkers quickly formed lines of battle in the vacant field. Ordering his troopers to draw their sabers, Hammond turned to his 14-year-old bugler, "Johnnie" Catlin, and nodded with a warrior's determination. Catlin's boyish face was still smeared with a pie he tried to swallow whole, given to him by a pretty young lass only moments before. Catlin knew what the nod meant and quickly wiped his mouth with his sleeve, lifted his bugle to his purple lips, and blew as hard as he was worth.[100] With "a terrific yell" Hammond and his New Yorkers, with Company A in the lead, hammered their mounts' flanks with their spurs and galloped toward the enemy, crashing into the Confederates gathered on Frederick Street.[101] "I believe I have the honor, with the Fifth, of leading the first charge and fighting the first battle on free soil since this war commenced," Hammond proudly proclaimed to his wife a few days later.[102]

Companies D and M, both of Lt. Col. Addison Preston's newly arrived 1st Vermont, joined the counterassault delivered by Hammond's New Yorkers. "There was mounting in hot haste," recalled Sgt. Horace K. Ide of Company D. "The order was given to our Squadron . . . to 'Right about wheel,' which we did . . . Then the order was given to charge and away we went."[103] The 1st Vermont's Captain Parsons watched as

> Maj. Hammond, with a portion of the 5th N.Y., and Capt. [John W.] Woodward, with a portion of the 1st Vt., occupied an elevated position in a cross-street, where they could watch their opportunity and direct a counter-charge. They struck the head of the pursuing column, with its disordered ranks and spent horses, a fierce and resistless blow, cutting down the leaders and capturing men and horses.[104]

The 5th New York's Company A led the charge and suffered heavily as a result. Sergeant Selden Wales spurred his horse hard, galloping ahead of his company. As he turned in the saddle to urge his comrades forward a Confederate bullet slammed into his heart, knocking him off his mount and killing him instantly.[105] Lieutenant Frazier A. Boutelle's horse was shot out from under him and the officer seriously injured when the poor beast crumpled on top of him.[106] Both Sgt. Michael J. Hayes and Pvt. Brad Wessart suffered nasty saber cuts in the swirling Hanover fight.

Major Hammond's staff officers were not immune to Southern lead. His adjutant, Lt. Alexander Gall, was killed instantly at close range when a bullet struck him in the left eye. The ball passed completely through his head and spattered bits of brain, bone, and blood on the New Yorkers riding behind him.[107] Major Amos H. White, also of Hammond's staff, took a spent ball in the leg that cracked the bone above his right ankle.

The nearly unbearable pain from the wound hunched the major over his skittish mount, and his boot filled with blood. White kept his composure and remained with his men long enough to witness their countercharge put the Confederates to flight. Confident of the tactical victory, White turned his horse to the rear to find medical treatment for his agonizing wound.[108]

Lieutenant Potter and some of his 18th Pennsylvania rear guard detail joined the 5th New York in the town square after the opening clash. They, too, joined in Hammond's counterattack, along with troopers of Col. Nathaniel P. Richmond's 1st West Virginia. Privates John F. Roller and Jacob R. Harvey of Potter's Company M were both shot and killed. Harvey was galloping alongside Lieutenant Potter when he fell from his mount and sprawled senselessly across the lieutenant's horse. "I had to push him off and he slid to the ground between the horses," Potter later wrote. "He was either killed outright or was tramped to death by the horses."[109] Twelve-year-old Edward F. Parker, or "Little Ed" as he was called by the troopers, was the "mascot" of the 18th Pennsylvania. The brave boy charged with the troopers of Company I. He emerged from his first combat unscathed, although he suffered the harrowing experience of having his horse shot out from under him.[110]

Corporal John Hoffacker, Company E, 18th Pennsylvania, grew up just a few miles south of Hanover, a town he almost certainly visited during his formative years. The 24-year-old had joined the regiment only two months earlier and was "universally popular" with his comrades. Hoffacker was killed during the charge and was laid to rest in Hanover's Mt. Olivet Cemetery soon after the battle ended.[111]

Sergeant James P. Allum of the 1st West Virginia's Company B recalled the carnage later in life. "I remember very well seeing some of the 18th [Pennsylvania], or afterwards they belonged to the 18th, lying in the street, our horses jumping over their dead bodies. Just after we got through the town we met the rebels in line of battle. We had quite a skirmish." Perhaps Hoffacker's corpse was one of the bodies Allum remembered littering the street.[112]

In the whirlwind of the thundering cavalry charge, Allum somehow took notice of how the ladies of Hanover reacted to the violent and bloody street fighting. "I have often said that the women of that place were the bravest that I ever saw," he wrote. "They stood in the doors of their houses and waved their handkerchiefs and cheered us as we charged through the town, although the bullets were flying thick and fast."[113]

The commander of the 13th Virginia, the sullen-eyed and heavily bearded Maj. Joseph E. Gillette, took a serious gunshot wound to his neck while at the head of his regiment. Toppled from the saddle, a member of his staff scooped up Gillette and carried the injured officer to relative safety in the rear.[114]

Outnumbered, with one regimental commander down, and with the momentum now swinging to the Federals, the Virginians and North Carolinians were driven back down the street and about one mile out of the town to where some of Chambliss's North Carolinians were driving Kilpatrick's ambulance wagons and stores south toward Mudtown and away from the rest of the bluecoats. "For a few moments the enemy made heroic resistance, but finally broke and fled," Chaplain Boudrye later noted.[115] "[Q]uite a severe fight ensued" along the Littlestown Road, reported the 1st Vermont's Sergeant Ide.[116] According to Chaplain Boudrye, the stubborn Confederates "rallied again and again but were met with irresistible onsets, which finally compelled them to retire behind the hills under cover of their guns."[117] The momentum of the charge fell away, however, reported Major Hammond, when "we found a large force [of the Confederates] drawn up in the road as a reserve, and received from them a severe fire, causing the men to halt for a moment."[118]

The "large force" was Colonel Beale's 9th Virginia Cavalry, nearly 500 Southern troopers waiting for the Federals near the intersection of Frederick Street and the Westminster Road. Their murderous volley emptied many saddles of the 5th New York. "Our men in the road opened fire on them," reported Beale, "and as soon as the fence could be broken down, a small party charged with the sabre. The mounted Federals retreated behind a line of dismounted men, who now advanced, extending across our front and as far to the right as we could see."[119] The 5th New York and 18th Pennsylvania retired down Frederick Street, which was now littered with the victims of mounted charges and countercharges. At least a dozen blue and gray troopers lay dead, many more lay wounded, and more than two dozen horses lay strewn on the street from the square to the edge of town.[120]

Taking advantage of the confusion, several Confederate troopers set out to cut down the American flag flying over the *Hanover Spectator* newspaper office on Frederick Street. Pennsylvanians and New Yorkers alike spotted the move and chased them off, leaving the banner to fly defiantly atop its post of honor.[121]

By this time Elon Farnsworth, sitting tall in the saddle, had ridden directly into the action. "Gen. Farnsworth was at the head of the column when the firing began," remembered the 1st Vermont's Lieutenant Clark. "He quickly turned, and was at the scene of the conflict in short order."[122] Listening to hasty reports from his regimental leaders while rallying his scattered men, Farnsworth's determination was palpable. "As he passed the regiments, he gave orders where each regiment should form," wrote Clark. "The 1st Vermont was ordered to form in an open field to our right. General Farsworth soon had the 5th N.Y. and 1st. W. Va. Cav. at work."[123] When everything met his satisfaction, Farnsworth drew his saber with a flourish, ordered his troopers to do the same, and bellowed out orders to charge. With their blades pointed at their foes, the screaming New Yorkers, Vermonters, and West Virginians again put spur to horseflesh and began, as Hammond reported, "driving the rebels in confusion along the road and through the fields."[124]

The young brigadier's mettle made a lasting impression on his new command. "General Farnsworth had wheeled [us] into line and with lightning speed charged the rebel foe driving them in hot haste before us," Sgt. Atchinson Blinn of the 1st Vermont scribbled that night in his diary.[125] "Farnsworth's generalship in handling the position at Hanover," declared Lieutenant Clark, "placed him at once as A No. 1 with his men."[126]

During this second charge, Pvt. Thomas Burke of the 5th New York's Company A spotted a wounded comrade engaged in a hand-to-hand struggle with a color bearer of the 13th Virginia. Spurring his mount, Burke dashed to his rescue, shot the Southerner dead with one shot, and grabbed his flag, which he later turned over to General Kilpatrick. Burke also captured the two remaining Virginians of the color guard.[127]

Shortly after 11:00 a.m., Kilpatrick's hell-bent-for-leather run brought him to Hanover's square just as Farnsworth's charge repulsed the Southerners. A rousing cheer by his troopers greeted Kilpatrick, whose stirrups, remembered one witness, sported pieces of grass, corn, and wheat stalks.[128] Captain Parsons remembered the moment Kilpatrick arrived and later recorded his observations for posterity:

As he reached the line of battle he turned in front of the Vermont troops, who were new to him, seized [his] flag, and standing in his stirrups, without drawing rein, cried out, 'Men of Vermont, you don't know me; I don't know you. To-day we make an acquaintance on the battlefield. I know I shall like you; I think you shall like me,' and passed around to the left.[129]

Kilpatrick selected the tall Central Hotel as a post from which to observe the enemy.[130] Reining up in front of the building, the general dismounted, his horse gasping deeply for air. The loyal beast, which had carried him nonstop across eight miles of crops and over countless fences, swaggered for a moment, dropped to its knees, and collapsed in a heap. The recently captured Confederate mount, sporting the brand "CSA," died within a few hours.[131]

While his counterpart galloped for the front, Stuart and his headquarters staff pushed rapidly up the Westminster Road toward the sound of the fighting. They had some distance to traverse, riding from their position at the rear of Chambliss's Brigade. "Have the artillery put in position yonder on the road," the general cried out as he galloped past. "Tell it to open!"[132]

Stuart planned to take immediate control of his men by galloping beyond his column and onto the brow of the ridge where McGregor and Breathed had unlimbered their guns only 300 yards from town.[133] From the commanding heights south of town, Stuart watched Chambliss's Virginians and North Carolinians wither away before Farnsworth's determined countercharge. "As General Stuart saw them rushing out of the place, he started down the road to meet them, calling me to follow him," recalled Adjutant Blackford. "We tried to rally them, but the long charge *in* and the repulse *out* and the hot skirmish fire . . . had thrown them into utter confusion."[134]

As the fighting south of town rolled northward, scores of Union and Confederate troopers, locked in hand-to-hand combat, filled the streets and yards of Hanover, the bulk of the action unfolding on and around Frederick Street. The fighting was up close and personal. By this time many of the troopers were fighting like madmen to save their own lives. Personal duels featured exhibitions of strength and examples of bravery everywhere one looked. Slashing sabers emptied saddles and pistols fired at point blank range dropped grown men to the ground.

Lieutenant Colonel
William Payne,
2nd North
Carolina Cavalry.

National Archives

Citizens found it difficult to avert their eyes from the small knots of two and three troopers locked in mortal combat just outside their front windows. One witness watched in horror as a Union soldier who refused to surrender was blasted out of his saddle. It was obvious to the onlooker that the trooper was dead before he hit the street.[135] The town square, too, witnessed its share of combat. A shot from a Yankee weapon struck Sgt. Isaac Peale of the 2nd North Carolina squarely in his chest, knocking him from his mount. Peale fell senselessly to the ground, cracking open his skull on the cobblestone-paved sidewalk at the northeast edge of the square. By the time he was carried to the front of a nearby store, Peale was "raving in his delirium . . . denouncing the Yankees," remembered one witness to the affair.[136] The Tarheel died in a makeshift Hanover hospital the following day and was buried in the nearby Conewago Church Cemetery.[137]

Sergeant Peale's commanding officer, Lt. Col. William Payne of the 2nd North Carolina Cavalry, found himself in a twist near the Winebrenner Tannery on Frederick Street. Slightly wounded and unhorsed, Payne somehow landed in one of the tannery's open dye vats while trying to escape. He sank up to his shoulders. The officer had been wounded and captured in May 1862, so Payne was no stranger to difficult situations. This day's episode, however, would be especially memorable.

William Payne was an 1849 graduate of the Virginia Military Institute and had studied law at the University of Virginia. He was working as an attorney and volunteering as a Virginia militia captain when the war began.[138] Payne enlisted as a private but was quickly promoted to a captaincy in the 4th Virginia Cavalry in April 1861. He was bumped up again to lieutenant colonel in June 1862 while a prisoner of war, and after his return to the army that September took command of the 2nd North Carolina.[139] Now, one year later, Payne was sitting in a barrel of brown dye in Pennsylvania, clenching his side to stem the bleeding from a saber cut. Worse still was the fact that Pvt. Abram Folger of the 5th New York's Company H towered over him, demanding his surrender. Folger recalled that Payne's "gray uniform with its velvet facing and white gauntlet gloves, his face and hair had all been completely stained, so that he presented a most laughable sight."[140]

Dripping with the vile whiskey-colored liquid, Payne was not as amused as his captor, who marched the Southern officer into Kilpatrick's presence. The general snickered in delight at Payne's plight and "congratulated him on his appearance."[141] Folger fully appreciated the irony of the situation, for he had been captured by Payne's command in 1862. As the private later put it, he was "glad to return the compliment with interest."[142]

The 2nd North Carolina suffered heavily at Hanover. The regiment was, Lieutenant Colonel Payne correctly noted, "almost cut to pieces."[143] The urban combat left Capt. William A. Graham, a company commander with the 2nd North Carolina, a bitter man. He believed Jeb Stuart had abandoned the Tarheels to their fate. "General Stuart . . . left the regiment to its own defense," he seethed after the war. "Hardly thirty men escaped being killed or captured. Most of these came out on foot through gardens or enclosures which offered protection." The Tarheels lost 22 enlisted men and two officers out of just 50 men.[144]

Elon Farnsworth's hammering countercharge had swept most of the North Carolinians and Virginians from the town when Stuart and his staff reached the fields south of Hanover. They arrived just in time to witness the Confederate mass exodus from Hanover. "[I]n spite of all we could do they got by us," lamented staffer Blackford, "and before we were aware of it we found ourselves at the head of the enemy's charging column."[145] It was a hot place, especially for Stuart and his lieutenants. One Confederate captain, attempting to escape, suffered a nasty saber blow to his head and "remained insensible for about six hours."[146] Blackford later wrote of their dangerous position:

> The [Westminster] road was lined on each side by an ill-kept hedge grown up high, but at some places, fortunately for us, there were gaps of lower growth. Stuart pulled up and, waving his sabre with a merry laugh, shouted to me, 'Rally them, Blackford!' and then lifted his mare, Virginia, over the hedge into the field. . . . As we alighted in the field, we found ourselves ten paces in the front of a flanking party of twenty-five or thirty men . . . accompanying the charging regiment, and they called us to halt.[147]

Colonel Beale of the 9th Virginia, who was watching the affair unfold, feared his chief's small party was doomed. "General Chambliss, commanding the brigade, was met and told that General Stuart had been seen surrounded, and was probably captured," explained Beale.[148] Fortunately for the Southerners, however, Stuart and Blackford were riding fresh mounts that had been led instead of ridden that morning. The Federals galloped after the officers into a field of timothy east of the road in "hot pursuit," recalled Blackford, "firing as fast as they could cock their pistols."[149]

With his trademark plumed hat raking the humid air, Stuart galloped just a handful of strides ahead of his pursuers, his mare Virginia straining to escape. Suddenly, an obstacle appeared in front of the fleeing officers. Blackford recounted the scene:

> [W]e did not see, nor did our horses until close to it, a huge gully fifteen feet wide and as many deep stretched across our path. There were only a couple strides of distance for our horses to regulate their step, and Magic [Blackford's horse] had to rise at least six feet from the brink. Stuart and myself were riding side by side and as soon as Magic rose I turned my head to see how Virginia had done it, and I shall never forget the glimpse I then saw of this beautiful animal away up in mid-air over the chasm and Stuart's fine figure sitting erect and firm in the saddle. . . . The moment our horses rose, our pursuers saw that there was something there, and it was with difficulty they could pull up in time to avoid plunging headlong into it.

Instead of following suit, the Federals wisely pulled up rein and halted, but not before some of Stuart's less fortunate riders slid and fell into the drainage ditch cleared by Stuart's panting mare just moments before.[150] The disappointed bluecoats were left on the wrong side of the ditch, watching helplessly as the Confederate cavalry chieftain galloped away. They decided not to extract the others, leaving them instead to scrape the muck from their uniforms and fend for themselves.

Without breaking stride, Stuart and his staff galloped up the hill to the fields of the Rice and Keller farms, where his horse artillery was still banging away at the Federals milling below. Blackford, however, decided to lead his winded mount Magic to safety by another route. "I, wishing to get Magic cooled down away from the excitement . . . took a path which wound round the foot of the hill. I had just quieted her, so that she had put her head down . . . when I heard the clatter of a horse's hoofs behind me at full speed."[151] At first Blackford believed the hooves signaled another staff officer riding to join him. "I looked back, and there . . . came dashing a Yankee sergeant bending low on his horses' neck with his sabre 'en-carte' ready to run me through," recalled the stunned rider. Blackford snatched his reins and plunged his left spur hard into Magic's side. "As quick as lightning Magic bounded . . . and at the same instant there gleamed the bright blade of a sabre between my arm and body as my pursuer made his thrust." By the time Blackford gathered his reins and turned his mount, "the man was fifty yards away." Cheering caused Blackford to look up to the left. On a nearby hill were "a [Federal] general officer and his staff, toward whom my man was making his way. It was evident that, seeing me alone, this man had made the pass as a little sword practice for the amusement of his comrades and his own glorification," explained Blackford. "I could only show my feelings upon the subject by shaking my fist at them as I moved slowly on to the battery on our hill."[152]

While Blackford was playing the unwilling subject of a "little sword practice," Stuart directed the fire of Breathed's guns from the eminence south of town. His troopers and gunners cheered when the general emerged unscathed from the scrap that had unfolded below them. "To our great joy," recalled Beale, "we met General Stuart, smiling as ever."[153] Stuart's trademark grin belied his harrowing brush with death. He also knew there was more work to be done if he was to shove the Federals out of his way and continue his northward progress. Stuart ordered a line of skirmishers formed to discourage any thoughts of assault by the bluecoats while dozens of cannon lanyards dropped to the ground as his horse artillery pounded the town with shell. The combination of McGregor's rapid fire from the east side of the road and the timely arrival of the rest of Chambliss's Brigade convinced Farnsworth to move his

Lieutenant Samuel S. Elder, commander of Battery E, 4th U.S. Artillery, which served with Farnsworth's brigade.

Dave Shultz

men back toward the town square.[154] It was shortly after noon; Stuart had been utterly blocked for more than two hours.

About this time, just after the first two assaults by Farnsworth's regiments, Judson Kilpatrick scrambled up to the roof of the Central Hotel. His staff followed him there and shared the outstanding view of the town and surrounding fields and roads. Below them stretched the scattered remnants of the dreadful street fighting. Private Gillespie, Kilpatrick's bugler, recalled that "dead horses were lying along the streets and upon the sidewalks, where the battle had raged, with here and there a gray coat and then a blue, sleeping their last sleep together in the dust."[155] Chaplain Boudrye of the 5th New York similarly recalled, "The dead and wounded of both parties, with many horses, lay scattered here and there along the streets, so covered with blood and dust as to render identification in many cases very difficult."[156]

Taking advantage of this temporary lull in the fighting, the bravest of the citizens emerged from their doors and curtains to assist Kilpatrick's troopers in barricading the streets to retard more Confederate attacks. They grabbed anything and everything they could and rolled, pushed, and threw it all into the streets. "Baltimore, York, and Frederick streets were barricaded. . . . Store boxes, wagons, hay ladders, fence rails, barrels, bar iron and anything that would prevent the enemy from dashing into town were placed across the streets," remembered one of them.[157]

North of Hanover, the guns of Lt. Samuel Elder's Union battery, after countermarching down the Abbottstown Road, bounced across farm fields and through fences to reach a hill on the eastern side of the Carlisle Pike. Locally known as Bunker Hill, the eminence mirrored that of their

Lieutenant Alexander C. M. Pennington, commander of Battery M, 2nd U.S. Artillery, which usually served with Custer's Michigan Brigade.

Library of Congress

Southern counterparts south of town. Once in position, the Union gunners unlimbered their four 3-inch Ordnance Rifles and began firing at Stuart's position, barely 800 yards distant.[158] Samuel Althoff was still on the roof of his Baltimore Street home, mesmerized as he watched the opposing guns engage in counterbattery fire over the embattled town. A 5th New York Cavalry officer spotted Althoff and ordered him to "get off the roof of the house," remembered the civilian, "for I was in danger of being shot." Convinced of the accuracy of the officer's admonition, Althoff crawled through his trap door and bounded downstairs. He did not join his family in the basement, however, for the urge to continue watching the action from his first-floor windows proved too great to resist.[159]

When Elder's rifles challenged Stuart's ordnance, the Southern gunners returned the favor by turning their pieces against Elder, who was reinforced by Lt. Alexander Pennington's six 3-inch Ordnance Rifles (minus a crewman and limber that were accidentally blown up on the Abbottstown Road earlier that same day). Thundering down the road, Pennington's battery bounced and rolled up the hill on the western side of the Carlisle Pike and unlimbered in line with Elder's rifled pieces. The vigorous artillery duel, staged with the town of Hanover caught squarely in its middle, raged between the proud gun crews for nearly two full hours.[160]

Shells fired by Breathed's artillerists hit a number of homes and killed and wounded several Federal troopers and horses. One of the first projectiles, a 12-pounder, struck the rear balcony door of Henry

Winebrenner's home on Frederick Street, just moments after Winebrenner's wife and daughter closed the door and stepped inside to escape the artillery fire. The shell failed to explode. Instead, it shattered a chest of drawers, plowed through the second story floor, and punched into the family's parlor below before lodging itself in a brick wall.[161] Two more shells struck the Winebrenner house before the fight ended.[162]

Kilpatrick was studying the situation from the hotel roof while Major Hammond reformed his depleted 5th New Yorkers near the town's commons. Hammond posted skirmishers and a reserve line at the town limits near the Winebrenner Tannery and the Karl Forney farm along Frederick Road. Farnsworth's other regiments reorganized while the scattered remnants of companies fell back into line. In an effort to restore cohesion and order to his brigade, Farnsworth ordered Hammond to withdraw most of his troopers to Bunker Hill and support Elder's guns.[163]

Before Hammond could do so, however, Kilpatrick issued orders of his own. "I was ordered by General Kilpatrick to flank the enemy's position, and capture [Breathed's] battery, if possible, and to order an advance of the skirmishers on the right, which was done," Hammond reported.[164] The worn-out New Yorkers, consisting by this time of eight depleted companies, rode obediently to the eastern edge of town between Abbottstown and York streets. To replace Hammond as Elder's battery support, Kilpatrick directed Lt. Col. Addison Preston's 1st Vermont Cavalry to move from the town commons to Elder's position on Bunker Hill. Because only two of Preston's companies had brawled with Stuart's horsemen that morning, most of his regiment was fresh. Kilpatrick's directives proved unpopular with the men of both regiments; knowingly or not, Kilpatrick had dispatched a fresh unit to support Elder's battery, and the tired and shot-up New Yorkers to a position from which they were expected to attack a very active enemy battery.[165]

While the horse regiments were riding to assume their new positions, Col. Nathaniel P. Richmond's 1st West Virginia troopers followed their orders to correct their skirmish line. Richmond connected his left flank with Preston's right and hunkered his men down behind the hasty barricades thrown up across Baltimore Street and nearby side streets. To Richmond's right rear were members of the 18th Pennsylvania, who supported his exposed flank along Frederick Street.[166]

The horsemen had no way of knowing that the fight at Hanover was only just beginning.

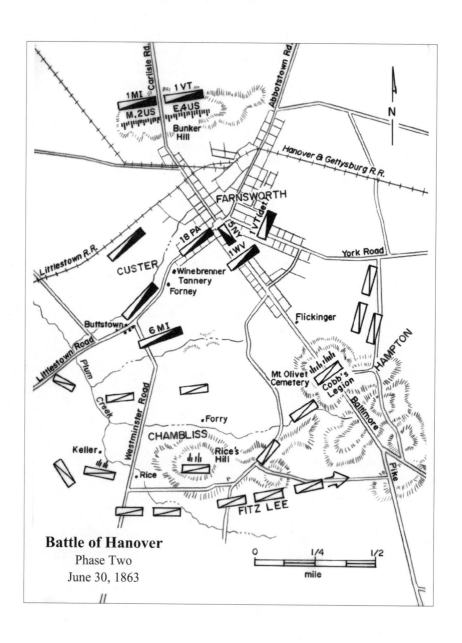

Battle of Hanover
Phase Two
June 30, 1863

0   1/4   1/2
mile

Chapter 5

The Second Phase of the Battle of Hanover

"We are put in all of the worst places on account of [the] seven shooters."
— Pvt. William H. Rockwell, 5th Michigan Cavalry

Bringing up the rear of the 2nd Brigade were Col. William D'Alton Mann and his 7th Michiganders. These Wolverines were the first of George Custer's troopers to return to embattled Hanover.[1] Spurring ahead of his men, Mann sought out Custer, who after returning to Hanover, had established his headquarters at Jacob Wirt's Frederick Street home. This was the same spot where Kilpatrick had conferred with his staff and General Farnsworth when the division commander arrived in town. Once Custer reached the square, he tied his own panting horse to a stout maple tree in front of one of the homes and left his body servant to care for the animal.[2]

While Pennington swung his battery alongside Elder's on Bunker Hill, with elements of the 1st Michigan Cavalry deployed in support, Custer ordered Mann and his 7th Michigan to deploy on the hill's southern slope north of the Carlisle Pike. A four-company battalion dismounted and advanced toward the railroad to form a skirmish line.[3] Kilpatrick sent for his two brigadiers to attend a conference at the Central Hotel.[4]

The generals were deep in discussion when the luckless Lieutenant Colonel Payne of the 2nd North Carolina, dripping brown tanning dye from his already filthy uniform, was marched before them. The Tarheel had already endured endless derision about his unfortunate condition;

now he was forced to undergo an interrogation about the strength and disposition of Stuart's command. In a convincing performance designed "to prevent any further attack" by the young brigadier, Payne lied to Kilpatrick by saying Stuart was on the field with his entire cavalry corps of more than 12,000 troopers. Payne's ruse may have worked, for Kilpatrick's command decisions the rest of the day were tempered with a good deal of caution.

As the opposing batteries pounded away at one another over the town, Stuart knew his gunners could not maintain the contest for any sustained period. The firing on both sides was ineffective and ammunition was already running low. Unlike his counterparts, Stuart was far from his base of supplies, his gunners and troopers were already exhausted from the travails of their lengthy ride, and they still had a long journey ahead of them. Stuart's hope was to safely disengage from a fight he had never wanted in the first place. The clash, which had gotten considerably out of hand quickly, was burning up valuable powder, energy, horseflesh, and time. For the moment, however, Stuart's artillerymen would have to continue their fitful exchange with their Union counterparts. As Stuart contemplated his next move, enemy troopers appeared on a rise left and behind a section of McGregor's guns on the Keller Farm.

When they heard from a citizen that "a large force of the enemy" had been seen near Hanover, Colonel George Gray and his 6th Michiganders, left behind at Littlestown to reconnoiter that morning, rode to Hanover to join the rest of Custer's brigade.[5] The 6th Michigan's ride had been accompanied by "citizens, with shot guns in their hands . . . going on foot on the flank of the column, trying to keep pace with the cavalry, and apparently eager to participate," recalled Capt. James H. Kidd.[6] Neither the troopers nor the daring citizens knew that their route would lead them squarely into Jeb Stuart's flank, which lay between them and their destination.

The Michigan troopers turned east off the Littlestown Road and headed into a sprawling wheat field, riding toward the unmistakable sound of discharging artillery. When Gray's men crested a rise to the north, they immediately spotted the vanguard of what appeared to be Confederate cavalry riding just ahead, supporting an unlimbered battery. As they later discovered, the cavalry was Colonel Davis's 10th Virginia troopers, part of John Chambliss's Brigade, who were supporting two of

McGregor's Napoleons on the Keller Farm west of the Westminster Road.[7] The Southern gunners discovered their unwelcome guests quickly, and within a short time McGregor swung his two guns to the left and "opened upon the head of the regiment . . . with shell, wounding several men and horses."[8] Gray was as surprised to stumble upon the Southerners as Lieutenant Potter had been earlier that morning.[9]

Those troopers of the 10th Virginia Cavalry nearest to Gray's column of mounted Wolverines, lined up four abreast, joined McGregor's gunners. Gray quickly absorbed the situation and made a snap decision: he would attack. The 10th Virginia fielded fewer than 300 men, and its line was stretched thin for nearly a mile from McGregor's position all the way to the Littlestown Road. On his command, Gray's 600 Wolverines fanned out slightly from their column and pounded forward. The weight of their attack scattered many of the 10th Virginia's skirmishers and nearly carried them all the way to McGregor's guns. Before they could punch through the line that deeply, however, the balance of Davis's Virginians, mounted and ready for a countercharge, arrived to meet them. The Southerners put spur to horse and, despite Gray's superior numbers, drove the Union horsemen back. By this time McGregor's remaining section had abandoned its duel with the Federal cannons, swung around, and was pointing its guns squarely at the Michiganders.[10]

Fitz Lee's Brigade also began arriving on the scene, just in time for some of his horsemen to rush into Gray's right flank and check any deeper advance. Lee took a careful look through his field glass, turned to the 1st Virginia Cavalry, which led his column's advance, and yelled, "Charge them, boys, there isn't many of them!"[11] It took Colonel Gray only a few moments to realize he was now outnumbered and outgunned; without reinforcements he could not fight Chambliss and Lee with any prospect of success. After deploying Companies B and F of the 6th Michigan as a covering force, which he later wrote "met, by counter charges, three successive charges of the enemy," Gray led his remaining companies west for Hanover to report to Custer.[12] Allen D. Pease, a private in the 6th Michigan's Company B, later wrote to his mother that the two screening companies "were surrounded by two brigades of rebel cavalry [and] cut off from the regiment." Keller's Hill was a place the twenty-four-year-old Pease would not soon forget. "We took to the woods [with] about three hundred rebs after us," he wrote home. "We turned and made a charge with our sabers on them and they turned and run. They charged on us and shot a good many of our horses. We charged on them five times and they on us four. We had 14 men and our first lieutenant [Daniel H. Powers] taken prisoner," he continued. "They wounded one man in the neck after they had taken him." The remnants of the two companies did not rejoin the rest of their regiment in the town until well after dark.[13]

Littlestown's citizens could talk of little else but the cavalry battle. When Federal infantry arrived early in the afternoon, the soldiers got an earful. Brigadier General John W. Geary marched into Littlestown with his Second Division of the Union Twelfth Corps shortly after noon. When he heard reports of the shooting between opposing cavalry ahead, Geary prepared for a fight. "At 5 o'clock on the morning of the 30th, the division . . . marched through Taneytown and Littlestown, encamping near the latter place at noon," recounted Geary. "A half hour before reaching this place our cavalry had there [Hanover] a skirmish with that of the rebels. The command was hastened forward and dispositions at once made to receive the enemy, who, however, retired in the direction of Hanover."[14]

One of Geary's brigade commanders, Col. Charles Candy, went into more detail. "On the arrival of this division [Second] at Littlestown," he wrote, "this brigade was ordered to take a position in the woods on the right of the town [Littlestown], in the direction of Hanover, and on the right of the road, and hold it at all hazards. The cavalry skirmishing with the enemy in the front, formed in column by two battalion front, threw forward skirmishers, and picketed to my front and right."[15] Geary's foot soldiers did not participate in the fighting at Hanover. However, it is interesting to note that in addition to battling Kilpatrick in his immediate front, Stuart's left rear was being threatened by an antsy Federal infantry division only a few miles away.

As Gray parried with Chambliss and Lee, Col. Russell Alger moved his 5th Michiganders, also left behind at Littlestown that morning, toward Hanover just after noon. The Wolverines arrived from the south along the Littlestown Road sometime after 3:00 p.m. and promptly ran into some of Fitz Lee's troopers.[16] Alger ordered a charge and his men drew their sabers and spurred their mounts into Lee's riders, driving them back down the road. Flushed with success, Alger dismounted his entire command and pursued the Virginians on foot, "killing and capturing quite a number. My regiment was armed with the Spencer rifle," explained Alger in his report, "and [we were] required to do very much fighting on foot."[17]

The 5th Michigan's new rifle, which was also in the hands of four companies of the 6th Michigan, was a repeating long arm loaded with a tube of seven metallic cartridges. This new fast-firing weapon had a devastating effect on the Southerners.[18] The 5th Michigan's Pvt. William H. Rockwell wrote to his wife a few weeks after the battle about the weapon's effect. "We are put in all of the worst places on account of [the] seven shooters," he boasted. "The rebs call us the seven devils for they say we can load in the morning and fight all day. If they find the 5th [Michigan] is after them they skedaddle."[19]

These Michigan men had spent the first portion of their service assigned to the defenses of Washington, and so were unaccustomed to "the worst places." Henry Avery, another 5th Michigan man, recalled the first time orders deposited them into a fight. "We received orders to dismount to fight action front. As this was our first order of the kind and came so suddenly, we were somewhat flustered, officers and men," he admitted, "but we were quickly in line, leaving every fourth man to care for the horses." The Wolverines advanced through the town in their first real skirmish, losing Capt. George M. Dutcher to wound in the process. "Here we saw our first dead rebs, and we were highly elated at our victory," Avery proudly recounted.[20] Alger's men remained in position south of Hanover and west of Stuart, skirmishing until near dark. They, like many of their comrades of the 6th Michigan, did not join the rest of their brigade until later that evening.

Most of the balance of Custer's troopers were reunited in the town late that afternoon. After studying the Confederate line arrayed on the hills south of town, he directed his regiments, which were reforming near the railroad depot, to dismount. Every fourth trooper led his own horse and those of three comrades to the rear, standard procedure when cavalry fought dismounted. "It was here that the brigade first saw Custer," remembered the 6th Michigan's Captain Kidd.[21] "As the men of the Sixth ... were deploying forward across the railroad into a wheatfield beyond, I heard a voice new to me, directly in rear of the portion of the line where I was, giving directions for the movement, in clear, resonant tones, and in a calm, confident manner, at once resolute and reassuring." The surprised Kidd turned around to see whose voice he was hearing. "My eyes were instantly riveted upon a figure only a few feet distant, whose appearance amazed if it did not for the moment amuse me," he continued. "It was [Custer] who was giving the orders . . . and that he was in command of the line." This fight marked Custer's maiden combat as a brigadier. As Kidd and his comrades soon learned, the young general was determined to steer the ship with a resolute hand.

By the time Colonel Gray made his way into Hanover late in the afternoon, both Kilpatrick and Custer were watching the action from the lofty steeple of St. Matthew's Church on Chestnut Street.[22] Kilpatrick could see what appeared to be unsupported Confederate artillery at the Keller Farm because he could not see the 10th Virginia Cavalry or Fitz Lee's advancing brigade, both of which were hidden behind a ridge. Kilpatrick ordered Custer to dismount Gray's men and form a single battle line west of town.[23] With skirmishers in front, the troopers advanced forward in "a line of battle one mile in length" through the Forney Farm field, crawling on their hands and knees through brambles and brush, most of the way. The move caused some of Chambliss's and Lee's men to think a general advance of Kilpatrick's entire force was underway.[24]

About 2:00 p.m., Gen. Wade Hampton's Brigade, escorting the lumbering wagon train, arrived near Stuart's position. The horses and the famished and all but unmanageable mule teams had condemned Hampton's advance to a snail's pace, leaving the burly South Carolinian's command, in Stuart's words, "a long way behind."[25] Hampton moved the wagons along the Westminster Road before driving them into a large clearing on the east side, where he parked them in a giant circle.[26] Dense woods around the clearing hid the wagons from prying Federal eyes. A local named Robert Spangler, however, managed to spot the train. "Wood," wrote Spangler, "[was] piled around the wheels and bodies ready to put the torch to and burn them [to prevent them] from falling in the hands of Kilpatrick's troopers, in case of defeat, in the woods two miles south of Hanover . . . between the Westminster and Becker Mill roads on lands of Samuel Keller and Henry Gotwalt."[27]

Colonel Gray's men were moving toward Stuart's wagon park, and they eventually crawled and crept within 300 yards of Stuart's guns posted at Rice Hill. On Custer's order the Wolverines rose and let fly a volley from their Spencer repeaters and Colt revolvers. That amount of lead fired all at once shocked even the artillery crews, who began treading backward in anticipation of a large-scale enemy advance. Those not wounded in the initial fire scrambled for cover, but not before Gray's men took fifteen prisoners.[28]

Fitz Lee hastened enough troopers to the ridge to force Gray back down the slope, but Custer rallied the 6th Michigan and sent them forward a second time. Although they failed to dislodge the Southerners, the fearsome rapidity of the bluecoats' firepower momentarily silenced the field pieces and wreaked havoc among the artillerists. Taking up strategic positions while shot and canister boomed and shrieked in the warm air around them, the men of the 6th Michigan hung on, forcing Fitz Lee to rush a majority of his brigade into position to hold the ridge.

Sergeant Jerry Haden of the 1st Virginia Cavalry dismounted to procure the weapon and horse of a wounded Wolverine. He was in the act of pilfering his less fortunate opponent when Haden's friend Billy McCausland rode by at high speed yelling at Haden to mount and get away as quickly as possible: the Federals were charging with a heavy force! "I knew when he left times were getting squally," recalled Haden, "so I mounted, putting the captured horse in front of me, drew my saber and struck him a few times, and brought him out safely." Trooper C. H. Koiner of Haden's company was not as lucky. Koiner was mortally wounded when a Yankee ball passed through the front of his saddle and continued on through him. The enemy, wrote a relieved Haden, "Pursued us until we reached our support and then retired."[29]

Rufus Peck served in the 2nd Virginia Cavalry of Fitz Lee's Brigade. "One of our young men, Walter Gilmore, was shot in the shoulder, as he was riding between Chas. Price and myself, as we were trying to get him to the rear, he was shot in the left eye, but we finally got to a house and asked the lady of the house to take care of him, while we went on and took the garrison," recalled Peck. "I never knew anything more of young Gilmore until the summer of 1911, [when] I met him at New Port News at a reunion. He told me he was sent to a hospital in Baltimore by the Yankees and received the kindest of treatment and the best of medical aid, and soon recovered."[30]

After trading shots with Lee's and Chambliss's troopers for about an hour, the Wolverines pulled back into town about sunset and reformed near the railroad, their participation in the fighting at an end.[31] A mutual cessation of the artillery duel brought a second lull to the contest. Perceiving a possible threat from Hampton's newly arrived troopers to the southeast, Kilpatrick ordered Elder's and Pennington's batteries off Bunker Hill and down into the town, directing them to new spots near the depot and the Commons.[32] However, Hampton only feigned a charge down the York Road with his 1st South Carolina, causing some consternation among the pickets of the 1st Vermont Cavalry posted there. Hampton then wheeled his gray riders around and returned to his original position on Stuart's right.[33]

Samuel Althoff, the citizen who had watched the first part of the Hanover fight from his roof, and then much of the rest from his windows, believed things had quieted down enough to leave the safety of his home. "Late in the afternoon, I went to the square, where I saw half a dozen dead horses lying," he recollected. "The wounded soldiers had been carried to Marion Hall . . . where they received careful surgical attention."[34] Several of the larger buildings in town were pressed into service as temporary hospitals, and Kilpatrick's surgeons, local doctors, and many of the citizens pitched in to treat the wounded of both sides.

Samuel and John Forney, the boys who had taken a break from their plowing to watch the Federal troopers march through Mudtown earlier that morning, cautiously returned from hiding. They spotted several horses lying dead in the road fronting their farm along the Littlestown Road. The boys helped other men drag the heavy beasts away to be burned the following day. When they returned home they discovered four wounded soldiers, three Federals and one Confederate, bleeding in their father's front parlor. The Southerner, Sgt. Samuel Reddick of the 2nd North Carolina, had been shot in the chest and was "struggling with death," recalled Samuel. Reddick had been shot in front of Forney's home early in the fight, struggled his way into the yard, and crawled up their steps to the front porch, where he collapsed into unconsciousness. While the Forney family cared for him, Reddick took a New Testament from his coat and handed it to Samuel's sister. "Take this book and send it to my home," Reddick pleaded, "That address will reach my sister. She gave me this book when I left home two years ago, and she asked me to keep it and bring it back again when the cruel war shall have ended. It has ended for me now." He died at the Forney home the following day and was buried near the road along the fence the boys had sat upon to watch Kilpatrick's column march to town. The boys' mother sent the Bible home with a letter to inform the deceased's sister of Reddick's final hours. The following summer a small group of relatives arrived to claim

Lieutenant Colonel Andrew J. Alexander, commander of a detachment of cavalry Regulars sent by General Pleasonton to gather intelligence on Jeb Stuart's whereabouts.

USAMHI

his remains, which were exhumed, carried back to North Carolina, and buried in his village's graveyard.[35]

Everyone had had enough fighting for one day by the time the sun began setting behind the horizon. Except for occasional small arms fire on the outskirts of town, the meeting engagement at Hanover had ended. As the fighting was drawing down, Kilpatrick sent a rider to Littlestown asking for reinforcements. General Pleasonton's chief of staff, Lt. Col. Andrew J. Alexander, received the message and sent Kilpatrick "every cavalryman that I could get hold of."[36] Pleasonton, who had his headquarters at Frederick, sent Alexander along with a detachment of forty troopers of the 2nd U.S. Cavalry to try to find out what Robert E. Lee's army was up to, and where it was moving. Alexander stopped in Littlestown for breakfast on the morning of June 30, and then moved on toward Hanover. His little detachment drove back some of Stuart's pickets and advanced to Hanover, where he engaged the main body of Stuart's force for several hours. Alexander dispatched two couriers to report to Kilpatrick, one of whom was captured. "The other would have shared the same fate, but just as he was about to be overtaken by the rebel pursuers, a patriotic citizen gave him a stout, fresh remount which carried him safely through, and was returned to its owner by Alexander the next day." As the fighting progressed, Alexander and his dogged little band joined Kilpatrick's division.[37]

For the most part, Farnsworth's brigade had carried the morning's fight, while Custer's brigade managed most of the afternoon's brawling. As the hazy summer sky dimmed and dropped into dusk, both Stuart and Kilpatrick regrouped their commands. Stuart decided to withdraw from Hanover under cover of darkness. "[N]ot until night had fallen did Stuart deem it prudent to withdraw from Kilpatrick, who still maintained his threatening position in front of Hanover," Henry McClellan recalled.[38] Once the companies and scattered regiments of Kilpatrick's division found each other and counted their losses, they remained in a defensive formation for most of the evening. The Yankees, explained McClellan, showed "no disposition as to hinder Stuart's withdrawal."[39] The troopers of the 18th Pennsylvania, which had opened the unexpected saber dance at Hanover and thus earned their veteran spurs, remained in formation along bloody Frederick Street as the sun set on the western horizon. Farnsworth's and Custer's other regiments were scattered outside and throughout the town from the Hanover Junction Railroad to the Littlestown Road.[40]

Most of the Confederate prisoners captured during the day were marched to the town jail, located beneath the open-ended Market House building in the center of the square. Because only a plank floor covered the jail, many of the Southerners thought the building was a covered bridge as their mounts clattered through it early in the fight.[41]

After helping the surgeons and citizens attend to the wounded of both sides, Chaplain Beaudrye of the 5th New York sat down to write of the day's events. After jotting notations about the welcome received from the townsfolk upon their arrival and the clash that disrupted what began as a peaceful ride through an otherwise indistinguishable Pennsylvania hamlet, the chaplain welcomed the calming dark of night by writing simply, "It has been an awful day."[42]

At his headquarters in Room 24 of the Central Hotel that evening, Kilpatrick dictated a dispatch to General Pleasonton at army headquarters in Taneytown, Maryland. Kilpatrick recapped the day's action and boasted that his first battle as a division commander had been a rousing success. "After a fight of about two hours, in which the whole command at different times was engaged, I made a vigorous attack upon their center, forced them back upon the road to Littlestown, and finally succeeded in breaking their center. . . . My loss is trifling. I have gone into camp at Hanover. . . . We have plenty of forage, the men are in good spirits, and we don't fear Stuart's whole cavalry."[43]

Only some of what Kilpatrick related to his superior was true. He blatantly lied about breaking Stuart's line, and about permitting the Confederates to withdraw at his convenience. In fact, Stuart slipped away into the gathering darkness entirely unmolested. Kilpatrick's wording may have, for a time, assuaged his own embarrassment over the surprise attack on his column, and for not having discovered Stuart's location at Union Mills.

In the official report he submitted six weeks later, Kilpatrick claimed his Hanover losses were 19 killed, 41 wounded, and 123 missing. "For a moment, and a moment only, victory hung uncertain," the young brigadier dramatically wrote. "For the first time our troops had met the foe in close contact; but they were on their own free soil. . . . The foe turned and fled. He had for the first and last time polluted with his presence the loyal town of Hanover."[44]

Stuart's after-action report was noticeably less dramatic. The Southern general assessed the Hanover fighting, which had cost him fewer than 150 casualties from all causes, as the unintended and unfortunate delay that it was. The city itself was "by no means desirable for us to hold," he explained, "as it was in a valley completely surrounded by the heights in our possession, which were soon crowned by our artillery." He was, however, candid about the effect of the captured wagons and the more than 200 herded mules on his progress. "Our wagon train was now a subject of serious embarrassment, but, I thought . . . I could save it."[45]

Major McClellan was even more candid when he later opined that, once his commander had suspected the enemy was so near, "it would have been better had Stuart here destroyed the captured wagons. . . . But it was not in Stuart's nature to abandon an attempt until it had been proven to be beyond his powers; and he determined to hold onto his prize until the last moment. This was unfortunate."[46]

Once darkness blanketed the countryside Stuart quietly began withdrawing from the ridges and fields south of Hanover along the Blooming Grove Road and several minor routes to the east.[47] After consulting with his brigade commanders, he decided to ride nine miles east to Jefferson and then turn north for York, a route he hoped would help him avoid any more contact with the enemy while he continued his search for General Ewell's infantry.[48] Stuart ordered the wagon train back onto the road and sent it out ahead of the column, placing Fitz Lee's brigade in charge of it, and the 400 new prisoners captured since the mass paroles at Cookesville. Hampton's troopers, finally relieved of overseeing the lumbering baggage, brought up the rear of the column while Chambliss's Brigade and the artillery rolled along, sandwiched in the middle.[49] Stuart's entire column was on the road to Jefferson by 10:00 p.m. The strained riders knew they weren't going to get any rest anytime soon.

The Confederates were just setting off when they spotted "a fat Dutchman" who was counting the Southern horse soldiers as they passed. Stuart decided the fellow was too well informed to be left behind with the enemy and "requested [he] come along" on the back of a huge horse taken from the rich countryside. "This request he treated with calm disregard, when a cavalry-man made a tremendous blow at him, which caused him to mount in hot haste, with only a halter to guide him his elephant," recalled an amused Capt. John Esten Cooke. "He had no sooner done so than the Conestoga ran off, descended the slope, bounded elephant-wise over an enormous ditch—and it was only by clinging close with knees and hands that the Dutchman kept his seat. Altogether the spectacle was one to tickle the ribs of death." The terrified man was caught in the throng, riding in the center of Stuart's trotting column. He was, as Cooke put it, "swept on it with it; passing away for ever from the eyes of this historian, who knows not what became of him thereafter."[50]

Despite puffing his exploits to his commander regarding the bloody nose handed to Stuart at Hanover, Kilpatrick made only a feeble attempt to keep tabs on the Southern cavalry. Kilpatrick seemed almost content to let the always-dangerous Stuart slip away. Once darkness fell, the Union brigadier bivouacked his division in the wheat fields of the Andrew Rudisill farm along the road to Abbottstown. A handful of small patrols were sent north and east toward Dover, York, and Carlisle.[51] Though he had reported the fight to Pleasonton, no orders were sent back from cavalry corps headquarters. Pleasonton's chief of staff, Lieutenant Colonel Alexander, along with Capt. Lewellyn Estes of Kilpatrick's staff and a detail of less than one hundred troopers, trailed Stuart's column that night as far as Rossville (just north of Dover) and captured a few stragglers along the way. The darkness convinced Alexander to break off the pursuit and return to Kilpatrick.[52]

The other patrols turned up little beyond the obvious fact that Confederate infantry and raiders had already passed through the region. "I think there is a considerable [Confederate] force at Berlin," Kilpatrick erroneously reported to Pleasonton.[53] Misinterpreting information gathered by his scouts from local citizens, Kilpatrick believed the bulk of Lee's army was in and around East Berlin, just ten miles north of Hanover. Pleasonton heartily endorsed and relayed the information to General Meade. Fortunately for the Army of the Potomac, by the time Kilpatrick's information reached headquarters on July 1, Meade was already aware of the disposition of forces in and around Gettysburg.[54]

The misinterpretation of intelligence was nothing new for Alfred Pleasonton. Known universally as a toady whose sights seemed eternally fixed on self-promotion, one of Pleasonton's many weaknesses was gathering and qualifying intelligence on the enemy's movements and intentions. He had assumed command of the Army of the Potomac cavalry corps shortly after the Federal debacle at Chancellorsville. A graduate of the West Point Class of 1844, Pleasonton gained his military experience as a dragoon officer in Florida and in the western territories. A lowly captain at the war's start,[55] he was promoted to brigadier general of volunteers by July 1862 and began oiling the machinery of his promotion to command the mounted arm.[56]

* * *

Even without hindsight it is difficult to fathom why Kilpatrick permitted Stuart, encumbered by a large slow-moving wagon train, to ride away into the darkness. June 30 should have been a day of decision for Union arms because Stuart was nearly surrounded at Hanover: Kilpatrick blocked his immediate front and denied him the use of the pass through the Pigeon Hills, General Geary's infantry division beyond Littlestown was only a few miles from Stuart's left rear, and two other Federal cavalry divisions flanked him. Rather than continue pressing Stuart while sending out requests for a concentration against the enemy cavalry column, Kilpatrick allowed Stuart to break away. A great opportunity broke away with him.

Instead of sticking to Stuart, and mistakenly deducing he would find a sea of gray to his north, Kilpatrick moved his column on and through Abbottstown. His troopers wandered the roads in search of Confederates,

Major General Alfred Pleasonton, commander of the Army of the Potomac's cavalry corps. Pleasonton was an inefficient publicity hound who missed at least one opportunity to devastate Stuart's command before the major showdown at Gettysburg.

a decision that would waste all of July 1.[57] Kilpatrick spent the first day of the new month flat on his back in one of his own ambulances. The pounding his kidneys took during his June 30 morning chase to Hanover prostrated him.

Stuart's column, meanwhile, pressed on. More adventures lay ahead, including another encounter with George A. Custer and his Wolverines.

Major General Jubal A. Early heard Jeb Stuart's guns booming at Hanover on June 30. Unfortunately for Southern arms, he did not attempt to make contact with the cavalry commander.

Chapter 6

The Long Road to Carlisle

"After a series of exciting combats and night marches,
it was a severe tax to their endurance."

— Jeb Stuart

tuart's decision to withdraw from Hanover and resume the increasingly desperate search for General Ewell's infantry was a good one, though it did not alleviate the debilitating exhaustion his men were suffering. "Being broken down & in no condition to fight, we turned off towards Jefferson, Pa.," noted one of Fitz Lee's officers in his diary that night.[1] Although Stuart remained worried about the threat posed by Kilpatrick, the Federals showed little inclination to launch a vigorous pursuit or otherwise hinder his withdrawal.

As his column moved toward Jefferson, information gleaned from citizens and local papers reached Stuart that Maj. Gen. Jubal A. Early's Division, part of Ewell's Corps, was at York. The enemy blocked his direct route north, and the whereabouts of additional Federal cavalry concerned Stuart greatly. The road to York would have to be a meandering one that added still more miles and hours to what had already been a grueling and slow-moving expedition. What Stuart did not know was that the intelligence regarding Ewell's whereabouts was six days old. By the time Stuart moved for York, the bulk of Ewell's command had already moved to the area around Carlisle, some twenty miles north and west of York. Early was already on his way south to Cashtown and had stopped at Heidlersburg for the night, many miles west of Hanover, by the end of Stuart's fight there. The poor intelligence and the Hanover fight prolonged Stuart's ride by forcing him to move five miles east, which in turn added to the misery of his already exhausted command. Contrary to what he believed, Stuart was now riding *away* from Ewell.

Jubal Early's division began leaving York on the morning of June 30 between 4:00 and 5:00 a.m., and by 7:00 a.m. his entire command had vacated the town. About noon, Early and his staff officers stopped for lunch at a hotel along the route of march toward Berlin. Early paid for his meal with Confederate money, stepped outside, and heard the dull grumbling thunder of artillery coming from the direction of Hanover, about ten miles distant. The general stopped to ponder the meaning of the artillery and concluded it was nothing more than skirmishing militia. But who were the militia skirmishing with? Whether that thought entered Early's mind will never be known. What we do know is that instead of trying to make contact with the Confederate forces engaging what he believed was merely "militia"—the sounds were, of course, Stuart's horse artillery battling Kilpatrick's troopers—the general mounted his horse and rode west toward Heidlersburg.[2] With each step of Early's horse, Stuart's chances of finding the Virginian's infantry column grew more remote.

William Swallow was a member of Early's Division on June 30. His regiment was marching near East Berlin that evening when "the whole command distinctly heard Stuart's guns," he noted after the fact. "But in a hilly country like that in which we were moving we could not tell either the distance or direction of firing. When Stuart's command was at Hanover, on Tuesday, and in its wanderings during that day, had any of his force met White's battalion, who moved on Gettysburg that day from York, by the turnpike, he no doubt would have continued his movements through the night, reaching Cashtown on Wednesday, and could have been with Lee and Longstreet before the battle opened on that day," Swallow correctly observed. The meeting that never was would have altered the course of the entire battle of Gettysburg.[3]

The "White" mentioned by William Swallow was Lt. Col. Elijah V. White, commander of the 35th Battalion Virginia Cavalry. "The Comanches," as White's battalion would become known later that fall, had been detached from Grumble Jones's Brigade to escort Early's Division into Pennsylvania. On June 30, Capt. Marcellus French, the commander of one of White's companies, learned Yankees were holding Gettysburg and Lee's army was concentrating near there. "The constant inquiry from the men was 'Where is Stuart?'" asked French. "Somehow,

Lieutenant General Richard
S. Ewell, commander of the
Second Corps, Army of
Northern Virginia.

in a veteran army men divine
pretty closely what is going
on, and all were wondering
what could be the matter,
that with scarcely 200 men
we should be left alone with
the infantry in the enemy's
country to do the most arduous service." Not surprisingly, French and his
men grew resentful at Stuart's conspicuous absence.[4] In spite of this
anxiety, Early did nothing to locate Stuart. However, Stuart remained
determined to obey Lee's orders and continued searching for Ewell's
infantry.

Obeying General Lee's orders to collect provisions for the use of the
army, Stuart kept the wagon train in tow. As previously observed, Stuart
described the train in his after-action report as "a subject of serious
embarrassment." This statement, however, has been misunderstood for
many years. Modern historians have applied the wrong definition of the
word "embarrassment" in describing Stuart's statements, misconstruing
his original intent. In Nineteenth Century parlance, "embarrass" meant
"to hinder with obstacles or impede."[5] Stuart admitted his wagon train
severely hindered his freedom of movement, but was not suggesting he
was personally "embarrassed" to the point of regret for having captured
the train and kept it with him. "I had this immense train in an enemy's
country, very near a hostile army, and, besides about 400 prisoners,
which had accumulated since the paroling at Cookesville." To add to
Stuart's woes, the terrain along the eastern roads leading to Jefferson was
just as hilly as that taken by the wagon train to reach Hanover, further
slowing the column's progress. In addition, the Southerner's troopers

and gunners were nearly out of ammunition as a consequence of the march's steady skirmishing and fighting. He had to do something to deliver his command, and he had to do it soon.[6]

With Fitz Lee's Brigade at the head of his column, Stuart ordered his protégé to push on to Jefferson and then York. Hampton's men, who did not depart from Hanover until nearly 10:00 p.m., brought up the rear. Leaving the scene of a sharp fight, their task was to stay vigilant and rebuff any pursuit. Hampton was well aware that Brig. Gen. David M. Gregg's Second Cavalry Division was operating somewhere in the vicinity of Hanover in response to the threat posed by Stuart's incursion.[7]

"During the night march to Jefferson the train became a great burden to us, especially the 400 prisoners that we had with us since leaving Rockville and what we had picked up on the road. Many of these prisoners were loaded into the wagons," recalled one of James Breathed's gunners. "The mules were weary—and so were we—and were suffering for the want of food and water, and frequently became stalled in the roads, thereby stopping the whole command. The drivers became negligent, and it was with the greatest difficulty that the train was kept in motion."[8]

The Southerners kept a sleepy eye out for provisions along the way. "[The Rebels] were short of horses, also cattle for food," noted a local, "so they visited every farm house and confiscated all the horses that had not been moved into the woods, as well as other animals." The men found impressing horses a difficult task—a "disagreeable necessity" was how one described it. When the soldiers led horses away from family farms, the families often made tearful pleas to save a child's pet or lament their inability to feed themselves. "Tears have always been more powerful than an enemy in arms, and it was not an unusual thing that the harsh armor of a soldier concealed a tender heart to which such appeals were irresistible," noted one of Stuart's troopers.[9]

One Pennsylvania farmer's wife, however, was not about to easily give up the horses needed to work her farm. "Two work horses and a prize black stallion were not moved from the George Dubs farm near Dubs' Church. . . . Mrs. Dubs was notified by a passerby that the Rebels were coming from Hanover." After Luisa Dubs hid the work horses in her barn and the stallion in her basement, Stuart's column approached and several troopers watered their mounts in her trough. A quick search uncovered the animals. As the Confederates began leading them off, "she jerked the reins out of their hands. During the argument an officer appeared on the scene. After hearing her story that she had to have the horses to work her farm, he ordered the men to apologize and return the horses to the stable." The feisty Mrs. Dubs was one of the few locals who stood up to Stuart troopers, and her determination helped preserve her farm as the Southern column trotted past.[10]

Most other residents along Stuart's route were not so lucky. Records of the Pennsylvania Auditor General's Department contain nearly 700 claims for damages caused by Stuart's forces in York County alone, most of them for the theft of horses following the battle of Hanover. These claims also list a multitude of goods taken by the Southerners, including thousands of bushels of wheat, corn, rye, and oats, as well as anything else of use the gray clad troopers could carry off.[11] Judging by the amount of wagons needed to haul away the booty, the cumbersome trains were re-loaded with fresh cargo as quickly as they were emptied.

One member of the 13th Virginia Cavalry presented a humorous sight. Unable to find a horse after his had broken down, he had to make do with a mule, "one which he seemed confident would answer every purpose." The mule looked docile and he hoped it would provide suitable transportation. As the column approached a Pennsylvania town, the mule refused to stop—even though the main column had halted to size up the situation. The mule's mortified rider, bellowing expletives and yanking on the bridle for all he was worth, was unable to halt the beast. "Appreciating his dilemma the poor fellow let go the reins, and falling on the mule's neck, caught the bit in both hands in the vain attempt to stop him," recalled an amused observer. "His expressions had now begun to pass from the strongly imperative to the beseeching, until all the latent tenderness of his soul seemed to find expression in that one word—'WHOA!'" After enjoying a good laugh at their friend's expense, several of his comrades came to the man's aid and finally persuaded the runaway mule to wait for the rest of the regiment to catch up.[12]

An unfortunate atrocity occurred while Stuart's command was riding north toward Carlisle. One of Stuart's officers had taken his black manservant with him into Pennsylvania, and the man was in the woods searching for horses hidden by local farmers. When the Confederate column pressed on the servant was inadvertently left behind, and so lost in the woods. A group of five Warrington Township farmers found the servant and shot him multiple times. They carried his lifeless body from the road and hid it under some brush. The Wells family, for whom Wellsville was named, heard of the incident and demanded an inquest. The farmers, together with a prominent local man, were charged with murder; some of the participants were jailed. A grand jury, however, declined to indict the six men and they were set free. More than forty years later, a local newspaper claimed the incident was York County's only recorded "lynching."[13]

The Southern column arrived in Jefferson about midnight. Stuart, Fitz Lee, and staff officer John Esten Cooke stopped at the town tavern to procure some badly needed coffee. Cooke rousted the owner of the establishment out of bed to brew a fresh pot of coffee and serve the officers ale and bread. When Stuart finished his coffee, "which always put the stout cavalier in a gay humor," noted Cooke, he turned to the young captain and said, "By the by, suppose you stay here until Hampton comes along; I am going on with Fitz Lee. Tell Hampton to move on steadily on the road to Dover, and show him the way." The two Virginians rode off, leaving Cooke to perform his lonely duty. Hampton arrived before long and Captain Cooke resumed his ride with the burly South Carolinian by his side. Exhaustion rode with them.

"Are you going to stop, general?" Cooke inquired, hoping his answer would be in the affirmative.

"Yes, for a little while," responded Hampton. "I am perishing for sleep." With that, Hampton swung out of his saddle, headed for a nearby haystack, pulled down some hay, wrapped himself in his cape, and drifted off quickly to sleep. Cooke was not far behind.[14]

While the general slept, Stuart's hungry horsemen helped themselves to the town's bounty. "The behavior of the soldiers was not in keeping with their conduct elsewhere in the county," explained one historian. "Many of them were tired and hungry from the exhaustive march." The troopers confiscated horses to replace their played-out mounts and stole a variety of goods from William T. Crist's store on the town square, including hats, caps, 22 pairs of boots and shoes, 300 yards of calico, 40 yards of muslin, six silk handkerchiefs, five table oil cloths, six pairs of traces, five pounds of tobacco, 200 cigars, and several other items.[15]

Although utterly enervated, the Confederates had a good laugh along the way. While the vast majority of York County horses were driven across the Susquehanna River to Lancaster County to hide them from the Rebels, some farmers kept theirs at home in a largely unsuccessful effort to hide them. Some of the locals had been duped by con men who sold them a "signal" to make if a Confederate tried to confiscate their horses. According to the con men, the signal would announce some sort of "secret" order to not confiscate the animals, and the Southern troopers would supposedly understand what it all meant. The con men took the money and passed on the so-called "signal," which of course meant nothing at all. "The soldiers laughed at the sign because they knew nothing about it or the secret order which claimed to have been in communication with the Confederate government," explained one writer. "About 100 fine horses were captured in Jefferson and immediate vicinity."[16]

With July 1 nearly upon them, however, laughs were few and far between for the Southerners. "We were not molested in our march, which, on account of the very exposed situation of our flank and the enemy's knowledge of it, was continued during the night," wrote Stuart. A night march through unfamiliar and hostile territory strained the limits of the worn out cavalrymen. "After a series of exciting combats and night marches, it was a severe tax to their endurance," Stuart admitted. "The night's march over a very dark road was one of peculiar hardship, owing to loss of rest to both man and horse. Whole regiments slept in the saddle, their faithful animals keeping the road unguided. Some men fell from their horses, overcome with physical fatigue and sleepiness."[17] Lieutenant John Holtzman, 4th Virginia Cavalry, noted in his diary, "We marched all night. Amusing time to see the boys lose their horses and hats."[18]

The Confederate troopers, 125 wagons, hundreds of captured horses and mules, and nearly 400 prisoners made for a lengthy procession, which also included civilian prisoners impressed by Stuart. It took several hours for the entire column to wind its way through Jefferson. All the while Stuart worried about the rear of the column, which was especially vulnerable to attack. He prudently ordered his horse artillery to unlimber on the hills overlooking Jefferson and posted guards around the town to make it more difficult for Brig. Gen. David M. Gregg's cavalry division to strike from behind. With his guns deployed and the column moving through Jefferson, Stuart convened a conference of his commanders at John E. Zeigler's farmhouse and tavern near Hanover Junction on the night of June 30. Zeigler was one of the wealthiest men in the Seven Valley area, and his home and substantial grounds acted like a magnet for Stuart and his staff. Before leaving, the Confederates lightened Ziegler's holdings by six horses, six tons of hay, several dozen bushels of oats, and 500 bushels of corn.[19]

The meeting did little to shed light on the strategic situation. Neither Zeigler nor any of the locals knew where Early's Division was camped or whether Union troops occupied York. In addition, none of Stuart's scouts had returned. Stuart deduced that if the opposing armies were not concentrating for a great battle on the level plains west of York, they must instead be in the Cumberland Valley near Carlisle.[20] Stuart decided to move north, guiding the men and wagons up Panther Hill past Zeigler's Church and on through the unusually named town of York New Salem. They reached Jefferson by dawn after a ride of 25 torturous miles.[21] "During the night march to Jefferson, the wagons and prisoners were a serious hindrance," wrote Stuart's adjutant, Maj. Henry B. McClellan, in an effort to describe the arduous night journey. "Nearly four hundred prisoners had accumulated since the parole at Cookesville. Many of these were loaded in the wagons; some of them acted as drivers. The mules were starving for food and water, and often became unmanageable." Frequent halts occurred because the mule driver at the front of the train had fallen asleep as a consequence of sheer exhaustion, and his untended mules had stopped to rest. "The train guard became careless through excessive fatigue, and it required the utmost exertions of every officer on Stuart's staff to keep the train in motion."[22]

After passing through Jefferson toward Seven Valley, or Siebenthaler, as it was known by the local German populace, the main body of Fitz Lee's command interrupted a funeral being conducted at Zeigler's Church.[23] The deceased was a resident of New Salem named John Miller. Despite having a wife and three children to support, the 40-year-old Miller enrolled in Company D, 166th Pennsylvania Volunteers (a nine-month regiment) on November 8, 1862. In April and early May of 1863, Miller and his comrades helped defend Suffolk, Virginia, against Lt. Gen. James Longstreet's 23-day siege of that Tidewater town. Miller perished in the Suffolk military hospital on June 3, apparently a victim of dysentery. His body was shipped to Glen Rock because the railroad bridges south of Hanover Junction had been destroyed by Confederate cavalry a few days earlier, and was then placed on a wagon and taken to Zeigler's Cemetery for burial. The Rev. Constantine Deininger officiated at the 8:00 p.m. service. The arrival of the Confederate horsemen caused the mourners to scatter, their day of sorrow deepened by the approach of the enemy. Many of the mourners rushed home to hide their animals from the marauding Confederates.[24]

Peter Diehl was a prominent merchant and farmer from New Oxford, a small town not far from Hanover. Diehl regularly hauled farm products, tanned hides, and local products to the port at Baltimore and returned with merchandise and dry goods for area stores. His son Charley and a kinsman, Amos Lough, were hauling goods near Ziegler's Church on June 30. While passing through Seven Valley, Lough and Charley Diehl encountered some of Stuart's men guarding a portion of the captured wagon train. The Confederates seized all of Diehl's horses, exchanging them for several worn-out mounts. The troopers ordered Diehl and Lough to fetch water for them and help care for their wounded from the fighting at Hanover before releasing the frightened civilians in the early evening.[25] Stuart's column, meanwhile, pushed on through the night.

The weary Southern horsemen arrived at Dover, about seven miles east of York, on the morning of July 1. Stuart decided it was time to alleviate some of his burden. Hampton paroled the 400 prisoners accompanying the column, releasing them in the town square. The South Carolinian established his headquarters in Dr. John Ahl's office in the center of the town. About 8:00 a.m., Stuart ordered local hotelkeeper Jacob Fries to serve his staff and brigade commanders. Stuart paid for the sumptuous breakfast with greenbacks; his famished troopers found what they could in the local countryside. After six hours of rest the column resumed its fitful journey toward York. The command now moved in two separate columns with squads of horsemen buzzing about on all sides, roving the countryside in search of food, fodder, and the enemy.[26]

If Stuart believed he was being shadowed, he was right. Although vastly outnumbered, Lt. Col. Andrew J. Alexander and his dogged little band of Regulars had followed Stuart's column as far as Rossville in northwest York County, hovering around the fringes of the long Southern column and occasionally trading shots with the Confederate rear guard.[27] The Union troopers captured a few prisoners who informed Alexander that Carlisle was Stuart's next destination.[28] As Alexander discovered, maintaining contact with Stuart was a rather routine affair. Had Kilpatrick shown some initiative and sent a larger force in pursuit, he might have bagged the entire command while the exhausted column was strung out across the Pennsylvania countryside. Stuart was fortunate his adversary was not determined to fight a decisive battle with him.

If Stuart was confident he would find friendly faces around York, his arrival there earned him nothing but another disappointment. "I found that General Early had gone, and it is to be regretted that this officer failed to take any measures by leaving an intelligent scout to acquaint me with his destination," complained Stuart in his campaign report months after the fact. "He had reason to expect me, and had been directed to look out for me. He heard my guns at Hanover, and correctly conjectured whose they were, but left me no clue to his destination on leaving York, which would have saved me a long and tedious march to Carlisle and thence back to Gettysburg." The benefit of knowledge gained with the passage of time permeated the general's after-action report.[29]

The citizens of York had spent the past few days under Confederate occupation, and the thought of Stuart's horsemen heading there next struck fear into their hearts. "Fitz Hugh Lee was at [York New Salem] about six miles from us—and told them that their whole force was coming here to York, and they were going to bring desolation to Pennsylvania!" recalled York resident Cassandra Small. "People outside and inside of our town—may talk as they please about what was done—it was right, and it is only those who ran off, and others who don't know, that talk so. All the Rebels say it was their intention to have the battle here, and then we would have been in the situation of Gettysburg."[30]

It was not desolating Pennsylvania but finding Confederate infantry that was foremost in Stuart's mind, and it looked more likely than not he would fail in his effort on July 1. All the general could ascertain was that Early's Division had marched toward Shippensburg, which Stuart learned was to be the concentration point for Lee's army. With that paltry news in hand, Stuart dispatched his most trusted staff officer, Maj. Andrew R. Venable, to ride ahead and locate Early. Later that day he sent Lt. Henry Custis Lee, Fitz Lee's younger brother and staff officer, riding toward Gettysburg with the same mission.[31]

The friendship between Stuart and Venable stretched back to their prewar Regular Army service. The general knew he could depend on him to carry out his orders.[32] Venable took a detachment of thirty men and set off to find Early. "I left Dover before daylight of July 1," he recounted, "and after skirmishing all day with a regiment that was pursuing us from

Major Andrew R. Venable, Jeb Stuart's staff officer. It was Venable who found Robert E. Lee and the bulk of the army around Gettysburg.

Robert J. Trout

Dover, we overtook General Early about 4 p.m., just approaching Gettysburg."[33]

Unfortunately for the Southern column, neither Venable nor Lee returned with news before Stuart reached Carlisle, which meant the cavalry chieftain's journey northwest from York continued as it had before—a blind grope on a large scale. Anxious for news, Stuart sent Major McClellan off on the same mission. After making sure the dispositions of his command were sound, the exhausted cavalryman lay down under a tree for a four-hour nap. That short respite, however, did little to refresh him or his exhausted command.

Major Venable and a single courier reached Gettysburg on the afternoon of July 1, drawing in their mounts as General Ewell was posting a battery on the high ground of Oak Hill. Ewell's stepson and staff officer, Maj. Campbell Brown, had recently arrived with a message from Robert E. Lee. Venable spotted several high-ranking officers huddled in discussion and approached with his own news. "Not five minutes after I joined Gen'l Ewell, Maj. Venable of Jeb Stuart's Staff with one courier, rode up to let us know where Jeb was, only a few miles off," remembered Major Brown. "Learning first of all that was important, Gen'l Ewell sent him on to report to Gen'l Lee, advising him to send the courier back to hurry up the cavalry."[34] Venable reported to General Lee as directed. After hearing the important news he carried, the army chief ordered a squadron of cavalry, probably troopers from Maj. John H. Richardson's 39th Battalion of Virginia Cavalry, to ride at once in search of Stuart.[35]

Perhaps exhaustion caused Venable to misstate the distance between Stuart's command and Gettysburg, for the Southerners were more than a few miles away. Perhaps Campbell Brown simply misunderstood the staff officer's message. With his news safely delivered, Venable mounted his horse, turned its head northward for Carlisle, and set his spurs. He carried orders for Stuart to ride for the battlefield at once.

Captain James Breathed, one of Stuart's horse artillery battery commanders, deployed his guns on a ridge in front of the Salem Church overlooking the town. A delegation entered Dover and threatened it with destruction if a ransom was not paid. The townsfolk could not raise the ransom, but the temporary respite in the town offered the weary Confederates a chance to dismount, parole prisoners, and visit Dover's shops, where they liberated hats, handkerchiefs, clothing, and horses.[36] While some pilfered, others undertook more mundane but necessary chores like feeding their horses and mules in the streets of the town.[37]

After allowing his men as much rest as possible Stuart resumed the march to Carlisle, where he hoped to find provisions and elements of the Army of Northern Virginia. "I still believed that most of our army was before Harrisburg, and justly regarded a march to Carlisle as the most likely to place me in communication with the main army," noted Stuart in an effort to justify his decision to continue on. "Besides, as a place for rationing my command, now entirely out, I believed it desirable. The cavalry suffered much in this march, day and night, from loss of sleep and the horses from fatigue."[38]

Colonel Richard L. T. Beale and the 9th Virginia Cavalry, Chambliss's Brigade, drew the unhappy duty of escorting the wagon train. The long column passed through Rossville and arrived in Dillsburg about midday. Colonel Beale's son, Lt. George W. Beale, expressed the opinions of the rank and file of Stuart's command about that long miserable day, when minutes seemed like hours and hours seemed like months. "Weak and helpless as we now were our anxiety and uneasiness grew to be painful indeed. Thoughts of saving wagons were now gone from many of us, and we began to consider only how we ourselves might escape," recorded the younger Beale in a letter to his mother. "But this was not so with Stuart. He seemed neither to suppose that his train was in danger nor that his men were not in condition to fight. He could not have appeared more composed or indifferent."[39]

Composed or indifferent, Stuart drove his men relentlessly. He rode alongside his friend and favorite companion, Fitz Lee. "Stuart and Fitz Lee were very like in temperament, and devoted as brothers. Both were full of fun, and their gaiety never forsook them even amid the darkest and most trying ordeals," recalled one Confederate. "On the march they generally rode together, and their songs and peals of laughter could often be heard far down the column, above the trampling of the horses and the clanking of the sabres, and were a solace to many weary and homesick hearts."[40] Fitz's tired brigade led the way, with Beale's 9th Virginia Cavalry, wagons, ambulances, and horse artillery trailing after it. Chambliss's Brigade was next in line, and Hampton's regiments composed the rear guard. Riding behind the miles-long column was an arduous task, and Hampton's men suffered accordingly. They had to contend with the billowing clouds of dust kicked up by the units ahead of them, as well as the numerous stragglers who fell behind.[41]

At Dillsburg, some of the men took possession of whatever they could find in the local stores and robbed the post office of its stamps and money. While the looting was underway Hampton, now in charge of the wagon train, moved it a mile and a half north of Dillsburg and set up camp on the farm of John Mumper. It was the end of the journey for the cumbersome rolling stock. By this time guarding the 125 wagons was simply too difficult for exhausted and hungry men, and the agonizingly slow pace had to be picked up. Their passage unfettered, Stuart's remaining pair of brigades pushed northward for Carlisle.[42]

Men fell out of line to forage. Despite their exhaustion, they still managed to have a bit of fun. Several members of the Old Dominion Dragoons, Company B, 3rd Virginia Cavalry, rode up to a farm house and knocked on the door. When a woman carrying a baby answered, they politely asked if they could buy some food because they had not had much to eat for several days. "I have nothing and if I did, I'd not give it to you," she responded. The response was not what the troopers were hoping to hear. When one of them edged closer, the woman proclaimed, "You dirty Rebels will get nothing from me. I'd like to see the whole murderous lot of you die." An unnamed Virginian snatched the baby from her arms. The woman screamed when the Virginian insinuated he would eat the baby if they couldn't get anything else. According to one of the participants, by this time "it was obvious that her former bravado was gone." The man with the infant "offered to trade her the baby for some bacon, whereupon she set out ham, fowl, bacon, bread, and butter. We had a glorious feast and took the remainder back to camp after paying her (in Confederate money) for all we had taken." Their comrades had a good laugh at the expense of the terrified woman.[43]

The failure of horses left many of Stuart's troopers dismounted. They had limited options: find new horses in the rich Pennsylvania countryside or walk. The local residents did what they could to hide their animals or discourage the Confederates from confiscating them. One woman protected her prize horse by smearing cow dung all over him. One of Stuart's foraging parties spotted the ridiculous looking animal, laughed, and continued on, convinced that discretion was the better part of valor. Searches turned up not only riding mounts but draft horses as well. By the time Stuart's column left York County, it had collected nearly 1,000 of the latter, which the Army of Northern Virginia would put to good use.[44]

Captain Frank S. Robertson's mount Bostona was near collapse, and Theodore S. Garnett's mount was also exhausted. The men, both on Stuart's staff, left the column to go horse hunting in the nearby woods. "Finding a dozen or more hidden in the brush, we selected two, abandoned ours in place of them and rejoined the General," recalled Robertson. "I rode my new mount for four days when she gave out and fell in the road at last," leaving Robertson to once again look for another mount. He ended up with a captured nag which was "the worst-riding horse I was ever on. This U. S. branded horse could do naught but trot, and such a trot that I felt my brains would be addled."[45]

One of Stuart's couriers, Pvt. J. A. Buxton, wasn't even that lucky. With his little sorrel utterly worn out by the time the fight at Hanover ended, Buxton turned her out on the night of June 30 and added her to the column of led horses. Needing a new mount, Buxton selected one of the herded mules Stuart had detached from the Federal wagon train before leaving Rockville. After catching up with Stuart, Buxton reported his plight to Major McClellan, who gave the courier permission to scour the countryside for a new mount. Unable to find one, Buxton plodded along on his mule all night and most of the next day. He finally captured a fine chestnut mare near Carlisle and gratefully returned the mule to the herd following the column. The mule had provided reliable transportation, but it was not much of a mount for a proud Confederate cavalryman, and Buxton gladly gave it up when a better choice came along.[46]

The obvious passage of such a long column of cavalry (and a wagon train for much of the journey) did not at this point in the journey pass unnoticed by Union forces. On June 30, Southern cavalry under Brig. Gen. Albert G. Jenkins fought a large-scale skirmish with infantry from the defenses of Harrisburg at a place called Sporting Hill, southwest of Camp Hill. Late in the afternoon, General Ewell ordered Jenkins to break off the engagement and ride toward Carlisle after he had received orders for the army to concentrate around Gettysburg. As Ewell's Corps marched for South Mountain, Union infantry led by Brig. Gen. William F. "Baldy" Smith followed. Joseph F. Knipe, a brigadier in command of one of Smith's brigades, led the slow pursuit, which reached Carlisle on the afternoon of July 1.

That same afternoon Smith sent a note to Knipe. "It is reported by a citizen . . . that there are 3000 rebel cavalry or mounted infantry on the road from Mechanicsburg to Dillsburg. I place no reliance on the report but want you to keep a sharp lookout and send word to [Maj. Gen. Darius N. Couch, commander of the Department of the Susquehanna, Smith's commander] that he may send what force he has into the fort if he thinks fit."[47] Though Smith doubted the news, it was quite accurate. Another opportunity to trap Stuart's fatigued command slipped through Union fingers. Had Smith placed a small blocking force in the mouth of Holly Gap—the only passage through South Mountain anywhere near Carlisle—he might have stopped Stuart dead in his tracks. Instead, Stuart's horsemen continued unimpeded toward Carlisle.

Carlisle was the county seat of Cumberland County. Dickinson College, a well-regarded liberal arts college established by Benjamin Rush, one of the country's Founding Fathers, had graced the town since 1773. The school was immediately popular with Southerners, and a number of prominent Confederate cavalrymen, including one of Chambliss's regimental colonels, were alumni of that distinguished institution. The British used the town as a major supply center and military outpost in Carlisle in the 1750s, and the Continental Army established its own outpost there during the Revolutionary War known as Washingtonburg. The U.S. Army maintained the post as the Carlisle Barracks ever since, garrisoning it with infantry, artillery, and cavalry. In 1838, the Army established a cavalry training school at Carlisle Barracks, where new cavalrymen learned the basic skills needed to operate effectively in the field. The training school closed in 1861 when the

Brigadier General Albert G. Jenkins's Brigade of mounted infantry accompanied Lt. Gen. Richard Ewell's Corps into Pennsylvania.

USAMHI

Barracks became the home of the U.S. Mounted Recruiting Service. All new recruits and officers passed through the new training and supply center before joining their regiments, making it crucial to the Union war effort. The garrison from the Barracks was evacuated to the defenses of Harrisburg in June 1863 when it appeared likely that the Confederates were going to pay Carlisle a visit. By the time Stuart arrived its buildings and armory stood vacant and unguarded.[48]

Although Stuart did not have any direct personal ties to Carlisle Barracks, many associated with him did. His father-in-law, Union Brig. Gen. Philip St. George Cooke, had been in command of the Cavalry Recruiting Services from 1848 through 1852. Two of Stuart's brigade commanders, Fitz Lee and John Chambliss, were stationed at the Barracks during their prewar careers. Chambliss spent 1853 and 1854 there. Fitz spent two years at the cavalry school (1856-1858) and graduated first in his class in horsemanship. He grew fond of the town and its occupants. Colonel Beale of the 9th Virginia Cavalry was an alumnus of Dickinson, which shared Carlisle with the Barracks. All three senior officers carried warm spots in their hearts for the old town.[49]

By the time the Confederates reached the outskirts of Carlisle on the afternoon of July 1, they were out of rations. The troopers expected to find friendly infantry from Ewell's Corps occupying the town, "behind whose sheltering muskets we hoped to find one more night of sweet sleep," recalled an officer who rode with Chambliss.[50] Much to his dismay, he discovered not Southern infantry but Union soldiers holding the place. Baldy Smith's Northern militia, pursuing Ewell's infantry toward Gettysburg, had slipped into Carlisle just that afternoon. Enemy or no enemy, Stuart intended to levy the town for rations and fodder.[51]

The townsfolk of Carlisle had already had a rough week. Albert Jenkins's Confederate cavalry had occupied the town and levied it for supplies before heading north to try and capture Harrisburg. The balance of Ewell's Corps arrived on June 28, flooding the place with ragged and ravenous Southerners. The Confederates returned to Carlisle two days later after receiving instructions from Robert E. Lee to march to Gettysburg, where the Army of Northern Virginia was concentrating. With Jenkins's cavalry leading the way, the Southerners once again terrorized the citizens of the town. Fortunately for the locals, this time they only paused briefly as they passed through on their way south to Gettysburg, about thirty miles distant on the far side of South Mountain. Although Jeb Stuart's cavalry only visited Carlisle for a few hours, they proved to be some of the longest and most dangerous hours of the town's long and distinguished history.

Captain William H. Boyd's company of the 1st New York (Lincoln) Cavalry led Baldy Smith's Federal advance on Carlisle the afternoon of July 1. Boyd's troopers, who had escaped from Winchester, Virginia, before it fell to Ewell's infantry on June 14, dogged the Confederate move all the way up the Cumberland Valley, buzzing about the edges of Jenkins's column like mosquitoes, fighting delaying actions and harassing the Southerners. Boyd and his men were all Philadelphians who had traveled to New York to enlist in the war's first volunteer cavalry regiment. They proved their mettle that summer by performing admirably throughout the difficult campaign. That morning, Boyd's troopers captured a dozen wagons, together with a large number of horses and mules, and turned them over to Baldy Smith. The intrepid captain had other things on his mind as he rode with his command to Carlisle on the morning of July 1 in preparation for a daring expedition. Boyd's plan was nothing short of an attempt to capture Robert E. Lee at his headquarters near Cashtown. But his men needed rest, food, and fodder before undertaking such a dangerous mission.[52]

Thrilled to see friendly soldiers again after enemy hordes had descended upon them three times in one week, the relieved Carlisle townsfolk welcomed them with open arms and open pantries.[53] When the weary horsemen clattered into town they were "hailed with shouts of joy." Within minutes of their arrival, the citizenry filled the town square, anxious to hear the latest news. Boyd responded that he had no news, but that his men were hungry. "The announcement set the people flying to their homes and in a few minutes the market place was filled with eatables." After eating and resting for a while, the tireless Boyd and his energized horsemen mounted and headed toward Cashtown.[54]

Not long after the cavalrymen arrived, Smith's two brigades of foot soldiers entered the town. As the day wore on, regiment after regiment of militia, supported by artillery, filed into the town. Smith deployed his men around the town square and ordered his artillery to unlimber on Hanover Street. A member of the West Point class of 1845, William F. Smith was an experienced and skilled soldier. He had served as an engineer and mathematics instructor at West Point and commanded the Army of the Potomac's Sixth Corps at Fredericksburg. When Smith complained to President Lincoln about Maj. Gen. Ambrose E. Burnside's performance at Fredericksburg, Smith was transferred away from the Army of the Potomac and so missed the combat at Chancellorsville. When Darius Couch assumed command of the Department of the Susquehanna, Smith assumed command of his forces in the field on the west shore of the Susquehanna River. On July 1, 1863, "Baldy" Smith proved he was the right man in the right place.[55]

Brigadier General John Ewen's 4th Brigade of Smith's command consisted of two regiments, approximately 1,200 New York militiamen. Ewen was an inexperienced militia officer and had frozen in battle the day before (June 30) in the skirmish with Jenkins at Sporting Hill. Lieutenant Rufus King, Jr., the son of a Union general, was everything Ewen was not, militarily speaking. A Regular Army artillerist (though not a West Point graduate), King would receive two brevets for valor during the Civil War and be awarded the coveted Medal of Honor for his performance at the Battle of White Oak Swamp on June 30, 1862. On that day he succeeded to command of two batteries of the 4th U.S. Artillery while in action against a superior force of the enemy and fought his guns gallantly until compelled to retire.[56] Realizing Ewen was paralyzed by fear, King had assumed command of the New Yorker's militiamen at Sporting Hill, coaxing them to stand and fight Jenkins's veterans. Ewen was, at best, a weak reed for Smith to rely upon.

Major General William F. "Baldy" Smith, commander of the Union troops in Carlisle, Pennsylvania

National Archives

Colonel William Brisbane's 5th Brigade consisted of two regiments of Pennsylvania emergency troops, about 1,400 officers and men. They were almost completely untried and were of questionable quality. Smith also had with him Capt. Henry D. Landis's 1st Philadelphia Battery, two guns temporarily commanded by Lieutenant King and manned by 30 Regulars of the 4th U.S. Artillery drafted from the garrison at Carlisle Barracks.[57] By 3:00 p.m., these ragtag forces were in position in Carlisle. "The rebs had left there in the forenoon, and the citizens were glad to greet the blue uniforms again," recalled a member of the 28th Pennsylvania Emergency Infantry, part of Brisbane's command.[58] "Found a first rate supper waiting for us in the Market House," reported one of Landis's gunners. "Bread, butter, coffee, apple butter jelly and young ladies to wait on us."[59] Their pleasant respite would not last long.

All told, Smith had some 2,600 inexperienced and unreliable infantry, supported by a single battery of artillery and Boyd's small detachment of cavalry to defend the Barracks and the town. Few of these men were accustomed to the vicissitudes of hard military service, and all of them were tired from their long march from Harrisburg. Indeed, stragglers from Smith's column littered the roadside.[60]

About 3:00 p.m. a citizen rode into town with word that Confederates were advancing on the Baltimore Pike. The militia disregarded these reports after a Northern officer, supported by a company of infantry, rode out to investigate and reported no enemy within sight. Two other citizens who had ridden in from Petersburg reported that there were no rebels on the west side of Piney Mountain. "The Company then returned to town, and a laugh was had at the scare," recalled one of the soldiers.[61]

The alarm came a second time, however, and this time it was no laughing matter. A New York militiaman, exhausted from the unfamiliar tribulations of campaigning, noted, "We had just begun to be rested, and to get acquainted with the fair girls who were serving us with refreshments, [when] word came that the rebels were returning."[62]

The soldiers had stacked their weapons in the town square and were resting, eating, and swapping stories. "While eating, the alarm was given 'the rebels are on us!'" recalled an artillerist. The infantrymen rushed to grab their weapons.[66] "Suddenly the presence of Rebels became known and then a stampede of course followed."[67]

Carlisle's long night of terror was about to begin.

Chapter 7

A Night to Remember: Carlisle

"Shell away and be damned!"
— Brig. Gen. William F. "Baldy" Smith

B aldy Smith arrived in Carlisle about 6:00 p.m. According to the local paper, the general was "cheered by soldiers and citizens as he entered but paid no attention to the compliment. He proceeded on in his carriage for the purpose of selecting a prominent position for his artillery."[1] Smith fully realized the difficult task facing his inexperienced command, and "determined to content myself till morning with simply holding the town."[2] Even that would be a tall order.

Smith began by deploying his four regiments on the eastern side of Carlisle in a line running north to south. Brisbane and his Pennsylvanians held the northerly portion of the line, while Ewen's New Yorkers deployed on the southern end. Smith assumed personal command of the center of the line. Skirmishers moved well in advance of the main line of battle, whose sole purpose was to protect the town and keep the approaching Confederates out. "Gen. Smith distributed his handful of men to the best advantage in the different portions of the town," recalled a member of the 22nd New York Militia.[3]

Several companies of local militia hailing from Carlisle willingly answered the call to defend the town. Four captains commanded the militia: Low, Kuhn, Black, and Smiley. They quickly deployed their troops on the eastern edge of town and opened "a very telling fire" that compelled the advance elements of Stuart's column to pull back from what one of Fitz Lee's men called "a sharp fight."[4] A hot skirmish broke out along the eastern edge of town as Ewen's New Yorkers traded shots with the Virginia horse soldiers, a steady rattle of musketry that continued all evening.[5] After escorting General Smith's advance, some of Capt. William H. Boyd's tireless troopers of the 1st New York (Lincoln) Cavalry dashed down Pomfret Street toward the approaching Confederate horsemen. After crossing the bridge over Letort Creek, however, they ran into a detachment of Southern troopers secreted in bushes in an adjoining field. The enemy popped up and unleashed a short-range volley directly into the faces of the trotting Federal horse soldiers that compelled them to fall back in some confusion, a withdrawal that left the east bank of the creek entirely in Stuart's hands.[6] The repulse of Boyd's horsemen and Smith's deployment east of town left the Barracks buildings undefended and vulnerable.[7]

Only moments after Boyd's New Yorkers fell back Southerner Lt. Henry Lee entered Carlisle. In his hands was a flag of truce. James Sullivan, a Carlisle youth approaching his teen years, watched in rapt awe as Lee approached with the flag, accompanied by two privates. "The officer bore on a staff held sidewise, horizontally, plainly visible to us, a white flag of quite large size, I should judge a third of an ordinary bed sheet." Sullivan watched silently while two of Ewen's soldiers stopped the truce

Lieutenant Henry C. Lee, Fitz Lee's younger brother.

The Museum of the Confederacy

bearers to find out what they wanted. After a short exchange the Union troopers conducted Lee and his companions to Baldy Smith's headquarters on the town square.[8]

The truce offer came about because Jeb Stuart had no desire to "subject the town to the consequences of attack." In an effort to avoid shelling it, he directed Fitz Lee to send in a flag of truce demanding the unconditional surrender of Carlisle, threatening its bombardment only if the demand was rejected. The man carrying the flag and the important message was Fitz's twenty-one-year-old brother Henry.[9] He arrived at Smith's headquarters and reported that Fitz Lee's cavalry, 3,000 strong and supported by artillery, was preparing to shell the historic town unless Smith unconditionally surrendered. Henry Lee concluded by telling Smith to send the women and children out of town if he was unwilling to capitulate. "To this," explained the *Carlisle Herald*, "Gen. Smith gave a decided refusal, when the rebel officer informed him that the shelling would proceed."[10]

Old Polly McGinness was making coffee for General Smith and some of his soldiers when Henry Lee arrived with his flag. When she heard Lee's surrender demand, Polly clapped Smith on the back and loudly proclaimed, "Don't do it, General! Don't do it as long as one brick remains on another." The pugnacious Smith surely appreciated Polly's words, though he did not need the fortitude to muster his response to Lieutenant Lee: "Shell away and be damned!"[11]

Once Lee left to convey Smith's reply, the general dispatched his volunteer aide, a Mr. Ward of Harrisburg, to inform Joseph F. Knipe, one of his brigade commanders also in Carlisle, to march his men at 3:00 a.m. and report the state of affairs in Carlisle to General Couch. Later that evening that general would, in turn, pass along information on the developing situation in Carlisle to General-in-Chief Henry W. Halleck. "I have sent out a force in the direction of Carlisle," explained Couch. "It has been attacked by a body of cavalry, at least, and just now things do not look well."[12] While Ward rode for Knipe, Smith worried about the reliability of his artillery and the limited supply of his fixed ammunition. His solution for both issues was to order Lt. Rufus King, Jr. not to return enemy artillery fire.[13]

Whether Jeb Stuart actually expected Smith to surrender is unknown. He responded to Smith's bold refusal by placing Capt. James Breathed's battery of horse artillery on commanding high ground east of Smith's defensive position, taking possession of the main thoroughfares leading into the town, and repeating the demand for Smith's surrender. "It was again refused," wrote the Southern cavalry chief in his after-action report, "and I was forced to the alternative of shelling the place."[14] Thus opened what one Federal soldier described as "a perfect hail of shot and shell" that continued for three and one-half hours.[15] The citizens of Carlisle had no idea what was coming, remembered one newspaper. "The people not anticipating such a thing—not even knowing that the rebels had cannon, were walking the streets. The first announcement was the whizzing of shells and the terrific report of their explosions. The utmost alarm and consternation ensued."[16]

Frank Robertson, one of Stuart's staff officers, remembered watching from afar as women and children walked about in the town square. It was their final blissful moments before the heavens began raining iron. The staffer looked on as Breathed's gunners unlimbered their pieces, took aim, and opened fire. "After seeing all those ladies and children, I remember somehow I didn't like the crashing of shells among the houses," Robertson recalled. "Suddenly a volley was fired upon us, a bullet striking a box tree by me." The realization that he was also in a killing zone prompted Robertson to beat a hasty retreat.[17]

Margaret Fleming Murray lived in Carlisle. She had spent part of the day writing a letter to her brother, recounting the terror they had all

Harper's Weekly

"The Shelling of Carlisle."

suffered during the past week. "My last letter was written in rather a hopeful strain," she later stated, "and we never dreamed that very evening the Rebel demons would . . . shell the town, and that, too, without giving the usual warning." Before the shelling began, Margaret and her sister Mary walked to the town square to meet and talk with Smith's soldiers. "We were having a very nice time, when the cry 'the Rebels are coming!' was raised." The townsfolk could see the Confederates near the town gas works, and "such a stampede of women and children you never saw in your life," continued Margaret. "You cannot imagine the confusion that ensued. It was a disagreeable surprise. Officers calling to their men, who were scattered in all directions, some eating, others worn out with their long march, fast asleep on the square and pavements; soldiers loading their pieces; the gunners away from their armor and nowhere to be seen; the excitement was intense."[18]

As Margaret and her sister ran for their lives, the terrifying sound of descending artillery shells slicing through the air reached their ears. "The shot and shell were coming thick and fast, and we all retreated to the cellar for safety, the sound of the shells as they came over the house and exploded nearby was terrific. I cannot use a more significant expression than to say that they had an infernal sound. I liked the booming of the cannon but the whizzing of those shells, I hope to never hear again."[19] As another citizen aptly noted, though with great understatement, "Cellars were in demand during the shelling."[20]

The impact of the shelling on the town's women and children was not lost on the Southern horsemen. "Above the roar of cannon, and the rumbling of falling walls could be heard the screams of the women and children, which were heart rending in the extreme," was how one of Fitz Lee's troopers remembered the occasion.[21]

The unearthly screaming of incoming artillery shells was the first warning many residents of Carlisle had that their town was under any serious threat, let alone an outright attack. "Women and children had to fly from the town. Alex Cathcart and Sue had to leave their home, and got shelter with a number of others under a tree," reported a resident of York, Pennsylvania. "Soon the shells came so near them that they had to go farther to another tree where they stayed all night and until 10 the next day."[22] If Stuart wanted to strike terror into the hearts of the townsfolk, he succeeded.

The first round of shelling lasted about thirty minutes before ceasing abruptly. Hoping he had made his point, Stuart sent a second flag of truce into town with a second demand for the unconditional surrender of Carlisle and its contingent of Federal troops. The shelling had done nothing to soften Smith's resolve, however, and for a second time he colorfully refused Stuart's offer.[23] Serious about the work before him, Stuart resumed shelling Carlisle, only this time his guns fitfully hammered away for several hours. Conway Hillman, whose father taught at Dickinson College, estimated the Confederates threw as many as 300 shells into the town during that long, terrifying night. Confederate records, however, indicate the actual shell count was closer to 135.[24]

One of these Southern shells struck a stone wall extending along the north side of West Louther Street from the Pennsylvania Hotel, the same building that served as Smith's headquarters. The round ricocheted and passed through a nearby house, lodging unexploded between the ceiling and floor. Two more shells struck Adam Humerich's house at 147 West Louther Street, passing through the east gable. Once through the home's outer wall the shell exploded in the chimney, blowing a large hole in its side and splintering a mantle above the fireplace. A second shell struck the same side of the house, passed through the wall, struck a joist, ricocheted, and lodged against the outside wall unexploded. These shells had the desired result of spreading fear and confusion among the town's citizenry.[25]

One of Breathed's shells hit South College on Dickinson's campus, tearing through the roof, beam after beam, until it struck a heavy post, where it left a perfect impression. Fortunately, the impact with the beams snuffed the shell's fuse, rendering it otherwise harmless. Young Conway Hillman's father eventually retrieved the unexploded shell and presented it to the college. Another shell exploded in one of the college's classrooms and damaged it extensively. Others struck the Cumberland County Courthouse on the town square. Once the tide of battle passed Carlisle by for good, locals marked the damage on one of the courthouse columns with the date: "July 1, 1863."[26]

About 11:00 p.m., while Stuart's gunners rained intermittent destruction upon the town, General Smith sent another of his volunteer aides, James Dougherty, to ride to General Knipe with orders for him to march his brigade immediately to Carlisle. Dougherty, however, was captured and his orderly badly wounded before the message could be delivered. When Stuart learned Smith was sending for reinforcements, he decided it was time to demand the surrender of the town and its defenders one last time.[27]

"The shelling was kept up at intervals till 3 o'clock in the morning, but a great part of the time, there was no firing," recounted Thomas Griffith, whose father also taught at Dickinson. About midnight, several citizens ventured to Baldy Smith's headquarters to ask if any time had been allowed for removing the women and children from the line of fire. Smith told them the Rebels did not give any time for that purpose except just before the shelling began, but that he had arranged for a cessation of hostilities to allow for the removal of the women and children from the line of fire.[28]

During this second shelling of the town, Stuart sent Captain Robertson to Col. Williams C. Wickham, commander of the 4th Virginia Cavalry, Fitz Lee's Brigade, with orders to burn Carlisle Barracks. Robertson dutifully related the order to Wickham. "In a few moments I saw the grand cavalry barracks begin to glow from many points and then, with a great burst of flame, light up the scenery for miles around," remembered Robertson. "I was too sleepy and exhausted even to know how I got back to General Stuart."[29] The Virginians also torched a lumberyard not far from where Breathed's guns were unlimbered and pounding the town.

As might be expected, the sight of fires raging here and there while shells sparked their way across the dark summer sky struck terror into the souls of the local residents, who worried the Confederates would set the entire town ablaze.[30] "Although the houses were used by their sharp-shooters while firing on our men, not a building was fired excepting the United States cavalry barracks, which were burned by my order," wrote Stuart, "the place having resisted my advance instead of peaceful surrender, as in the case of General Ewell."[31] At 10:00 p.m. that night, "the torch was applied to the Barracks," reported a local newspaper, "simultaneously to each row of buildings, and by eleven o'clock a great sheet of flames spread over the sky in the northeast, turning the terrible scene into sublimity. The hungry flames shot their red tongues high into the Heavens, and their fury could be heard amidst the roar of the artillery."[32]

Fitz Lee's men also torched the town's gas works. "The match was applied to the Purifying house, and it was soon in flames," recounted an

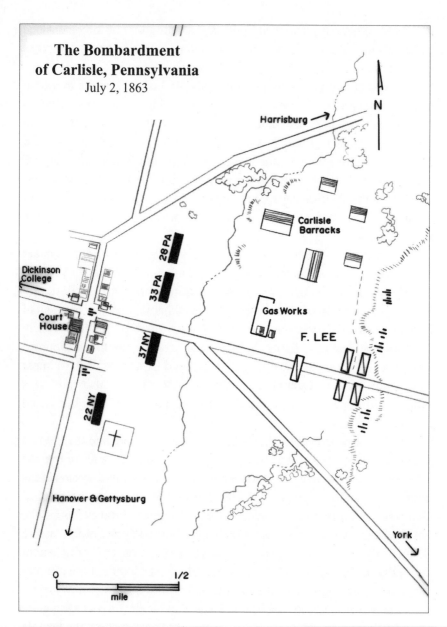

The Bombardment of Carlisle, Pennsylvania
July 2, 1863

Harrisburg →

N

Carlisle Barracks

Dickinson College

28 PA

33 PA

Gas Works

F. LEE

Court House

37 NY

22 NY

Hanover & Gettysburg ↓

York ↘

0   1/2
mile

eyewitness. "The Gasometer, which contained 35,000 feet of gas, was made a target and a number of shell and shot were sent into it." Flaming jets of gas poured out of the brick buildings of the works. George Wise, the superintendent of the gas works, was horrified by the act and believed the shelling would trigger a gigantic deadly explosion. Wise bravely tried to reach the works in the hope of saving them, but Union soldiers prevented him from getting too close. Rebuffed, Wise took the precaution of cutting off the main gas pipe near the edge of town, an act that ensured civilian homes would be spared if an explosion occurred.[33]

The burning gas works presented quite a spectacle. "To add terror to the scene the Rebels fired the board yard near the gas works and soon the flames were leaping up against the lurid sky," reported the *Carlisle Herald*. "The fire communicated to the stable and dwelling connected with the yard and soon they were enveloped in flames. This increased the consternation and those people living in the eastern section of the town fearing that the torch would be applied to their dwellings, and not being aware that our militia still held their positions near the bridge and other points, fled wildly from their dwellings, and amidst the iron rain, hurried into the fields."[34]

Townsman James Sullivan had a good view of the raging conflagration. "From a rear second story window I looked northeast and east over open plots and fields. . . . I saw striking evidence that the Confederates knew their job. Long rows of the brick barracks buildings, in a direct line half a mile away, were in flames," he recalled. "The big lumber yard, much nearer, was also brilliantly burning."[35] It was a night the young man would never forget.

Stuart's horse soldiers did not have much to do once the Barracks, lumberyard, and gas works were set alight. In spite of the noise generated by the shelling and the brightness of the inferno, the exhausted horse soldiers welcomed the respite, and many fell asleep where they stood, sat, or leaned. "From our great exertion, constant mental excitement, want of sleep and food, the men were overcome and so tired and stupid as almost to be ignorant of what was taking place around them," reported Lt. George W. Beale in a letter to his mother. "Couriers in attempting to deliver orders to officers would be compelled to give them a shake and call before they could make them understand. This was true of Colonels. As for men though in line and in momentary expectation of being made to charge, they would throw themselves over on their horse's necks, and some even down on the ground and fall asleep."[36] No matter the era, every soldier learns how to catch sleep whenever he has the opportunity. For many of Stuart's Confederate horse soldiers, slipping into the arms of Morpheus was not by choice.

The Southern guns fell silent about midnight. "The town had been considerably battered," observed one of Fitz's officers.[37] Stuart sent James Dougherty, Baldy Smith's captured aide, into the town with a third flag of truce to once again demand the surrender of Carlisle and its defending host. True to form, Smith rejected the demand a third time, informing the bearer of the truce that this message had been twice answered before. Smith concluded by requesting "that the bearer inform General Lee that he would see him in a hotter climate first."[38] Stuart responded by ordering his gunners to open fire once again. This time the shelling would be short-lived, however, because Stuart's horse artillery was running low on fixed ammunition.[39]

James Sullivan used the lull in the shelling to slip out of the safety of his basement to discover what, exactly, was going on. He wandered slowly to the town square, where he found a mass of soldiers in line of battle. "What regiment?" he inquired.

"The Twenty-Second New York."

Sullivan did a rough head count and concluded only about 200 were in line. "Wishing to see Union soldiers similarly posted in waiting elsewhere, ready to repel an attack, I innocently inquired, 'Where [is] the rest of the regiment?'" A joker in the ranks responded, "In the cellars!" A wave of laughter rippled up down the line of soldiers, some of whom warned James to head back home because they expected the enemy cavalry to charge any moment. Prudently heeding the good advice, Sullivan hastily retreated to the safety of his mother's cellar.[40]

*   *   *

After the brief third shelling Stuart finally received the news he and his worn out troopers longed to hear: General Lee's army was concentrating around Gettysburg and Stuart was to join it with all possible haste. Major Venable and Lieutenant Lee had returned with the orders from Lee after crossing South Mountain for the second time that day. Young Herbert Shriver, who was still accompanying Stuart's column, believed if Stuart had not received orders from General Lee to ride for Gettysburg, "there would not have been one whole house [in Carlisle] standing. As it was, we burnt a good many." Venable and Lee had used the flames from the Carlisle Gas Works to guide them to Stuart's location.[41]

Captain Blackford, Stuart's engineer officer, was with his cavalry chief when the officers made their appearance. "About midnight Venable and Lee returned with the first information we had received from our army and with orders from Gen. R. E. Lee for Stuart to march to Gettysburg at once," remembered Blackford. "They also brought us intelligence of the successful combat of the day at Gettysburg." The relieved Stuart immediately made preparations for his weary troopers to make one more long, final ride.[42]

In order to make sure Stuart received his orders, General Lee also dispatched a squad of riders to Stuart with written orders to return to the army at Gettysburg. Corporal Edwin Selvage of the 1st Maryland Cavalry (CSA) and eight men of his Company D set off to find Stuart. "When we left headquarters, we inquired the shortest way to Carlisle, but, being in hostile territory, we could get little or no information that would be of service to us, and we were left to our own resource in finding the road," Selvage wrote long after the war.[43] He and his troopers arrived at Carlisle about 11:00 p.m. (perhaps a little ahead of Venable and Lee), where brusque calls from Federal pickets brought them to a halt. "How to get past without being recognized was the puzzling question," mused the corporal. One of his industrious comrades devised a ruse to slip through the picket line. "'Buddy' Obenderfer, the 'kid' of the squad, as he was then called . . . said: 'Corporal, I'll bluff them, and you rush past.' Obenderfer rode up to the picket, without heeding the challenge to dismount, and engaged the sentinel in conversation. The rest of the squad, taking advantage of the distraction, dashed through the line, Obenderfer following in the rear. We were pursued for about five miles, but by cutting across fields we outwitted the Yanks."[44]

After slipping through the outer picket line, Selvage and his men spent nearly two anxious hours searching for Stuart or Major McClellan. They finally located the latter officer about 1:00 a.m. and related the news from General Lee, which Stuart had already received from Venable and Henry Lee. McClellan told the weary couriers to rest while he carried the additional dispatch to Stuart. Within a short time Selvage and his band were rewarded with an audience with Stuart. The general asked Selvage if he could lead the column to the Gettysburg battlefield, a task Selvage confidently replied he could manage. His important assignment conferred, Selvage rode near the head of Stuart's column as it disengaged from Carlisle and rode south for Gettysburg. The corporal made the dangerous roundtrip journey without losing a man. Selvage proudly recalled the experience he would remember for the rest of his life, adding that he "was warmly commended for the service rendered the cause."[45]

The news from General Lee energized Stuart, who later reported he "gave orders to the other brigades, with a view of reaching Gettysburg early the next day, and started myself that night." McClellan was quickly dispatched to Wade Hampton's position north of Dillsburg, where the brigadier was ordered to turn south on the well-maintained Gettysburg Turnpike and ride directly to the battlefield. "I myself delivered the order to Hampton," McClellan recalled, "and I saw no more of his command until he came on the field of the cavalry battle on the 3rd." Hampton made good time to Gettysburg, even though he probably stopped for a short rest near Petersburg about daybreak.[46]

Stuart left Carlisle for Gettysburg after 1:00 a.m. accompanied only by Major McClellan, Captain Blackford, Captain Cooke, Major Venable, his ordnance officer Lt. Chiswell Dabney, and a handful of aides. John Chambliss's Brigade led the main column, which left a short time after Stuart and his staff pulled out. The 9th Virginia Cavalry drew the short straw and was placed in charge of the wagon train. "In spite of the broken-down condition of his command, Stuart moved at once," remembered Cooke, "and whole columns went to sleep in the saddle. Pennsylvania had so far proved to be a veritable 'Land of the Drowsey-head.' This night march was the most severe I ever experienced. The long succession of sleepless nights had prostrated the strongest, and General Stuart and his staff moving without escort on the Willstown road, passed over mile after mile asleep in the saddle."[47]

Fitz Lee's troopers remained in place while Chambliss's men headed south. "We were kept in a few hundred yards of the town, every man holding his bridle in his hand during the night," recalled a sergeant.[48] Fitz's pickets captured a few militia soldiers and townsfolk who tried to escape.[49] Although he had plans to attack Carlisle again, no attack was forthcoming. At 3:00 a.m. on July 2 Fitz Lee ordered Breathed's gunners to lob three more shells into the town "to let them know that he was still about." With the final salvo, the gunners limbered their pieces and left by way of Boiling Springs. Lee's Confederates rode to Papertown (present-day Mt. Holly Springs), where they caught up with Colonel Beale's 9th Virginia Cavalry, which was leading the way with the wagons in tow.[50]

Throughout the ordeal at Carlisle, Baldy Smith's artillerists had for the most part held their fire as ordered, suffering in silence while the enemy owned the skies above them. The men of Landis's battery endured the worst of the shelling. They fired only a handful of shots that dreadful night. Gunner John Gunmere fell asleep during the firing and slept until 3:00 a.m., when the final trio of Confederate shots shook him from his slumber. "We fired three shots and were then ordered to lie down at the guns," he recalled, "the rebs had the range so perfectly that they exploded shells directly in our guns. It was so dark that we could not see where to fire, but learned afterward that our first shot upset 15 of them," he concluded.[51]

None of the townsfolk were sorry to see Fitz Lee and his gunners go. "Pocketing the loud threat of capture and demolition, and after exhausting his artillery ammunition, which he could fire at a safe distance," facetiously commented a writer with the *Carlisle Herald*, "he slunk away, immortalized by his brave attack upon the defenseless women and children of a town where he had in past days been treated with the civility and courtesy which his dastardly conduct has shown him so undeserving."[52] The events at Carlisle foreshadowed the darker turn the war would soon take. Until July 1863, the good people of Carlisle labored under the archaic thought that war avoided civilians.

Once the sun rose on July 2, the townsfolk ventured out to see what damage had been wrought by Stuart's artillery and cavalry. "A few bricks and a little mortar will restore the walls of the houses to their old condition," reported one happy civilian who survived the shelling.[53] Mary Murray, who witnessed the firing of the first Confederate shells with her sister Margaret, ventured out to see the ruins of the Carlisle Barracks. "It is really a desolate looking place," she wrote her brother. "The old magazine was not destroyed, neither was . . . the old stable and two or three houses (the bakery's I suppose) situated at the western part of the garrison ground, but the other buildings have all been destroyed." The scene stirred her patriotic blood. "The bare and smoked walls alone are standing monuments to rebel barbarism," she wrote proudly, "but our flag is again waving from the flag-staff and looks more beautiful than ever."[54] Another citizen looked a bit more glumly on what his eyes saw, noting that "It will be some years before the grounds are as beautiful as they were."[55] The fire caused about $70,000 in damage to the Barracks but no lasting damage that could not be fixed. By July 14, the Army had reestablished its supply depot there. The burned buildings were rebuilt and the Barracks never missed a beat, resuming its important role as a training center for new Union recruits.[56]

Local businesses also sustained damage during the nighttime shelling. The local hardware store, druggists, shoe store, grocery store, a number of merchants, blacksmiths, and other prominent citizens suffered injury from the Southern barrage, losing business and revenues as a consequence. By July 15, however, every damaged business in Carlisle had reopened with full supplies, and the railroad bridge across Letort Creek was repaired and back in service.[57] Although Stuart's visit terrified the town, it did little damage that could not be quickly rectified.

Like most of his neighbors, James Sullivan emerged from his mother's house to inspect the damage that morning. As he stepped outside, a member of Ewen's 22nd New York greeted him with a request for a cup of coffee. Sullivan's mother invited the soldier in for breakfast, fascinated by the opportunity to hear war stories from a real soldier. "He was deeply sensible that he was encountering the hardships of war," recalled James. "The long march of sixteen miles the day before, the horrible surprise jar given him and his comrades by the appearance of the Confederates, the disagreeable shocks of the shelling, the fatiguing wait of his group during the night in expectancy of a bloody charge on them at the Louther Street corner—all these trials, with little food or sleep, to one, like himself, soft muscled and unaccustomed to roughing it, had been painfully wearing. His comrades were men of gentle breeding, like himself, he admitted." More tribulations awaited the young soldier.[58]

Despite the length of the bombardment and proximity of opposing forces, Baldy Smith reported only a dozen wounded and none killed. Stuart did not suffer a single injury in the lengthy exchange.[59] The handsome limestone buildings of Dickinson College served as a hospital for those wounded in the shelling, adding to the college's long historic legacy. Within days, the idyllic college campus would be completely overwhelmed with battle wounded from the charnel house at Gettysburg.[60]

The shelling created a great deal of indignation among the townsfolk. "By this inhuman and most brutal act this man Lee has written his name in history a niche higher than Haynan, the Austrian woman whipper," righteously proclaimed the *Carlisle Herald* newspaper a few days after the episode. "If he should ever fall into the hands of the Union soldiers, as we most devoutly hope he may, let mercy such as he showed be meted out to him."[61] While this overstated the case, there was little precedent for this sort of shelling of civilians, and the citizens were justifiably outraged. Margaret Murray echoed similar sentiments. "I think the attack was the most inhuman and barbarous I ever heard of, attempting to destroy a town with the women and children in it. Fitzhugh Lee was the commander of the Rebs: it just shows what they would do if they had the opportunity."[62]

Years later, when passions had cooled somewhat, Fitz Lee defended his actions. "I did not know Carlisle was occupied by hostile troops until I got into a mile or two of the place—& in all statements as to the affair of July 1st then, it must be borne in mind that Carlisle was occupied by troops & their commander refused to surrender it. Of course there was nothing left but to fight for it. It was with much regret I proceeded with hostile intent against Carlisle," admitted Lee. "My first military service after graduating from West Point was there—I knew & had received the hospitalities of most of its citizens—I had warm and earnest & good friends among its inhabitants—Some of the most pleasant days of my life was passed in the hospitable homes of her people—but war—horrid war—raging then between them and those with me & my paths & their paths had separated."[63]

In the years following the Civil War, the people of Carlisle have proudly recited a couplet summarizing their experiences of July 1:

> In eighteen hundred and sixty-three
> Carlisle was shelled by Fitzhugh Lee.[64]

Fortunately, the extended shelling by Breathed's guns did little lasting damage to the town. "Carlisle would undoubtedly have been burned as was Chambersburg the next year had not Baldy Smith and his command hit in their wanderings," noted a grateful civilian years later.[65]

That September, several ladies of the town sent General Smith a silver pitcher "as a testimonial from them, by which they desire to express to you their appreciation of your firmness, gallantry and skill, as manifested in the defense of this town on the night of the 1st July, 1863, a night ever memorable to us all." Their praise continued:

Accept then, General, this token of our high regard which the Ladies of this Borough desire thus to convey to yourself and your gallant soldiers for saving them from the plundering of a Rebel soldiery, and from the humiliation of a town surrendered with national and local defenders within it, and also for giving them occasion for the feeling of a patriotic pride in the knowledge of their own homes being successfully defended against a cruel marauding foe.[66]

Baldy Smith responded rather modestly a few weeks later by thanking the ladies for their kind gift, but giving the credit for his defensive victory to a more heavenly source and to the men under his command. "God, who gives not always the victory to the many, gave me brave men around me, and to Him and them belong the thanks for the successful defense of your town that night." With a nod to chivalry, he added, "I trust the storms of War may never again visit your beautiful country, or disturb its brave women, but should such be the case no one would more zealous or devoted in your service than I, were it my good fortune to be near your homes."[67] Although the citizens of Carlisle had a bad scare during the Chambersburg Raid of 1864, Smith's earnest wish for them came true. Their exposure to the vicissitudes of war was over.

The citizens of York, through which Stuart and his troopers had but recently passed, were grateful they did not suffer Carlisle's fate. "Why didn't we suffer as they did at Carlisle?" asked Cassandra Small. "Now we know why we were spared; they told themselves they expected to make this their headquarters. The battle was to be here and that was the reason they guarded our warehouses and mills so well," she wrote. "They inquired whether there was anything in them and when told, 'Full of Grain and Flour,' they said at once, 'A guard shall be placed there.' They intended it for their own use, but they hurried off too unexpectedly. Were they to return again, nothing would be spared, so we would all leave."[68]

The ordeal was over for the citizens of Carlisle, but Jeb Stuart and his exhausted horsemen were still trapped in the middle of a seemingly endless nightmare. "We proceeded at a trot, pushing our fatigued animals as much as we dared, for they had been constantly on the march during the last ten days," recalled a sergeant riding with the 3rd Virginia Cavalry.[69] With the now thoroughly despised 125 wagons lumbering in tow, Southern cavalrymen belonging to Fitz Lee's and John Chambliss's brigades pressed on, riding for hours through the pitch black

Pennsylvania night. Leaving Dickinson College behind again, as he had upon graduation twenty years earlier, Colonel Beale led the way south toward Gettysburg. When he reached the foot of South Mountain at Papertown, "a command was made for the command to close up. Here some of our men were busy in a search for rations, but most of them, suffering an agony for sleep, lay on the road with bridles in hand, some on rocks, and others on the wet earth, slumbering soundly." Their respite lasted but a single hour. "Resuming the saddle, we moved over the mountain spurs along a broad macadamized road leading towards Gettysburg."[70]

The Southern horsemen struggled up South Mountain with the bright conflagration raging at Carlisle lighting their way. "Tired—exhausted—as I was—I could not but reflect as I looked back on the burning town on the wickedness, the horrors of this felt war," recalled Colonel Beale's son, a lieutenant in the 9th Virginia Cavalry.[71] What none of them knew was that they were sleep-riding their way toward one of the hardest cavalry fights of the war on the John Rummel farm east of Gettysburg.

"This night march was the most severe I ever experienced," recalled Captain Cooke of Stuart's staff. "The long succession of sleepless nights had prostrated the strongest, and General Stuart and his staff moving without escort on the Willstown road, passed over mile after mile asleep in the saddle." At dawn, Stuart dragged himself from the saddle, found a clump of trees by the roadside, and said, "I am going to sleep two hours." The cavalier wrapped himself in his cloak, leaned against a tree, and was instantly sound asleep. The rest of his entourage quickly followed suit. "I was awakened by the voice of one of the couriers," recalled Cooke, "who informed me that 'the General was gone.'" Stuart had awakened precisely two hours later, mounted his horse, and continued riding across the Pennsylvania countryside to reach Lee and the embattled Army of Northern Virginia.[72]

During the ride south, men fell asleep in the saddle and some crashed to the ground, opening their eyes to the snickers and jeers of their companions. "I only remember when we reached Gettysburg the next morning I could hear cannonading south of us," recalled Captain Robertson. "I was nearly dead with fatigue and loss of sleep. I was riding my third horse since crossing the Potomac, my own Bostona, one I borrowed from a farm and lastly one captured in a picket scrimmage, and he was the meanest cuss I ever rode."[73] A lieutenant of the 4th Virginia

Cavalry noted much the same thing in his diary the next morning: "This makes the fifth night without sleep with the exception of four hours. Traveling all the time."[74]

The bulk of Stuart's command finally reached the battlefield at Gettysburg on the afternoon of July 2. "What a pleasing assurance, to think that after so many days & nights of incessant toil, we were within our lines & there would be some prospect for rest, for at least one night!!" was what one of Fitz Lee's happy officers scribbled in his diary that evening.[75] "About 12 m. we reached the pickets of our army," noted a Virginian. "This ought to have been a source of profound relief and gratification, but was not, for our army was then engaged in the great battle of Gettysburg, and we well knew that as tired as we were there was to be no rest till it was over. We marched straight into position and commenced the fight about dark."[76]

*   *   *

The First Troop Philadelphia City Cavalry, which traced its roots to the American Revolution, was an elite militia unit. The original First City Troop was organized in 1774 to serve as George Washington's personal bodyguard.[77] The next generation of troopers served with distinction during the War of 1812. Membership in the First City Troop was by election only, and was highly desired by members of the city's social elite.[78] The First City Troop mustered into Federal service as part of Pennsylvania's emergency response during the Confederate invasion. The troopers were serving in York and Lancaster counties in defense of Harrisburg.

On July 2, a scouting party comprised of 21 members of the First City Troop crossed the Susquehanna River from Columbia using flatboats. From there, they rode westward toward York. Betrayed by an informer, the troopers broke off their ride and took up defensive positions in a cemetery near Heidlersburg. Some acted as sentries while others rested. In the early evening they heard the thunder of hooves on the main road from Harrisburg to Gettysburg and on a parallel road that branches off from York Springs and runs to Hunterstown. The noise was Stuart's main body of cavalry heading for Gettysburg after its long ride. The Southern troopers continued clomping past until well after sundown. Although they surrounded the cemetery, they never discovered the squad of

Philadelphia horsemen hiding inside. Because there were too few Union troopers to make a difference, the men from Philadelphia wisely did nothing to hinder the passage of Stuart's column.[79]

Once Stuart's troopers reached Gettysburg they took up a position on the York and Heidlersburg roads to screen the left flank of the Army of Northern Virginia.[80] Elements of Fitz Lee's Brigade did not reach the field until nearly midnight.[81] Stuart himself rode off to report to Robert E. Lee. As the fighting for Little Round Top, the Peach Orchard, Devil's Den, and the Wheatfield raged, Stuart headed to Lee's headquarters on Seminary Ridge, where a dramatic scene was about to play out. Lee spotted his cavalry chief and reined in his mount. "General Stuart, where have you been?" inquired the army commander in a sharp tone.

Stuart explained his odyssey to Lee, who answered, "I have not heard a word from you for days, and you the eyes and ears of my army."

The cavalry chief feebly responded, "I have brought you 125 wagons and teams, general."

"Yes, general, but they are an impediment to me now," retorted Lee. Abruptly changing his tone, the army commander stated, "Let me ask your help now. We will not discuss this matter longer. Help me fight these people."[82]

Many writers have claimed that Stuart received a dressing down from the army commander, but there are no surviving accounts of that confrontation other than Major McClellan's statement that the meeting between the two officers was "painful beyond description."[83] However things played out between the two, General

General Robert E. Lee, commander of the Army of Northern Virginia.

Library of Congress

Lee was undoubtedly relieved to see the safe return of one of his favorite subordinates and his cavaliers.

That night some unwelcome orders reached the horsemen. Stuart issued a directive to his exhausted men to remain in the saddle all night, "with the assurance that the promise was fair that Pennsylvania would on the morrow be open to our army," recalled Colonel Beale. "The reply was sent that the request would be cheerfully complied with; but that the utmost verge of endurance by men and horses had been reached, and that whatever the morrow might bring, we feared that neither horses nor men could be used either to march or fight." Men sank at the heads of their horses, instantly falling deeply asleep, "the grassy sod [supplying] a couch softer to the wearied limbs than any down bed in days of moping peace."[84] Many similar recollections survive from Stuart's command. "As we had been marching so much and had so little rest since June 20, we all laid down in a stubble field and were soon fast asleep," recalled one of the grayclad horsemen. "I tied my horse's halter slap to my gun sling and just left saddle and all on, and when I awoke the next morning, I was about 30 yards farther down in the field than where I went to sleep. She had just dragged me on as she ate, but I was too dead asleep to know it."[85] Another recalled simply, "What a pleasant night!"[86] "For eight days and nights, the troops had been marching incessantly," observed Major McClellan. "On the ninth night they rested within the shelter, with a grateful sense of relief words cannot express."[87]

"That night was the first night's rest we had had in seventeen days," noted an officer riding with the 5th Virginia Cavalry, "all of which time I had not taken off my boots nor the saddle from my horse except to adjust the blanket, or [had] a square meal except what we could pick up along the line of march."[88] A lieutenant with the 4th Virginia Cavalry recorded on July 3 the toll exacted by the ordeal: "Only some twenty men with Company D out of fifty-six who started. Our raid is at an end. It makes ten days."[89] Turner Holley of Wade Hampton's 2nd South Carolina Cavalry agreed. "We have been marching and fighting all most every day," he wrote. "I have not slept in a tent for twenty days nor had my cloths off."[90]

Virginians were not the only ones who suffered from the lack of sleep. S. A. J. Creekmore, a Mississippian in the Jeff Davis Legion, echoed a similar note. "We were ten days making our way from Brandy Station in Culpeper Co., Va. to the Potomac River near Dranesville, Va. During which time we were skirmishing with the enemy or pursuing them or being pursued by them every day. We traveled day and night, stopping occasionally long enough to feed our horses or whip the Yankee cavalry out of our way." [91] One of James Breathed's gunners made a good point when he penned his recollections years later. "For eight days and nights the command had been in the saddle, marching day and night. On the ninth night they reached within the shadow of Lee's army, with a grateful sense of relief, which words cannot express. No one except those who were on this expedition can imagine the condition of the men and horses. We had to substitute. Conestoga horses for our faithful animals. Time and time again we had to borrow horses from our friends in Pa., very much against their will; but remonstrance was of no avail." [92] The ordeal of their long march was finally over, but plenty of hard and bloody work remained ahead.

The men of Wade Hampton's Brigade, however, were still facing another challenge that would unfold near the hamlet of Hunterstown, six miles from Gettysburg as they slogged their way toward Lee's army. The final chapter of their odyssey remained to be written.

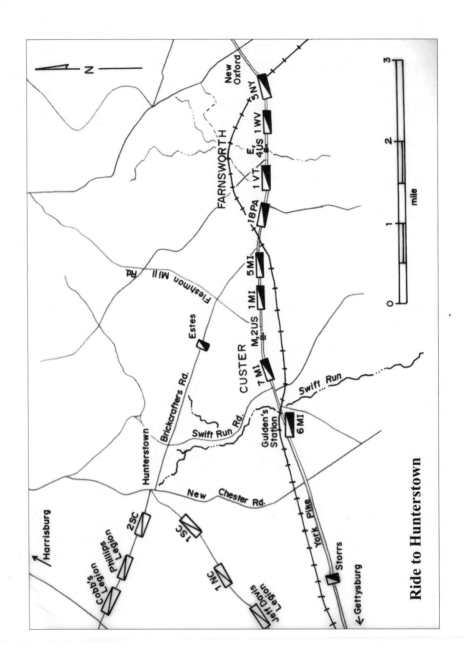

Ride to Hunterstown

Chapter 8

The Battle of Hunterstown

"I'll lead you this time, boys. Come on!"

— Brig. Gen. George A. Custer

A fter the sharp battle with Jeb Stuart at Hanover on June 30,
Judson Kilpatrick missed an outstanding opportunity to capture
or seriously cripple the Southern cavalier's command.

If Kilpatrick had at least maintained contact with Stuart and driven
his own Union troopers just a dozen or so miles from Berlin to Dillsburg,
Stuart almost certainly would have been forced to turn and fight another
battle, perhaps at a severe disadvantage given his long wagon train and
the state of exhaustion his troopers were experiencing. Instead of the
vigorous pursuit the situation demanded, however, "Little Kil" refused to
permit his troopers to venture beyond the outskirts of Hanover. This, in
turn, allowed the Confederates a ten-hour head start on the road to York
and Carlisle. When he did finally move out the next morning, Kilpatrick
rode slowly north in a failed effort to prevent Stuart from moving farther
west. Kilpatrick cited the pounding taken by his back and kidneys during
the previous morning's hell-bent-for-leather ride into Hanover at the
outbreak of the fight as an excuse for his dawdling. Unable to mount a
horse, he spent all of July 1 flat on his back in one of his own ambulances
while Stuart rode through York, angled northwest toward Carlisle, and
inaugurated his infamous nighttime bombardment of the town.[1]

Late on the evening of July 1, after riding fewer than 20 miles,
Kilpatrick's division went into camp between Berlin and Abbottstown.[2]
In the otherwise lengthy official report he would eventually file,

Kilpatrick devoted the least ink to July 1. Of that day he wrote simply, "marched to Berlin, via Abbottstown, to intercept Stuart, but failed."[3]

While Stuart's horsemen plodded toward Gettysburg on their all-night march following the Carlisle bombardment, Kilpatrick's men slumbered soundly in farm fields near Berlin. As the sun rose on July 2, Kilpatrick's troopers awoke to news from General Pleasonton's headquarters: the Yankee horsemen had been ordered to march in haste toward the sound of the guns booming to the west, guns Kilpatrick's men had heard much of the previous day.[4] Division staff roused the brigade officers from sleep, which in turn brought the regiments to their feet. In short order, Kill-Cavalry's division marched toward Gettysburg where, as Sgt. Atchinson Blinn of the 1st Vermont dolefully reminisced, "nothing is heard but the roar of artillery & rattle of musketry mingled with the groans of the dying."[5]

With George Custer's brigade in the lead, the division rode to the Gettysburg-York Pike and turned west.[6] "I proceeded rapidly across the country in the direction of the firing," reported Kilpatrick. "Reached the battlefield at 2 p.m. Received orders from headquarters Cavalry Corps . . . to move over to the road leading from Gettysburg to Abbottstown, and see that the enemy did not turn our flank."[7] The unmistakable din of two giant armies locked in combat was more audible now as the Northern troopers drew near the field. "The sound of the conflict was sufficient guide," explained the 18th Pennsylvania's Capt. John Phillips. "The peaceful and fertile fields of Pennsylvania never looked prettier . . . all unconscious of the carnage that was reddening the fields of the beautiful valley of Gettysburg. . . . On we rode, no man left his place, no man faltered."[8] The horsemen trotted to within four miles of Gettysburg, near Gulden's Station. They found the pike choked with retreating and advancing columns of shuffling blue infantry. Near Gulden's Station Kilpatrick was met by one of Pleasonton's staff officers, who ordered him to picket the army's right flank in concert with Brig. Gen. David Gregg's Second Cavalry Division. Kilpatrick chose a position from which he could see well north of the road.[9] After meeting briefly with Custer and Farnsworth to apprise them of their orders and responsibilities, Kilpatrick directed the division's pickets and patrols be called in so the troopers could continue onward. One small patrol comprised of 6th Michiganders riding in advance of the division, however, had already bumped into some of Wade Hampton's troopers near the intersection of the York Pike and the road to Hunterstown, a small and ancient crossroads a few short miles northeast of the bloodletting just getting underway once again at Gettysburg for a second straight day.

Founded in 1741 by Irish settler David Hunter along an old Indian trail, Hunterstown had once vied with Gettysburg to be the seat of Adams County. In the latter part of the 1700s, when the place was known as "Woodstock," Hunterstown was a burgeoning village, the focal point of the county, and known as "the Hot-Bed of Rebellion" during the American Revolution.[10] Hunter distinguished himself as an officer in the Continental Army.[11] After Gettysburg reaped the rewards that followed its designation as the county seat, Hunterstown faced a slow decline in its vibrancy, settling into a "sleepy little town" of wagon-makers, gunsmiths, cigar-makers, and farmers.[12] Late on the afternoon of July 2, 1863, the town was rudely awakened when Jeb Stuart's bedraggled and drained horsemen rolled through Hunterstown on their way to Gettysburg. The place had no inherent military value, though it could boast of a network of roads that had suddenly become quite important in the campaign. One modern writer described 1863 Hunterstown as "a Gettysburg in miniature," crucial for its access to the Confederate left flank.[13]

An officer with Cobb's Legion, riding in advance of the column, announced to the Hunterstown citizens that Jeb Stuart's cavalry was coming and "all who desired to see them should come up to the square." Within minutes throngs of curious, though cautious onlookers flooded the square to catch a glimpse of one of the most famous men in America.[14]

Stuart's long gray column, with the captured wagons lumbering in tow, required two full hours to pass through the little town and out the road leading to Gettysburg. The front of the column stopped a few miles southwest at Brinkerhoff's Ridge, while Hampton's Brigade, bringing up the rear and escorting the wagons, passed through Hunterstown under the suspicious stares of its citizens.[15] While Stuart continued riding toward Gettysburg to report to Robert E. Lee, Hampton remained at the tail of the column about one mile south of Hunterstown, where the South Carolinian halted his troopers for a short respite in the hot summer sun.[16]

The main body of Kilpatrick's division was riding northwest from the York Pike toward Hunterstown along a narrow farm lane when one of

Hampton's patrols galloped up to the resting South Carolinian with important news: blue cavalry was approaching in "heavy force."[17] After ordering all six of his regiments to countermarch nearly to the Harrisburg Pike, Hampton fired off a message to Stuart to apprise him of the development before galloping forward to join the Jeff Davis Legion at the front of his column.[18] When he heard the news that the enemy was approaching in force, Stuart instructed Hampton to "hold the enemy in check."[19] About 4:00 p.m., Hampton's troopers rode through Hunterstown and rode south along the Gettysburg-Hunterstown Road. A patrol comprised of some 40 troopers under Col. Pierce M. B. Young, the Cobb Legion Cavalry, remained in the streets to keep a close watch on the rear of the the gray column.[20] Young's mission was identical to Lieutenant Potter's two days earlier: guard against a surprise attack. One of Kilpatrick's advance patrols, led by Capt. Llewellyn Estes of the U.S. Volunteers, was paralleling the Union division's right flank. Kilpatrick was advancing toward General Lee's left flank, and Wade Hampton had orders to protect it. Another potentially major collision was in the making.[21]

Estes had a handful more men riding with him than did Pierce Young, all hailing from the 18th Pennsylvania Cavalry's Company A. Each was a veteran of the Hanover fight, where Company A had received its baptismal fire. This time, however, the Union troopers would turn the tables on the rear guard of their opponents, and they took advantage of both speed and surprise to do so.

"In a minute somebody fired a shot," recalled a Hunterstown boy named Jacob Taughenbaugh, "[and] then, the [Federal] officer called out, 'Draw . . . SABERS!' There was a rattling, then, 'CHARGE!' Down the street they came, hard as they could go, waving their sabers and yelling."[22] Moving quickly, Estes caught Young's troopers off guard, firing as they charged. "I was in the front and came near being killed," declared Bugler H. E. Jackson of Company C, Cobb's Legion. "Gen. [*sic*] P. M. B. Young came flying down the pike, hat in hand, with [Estes's] men in close pursuit, firing at him constantly."[23] Young and his Georgians raced back into Hunterstown, where they quickly reformed. "[Young] ordered a charge," continued the private, "and the two lines rushed at each other and had a hand to hand conflict."[24]

In short order the Pennsylvanians drove the Georgians completely out of Hunterstown.[25] Following behind them were George Custer's

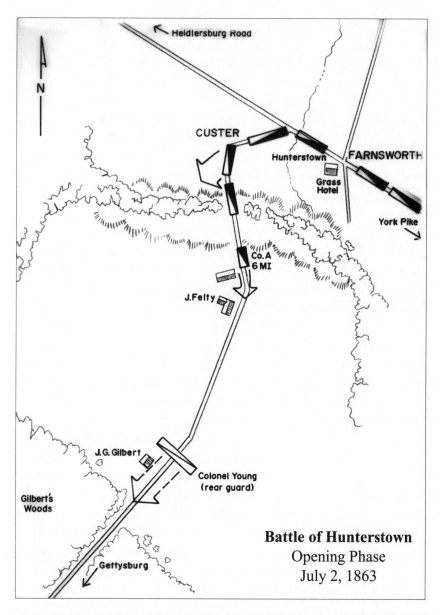

Battle of Hunterstown
Opening Phase
July 2, 1863

leading regiments, the 6th and 7th Michigan. They had just arrived on the outskirts of Hunterstown, and Custer was in the lead. Hearing shots to his front, Custer ordered Colonels Gray and Mann to dismount skirmishers in the elevated fields surrounding the Henry Harman and Samuel McCreary farms about one-half mile outside town.[26] A squadron of Colonel Town's 1st Michigan, commanded by Capt. A. W. Duggan, was detached to the east to hold the road leading into town from the rear.[27] As the cavalrymen deployed, Pennington's Battery M, 2nd U.S. Artillery, galloped into the fields and dropped trail, its six three-inch rifles taking up position in front of McCreary's home. "A moment later cavalry came dashing at full speed into the town, firing as they came at the fleeing pickets with their carbines," recalled a Hunterstown citizen who watched the action unfold in breathless excitement.[28]

The smattering of small-arms fire wafting over the humidity of the late afternoon alerted Hampton to the fact that his rear guard was becoming seriously embroiled with an enemy of unknown size and intention. Ordering his brigade to turn about, Hampton raced two miles through his ranks to get to the Cobb's Legion's position. He arrived near the John Gilbert farmhouse along the Gettysburg-Hunterstown Road just in time to witness the repulse of Young's Georgians.[29] Hampton's position was along a low tree-lined rise that ran perpendicular to the road, parallel to a similar rise held by Custer opposite him less than one mile to the north. Between them lay fields of corn and wheat surrounded on the east and west by thick woods, the whole interlaced with the characteristic rail fences of the era. The road cut the basin of fields below nearly in half. Although no one could yet know it, a bend in the road along another lower rise, this one closer to Hampton's position, would prove critical in the action that was about to unfold.[30]

As the action was getting underway, Kilpatrick rode into Hunterstown and established his headquarters on the southwest corner of the town square in a two-story brick hotel owned by George Grass. After sending out pickets on all the roads leading out of town, Kilpatrick ordered Custer "out the York Springs road . . . and that officer soon returned and reported the woods 'swarming with rebels,'" recalled one local.[31] On Kilpatrick's orders, Custer led his 6th Michigan on the Gettysburg Road, where the young brigadier pulled up rein at the top of the ridgeline overlooking the basin of the valley. "We came upon a small hill just out of town where was located a small squad of rebel cavalry near some woods," wrote Pvt. Nathan H. Green of the 6th Michigan's Company D.[32] Just 200 yards ahead Custer took note of Colonel Young's small yet defiant rear guard. Custer and Georgia-born Young had been classmates at West Point, but the Georgian left the Academy in May 1861 when the storm clouds of war had opened over the country.[33] The boy

Captain Henry E. Thompson of the 6th Michigan Cavalry. His company charged Wade Hampton's men with George Custer at Hunterstown.

general turned to Capt. Henry Thompson and ordered his Company A to sweep Young's Southerner troopers out of the way.[34]

"All was ready, and Thompson was preparing to charge," Custer's trooper noted, "when to everyone's surprise, the boy general flashed out his long Toledo blade, motioned to his staff to keep back, and dashed out in front of Co. A with the careless laughing remark, 'I'll lead you this time, boys. Come on!' Then away he went at a gallop . . . while the men raised a short yell of delight and followed. Down the road in a perfect cloud of blinding dust went the boy general, riding in front of that single company."[35]

As Custer and about 50 troopers charged four abreast toward Young's band of Confederates, three more of the 6th Michigan's companies dismounted and quickly rushed down the slope on the western side of the road. Some members of Company E ran to the large brick barn of local magistrate John Felty and took up positions, while Companies C and D scurried determinedly through the waist-high wheat. Pennington's battery had followed the action and unlimbered behind these men.[36] With the 6th Michigan covering the fields west of the road, the majority of the troopers from the 7th Michigan trotted ahead, dismounted, and formed a skirmish line along the ridge on the road's east (or left) side.[37]

Custer's charge with his squadron down the road was his first mounted assault as a brigadier general. Young's Confederate troopers formed to receive the collision near Gilbert's farmhouse. The brigadier

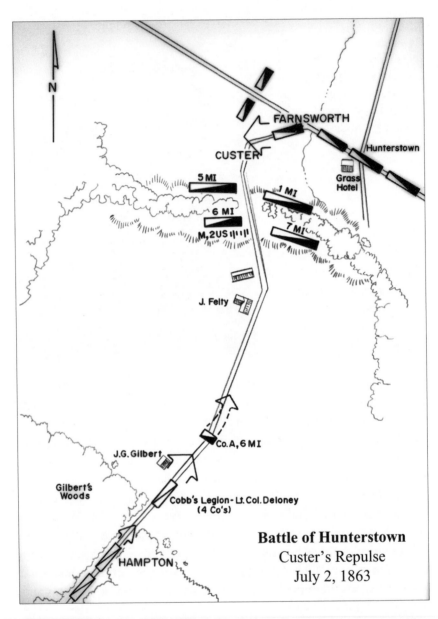

Battle of Hunterstown
Custer's Repulse
July 2, 1863

followed the bend in the road to the right and struck his enemy with a crash, bringing to bear a force greater than Young's stationary troopers could withstand. Swords slashed and parried and revolvers blasted away at point blank range. Saddles were quickly emptied as the melee raged in the narrow road, the participants hemmed in by stout wooden Pennsylvania fences.[38] Initially Custer held the upper hand, but the bend in the road behind him concealed more of Hampton's force than just Young's squadron. "[Custer's men] were received with a rattling fire of carbines, more efficacious than common, and the next moment down went the general, horse and all, in the road, the animal shot stone dead."[39]

Like his opponent, Hampton had also placed dismounted skirmishers on both sides of the road. The perfectly positioned Southern troopers poured a galling fire into Custer's exposed flank. "I threw the Phillips Legion and the Second South Carolina as supporting forces on each flank of the enemy," Hampton explained in his official report of the campaign's fighting.[40] Within moments Custer found himself trapped under his lifeless horse. While he struggled to get free, the close-up fighting raged around him as more Southerners closed in. Companies C and H of Colonel Young's Cobb's Legion charged down the slope into the combat, with Companies A and I following shortly thereafter.[41] "Here I lost in one charge during ten minutes six commissioned officers killed out of my own regt," recalled Young. "This was a great mortality for the length of time engaged."[42]

Lieutenant Wiley C. Howard of the Cobb Legion had a bird's-eye view of the unfolding events. His recollection of the action confirms Young's account. "Our command had a thrilling experience and while charging a body of cavalry down a lane leading by a barn, ran into an ambuscade of men posted in the barn who dealt death and destruction upon us," he recalled. "Within five minutes some four or five officers were killed and wounded and about fifteen men were slain or wounded."[43]

Captain Barrington S. King was a trained physician in command of a company of the Cobb Legion Cavalry. King had his own peculiar adventure at Hunterstown. "My horse ran away with me carrying me through almost the entire column of the enemy. [W]hen running against the fence he fell, throwing me heels over head. I was considerably bruised but the fall saved my life," he explained to his wife. "My horse jumped up and joined the Yankees with all my arms & [accoutrements] & my saddle bags with many little valuables in them my needle book with my sleeve buttons in it all my [handkerchiefs] & towels soap brush & comb &c. A serious loss to me but thank God my life was saved. Lost five Lts. killed and five privates, one of my Lts. among the number." Badly bruised, King was sore for days after his fall. Unlike so many, however, he was alive.[44]

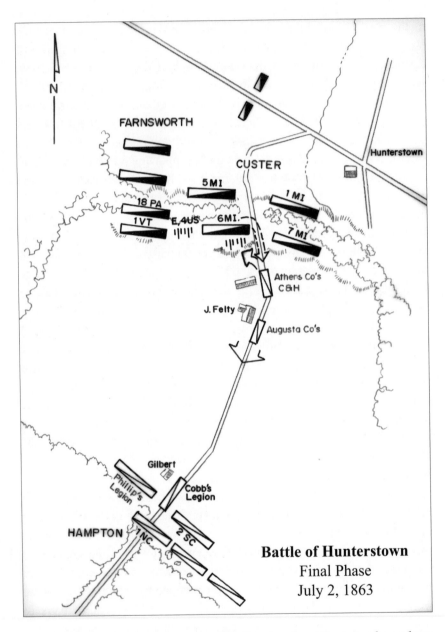

Battle of Hunterstown
Final Phase
July 2, 1863

Within a short time, the overwhelming numbers Hampton brought to bear in his counterattack forced Thompson's Michiganders rearward. Lieutenant Colonel William Delony of the Cobb Legion pitched into the counterassault on his war horse named Marion. His impetuousness nearly cost him his life. Delony recounted in a letter to his wife that he

Lieutenant Colonel William G. Delony, commander of the Cobb Legion. Delony was severely wounded with saber cuts to the head at Hunterstown on July 2, 1863.

University of Georgia

suffered "three sabre cuts on the head, two of them slight and one of them apparently severe."[45] Bugler Jackson recalled watching Delony go down. "My colonel [was sabered] over the right eye near the temple," wrote the bugler, "and he fell paralyzed on his horse's neck."[46]

Soon after Delony was sabered, his bay Marion was shot. Like Custer, the hapless animal fell on Delony and trapped him for a short time before jumping up and galloping off. The fall knocked Delony to his senses like a brisk slap on the face shakes a drunk out of a stupor. "Our men had passed him meantime, driving and routing the force in front, when three Yankees seeing his almost helpless position and that he was an officer of note, dashed upon him to subdue, capture him, or kill him, shooting and cutting him from their horses," wrote the Cobb Legion's historian.[47] After struggling to extricate himself, Delony—blood running down his face in rivulets—fought off mounted attacks while balanced unsteadily on his knees, all the while trying to keep from being trampled to death. He was finally assisted to safety when the bugler spurred to his side, doggedly repulsed the closest attackers, and carried the badly wounded officer to safety within Hampton's lines.[48]

"Henry Jackson," Delony proudly recounted, "behaved very gallantly, and I have no doubt saved my life after I was disabled. I fell from my horse and for a few moments was insensible & he fought desperately over me until he was relieved—his clothes & bugle and saber are all badly cut but he escaped, I am happy to state, entirely unhurt."[49] Like Captain King's mount, Delony's faithful Marion continued galloping after its rider was unhorsed. "I lost old Marion," he reported to his wife. "After I fell from him, he continued on in the charge and when our men halted he kept on and went into the enemy's line, much to my regret."[50] He was, however, able to capture "a beautiful little Pennsylvania pony for him" a few days later.[51]

Jackson's blade had several notches chipped into it as result of having crossed sabers with the Wolverines. That night, the wounded Delony sent for Jackson to thank him for his timely and courageous defense.[52] Jackson showed the colonel his slashed coat and shirt, and the dented bugle he used to help defend himself during the charge. As Delony concluded in his letter to his wife, the young bugler had "behaved like a hero."[53]

The loss of several fine officers and troopers tempered Delony's elation. "I have lost some warm friends in the late battle," he confessed to his wife. "Lt. Houze was killed instantly . . . shot through the head. . . . Lt. Brooks of Ritch's company, Lt. Pugh and Lt. Cheeseborough . . . and Lt. Smith of Capt. King's company were all killed at the same time. . . . Several privates were killed and wounded."[54]

Pierce Young nearly found himself on the lengthy casualty report. His mount was also shot under him, pitching the dashing young Georgian head over heels into the dust amid the human and equine wreckage of mounted saber charges. Young was unhurt by the tumble. He secured another mount and continued the attack.[55]

The Cobb's Legion's frontal counterassault, combined with the accurate carbine and revolver fire delivered from the wheat fields on both flanks by the Phillips Legion and 2nd South Carolina, proved too much for Thompson's bluecoats to bear. "For several paces the blue and gray were mixed up, knocking, cutting, and shooting each other," recalled Jackson.[56] "We charged them, running them back under cover of their artillery," an enlisted man who fought with the legion penned in his diary that night.[57]

Unlike Delony, it took Custer much longer to struggle free and get to his feet. As soon as the prone officer was spotted, he became the target of several Confederate thrusts to kill, wound, or capture him. Those lucky Federals still in their saddles watched as "the enemy raised a yell, and came rushing on. Thompson was shot down . . . and a man rode at Custer, who was struggling up from his dead horse."[58] Intent on killing or capturing the sprawled-out brigadier, a Southerner reined his horse up to Custer, a cloud of dust billowing out from beneath the horse's hooves. Private Norvill F. Churchill, one of Custer's orderlies, realized what was about to take place and spurred his horse toward the antagonist. By this time the Michiganders fighting with Custer were looking for ways to cut themselves out of the melee. All, that is, "but one boy named Churchill, who was near the general. He shot down Custer's assailant, took up the general on his horse, and started back with him."[59] The 23-year-old private, with his golden-haired commander's arms clutching his waist, beat a hasty retreat up the dusty road to the safety of the brigade's lines near the Felty farm.[60]

Unable to withstand further the killing zone into which they had ridden, those Michiganders still in the saddle and able to ride began slapping their reins, setting their spurs, and galloping furiously up the road in Churchill's tracks. "The charge was most gallantly made, and the enemy was driven back in confusion," reported Hampton.[61] "Custer came back . . . with about as many rebs mixed up with them as there was members of Company A—all cutting and slashing as best they knew how," recalled the 6th Michigan's Pvt. Nathan H. Green of Company D. "The rebs broke away when near us and got back to their main body just as they started to charge us."[62] The 6th Michigan's Company A left behind two killed and twenty-five wounded, including Lt. Stephen Ballard, who was lightly wounded and taken prisoner.[63] "Only about 28 men of the company came back," noted Pvt. Gershom W. Mattoon of the 6th Michigan's Company E, "the rest being killed, wounded, or prisoners . . . many of the men were left on the field dangerously wounded."[64] When he later wrote of the charge in which a cavalry company lost half its numbers, Custer didn't even mention his own participation. "Though suffering great loss, he checked the enemy," Custer wrote of Thompson's band, "so as to enable our battery to be placed in position."[65]

"The batteries were not idle" when the hand-to-hand melee took place in the road, reported one of the locals. Pennington's gunners, in position west of the road behind the Felty farm buildings, "kept up an incessant shelling until finally our cavalry fell back."[66] While the guns crews kept their ordnance smoking,[67] "Kilpatrick ordered the rest of the [6th Michigan] regiment to dismount and run to [the Felty] barn that was just under the hill near by. He sat there on his horse hollering: 'Run to that barn! Give them hell!'"[68]

Young's inspired Georgians, engaged with the retreating bluecoats, launched a countercharge against the Federal position on the Felty place. Awaiting their arrival were the dismounted troopers of the 6th Michigan, hiding among the buildings and mature wheat stalks. "As the rebs came toward us the man that was leading the charge was three or four lengths ahead of the other horsemen," recalled Green. "He was swinging his saber and giving that rebel yell. My gun cracked and he went over his horse's head."[69] Captain James H. Kidd watched the withering fire delivered by his Michigan comrades take a deadly toll. "[T]he dismounted men on the right of the road kept up such a fusillade with their Spencer carbines, aided by the rapid discharges from Pennington's battery, that he was driven back in great confusion," he recalled.[70] A 5th New York trooper remembered the Georgians "went back faster than they came" after being greeted by the shower of canister shot and rifle balls.[71] "[T]here wasn't a reb that got past that barn," Private Green announced with pride. "They simply jammed up against the rail fence in front and could not turn around. . . . We gave them a hot reception. I can't see how any of them got out alive."[72]

The dismounted troopers of the 7th Michigan on the left side of the road added the weight of their lead. Bugler Jackson charged into the flanking fire with his Cobb's Legion comrades. "Finally, we ran into [the] dismounted men, who were on both sides of the road, and into a large barn on the left," he wrote. "Every door and window was a blaze of fire, and every man who was with me fell." Jackson quickly recognized that it was suicidal to stay. "I looked back, and saw that my nearest men were fifteen or twenty steps back, and were making to the rear. I did likewise."[73]

While the momentum of the Southern countercharge was thundering toward Custer's position, Hampton was advancing the balance of his brigade to the ridge along the Gilbert farm fields, where he deployed his men in a line of battle. The remaining seven companies of Cobb's Legion trotted into the road, while the Phillips Legion and the 2nd South Carolina finished deploying to the left and right, respectively.[74] The 1st North Carolina established a reserve line behind them, partially concealed by the tree line of Gilbert's woods. Opposite the Southerners, Elon Farnsworth filed his brigade into line on Custer's right flank, where his troopers tore down fences and manhandled some of Elder's guns into position. "General Kilpatrick came along," recalled Sgt. Horace K. Ide of the 1st Vermont's Company D, "and ordered the battery to fire away for some time. 'Pitch a lot of shell over in there so as to make them believe that there is a hell of a lot of us here.'"[75] Other than supporting the artillery, however, Farnsworth's troopers were not engaged on July 2.[76]

Both Hampton and Kilpatrick enjoyed ideal fields of fire for artillery but, as Hampton lamented, "I had no artillery with me at this time."[77] The South Carolinian could only watch while survivors from Cobb's Legion raced back toward him after the repulse on the Felty Farm, Pennington's guns raking their fleeing ranks the entire ride back. Adding to his consternation was the second battery he could see through his glass—four rifles belonging to Lieutenant Elder swinging into line on Kilpatrick's ridge. The cannons, reported Hampton, "opened on me heavily."[78] If he was going to hold his position, he would need artillery to do so. Hampton dispatched a courier to seek out long-arm support. It would not be long in coming.

"Thursday evening, July 2, just before sunset, I was ordered to report with my section of [10-pounder] Parrott guns to General Hampton, at Hunterstown," reported Capt. C. A. Green of the Louisiana Guard Artillery. Green's guns were attached to General Ewell's Second Corps. "Arrived at dusk, and immediately engaged a battery attached to the enemy's cavalry. . . . The engagement lasted until dark."[79] The 6th Michigan's Private Green was still posted in Felty's barn when the Louisiana guns arrived on the field. "[T]hey began to shell us," he remembered. "They put a shell through the house and when they dropped one in the barn we thought it time to get out."[80]

Captain Green and Kilpatrick's gunners hammered each other well into the night, by some accounts as late as 11:00 p.m.[81] Despite poor visibility and being outnumbered, Green managed to disable one of Pennington's guns and kill four of his horses.[82] Facing two enemy batteries, however, Green had the worse of the iron exchange. One of his men was killed outright and a sergeant and 14 others were wounded.[83] In addition, one of his 10-pounder Parrotts was dismounted when Pennington fired a shell straight into the weapon's carriage.[84]

Darkness, nature's interrupter of pre-20th century battles, neutralized any thoughts Kilpatrick may have had of exploiting his numerical superiority over Hampton's 2,000 troopers. The unplanned encounter at the small crossroads town, which began with a handful of shots along a few streets two hours earlier, fell into stalemate. Stuart later lauded Hampton for his brigade's "gallant service" at Hunterstown.[85] Like the Hanover fight two days earlier, losses compared to numbers engaged were insignificant. Kilpatrick took 33 killed, wounded, and missing, with the majority in the 6th Michigan's Company A.[86] Hampton's Brigade suffered nine killed, five wounded, and seven missing.[87] The significance of these numbers, however, can only be fully appreciated by realizing that a single company of Custer's brigade and five companies of Cobb's Legion (250 total men, blue and gray) bore the brunt of the sharp Hunterstown brawl. Despite the larger battles those men had and would yet participate in, each long remembered the hellish vortex on a dusty road outside Hunterstown.

About 11:00 p.m. that night, Kilpatrick received orders to march south to Two Taverns along the Baltimore Pike. At approximately the same time that Kilpatrick vacated Hunterstown, Hampton withdrew part of his brigade one mile south near the William Stallsmith farm, where Stuart had set up his division's camp.[88] The bulk of Hampton's troopers held their position along the Gilbert woods line throughout the night. At daybreak, Hampton was "ordered to move through Hunterstown, and endeavor to get on the right flank of the enemy."[89] Ahead of them, sprinkled across the landscape, lay the corpses of both men and animals from the previous evening's fight. Nearly every building in town was pressed into service as a hospital, primarily for members of the Cobb Legion and the 6th Michigan.

Bugler Jackson spent a fitful night wondering what happened to a missing relative from his regiment. With the daylight came sad news. "We rode up to Hunterstown next morning and found our men lying here and there at the [Felty] barn. My brother-in-law had been killed and his pockets had been turned inside out."[90] Hampton's Brigade rode onward, where it would face an even more arduous test east of town on the afternoon of July 3. "About six o'clock we carried the wagon train into Lee's lines not having lost a single vehicle," proudly noted one of Hampton's men, who had escorted the wagons from Dillsburg.[91]

Years later, Capt. John M. Lamb of Company D, 3rd Virginia Cavalry, looked back on the week he had experienced. "We had not slept for six nights save on horse back and horses and men were more dead than alive," was the best way he could sum it up.[92] Although plenty of fighting remained to be done by his exhausted and saddle sore comrades, the long ordeal of Jeb Stuart's ride was finally at an end. The journey had consumed eight days, nearly 200 miles, and included four sizeable skirmishes (Thoroughfare Gap, Fairfax Court House, Rockville, and Carlisle), the encounter with Corbit's courageous Delawareans at Westminster, and two battles at Hanover and Hunterstown.

The end of the ride, however, marked only the beginning of a controversy that has raged for more than 140 years. It continues to this day.

Chapter 9

The Controversy Begins

"General Stuart is much criticized for his part in our
late campaign, whether rightfully I cannot say."
— Capt. Charles Minor Blackford, Judge Advocate, Longstreet's Corps

Recrimination over the manner in which Jeb Stuart's ride was
conducted began almost immediately. Indeed, the controversy
began within days of the end of the fighting at Gettysburg.
Someone had to take the blame for the loss there, and Stuart, along with
Lt. Gen. James Longstreet, was the most logical candidate.

"There are many wild reports in circulation today regarding General
J. E. B. Stuart, the Chief of Cavalry in Virginia," wrote a newspaper
correspondent based in Richmond in early August 1863. "It is said that he
will be deposed, and that Gen. Hood will be put in his place. For some
time back many serious charges have been made against Stuart, reflecting
severely upon him. His vanity seems to have controlled all his actions,
and the cavalry was used frequently to gratify his personal pride and to
the detriment of the service." Stuart had been heavily criticized since he
was surprised and nearly thrashed at Brandy Station on June 9, 1863. His
far-ranging ride before the fighting at Gettysburg dredged up those
unpleasant discussions again. "At the Battle of Gettysburg he was not to
be found," continued the editorial, "and Gen. Lee could not get enough
cavalry together to carry out his plans."

The correspondent concluded his attack with a condemnation of the
cavalier. After damning with faint praise by pointing out that Stuart had
many good and admirable traits, he added, "but that inordinate personal

pride—that weak-minded vanity, so subject to flattery and praise, ruin entirely his character as an officer."[1]

"General Stuart is much criticized for his part in our late campaign, whether rightfully I cannot say," wrote Capt. Charles Minor Blackford, brother of Stuart's adjutant William Blackford, in a July 18 letter to his wife. "During his many reviews in Culpeper he was said to have twelve thousand cavalry ready for duty. He crossed the river with six thousand, but they played a small part in the great drama either as the 'eyes of the army' or any other capacity. In his anxiety to 'do some great thing' General Stuart carried his men beyond the range of usefulness and Lee was not thereafter kept fully informed as to the enemy's movements as he should have been, or as he would have been had Stuart been nearer at hand." As judge advocate of Longstreet's Corps, Blackford was in a position to testify to the explicit grumbles regarding Stuart's performance bouncing about in the upper echelon of Lee's defeated army.[2]

Instantly and widely besieged, Stuart took it upon himself to defend his record in the report he prepared for his role in the Gettysburg Campaign. What follows is an extensive excerpt from that report. "In taking a retrospect of this campaign," began Stuart,

> it is necessary, in order to appreciate the value of the services of the cavalry, to correctly estimate the amount of labor to be performed, the difficulties to be encountered, and the very extended sphere of operations, mainly in the enemy's country. In the exercise of the discretion vested in me by the commanding general, it was deemed practicable to move entirely in the enemy's rear, intercepting his communications with his base (Washington), and, inflicting damage upon his rear, to rejoin the army in Pennsylvania in time to participate in its actual conflicts.

> The result abundantly confirms my judgment as to the practicability as well as utility of the move. The main army, I was advised by the commanding general, would move in two columns for the Susquehanna. Early commanded the advance of one of these columns to the eastward, and I was directed to communicate with him as early as practicable after crossing the Potomac, and place my command on his right flank. It was expected I would find him in York. The newspapers of the enemy, my only source of information, chronicled his arrival there and at Wrightsville, on the Susquehanna, with great particularity. I therefore moved to join him

in that vicinity. The enemy's army was moving in a direction parallel with me. I was apprised of its arrival at Taneytown when I was near Hanover, Pa.; but believing, from the lapse of time, that our army was already in York or at Harrisburg, where it could choose its battle-ground with the enemy, I hastened to place my command with it. It is believed that, had the corps of Hill and Longstreet moved on instead of halting near Chambersburg, York could have been the place of concentration instead of Gettysburg.

This move of my command between the enemy's seat of government and the army charged with its defense involved serious loss to the enemy in men and *matériel* (over 1,000 prisoners having been captured), and spread terror and consternation to the very gates of the capital. The streets were barricaded for defense, as also was done in Baltimore on the day following. This move drew the enemy's overweening force of cavalry, from its aggressive attitude toward our flank near Williamsport and Hagerstown, to the defense of its own communications, now at my mercy. The entire Sixth Army Corps, in addition, was sent to intercept me at Westminster, arriving there the morning I left, which in the result prevented its participation in the first two days' fight at Gettysburg.

Stuart continued:

Our trains in transit were thus not only secured, but it was done in a way that at the same time seriously injured the enemy. General Meade also detached 4,000 troops, under General French, to escort public property to Washington from Frederick, a step which certainly would have been unnecessary but for my presence in his rear, thus weakening his army to that extent. In fact, although in his own country, he had to make large detachments to protect his rear and baggage. General Meade also complains that his movements were delayed by the detention of his cavalry in his rear. He might truthfully have added, by the movement in his rear of a large force of Confederate cavalry, capturing his trains and cutting all his communications with Washington.

It is not to be supposed such delay in his operations could have been so effectually caused by any other disposition of the cavalry. Moreover, considering York as the point of junction, as I had every reason to believe it would be, the route I took was quite as direct and more expeditious than the alternate one proposed, and there is reason to believe on that route that my command would have been divided up in the different gaps of South Mountain covering our flank, while the enemy, by concentration upon any one, could have greatly endangered our baggage and ordnance trains without exposing his own.

It was thought by many that my command could have rendered more service had it been in advance of the army the first day at Gettysburg, and the commanding general complains of a want of cavalry on the occasion; but it must be remembered that the cavalry (Jenkins' brigade) specially selected for advance guard to the army by the commanding general on account of its geographical location at the time, was available for this purpose, and had two batteries of horse artillery serving with it. If therefore, the peculiar functions of cavalry with the army were not satisfactorily performed in the absence of my command, it should rather be attributed to the fact that Jenkins' brigade was not as efficient as it ought to have been, and as its numbers (3,800) on leaving Virginia warranted us in expecting. Even at that time, by its reduction incident to campaign, it numbered far more than the cavalry which successfully covered Jackson's flank movement at Chancellorsville, turned back Stoneman from the James, and drove 3,500 cavalry under Averell across the Rappahannock. Properly handled, such a command should have done everything requisite, and left nothing to detract by the remotest implication from the brilliant exploits of their comrades, achieved under circumstances of great hardship and danger.

Arriving at York, I found that General Early had gone, and it is to be regretted that this officer failed to take any measures by leaving an intelligent scout to watch for my coming or a patrol to meet me, to acquaint me with his destination. He had reason to expect me, and had been directed to look out for me. He heard my guns at Hanover, and correctly conjectured whose they were, but left me no clue to his destination on leaving York, which would have saved me a long and tedious march to Carlisle and thence back to Gettysburg. I was informed by citizens that he was going to Shippensburg.

I still believed that most of our army was before Harrisburg, and justly regarded a march to Carlisle as the most likely to place me in communication with the main army. Besides, as a place for rationing my command, now entirely out, I believed it desirable. The cavalry suffered much in this march, day and night, from loss of sleep, and the horses from fatigue, and, while in Fairfax, for want of forage, not even grass being attainable.

In Fauquier, the rough character of the roads and lack of facilities for shoeing, added to the casualties of every day's battle and constant wear and tear of man and horse, reduced the command very much in numbers. In this way some regiments were reduced to less than 100 men; yet, when my command arrived at Gettysburg, from the accessions which it received from the weak horses left to follow the command, it took its place in line of battle with a stoutness of heart and firmness of tread impressing one with the confidence of victory which was astounding, considering the hardness of the march lately endured.[3]

Jeb Stuart's report was written on August 20, 1863, six weeks after the end of the battle of Gettysburg. By then, Stuart had already received a great deal of blame for the Confederate defeat in Pennsylvania. Wade Hampton, who succeeded Stuart in command of the Army of Northern Virginia's cavalry corps in 1864 following Stuart's mortal wounding at Yellow Tavern, was anything but kind in describing the veracity of Stuart's report. "I never read a more erroneous—to call it no harsher name—one than it was," he wrote.[4] Hampton's caustic assessment was only the beginning.

In 1887, Col. Charles Marshall, who served as Robert E. Lee's military secretary for most of the war, made a stunning revelation at a dinner party. The guests included several former Confederate generals, so conversation naturally turned to the Late Unpleasantness. The battle of Gettysburg was one of the primary topics discussed. During the course of the conversation Marshall revealed that he had tried to have Jeb Stuart court-martialed for his role in the campaign.

"Who?" asked more than one of the stunned guests. "Not J. E. B. Stuart?"

"Yes, J. E. B. Stuart," replied Marshall.

Colonel David G. McIntosh, the evening's host, left the following detailed account of Marshall's words:

It was my habit and duty to prepare Genl. Lee's reports, that is a skeleton, which he would upon submission to him, modify as he saw fit, and to this and all the official reports from corps commanders down to Captains of infantry companies were referred to me, and I carefully read them and would oftentimes to reconcile conflicting statements, and to enable me to do this would frequently have to send for different officers, point out in their presence the discrepancies in their reports, and require them to modify and harmonize them. I never could get a report from Stuart of the Gettysburg campaign, I sent for it repeatedly. Finally Genl. Lee said he must have it, and I went to see Stuart; he gave me a first rate dinner—the best he had, but he had no report. He promised however it should be prepared by a certain fixed day, and I then prepared a report for Genl. Lee. I dealt with Stuart in the plainest language, in fact I had told him before that I thought he ought to be shot. Genl. Lee was unwilling however to adopt my draft. I had charged upon him explicit disobedience of orders, and laid the full responsibility at his door.

Marshall went on to describe in detail the orders Stuart rec'd. That they were given to him to move forward along our flanks and that after Genl. Lee had crossed into Maryland and Genl. Stuart had not occupied the position he was expected to, another explicit order was given him on the most peremptory terms as to the course of his march, and that in the very face of these orders, he had seconding to his own confession pursued a different course. In declining to adopt Marshall's report prepared for him, Genl. Lee did not question the accuracy of the facts as stated by his Aide, but said (as I understood Marshall) that he could not adopt the conclusions, or perhaps charge him with the facts as stated, unless or until they should be established by a court martial. He then added that Genl. Lee was excessively fond of Stuart, as he was himself, that he was a most noble, loveable man, and he then described how Genl. Lee was affected at hearing of Stuart's death, leaning forward and putting both hands over his face for some time to conceal his emotion. At this point Marshall himself became much moved as did those who were present.[5]

Marshall left one other interesting comment regarding James Longstreet's role in the cavalier's ride. "During this recital Marshall spoke very pointedly of how Genl. Longstreet acted and talked as if Stuart and all the cavalry were under his, Longstreet's orders and directives, when there was no sort of ground for such a pretention."[6]

Marshall penned two reports for the Gettysburg Campaign. The first was dated July 31, 1863. Here is what Marshall wrote that is of interest to this discussion:

General Stuart was left to guard the passes of the mountains and observe the movements of the enemy, whom he was instructed to harass and impede as much as possible, should he attempt to cross the Potomac. In that event, General Stuart was directed to move into Maryland, crossing the Potomac east or west of the Blue Ridge, as, in his judgment, should be best, and take position on the right of our column as it advanced.[7]

Colonel Charles Marshall, Lee's military secretary. He was the author of the fateful orders that sent Stuart on his infamous ride.

Tulane University

Lee's former military secretary continued: "General Stuart continued to follow the movements of the Federal Army south of the Potomac, after our own had entered Maryland, and, in his efforts to impede its progress, advanced as far eastward as Fairfax Court-House. Finding himself unable to delay the enemy materially, he crossed the river at Seneca, and marched through Westminster to Carlisle, where he arrived after General Ewell had left for Gettysburg. By the route he pursued, the Federal Army was interposed between his command and our main body, preventing any communication with him until his arrival at Carlisle. The march toward Gettysburg was conducted more slowly than it would have been had the movements of the Federal Army been known."[8] This preliminary report was very matter-of-fact, and did not so much as offer a hint of condemnation of Stuart for the manner in which he conducted his expedition.

However, in January 1864, Marshall penned a more detailed Gettysburg report. This time he set up Stuart's ride with his own personal interpretation of Stuart's operational orders:

> General Stuart was directed to hold the mountain passes with part of his command as long as the enemy remained south of the Potomac, and, with the remainder, to cross into Maryland, and place himself

on the right of General Ewell. Upon the suggestion of the former officer that he could damage the enemy and delay his passage of the river by getting in his rear, he was authorized to do so, and it was left to his discretion whether to enter Maryland east or west of the Blue Ridge; but he was instructed to lose no time in placing his command on the right of our column as soon as he should perceive the enemy moving northward.

Marshall continued by condemning the lack of communication flowing from Stuart: "The cavalry force at this time with the army, consisting of Jenkins' brigade and [E. V.] White's battalion, was not greater than was required to accompany the advance of General Ewell and General Early, with whom it performed valuable service, as appears from their reports. It was expected that as soon as the Federal Army should cross the Potomac, General Stuart would give notice of its movements, and nothing having been heard from him since our entrance into Maryland, it was inferred that the enemy had not yet left Virginia."[9]

Marshall went on to condemn Stuart's conduct during the campaign. "The movements of the army preceding the battle of Gettysburg," began Marshall,

had been much embarrassed by the absence of the cavalry. As soon as it was known that the enemy had crossed into Maryland, orders were sent to the brigades of [Beverly H.] Robertson and [William E.] Jones, which had been left to guard the passes of the Blue Ridge, to rejoin the army without delay, and it was expected that General Stuart, with the remainder of his command, would soon arrive. In the exercise of the discretion given him when Longstreet and Hill marched into Maryland, General Stuart determined to pass around the rear of the Federal Army with three brigades and cross the Potomac between it and Washington, believing that he would be able, by that route, to place himself on our right flank in time to keep us properly advised of the enemy's movements. He marched from Salem on the night of June 24, intending to pass west of Centreville, but found the enemy's forces so distributed as to render that route impracticable. Adhering to his original plan, he was forced to make a wide *detour* through Buckland and Brentsville, and crossed the Occoquan at Wolf Run Shoals on the morning of the 27th. Continuing his march through Fairfax Court-House and Dranesville, he arrived at the Potomac, below the mouth of Seneca Creek, in the evening.

He found the river much swollen by the recent rains, but, after great exertion, gained the Maryland shore before midnight with his whole command.

He now ascertained that the Federal Army, which he had discovered to be drawing toward the Potomac, had crossed the day before, and was moving toward Frederick, thus interposing itself between him and our forces.

He accordingly marched northward, through Rockville and Westminster, to Hanover, Pa., where he arrived on the 30th; but the enemy advanced with equal rapidity on his left, and continued to obstruct communication with our main body.

Supposing, from such information as he could obtain, that part of the army was at Carlisle, he left Hanover that night, and proceeded thither by way of Dover.

He reached Carlisle on July 1, where he received orders to proceed to Gettysburg. He arrived in the afternoon of the following day, and took position on General Ewell's left. His leading brigade, under General Hampton, encountered and repulsed a body of the enemy's cavalry at Hunterstown, endeavoring to reach our rear.

General Stuart had several skirmishes during his march, and at Hanover quite a severe engagement took place with a strong force of cavalry, which was finally compelled to withdraw from the town. The prisoners taken by the cavalry and paroled at various places amounted to about 800, and at Rockville a large train of wagons coming from Washington was intercepted and captured. Many of them were destroyed, but 125, with all the animals of the train, were secured.

The ranks of the cavalry were much reduced by its long and arduous march, repeated conflicts, and insufficient supplies of food and forage, but the day after its arrival at Gettysburg it engaged the enemy's cavalry with unabated spirit, and effectually protected our left.[10]

As strong as his wording was, General Lee almost certainly toned down Marshall's vitriol.[11] Although the commanding general's report lavishly praised the performance of many of the Army of Northern Virginia's subordinate commanders, praise for Stuart was muted at best. Marshall shed some light on how Lee handled this sensitive matter:

The official report of General Lee is I believe substantially true, as far as it goes. But it is not complete in many particulars which should be known to understand the campaign fully. He struck from the original draft many statements which he thought might affect injuriously, his sense of justice frequently leading him to what many considered too great a degree of lenience. It is well known that he assumed the entire responsibility of the issue of the battle of Gettysburg, and thus covered the errors and omissions of all of his officers. He declined to embody in his report anything that might seem to cast the blame of the result upon others, and in answer to my appeal to allow some statements which I deemed material to remain in the report, he said he disliked in such a communication to say aught to the prejudice of others, unless the truth of such statements had been established by an investigation in which those affected by them had been afforded an opportunity to defend or justify their actions.[12]

If Marshall was telling the truth, Lee sanitized his report to remove Marshall's stongest criticisms of the actions of several subordinates, Stuart and Longstreet among them.

In January 1897, Marshall gave an address to the Confederate Veteran Association of Washington, D.C., on the occasion of Robert E. Lee's birthday. The address was printed in two installments for the popular "Our Confederate Column" in *The Richmond Dispatch*.[13] Many facets of the Gettysburg Campaign were discussed, but most of his long speech was devoted to the movements of Lee's army prior to the battle. Marshall wasted little time voicing his opinion of Stuart's ride. "As the movement of the cavalry at this time has been much discussed," began Lee's military secretary,

and perhaps had more to do with the events that immediately followed than any other circumstance, I shall confine myself in stating those movements to the contemporaneous orders and correspondence.

That a great error was committed in the movements of General Stuart cannot be questioned. The object of the movement proposed by him in the rear of the enemy was to strike the line of the latter, who was then marching towards the Potomac from opposite Fredericksburg, his line of march being east of the Bull Run Mountains, and it will be observed that while General Stuart had the discretion to cross the Potomac river, either east or west of the Blue Ridge, his instructions to lose no time in placing his command on the right of our column as soon as he should perceive the enemy moving northward, were imperative.[14]

Marshall went on to read Lee's June 22 orders to Stuart. Thereafter, Marshall asserted that Stuart was under Longstreet's orders:

> This order was sent through General Longstreet, under whose immediate command General Stuart then was, leaving General Longstreet to decide whether the cavalry could be spared to execute the order, and also to direct how it should best move to carry it out in view of the state of things existing when the order was delivered to General Stuart.

> The letter of General Lee to General Stuart, however, shows that when it was written General Lee expected that General Stuart would pass with all of his cavalry, except two brigades, to the west of the Blue Ridge, and cross the Potomac on that side of the mountains . . .[15]

After reading Longstreet's June 22 letter to Stuart for his listeners, Marshall continued:

> In effect, General Longstreet tells General Stuart that he had better not leave the army unless he could take the proposed route in the "rear of the enemy" and his "suggestion" substantially amounted to an order to Stuart not to leave the army for the purpose of crossing into Maryland as directed by General Lee's letter, unless he could do so by that route.[16]

Marshall then read Lee's second order, dated June 23, and explained that it left no room for doubt as to how Stuart was to proceed. This explicit order precluded any movement by Stuart that would prevent him from "feeling the right of Ewell's troops," after crossing the Potomac, and it was the last order General Stuart received before leaving Virginia:

> In any case, General Stuart, after crossing the Potomac, was to put himself on the right flank of General Ewell, and that any movement on the part of the former which tended to prevent this was entirely inconsistent with General Lee's reiterated instructions. So, that, under this restriction, General Stuart was practically instructed not to cross the Potomac east of the Federal army, and thus interpose that army between himself and the right of General Ewell.[17]

Marshall continued by telling his listeners that any delays Stuart suffered were brought upon himself by not following Lee's orders, and that Stuart completely misinterpreted his own role in the army's movement north:

> General Stuart appears to have thought that his movement was intended to threaten Washington. He lost much valuable time in pursuing and capturing trains coming from that city to General Hooker's army, but as he moved northward the Federal army was also moving northward on his left, and separating him from the right of the Confederate army, where it was all important that the cavalry should be.
>
> The line of march taken by General Stuart on the right of the enemy brought on several skirmishes, which consumed much more time, the consequences of the loss of which will be presently described.
>
> Considerable delay was also caused in an effort to save the captured wagon train... The movement of General Stuart, as will be perceived, left the army which had passed into Maryland with no cavalry, except the brigade of Jenkins's and White's battalion, which accompanied General Ewell. It could not look for supplies in a hostile country, except by the use of artillery and wagon-horses, of which, of course, but a small number could be spared for that purpose, and it was, as we shall see, entirely without knowledge of the enemy's movements.[18]

Having set the hook, Marshall softened the importance of the cavalry brigades left with Lee and continued his indictment of Stuart by describing the commanding general's growing anxieties about the intention and location of the Federal army. "General Lee had the most implicit confidence in the vigilance and enterprise of General Stuart," explained Marshall. He continued:

> He had not heard from him since the army left Virginia, and was confident from that fact, in view of the positive orders that Stuart had received, that General Hooker's army had not yet crossed the Potomac. He remained at Chambersburg from the 27th to the 29th, and repeatedly observed while there that the enemy's army must still be in Virginia, as he had heard nothing from Stuart.
>
> Assuming that such was the fact, and that the movement of the Confederate army into Pennsylvania had failed to withdraw that of

General Hooker from Virginia, contrary to his confident expectations, General Lee began to become uneasy as to the purpose of the Federal commander, and to fear that he contemplated a strong movement against Richmond.

He remarked that such a proceeding on the part of the enemy would compel the immediate return of his own army to Virginia, if it could, indeed, reach Richmond in time to defend the city. The possession of Richmond was absolutely necessary at that time to preserve communication with the South, and its loss would have led to the evacuation of the whole of Eastern Virginia, at least as far south as the Roanoke. I heard General Lee express this apprehension more than once while we lay at Chambersburg, and the apprehension was due entirely to his hearing nothing from General Stuart. Under these circumstances he determined to take such action as would compel the enemy to leave Virginia, and deter him from any attempt upon Richmond. General Longstreet's Corps was at Chambersburg with the commanding general. General A.P. Hill's Corps was about four miles east of Chambersburg on the road to Gettysburg. General Ewell was then at Carlisle. On the night of the 28th of June I was directed by General Lee to order General Ewell to move directly upon Harrisburg, and to inform him that General Longstreet would move the next morning (the 29th) to his support. General A.P. Hill was directed to move eastward to the Susquehanna, and, crossing the river below Harrisburg, seize the railroad between Harrisburg and Philadelphia, it being supposed that all reinforcements that might be coming from the North would be diverted to the defence of that city, and that there would be such alarm created by these movements that the Federal Government would be obliged to withdraw its army from Virginia and abandon any plan that it might have for an attack upon Richmond.

Marshall explained that he sent off Lee's orders to Generals Ewell and Hill, and then was called to Lee's tent, where he found his commander involved in a conversation with "a man in citizen's dress, whom I did not know to be a soldier." The man was Henry T. Harrison, Longstreet's paid scout. Harrison had important information for Lee: the Federal army had already crossed the Potomac in force, Joe Hooker was gone, and George G. Meade was now in command.[19] The news, Marshall explained, was "the first information that General Lee had received since he left Virginia." Based on Harrison's intelligence, Lee directed Marshall to countermand the orders to the corps commanders. A. P. Hill was to "move eastward on the road through Cashtown and Gettysburg," and

Richard Ewell would "march from Carlisle, so as to form a junction with Hill either at Cashtown or Gettysburg." Longstreet was to follow Hill.[20]

Having explained for his listeners the state of affairs only 48 hours prior to the opening of the battle, Marshall postulated what may have been—if only Stuart had maintained contact with Lee's army:

> The army moved very slowly, and there would have been no difficulty whatever in having the whole of it at Gettysburg by the morning of the 1st of July had we been aware of the movements of the enemy on the other side of the mountains.
>
> You will thus see that the movement to Gettysburg was the result of the want of information, which the cavalry alone could obtain for us, and that General Lee was compelled to march through the mountains from Chambersburg eastward without the slightest knowledge of the enemy's movements, except that brought by the scout....
>
> It would have been entirely within the power of General Lee to have met the army of the enemy while it was moving on the road between Frederick and Gettysburg, or to have remained west of the mountains. It had not been his intention to deliver a battle north of the Potomac, if it could be avoided, except upon his own terms, and yet, by reason of the absence of the cavalry, his own army marching slowly eastward from Chambersburg, and southward from Carlisle, came unexpectedly on the Federal advance on the 1st day of July, a considerable part of the Confederate army having not yet reached the field of battle.[21]

With all the pieces in place, Marshall delivered his *coup de grace* by laying the blame for what unfolded at Gettysburg at Jeb Stuart's feet:

> It has been my object to correct the impression that has prevailed to some extent that the movement of the cavalry was made by General Lee's orders, and that at a critical moment of the campaign he crossed the Potomac river and moved into Pennsylvania, sending the entire cavalry force of his army upon a useless raid. That this is not true I think the evidence I have laid before you abundantly establishes. The suggestion of General Longstreet in communicating the order of General Lee to General Stuart that the latter should pass by the enemy's rear need not have led to the results which I have described...

The first movement of General Stuart after leaving Salem Depot early on the morning of the 25th brought him in conflict with General Hancock's brigade [*sic*], near Haymarket, and finding that he could not pass around the rear of the enemy, the discretion so given him by General Longstreet was at an end, and there was yet time for General Stuart to retrace his steps and obey the order that he had received from General Lee in the letter of the 23rd of June, to cross the Potomac west of the Blue Ridge and move on until he felt the right of Ewell's column. But, instead of pursuing this course, General Stuart, as I have already pointed out, moved to Buckland, east of Bull Run mountains, and proceeded to that place through Brentsville, down to Wolf-Run shoals, and thence across the country by way of Fairfax Station to the Potomac river. This latter movement was not sanctioned either by the suggestion of General Longstreet or by the positive orders of General Lee, and from the tenor of Stuart's report it would seem that he entirely mistook the part that he was expected to take in the movement of the army. He placed himself east of the Federal army, with that army between his command and the Confederate force. He left General Lee without any information as to the movements of the enemy from the time he crossed the Potomac river until the 2nd of July.

By his silence, as I have described, he caused General Lee to move his army to Gettysburg, not with the expectation or purpose of meeting the enemy, but simply to prevent a movement which he supposed the enemy was making to obstruct his line of communication with Virginia, and caused him to fight the battle of Gettysburg without having his whole force present except on the third day, when it was equally possible, had General Lee been informed of what the enemy was doing, for him to have fought that battle with his entire force while the enemy's forces were approaching Gettysburg.[22]

With the flair and dramatics of a great orator, Marshall concluded his address with a strong parting shot intended to show that Stuart's ride had dissected the Southern army at a critical moment in time: "The result of General Stuart's action was that two armies invaded Pennsylvania in 1863, instead of one. One of those armies had no cavalry, the other had nothing but cavalry. One was commanded by General Lee, the other by General Stuart."[23]

In his later years, Marshall wrote a memoir of his service during the Civil War. He saved most of his venom for this volume. By the time *Lee's Aide-De-Camp* was published both Lee and Stuart (and most of the major players) had been dead for many years, meaning that Marshall was free to castigate the cavalier without fear of recriminations from anyone. He did so with gusto. In fact, Marshall vented his spleen and laid the blame for the defeat at Gettysburg squarely upon the shoulders of Jeb Stuart. First, however, Marshall set forth his version of General Lee's expectations for Stuart's ride in detailed fashion. Marshall wrote the following in reference to the letter of June 22, 1863:

> After this letter was sent off General Lee explained to me that he had had a conversation with General Stuart when he left him near Paris, and that his own view was to leave some cavalry in Snicker's and Ashby's Gaps to watch the army of General Hooker, and to take the main body of the cavalry with General Stuart to accompany the army into Pennsylvania. It is much to be regretted that this course was not pursued. General Lee added that Stuart suggested that he could move down with his cavalry near Hooker, and annoy him if he attempted to cross the river, and when he found that he was crossing he could rejoin the army in good time.
>
> General Lee said that General Longstreet thought well of the suggestion and had assented, but he added that he had told General Stuart that, as soon as he found that General Hooker was crossing the Potomac, he must immediately cross himself and take his place on our right flank as we moved north. General Lee then told me that he was anxious that there should be no misunderstanding on General Stuart's part, and that there should be no delay in his joining us as soon as General Hooker had crossed. He said that in reflecting on the subject, while it had occurred to him that it might be possible for General Stuart, when the time came for him to cross the river, to cross east of the Blue Ridge and above General Hooker, thus avoiding the delay of returning through Snicker's or Ashby's Gap and crossing above Harpers Ferry, yet he added that circumstances might prevent Stuart from crossing east of the Blue Ridge. He said that he desired to impress upon General Stuart the importance of his rejoining the army with the least possible delay as soon as General Hooker had crossed, and he then directed me to write to General Stuart expressing these views.[24]

Having set the stage, Marshall attacked. He explained the operational orders for the expedition and assaulted Stuart's conduct:

> General Lee's letter to General Stuart, which I have quoted, and which General Stuart received through General Longstreet,

contained an order to the former, in case he found that the enemy was moving northward and that he could protect his rear with two brigades of his force, to move the other three into Maryland and take position on General Ewell's right, place himself in communication with him, guard his flank, and keep him informed of the enemy's movements. This order was sent through General Longstreet, that he might decide whether cavalry could be spared to execute the order, and also that he might direct how the cavalry should best move to carry it out, in view of the state of things existing when the order was delivered to General Stuart.

General Lee's letter, however, shows that when it was written, he expected that General Stuart would pass, with all his cavalry except two brigades, to the west of the Blue Ridge, and cross the Potomac on that side of the mountains, leaving two brigades in the gaps to guard his rear as long as the enemy threatened to attempt to penetrate through the gaps into the Valley.

The letter which General Lee sent to General Ewell informing that officer of the order to be given to Stuart, if General Longstreet decided that Stuart could be spared, makes it very clear that General Lee assumed that Stuart would cross into Maryland and put himself on Ewell's right.[25]

There were inconsistencies between Lee's June 22 order and Longstreet's of the same day, which Marshall pointed out in detail:

This letter of General Longstreet's appears to have been entirely controlled by the idea that General Stuart was to cross the Potomac in such a way as would best conceal the movements of the Confederate army, but it does not notice the positive instruction contained in General Lee's letter to General Stuart, that should the latter cross the Potomac he was to place himself as speedily as possible, after the enemy began to move northwards, upon General Ewell's right.

General Longstreet's suggestion that he should proceed by way of the enemy's rear to reach the Potomac and cross into Maryland contemplated the possibility of the entire detachment of the cavalry from the rest of the army. To obey the order, Stuart had to pass through the Bull Run mountains across the enemy's line of march from the Rappahannock to the Potomac river, if the way was open. That line of march was east of the Bull Run mountains. The cavalry under Stuart was on the east side of the Blue Ridge, and the enemy was already known to be assembling on the Potomac in Loudoun, so that Stuart's march as proposed by General Longstreet would take the cavalry east of the Bull Run mountains and bring it to the Potomac river, below where the enemy's army was concentrated. This might readily prove to be inconsistent with the chief aim of the movement ordered by General Lee, which was that General Stuart should place himself on the right of General Ewell after crossing the river, for there was evident danger that if General Stuart acted under the orders of General Longstreet and the enemy should cross the Potomac before General Stuart, the latter would be separated from General Ewell, who was moving west of the Blue Ridge.[26]

Interestingly, Marshall acknowledged that these inconsistencies were one of the causes for the manner in which future events unfolded. He recited the contents of the June 23 order verbatim, and then resumed his attack against Stuart:

> This letter was written and received before General Stuart started on his march "around the rear of the enemy," and was General Lee's last direction to him before the army left Virginia. It covers the case of the Federal commander remaining inactive, and also that of his not moving northward. In the former event Stuart was to leave two brigades to watch him and with the other three to withdraw, and in the latter event Stuart's whole command was to be withdrawn "this side of the mountains to-morrow" across the Potomac at Shepherdstown and move toward Fredericktown the next day.
>
> The order leaves Stuart to decide whether he can move around the Federal Army in either eventuality, without hindrance, doing it all the damage he can, and cross east of the mountains. In either case, after crossing the river, Stuart is directed to move on and feel the right of Ewell's troops, collecting information, etc.
>
> Whether Stuart should cross the Potomac at Shepherdstown, or in the exercise of the discretion given him, pass around the rear of the enemy and cross the Potomac east of the mountains, he was ordered unconditionally "after crossing the river" to move on and "feel the right of Ewell's troops." This explicit order precluded any movement by Stuart that would prevent him from "feeling the right of Ewell's troops" after crossing the Potomac. So that under these restrictions he was practically instructed not to cross the Potomac east of the Federal Army, and thus interpose that army between himself and right of General Ewell. There were places where the Potomac could be crossed between the enemy's army, at or near Edwards Ferry, and the Blue Ridge, and General Stuart had

discretion to use the fords east of the Blue Ridge, but he had no discretion to use any ford that would place the enemy's army between him and the troops of General Ewell.[27]

Marshall quoted extensively from Stuart's report of the Gettysburg Campaign as evidence of how the cavalier failed to obey his orders. After the lengthy quotations from Stuart's report, Marshall pitched into the cavalry chief. "During the winter of 1863-4 while we lay on the Rapidan," explained Marshall,

> I was engaged in preparing the report on the Gettysburg campaign. I had received all the reports of the infantry and artillery commanders, and I was only waiting for General Stuart's, to complete General Lee's official report. Some delay took place, and General Stuart was applied to more than once. He said he was busy preparing it, and promised me several times to send it in. General Lee was urging me to prepare his report before active operations should be resumed, and I think that when I told him the cause of the delay, he either wrote or spoke to General Stuart on the subject himself. I know that I was unable to complete and forward General Lee's report until some time in January or February 1864. At last General Stuart brought in his report and asked me to read it carefully, and to tell him what I thought of his conduct.

> In speaking of his having crossed the Potomac east of General Hooker on June 27th, instead of between Hooker and Harpers Ferry, General Stuart stated that he had at one time contemplated a dash on Washington, but did not undertake it because his orders were to join the infantry as soon as possible. He further stated that his orders had been to place his command on the right of our line of ranks, but argued that had he done so, he would have attracted the enemy's cavalry, which was more numerous than his, to that quarter. He said they could have broken through the mountains at some pass, as he was not strong enough to hold all, and thus endangered our trains which were moving north on the west side of the Catoctin. General Stuart asked me if I did not consider his excuse for not putting himself on our right satisfactory, alleging that his movement had drawn the enemy's cavalry away from the Catoctin to watch him, and thus secured our trains.

> I told him that I thought it would have been far better for him to have obeyed his orders; that General Lee had not ordered him to protect our trains, but had disposed his infantry so as to do that, most of the trains having crossed at Williamsport, while Hill's corps or most of

it crossed at Shepherdstown, and moved through Sharpsburg, to Hagerstown, thus keeping between the trains and the enemy, while the trains were so distributed that infantry support was near all parts of the line.

Marshall, who was trained as an attorney, continued to set forth his case against Stuart:

> I called his attention to the fact that the great object of having his cavalry on our right was to keep us informed of the enemy's movements. I pointed out the disastrous consequences of our being without cavalry to get information for us, and the fact that, owing to our not hearing from him, General Lee had been led to believe that General Hooker had not crossed the Potomac for several days after that event had occurred. I told him how General Lee, being confident that he would give him immediate information of Hooker's crossing, had assumed from not receiving the information that Hooker had not crossed and acted on that belief.
>
> Stuart said that when he crossed at Rowser's Ferry, and found that Hooker had crossed the day before above him, he had sent a dispatch to General Lee back by way of Ashby's Gap. We never got that dispatch, and, as I showed him, if we had, still we had no cavalry to get information for us.
>
> General Stuart admitted that he had made the movement at his own discretion, and that he had General Lee's letter written by me. He said that he was confident that he could get around Hooker and join us in Pennsylvania before the two armies could meet.
>
> I mention these facts to show that General Stuart felt it necessary to defend his course, which he would not have done had he been justified by his orders.[28]

Marshall concluded his condemnation of Stuart by characteristically placing all of the blame for the defeat at Gettysburg squarely on the cavalier's decision to complete the ride around Joe Hooker's army. Marshall's condemnation followed his address to the Confederate Veteran Association nearly verbatim, except that he tempered his final salvo by crediting Lee with having *some* cavalry at his disposal: "The result of General Stuart's action was that two armies invaded Pennsylvania in 1863, instead of one. One of those armies had little cavalry, the other had nothing but cavalry. One was commanded by General Lee, the other by General Stuart."[29]

Of significant interest is that fact that Marshall admitted there was a third previously *unpublished* order sent to Stuart on June 23, 1863.[30] With this damning condemnation, the controversy began in earnest.

* * *

Lieutenant Colonel Walter Herron Taylor, Lee's trusted adjutant, also felt obliged to comment at length on the wisdom of Stuart's decisions during the execution of his infamous ride. In his first postwar memoir published in 1877, he described the movements of the Army of Northern Virginia through June 27 before turning his pen against Stuart:

> With the exception of the cavalry, the army was well in hand. The absence of that indispensable arm of the service was most seriously felt by General Lee. He had directed General Stuart to use his discretion as to where and when to cross the river— that is, he was to cross east of the mountains, or retire through the mountain passes into the Valley and cross in the immediate rear of the infantry, as the movements of the enemy and his own judgment should determine—but he was expected to maintain communication with the main column, and especially directed to keep the commanding general informed of the movements of the Federal army.[31]

Lieutenant Colonel Walter H. Taylor, Lee's faithful adjutant. Although he never explicitly blamed Stuart for the Gettysburg loss, a reading of his postwar writings leaves no doubt he intended to divert blame from General Lee.

National Archives

Referring to the opening fighting at Gettysburg on July 1, Taylor made his case against the army's former cavalry chief:

> No tidings whatever had been received from or of our cavalry under General Stuart since crossing the river; and General Lee was consequently without accurate information on the movements or position of the main Federal army. An army without cavalry in a strange and hostile country is as a man deprived of his eyesight and beset by enemies; he may never be so brave and strong, but he cannot intelligently administer a single effective blow.[32]

Although Taylor did not explicitly blame Stuart for the defeat at Gettysburg, his intent was not difficult to divine. Lee's former adjutant blamed Stuart's ride for the lack of effective intelligence about the dispositions of the enemy army.

Thirty years later Taylor published a second memoir entitled *General Lee: His Campaigns in Virginia 1861 to 1865, with Personal Reminiscences.*[33] Instead of focusing on his service with Lee, this time around Taylor focused on the war itself, with a concentration on the Confederate commander's role in history. Taylor also expanded upon his previous analysis of the impact of the absence of Stuart and his horsemen. After describing the movement of the Army of Northern Virginia into Pennsylvania, he wrote the following:

> The cavalry force at this time with the army, consisting of Jenkins' brigade and a battalion under Colonel E. V. White, was operating with the advance of General Ewell's columns. No report had reached General Lee from General Stuart, who was ordered to give notice of the movements of the Federal army should it cross the Potomac; and as nothing had been heard from him, General Lee naturally concluded the enemy had not yet left Virginia. His confidence in General Stuart, who was so active, so vigilant, so reliable, was such as to reassure him and remove all solicitude concerning the movements of the enemy. Great was his surprise and annoyance, therefore, when on the 28th he received information from one of his scouts to the effect that the Federal army had crossed the Potomac and was approaching South Mountain. How materially different his plans would have been had he been kept informed of the movements of his adversary will never be known. Yet there is no word of censure in his official report, only a simple statement of the fact; a striking illustration of his tendency to always suppress all consideration of self and to spare the feelings and

reputation of others. His confidence in General Stuart was unlimited, and his admiration for him deservedly great. He realized that he made mistakes himself, and he was tolerant of those of others. His one great aim and endeavor was to secure success for the cause in which he was enlisted; all else was made subordinate to this. No possible good to the cause would result from exposing the errors of judgment of others, or by indulging in useless regrets at what had happened and was beyond recall. The possible effect upon himself of silence in such a case never operated as a motive to cause him to interpose another to shield him from the responsibility that he always assumed for the operations of the army under his command.[34]

Taylor offered these additional remarks regarding the impact on the army as a whole of not having Stuart's horse soldiers available:

In the absence of the cavalry it was impossible to ascertain the purpose of the enemy; but to deter him from advancing further west and intercepting our communication with Virginia, General Lee determined to concentrate his army east of the mountains. General Hill was ordered on June 29th to move to Cashtown, and General Longstreet was directed to follow the next day. On the morning of the 30th General Heth, who had arrived at Cashtown, sent Pettigrew's brigade to Gettysburg to procure supplies, where it encountered the enemy. This was a surprise, and being ignorant of the nature and extent of this force, General Pettigrew retired on the main body of the division.[35]

Implied, but not stated, is the idea that if Stuart been where he was supposed to be (i.e., with the army), Lee would have had accurate intelligence as to the dispositions of the Federals and would not have concentrated the army at Gettysburg. Taylor was consistent in his criticism of Stuart's conduct.

Although General Lee did not write on the subject before he died in 1870, at least one observer claimed the general also blamed Stuart for misconstruing his orders and taking liberties with them. In April 1868, Col. William Allen sat down for a discussion with Lee about the Gettysburg Campaign. Allen recorded what Lee told him. This makes Allen's account especially valuable because it is the only extant evidence that Lee disapproved of Stuart's conduct.

In response to a question about why he fought and lost Gettysburg, Lee (according to Allen) explained he did not intend to give battle in Pennsylvania "if he could avoid it." He continued:

> The South was too weak to carry on a war of invasion, and his offensive movements against the North were never intended except as parts of a defensive system. He did not know the Federal army was at Gettysburg, *could not believe it*, as Stuart had been specifically ordered to cover his (Lee's) movements, and keep him informed of the enemy's position and he (Stuart) had sent no word. He found himself engaged with the Federal Army, therefore, unexpectedly, and had to fight.

Allen also noted that General Lee explained that once the battle commenced, "victory would have been won if he could have gotten one decided, simultaneous attack along the whole line. This he tried his uttermost for three days and failed." Lee supposedly blamed Gens. Hill, Ewell, Longstreet, Robert Rodes, Early, and Edward Johnson for failing to coordinate their assaults. He also acknowledged he would have been unable to maintain his army in Pennsylvania all summer. Allegedly, Lee told Allen that "Stuart's failure to carry out his intentions forced the battle of Gettysburg, and the imperfect, halting way in which his corps commanders (and especially Ewell) fought the battle gave the final victory, which Lee says teetered for three days in the balance, to Meade and the Army of the Potomac."[36]

*   *   *

As time passed, it became *de rigueur* to blame Stuart for the disaster that befell the Army of Northern Virginia in Pennsylvania. Major General Henry Heth, whose division triggered the fighting west of town on the first day of the battle and was himself a target of criticism for initiating the combat, was a cousin of Robert E. Lee's. An unabashed admirer of Lee, Heth was known as the only man in the Army of Northern Virginia whom Lee called by his first name. It should come as no surprise that Heth stoutly defended Lee's conduct of the battle. "The failure to crush the Federal army in Pennsylvania in 1863, in the opinion of almost all of the officers of the Army of Northern Virginia, can be expressed in five words—*the absence of our cavalry* [emphasis added]," proclaimed

Heth. His criticism was severe and unambiguous. "Train a giant for an encounter and he can be whipped by a pygmy—if you put out his eyes. The eyes of an army are its cavalry. . . . It is thus evident that so far as deriving any assistance from his cavalry from the [twenty-fourth] of June to the evening of July 2, it might as well have had no existence. The eyes of the giant were out," Heth continued. "He knew not where to strike; a movement in any direction might prove a disastrous blunder."

Heth concluded his assessment with his strongest condemnation of all. "Had our cavalry been in position, the chances are that the battle never would have been fought at Gettysburg; but whether there or elsewhere, the battle would have been planned and digested with that consummate skill and boldness which characterized the plans of the greatest of American soldiers in his seven days' fights around Richmond, his discomfiture of Pope, his Chancellorsville fight, and his series of battles in 1864, from the Wilderness to Cold Harbor."[37]

*   *   *

Another major general and a staunch Lee defender was Jubal A. Early. The attorney-soldier eagerly looked for any scapegoat upon whom to pin the blame for the loss at Gettysburg. Early set his sights on two men: James Longstreet and Jeb Stuart. Perhaps his attacks upon the cavalryman came about from Early's own failure to communicate with Stuart at York. Was Early trying to misdirect criticism of his own conduct by blaming Stuart?

Early at least tried to appear evenhanded. He defended Stuart's decision to try and pass around Joe Hooker's army. Early conceded that Stuart's decision to cross east of the Blue Ridge had the desired effect of causing some confusion in the Federal rear, but went on to declare that cavalry raids were generally ineffective because they tended to "degenerate into mere marauding parties that merely annoyed the enemy without causing serious damage while the raiders came out badly worsted, at least in horseflesh; which latter was a very important consideration on our side." Early's nasty streak showed itself when he added, "The Dutch farmers and house-wives in Pennsylvania were probably very badly frightened, but the loss in disabled cavalry horses, which were left behind in exchange for useless Dutch farm horses, was not compensated by any damage to the enemy."[38]

Lieutenant General James Longstreet, Lee's senior corps commander during the Gettysburg Campaign. He was the officer responsible for the idea that led to Jeb Stuart's controversial ride into Pennsylvania.

Valentine Museum

James Longstreet, Lee's senior subordinate and commander of the First Corps, gave one of the orders that led to Stuart's ride. With the benefit of hindsight bestowed by the passage of time, Longstreet claimed Stuart disregarded Lee's orders by going off on his ride east of the Blue Ridge and around the enemy army. "The raid and the absence of the cavalry at the critical moment were severely criticized through the army and the country," observed Longstreet in his postwar memoirs. "If General Stuart could have claimed authority of my orders for his action, he could not have failed to do so in his official account. He offered no such excuse, but claimed to act under the orders of his chief, and reported that General Lee gave consent to his application for leave to make the march. So our plans, adopted after deep study, were suddenly given over to gratify the youthful cavalryman's wish for a nomadic ride," Longstreet concluded.[39] Longstreet, however, had wholeheartedly endorsed the idea in June 1863, which makes his postwar memoirs disingenuous and in conflict with his contemporaneous writings.

*   *   *

Fitzhugh Lee presents an interesting paradox in the evaluation and critique of Stuart's ride. Fitz Lee was both Gen. Robert E. Lee's favorite nephew and one of his biographers. However, Fitz was also Jeb Stuart's favorite subordinate and his handpicked successor should anything befall the plumed cavalier. Of all of Stuart's subordinates, Fitz most closely resembled him in personality and temperament, and shared Stuart's flamboyant, often cavalier, approach to warfare. Fitz Lee, therefore, was caught in an unenviable conflict of interest. He ultimately decided to publically defend his uncle and blame his friend, though his attacks were tempered, generally well reasoned, and not nearly as sharp as those being delivered by the likes of Henry Heth or Jubal Early. In private, however, Lee told a completely different story.

Although Fitz admitted the expedition was directly authorized, "the move selected was not the best under the circumstances." As soon as Hooker began to cross the Potomac, explained Fitz with years of hindsight as his guide, Stuart "should have marched to the west side of the Blue Ridge, crossed also, and moving rapidly to Lee's front, have placed himself at once in direct communication with him." Fitz further commented that if asked to name the reasons for the campaign's failure, his answer would be as follows: "1st. The absence of General Stuart's cavalry from the army."[40]

Fitz wrote at some length on this issue. As readers will quickly note, he tempered his words by offering at least a patina of defense on behalf of his former superior officer:

> General Lee heard of that event on the night of the 28th June through a scout. Up to that period he thought their army was still in Virginia, because he had heard nothing from Stuart. Knowing as I do Stuart's strict attention to forwarding all species of information, I am bound to believe he did not fail to send the notice of this important fact. It may have miscarried. It has been charged that Stuart disobeyed orders in crossing his command at a lower point on the Potomac than that at which the Federals crossed, and making the circuit which interposed the army of the enemy between his command and the force of General Lee. I deny that. I know that he was left to the exercise of his own discretion. Indeed, General Lee says in his report, that "in the exercise of the discretion given him, when Longstreet and Hill crossed into Maryland, General Stuart determined to pass around the rear of the Federal army with three brigades and cross the Potomac between it and Washington.
>
> Free to act, I think the move selected was not the best under the circumstances. As soon as the Federal army began to cross the river, he should have marched to the west side of the Blue Ridge, crossed

also, and moving rapidly to General Lee's front, have placed himself at once in direct communication with him. His bold activity would have developed the enemy's position, which, General Lee being no longer in ignorance of, could then have made his plans accordingly. In that event the battle would not in all probability have taken place at Gettysburg.

In justice to Stuart, it may be said that he had calculated upon the brigade of Jenkins and White's battalion of cavalry, which accompanied Generals Ewell and Early, and Jones' and Robertson's brigades, which were left to guard the passes of the Blue Ridge, and were to rejoin General Lee as soon as the enemy crossed the river, to do all that was necessary. The brigade of General Jenkins, Stuart estimated at 3,800 troopers when leaving Virginia, and, referring to the complaint of the Commanding General of a want of cavalry upon that occasion, says: "Properly handled such a command should have done every thing requisite."

In reference to the second point I have taken, there is evidence that a staff officer of General Lee carried an order to General Ewell on the afternoon of the 1st of July, that from where he, General Lee, was, he could see the enemy flying over the heights; to push on and occupy them. But in his official report of the operations of that day, General Lee says: "General Ewell was instructed to carry the hill occupied by the enemy if he found it practicable, but to avoid a general engagement until the arrival of the other divisions of the army;" and that Ewell "decided to wait for Johnson's division," of his corps, to get up, which had been left behind to guard the trains, and "did not reach Gettysburg until a late hour," and "in the meantime the enemy occupied the point which General Ewell designed seizing."

At the beginning of the war I occupied the position of chief of staff to General Ewell, and bear too much love for his heroic memory to say more than that I believe a little more marching, perhaps a little more fighting, would have given us the coveted position, and that in such an event the battle of Gettysburg, would have had another name, and possibly another result — who knows? It must be borne in mind, however, that at the time of these operations, I was only a general officer of cavalry, serving under Stuart. My brigade accompanied his movement, and I did not reach Gettysburg until the afternoon of the 2d July, going into line on the extreme left of our army, and fighting the enemy's cavalry in my front on the third.[41]

Given his role as Stuart's favorite and ranking subordinate, his defense of his friend and former commander should come as no surprise.

In a private letter to Stuart's adjutant, Henry B. McClellan, Fitz Lee declared, "Had Gen. Lee the same move to make over again I venture the prediction that Stuart would be kept where he could communicate with him every hour if necessary." The real blame for the loss at Gettysburg, argued Fitz Lee, belonged on Longstreet's shoulders.[42]

In 1894, Fitz Lee published a biography of his uncle, who had been dead for nearly a quarter of a century. The writing was remarkably candid and insightful. "This officer [Stuart] has been unjustly criticized for not being in front of Lee's army at Gettysburg, but Lee and Longstreet must be held responsible for his route," he wrote. "Lee crossed the Potomac west of the Blue Ridge, Hooker east of it, and Stuart between him and Washington."[43]

*　*　*

Another ex-cavalryman who opined on the Stuart's ride imbroglio was Thomas L. Rosser. The Virginian ended the war a major general, but was the colonel of the 5th Virginia Cavalry during the Gettysburg Campaign. Rosser achieved a rank beyond his talents because he was one of Jeb Stuart's favorites and because Stuart arranged for Rosser's promotion over more competent officers like Col. Thomas T. Munford of the 2nd Virginia Cavalry. However, the ungrateful Rosser grew to resent and then despise Stuart because he believed his commander took too long to arrange for his promotion.

Years after the war, Rosser wrote about his patron's performance during the campaign in question. After describing the ride up to and including the fight at Hanover, Rosser noted that "Stuart had been marching constantly, almost day and night, on scant forage and little rest for man or horse, for eight days, within the enemy's lines, and while his conduct displayed a daring almost to recklessness, he accomplished little, save the wear and fatigue of long marches. He had undoubtedly impaired the strength and vigor of his command." He was just beginning to sharpen his pen. "Major McClellan," continued Rosser,

> who so blindly worshipped Stuart that he could see none of his imperfections, while acknowledging the error of this move of

Stuart's is disposed to place the blunder on the shoulders of Gen. R. E. Lee (who was certainly able to carry them). But while every officer in those two grand armies, Confederate and Federal, ascribe great merit to Stuart as a cavalry general of great ability and unexceptional enterprise, courage and energy, we know that he was like all other men, *human* and liable to err, and did in my opinion on this campaign, *undoubtedly*, make the fatal blunder which lost us the battle of Gettysburg.[44]

In a postwar narrative of his service written at Wade Hampton's request—Hampton and Stuart were not close friends—Rosser spared little venom against Stuart's performance:

[A]ll of us who participated in the Gettysburg campaign know that the mistake committed by him [Stuart] then in leaving General R.E. Lee without 'eyes' and 'ears' and riding aimlessly about the country, not knowing where our army was, and without striking the communication of the enemy, contributed largely to our failure at Gettysburg. . . . I also think that if the cavalry had been with General Lee as he approached Gettysburg the battle would not have begun at Cashtown and the Battle of Gettysburg would not have occurred at all, but the armies would have met on ground selected by General Lee, and the result would therefore have been more favorable to our side.[45]

Rosser's words must be contemplated with a certain amount of skepticism. While some of his points have merit, his hatred for his benefactor knew no bounds.

Jeb Stuart's assailants were legion. In time, others would spring to his defense.

Chapter 10

The Controversy Continues

"I have seen a Jesuitical attack on Stuart by Colonel Charles Marshall, all a lie. Today I send the [*Richmond*] *Dispatch* a letter. It looks like I shall be at war forever."

— John S. Mosby

Colonel E. Porter Alexander, who served as James Longstreet's acting chief of artillery at Gettysburg, played an important role in how Pickett's Charge unfolded on July 3, 1863. Possessed of a brilliant mind and the ability to keenly observe events and report on them objectively, Alexander wrote at length about his experiences during the war. He also offered an evaluation of Jeb Stuart's conduct during the campaign that was balanced in its overall assessment.

According to Alexander, the idea of passing behind the Union army was "a very unwise proposition which Lee more unwisely entertained." The artillerist believed the expedition was a strategic error because it stripped Lee of three brigades of cavalry at a crucial time and resulted in a battle "of chance collision, with the Confederates taking the offensive, whereas the plan of the campaign had been to fight a defensive battle."[1]

In 1875, Samuel P. Bates, who was one of the most prolific and respected historians of the 19th Century, wrote an early account of the Battle of Gettysburg. Bates, who corresponded with many of the veterans, weighed in on the controversy. "Of Hooker's intention to march upon Williamsport, and break up his communications, or even of the passage of the Potomac by the Union army, up to this time, Lee knew nothing," explained the author. "That he should have so long remained in ignorance of these movements was due to the mishaps which befell the operations of that division of his cavalry under Stuart." Bates was the first of the many historians who would address Gettysburg to criticize Stuart for his absence and blame him for the Confederate defeat in Pennsylvania.

Bates continued:

> When about to cross the Potomac, Lee had ordered that daring cavalry commander to remain on guard at the passes of the Blue Ridge, leading to the Shenandoah Valley, and observe the movements of the Union forces, and should they attempt to cross the Potomac, he was to make demonstrations upon their rear, so as to detain them as long as possible in Virginia. But in the event of their passage, he was also to cross, either on the east or west side of the Blue Ridge, as to him should seem best, and take position upon the right flank of the main rebel column. So far south had his demonstrations carried him, however, that Stuart determined to cross at Seneca, some distance to the east of the point where the Union army had passed. When once over he found it impossible to reach his chief, and take position upon the flank as ordered, the Union army being interposed. He accordingly kept northward, passing through Hanover, and did not arrive at Carlisle, where he expected to find the main rebel column, until the 1st of July, after Ewell had been recalled from that place and was on his way to Gettysburg.
>
> He was at Carlisle met by a messenger from Lee ordering him forward to the scene of conflict, but did not arrive until the result of the battle had been well-nigh decided, and the star of his chief had gone down in blood. The need of cavalry was sorely felt by Lee in the maneuvers preliminary to the fight, as he was thereby stripped of the means for ascertaining the whereabouts of his antagonist, and his flanks and rear were indifferently protected. Thus are the plans even of great leaders the sport of fortune.[2]

Louis Phillippe Albert d'Orleans, better known as the Comte de Paris and a pretender to the French throne, spent the first year of the war serving as a volunteer staff officer in the headquarters of the Army of the Potomac. In 1886, the Frenchman published a history of the battle that is still considered a balanced treatment even today.[3] After a detailed rendition of the three days of fighting, the Comte de Paris laid out his conclusions as to the reasons for the Confederate defeat. From his vantage point, Stuart was due the lion's share of the blame. "We have seen how this battle was brought about, and, without pretending to say that the Confederates ought to have come out victorious, we have pointed out the errors which rendered their defeat inevitable," was how the Comte de Paris began before enumerating those "errors." The primary reason for Lee's defeat "was the absence of Stuart, which produced the fortuitous encounter at Gettysburg, delaying the concentration of the army, and rendering it impossible for that army either to resume a defensive position along South Mountain, where Meade would have been obliged to attack it, or to maneuver in order to dislodge him from those he occupied." The Comte de Paris also held General Lee at least partially responsible for the intelligence failure because he had "four brigades of cavalry with him, [but] failed to turn them to account: he left Robertson and Jones in Virginia, and sent Imboden as far as possible from the enemy, only retaining Jenkins, who at the critical moment found himself in the rear of the infantry."[4]

The Comte de Paris went on to recite the familiar litany of tactical errors committed by Lee and his subordinates, a cascade of circumstances that brought about the Confederate defeat at Gettysburg.

Major General Abner Doubleday, a Union general in the First Corps who briefly commanded the battlefield at Gettysburg on July 1, penned a history of the Chancellorsville and Gettysburg Campaigns as part of the "Campaigns of the Civil War" series published by Charles Scribner's Sons in the 1880s.[5] Doubleday was relieved of command of the First Corps on the evening of July 1, and remained bitter for the rest of his life about the way he was treated. The general used his book as a "bully pulpit" to criticize how George Meade and Oliver O. Howard performed at Gettysburg. Doubleday blamed both men for his removal from command. He also wrote with a very strong Northern bias, which is quite evident in his account. Therefore, much of what he wrote must be read carefully and considered in that context. However, Doubleday's analysis of Stuart's ride and its impact on the battle differed markedly from what others had written up to that time.

"It seems strange that Lee should suppose that the Union army would continue inactive all this time, south of Washington, where it was confronted only by Stuart's cavalry, and it is remarkable to find him so totally in the dark with regard to Hooker's movements," began Doubleday. Confederate writers, he noted, "extensively assumed . . . this ignorance was caused by the injudicious raid made by Stuart, who thought it would be a great benefit to the Confederate cause if he could ride entirely around the Union lines and rejoin Lee's advance at York. He had made several of these circuits during his military career, and had gained important advantages from them in the way of breaking up communications, capturing dispatches, etc." This campaign, however, was different, explained the general, because the distances were greater and the challenges substantially more difficult. Even so, the Southerners should not have been caught by surprise. Here is how Doubleday viewed the matter:

> It is thought that [Stuart] hoped by threatening Hooker's rear to detain him and delay his crossing the river, and thus give Lee time to capture Harrisburg, and perhaps Philadelphia. His raid on this occasion was undoubtedly a mistake. When he rejoined the main body, his men were exhausted, his horses broken down, and the battle of Gettysburg was nearly over. As cavalry are the eyes of an army, it has been said that Stuart's absence prevented Lee from ascertaining the movements and position of Hooker's army. Stuart has been loudly blamed by the rebel chroniclers for leaving the main body, but this is unjust; Lee not only knew of the movement, but approved it; for he directed Stuart to pass between Hooker and Washington, and move with part of his force to Carlisle and the other part to Gettysburg. Besides, Stuart left Robertson's and Jones's brigades behind, with orders to follow up the rear of the Union army until it crossed, and then to rejoin the main body. In the meantime they were to hold the gaps in the Blue Ridge, for fear Hooker might send a force to occupy them. These two brigades, with Imboden's brigade, and White's battalion, made quite a large cavalry force: Imboden, however, was also detached to break up the Baltimore & Ohio Railroad to prevent forces from the West from taking Lee in rear; all of which goes to show how sensitive the Confederate commander was in regard to any danger threatening his communications with Richmond.[6]

Written only two decades after the campaign and from a decidedly Unionist perspective, Doubleday's critique was balanced and rather surprising in that he pointed out the obvious: not all of the blame for the episode could fairly be laid at Stuart's feet.

Jesse Bowman Young was a lieutenant in the 84th Pennsylvania Volunteer Infantry and served on the staff of Brig. Gen. Andrew A. Humphreys, a division commander with the Third Corps at Gettysburg. Young was all of 19 years old in 1863. In 1913, on the fiftieth anniversary of the battle, he published a well-respected history of the engagement.[7]

"Stuart's role in the Gettysburg campaign," explained Young in a scathing evaluation of the merits of the expedition, "consisted in a venturesome skylarking expedition which led him around the Army of the Potomac—between that body and Washington—separating him from the rest of Lee's army for a full week, depriving Lee of the services of the cavalry, and bringing the mounted division to Gettysburg on the afternoon of the second day to little purpose, after days and nights of exhausting forays and several fierce encounters with Pleasonton's forces." Young concluded by proclaiming that the "judgment of the Army of Northern Virginia was nearly unanimous to the effect that this raid was a damage and a hindrance, and not a help to Lee's plans."[8]

Young's criticisms are interesting on several levels. He was a veteran of the battle, and his treatment of the fighting was evenhanded. Despite his comments, he downplayed the role of Stuart's cavalry by relegating it to the end of his long book on the campaign.

In 1914, Francis Marshal published his account of Gettysburg.[9] According to the author, he wanted his book to be a readable and enjoyable account for young and old alike. He wrote it in the present tense, and his style is engaging and at times, even elegant. Unfortunately, Marshal seems not to have given much original thought to the Stuart controversy. Instead, he parroted many of the standard criticisms of the day. The maneuvers of the armies, he wrote, "were in the nature of a still hunt for each other; as Lee's bold if dangerous strategy had befuddled the Federal commander, while the Army of Northern Virginia was without cavalry—its eye of observation." Marshal continued:

> [T]hrough a misunderstanding on the part of Gen. Lee or his cavalry commander, Stuart, or both, the latter in an attempt to mislead or to circle round the Federal army found himself with all but three brigades of the Confederate horse on the outer flank of the Federals moving towards the Susquehanna, and he was forced to continue on almost to that river before he succeeds in riding round the Federal front and reaching Ewell; his troopers more asleep than awake from several days and nights of almost continuous riding. Meantime Gen. Lee was ignorant of the position of Stuart and of his antagonist, but presumes the former was somewhere in the rear of the army, where strangely, he left three detached brigades of horse. Therefore Lee was without a single cavalryman in contact with his main forces spread from Chambersburg to the Susquehanna.[10]

In describing the fighting on July 2, Marshal—like others writing before and after him—called the ride an "ill-judged excursion" that bore "much evil fruit, for had [Stuart], as usual, been available during the preceding days, Lee would know that the Round Tops are now occupied by only a few Federal signalmen."[11] Stuart's expedition, he concluded, was "useless."[12]

Colonel James K. P. Scott served in the 1st Pennsylvania Reserve Cavalry in 1863, a unit that fought against Stuart's cavalry on many fields. The 1st Pennsylvania had borne more than its share of the fighting for Fleetwood Hill at Brandy Station on June 9, 1863. Scott intended to write a three-volume history of the Battle of Gettysburg but death intervened, capping his work to a single book that was published in 1927. Scott's first and only volume, therefore, addresses only the first day of the battle.[13] However, it includes a narrative of Stuart's movements that prevented the Southerner's three cavalry brigades from being at Gettysburg on July 1, and also discusses the fight at Hanover. After discussing the chain of events that led to the concentration of the Army of Northern Virginia at Gettysburg, Scott opined as follows:

> This radical change of the order of march upon Harrisburg, was due to the intelligence brought by Longstreet's scout and is so stated in General Lee's official report; and, that in the absence of his cavalry, it was impossible to ascertain the enemy's intentions, and it was to deter him from advancing farther west on his communications with Virginia that determined the concentration of the army east of the mountains.[14]

Colonel Scott quoted that portion of General Lee's report that criticized Stuart's failure to link up with General Ewell in a prompt fashion, and then concluded his condemnation of the cavalier by writing, "The reader has before him all that is pertinent or important to the discussion among Virginians over the absence of the cavalry at Gettysburg."[15]

*   *   *

Jeb Stuart's supporters vehemently disagreed that the critics had discussed all that was "pertinent or important" to the issue. Motivated by the often bitter and decades-long bickering over Stuart's decisions, they seized every opportunity to mount a convincing defense of his actions during the ride to Pennsylvania.

The raging storm of criticism among the aged veterans convinced some of Stuart's partisans to spring to his defense. His most vehement defenders were all well acquainted with the cavalry chieftain. Three of them—William W. Blackford, Henry B. McClellan, and Theodore S. Garnett—were former staff officers and members of Stuart's inner circle. The fourth Stuart advocate, John Singleton Mosby, had also played a major role in the 1863 ride. He leapt to defend not only Stuart but his own role in the events that played out above the Mason-Dixon Line.

William Blackford, Stuart's former engineering officer who was riding with the cavalier when they were nearly captured at Hanover, believed it was the defeat at Gettysburg that triggered most of the criticism of his boss. Blackford dodged the issue of blaming anyone directly for the loss by ascribing the defeat to General Lee's health problems. His medical condition, explained Blackford, had dulled the great general's normally impeccable military judgment. But for this illness, Blackford believed Lee would have identified the strong Cemetery Hill position on July 1 and would either have ordered Ewell to take it or he would have withdrawn to a better position. The ex-cavalryman concluded that "Lee's illness may have been sufficient to cause the loss of the battle," and not the absence of Stuart and his horsemen.[16]

As far as Blackford was concerned, the ends of the expedition justified the means. "It is easy enough to say that some other course would have been better than the one Stuart followed, looking back now with the knowledge of *what has since happened*," he chided, "but is it fair to blame him for acting with the best *knowledge he then had?* If the Battle of Gettysburg had been won by us, as it very nearly was," continued Blackford, "this expedition would have been called a magnificent achievement. As it was, the injury inflicted on the enemy by the diversion of troops was alone enough to justify it."[17] To Blackford's way of thinking, Lee probably missed Stuart himself far more than he missed his three cavalry brigades.[18]

Major Henry B. McClellan, Stuart's competent and well-regarded adjutant, also scrambled to Stuart's defense. McClellan was a native Philadelphian and a first cousin of Federal commander Maj. Gen. George B. McClellan. The former major analyzed the attacks others had launched against Stuart, picked up his agile pen, and produced a balanced defense of his old comrade in arms. "We may dismiss at once the inconsiderate charge that Stuart disobeyed or exceeded the orders given to him by General Lee," began McClellan, "for General Lee states that Stuart acted in the exercise of the discretion given to him." The major explained that the cavalier had submitted his plans to Lee "in a personal interview," the plans were "approved, and he was authorized to carry them out if in his opinion it seemed best to do so." The responsibility for the raid, concluded McClellan, "strategically considered, rests with General Lee. Many considerations may be urged in its favor. Two objects were placed before Stuart. He was desired to gain information of the enemy's movements, and to damage and delay him on his march."[19]

McClellan repeated the argument that the movement behind the Union army slowed and confused the enemy, and suggested that Stuart's ride deprived Meade of most of his own cavalry, meaning the pressure on General Lee's advancing army was less than it otherwise would have been but for Stuart's excursion.[20]

McClellan also claimed that when Brig. Gen. John Buford's cavalry division was withdrawn on July 2, Maj. Gen. Daniel E. Sickles lost his cavalry screening and scouting ability in front of the Union left flank, which in turn helped secure the success achieved by Longstreet's assault later that afternoon. Buford was withdrawn, explained McClellan, because Stuart was riding behind the Union army and the cavalry division was needed to protect the new Federal base at Westminster. In other words, Stuart's ride accomplished all that was anticipated by Lee.[21]

McClellan admitted that when Stuart's cavalry ran into Maj. Gen. Winfield Hancock's Second Corps on June 25, it was "clearly impossible" for Stuart to follow his intended route.[22] McClellan dismissed the contention that Stuart chose poorly in deciding to continue on around the Union army, and blamed Confederate cavalryman Brig. Gen. Beverly Robertson for the intelligence failures that followed.

An able defender of Stuart, McClellan reached conclusions that surprised some of his readers. His lengthy passage, which is worthy of reprinting, reads as follows:

> It remains to consider whether Stuart made proper arrangements to obtain information concerning the enemy's movements during his separation from the army. Had he decided to follow Longstreet's

crossing at Shepherdstown and operate on that flank, he could have attained this end only by using individual scouts or by making reconnaissances in force. For the latter purpose the force under Stuart's command was insufficient. After making the detachments which must necessarily have been made to observe or guard the passes of South Mountain, the handful of veterans left would have been unable to do more than hold their own in the presence of the Federal cavalry, which in recent encounters had proven itself an adversary by no means to be despised. Unless provided with an infantry support, Stuart could have made no reconnaissance which would have held forth any hope of piercing the cavalry which enveloped Hooker's advance. General Early speaks wisely when he says: "It is doubtful whether the former [alternative] would have enabled him to fulfill General Lee's expectations."

It seems necessary to emphasize the fact that Stuart carried but a portion of his cavalry with him, and that he left in direct communication with the army a force numerically superior to that under his own immediate command. Jenkins' brigade and White's battalion from Jones' brigade, which accompanied the advance of the army in Pennsylvania, numbered not less than 1,800 men, while Robertson's and Jones' brigades, which remained on the front vacated by Stuart, numbered about 3,000. Mosby and Stringfellow, two of the best scouts in either army, were, by Stuart's direction, operating within the enemy's lines; but Mosby was paralyzed by his failure to find Stuart in consequence of the movements of Hancock's corps, and Stringfellow had been captured and had allowed himself to be carried to Washington, intending to make his escape thence and return with the information he might gather. He had succeeded in this plan on a former occasion, but now was so closely guarded that he found no opportunity to escape, and only rejoined Stuart after the close of the campaign, and through the channel of regular exchange.

The arrangements which Stuart made for obtaining information appear to have been adequate to the occasion, and it seems strange that General Lee did not use Robertson and Jones for this purpose. He was aware that under the most favorable circumstances Stuart must be separated from the army for at least three or four days, and that during that time he must look to some one else for information; but although in daily communication with Robertson, he does not appear to have called upon him for such service; nor can it be discovered that Robertson made effort in that direction. He remained in the vicinity of Berryville until the 1st of July, on which day he was ordered by General Lee to join the army in

Pennsylvania. It is to be regretted that Stuart did not assume the risk of taking Jones with him, and that he did not leave behind him Hampton or Fitz Lee; for it is inconceivable that either of these officers, with or without orders, would have remained inactive under such circumstances. It was not the want of cavalry that General Lee bewailed, for he had enough of it had it been properly used. It was the absence of Stuart himself that he felt so keenly; for on him he had learned to rely to such an extent that it seemed as if his cavalry were concentrated in his person, and from him alone could information be expected. Hampton and Fitz Lee, better than any one else, would have supplied Stuart's place to the commanding general.[23]

Theodore S. Garnett served as an aide-de-camp to Stuart during the Gettysburg Campaign, joining his staff on May 15, 1863, at the age of eighteen. Garnett remained with Stuart until the cavalier's untimely death in May 1864. Recalling Stuart's interment in Richmond's Hollywood Cemetery, Garnett lamented, "all that was mortal of the best soldier I ever knew rests there."[24]

Following the war, Garnett was very active in the affairs of Confederate veterans and rose to command the Department of Virginia. As a member of the committee to erect an equestrian statue of Stuart in Richmond, Garnett was selected to give the dedication speech on May 30, 1907. He delivered his address in front of a crowd estimated at 50,000. Garnett defended his former commander's role in the Gettysburg Campaign, and castigated those who blamed the campaign's ills on Stuart:

> The fact that it took Stuart one day longer than expected to fight his way to Carlisle, Pennsylvania, arriving on the field of Gettysburg on the second day of battle, has been used to account for the failure of the Army of Northern Virginia to keep up its unbroken score of victories. To say that the battle would have been won if Stuart had arrived a day earlier is a tribute to him greater than his most ardent admirers could claim. General Lee believed that if Stonewall Jackson had been there the victory would have been assured. But Stuart was as blameless for his march to Carlisle as Jackson was for his absence in another and better world . . .
>
> General Lee's letters to Stuart on the 22nd and 23rd of June, 1863, establish the fact that General Lee authorized Stuart to use his discretion as to crossing the Potomac by way of the enemy's rear,

and General Longstreet, who communicated to him those instructions, distinctly advised General Stuart to choose that route. Two brigades of cavalry (Robertson and Jones) were left on the Blue Ridge to watch Hooker's army on the Potomac and keep General Lee advised of Hooker's movements, while Stuart with his other three brigades moved on through Maryland. A cavalry fight at Hanover took place on June 30th with Kilpatrick's division. It caused a wide detour, in the course of which we crossed the trail of Early's division. General Early heard our guns at Hanover and rightly conjectured that they were Stuart's Horse Artillery. Strangely and unhappily he failed to communicate with Stuart or leave any intimation that he was on the march for Cashtown . . .

To those who know General Stuart's character as we knew it, the bare suggestion that he was capable of disobeying any order of General Lee, either in letter or in spirit, is not only incredible, but absolutely untrue. General Lee himself, in his official report, makes not the slightest intimation of such a monstrous impossibility.[25]

Garnett continued by offering a prescient prediction that would ring truer than he could have ever envisioned: "The last word has not yet been said about Gettysburg. It will be discussed long after Waterloo has been forgotten, but history will not permit the fame of Stuart to be tarnished by the false claim that he disobeyed any order ever received by him from General Lee."[26]

The very public defenses offered by Blackford, McClellan, and Garnett were able, articulate, and generally well balanced. However, an even more eloquent defender rose to take the stage in defense of Jeb Stuart.

*   *   *

Colonel John Singleton Mosby found great fame as a partisan leader after the Gettysburg Campaign, when his men wreaked havoc on Federal operations in the Loudoun and Shenandoah valleys during the last two years of the war. When the war ended Mosby refused to surrender, choosing instead to disband his command and ride for home. The cavalryman became a prominent lawyer in Warrenton, Virginia. An extremely prolific writer, Mosby took up the cudgel to defend Jeb Stuart, to whom he was fiercely loyal. "He made me all that I was in the war,"

Colonel John Singleton Mosby, Jeb Stuart's most ardent, strident, and eloquent defender.

National Archives

Mosby proudly proclaimed of Stuart in 1896. "But for his friendship I would never have been heard of."[27]

Mosby repaid that debt and much more by staunchly defending Stuart's conduct during the Gettysburg Campaign in article after article, and finally in a book-length work that is one of the finest legal briefs ever written.[28] "I am writing a full history of the operations of the cavalry in the Gettysburg Campaign," he informed a friend in an 1896 letter.[29] He explained his theme in another missive. "I have seen a Jesuitical attack on Stuart by Colonel Charles Marshall, all a lie," he told another friend. "Today I send the [*Richmond*] *Dispatch* a letter. It looks like I shall be at war forever."[30]

Mosby's letter was a response to Marshall's address to a Confederate Veteran Association meeting in January 1896, a lengthy item carried by the *Dispatch*. (Excerpts from this address were reproduced in the previous chapter.) Marshall roundly criticized Stuart's ride and blamed the cavalier for the disaster that unfolded at Gettysburg.[31] Mosby's response to Marshall was direct, detailed, and didn't pull a single punch. "I have just read in the Post the report of Colonel Charles Marshall's speech at the celebration of the anniversary of General Lee's Birthday. It is the argument of an astute advocate and sophist, and utterly destitute of judicial candor." Mosby was only getting warmed up. "I shall briefly notice and answer the charge he makes that General Stuart, the Chief of

Cavalry, violated General Lee's order in the Gettysburg campaign. Fortunately, in this case, the truth does not lie at the bottom of a well."[32]

Mosby proceeded to dissect and refute Marshall's speech piece by piece, numbering each point as if he were making an argument in a court of law:

> 1. General Lee expressly says in his report that he gave Stuart authority to cross the Potomac in the rear of the enemy, which is the route he took. Colonel Marshall was a staff-officer of General Lee's, and, of course, knew this fact, yet he did not mention it.[33]

Mosby was referring to Lee's order of June 23, from which he quoted later in his response. Mosby was correct regarding Marshall's address in that the former staff officer discussed extensively Stuart's plan to pass around Hooker's rear, but in doing so implied Lee never authorized such a move. The implication formed the foundation for many of the arguments offered by Stuart's detractors. Lee's June 23 order (as does Longstreet's letter) clearly gave Stuart discretion to determine if he could "pass around their army without hindrance."[34]

Mosby moved on to an important second point: General Ewell and his infantry corps were already in Pennsylvania by the time Stuart received his orders. In order to make contact with Ewell, Stuart would first have to find him:

> 2. He [Marshall] states that Stuart was ordered to place himself on Ewell's right flank, and did not do it. Any one reading the speech would infer that at the date of the instruction Ewell was with General Lee in the Shenandoah Valley, and that Stuart was in default in this respect. He ignores the important fact that Ewell was then several days' march in advance of General Lee, in Pennsylvania. Of course, Stuart could not be at the same time with General Lee in Virginia, and with Ewell in Pennsylvania. He says that Stuart's instructions were to cover the Confederate right as the enemy moved northward. No such instructions were given, but just the reverse. At 5 P.M., June 23d, General Lee wrote to Stuart, who was then east of the Blue Ridge, in Loudon county.
>
> If General Hooker's army remains inactive, you can leave two brigades to watch him, and withdraw with the three others; but should he not appear to be moving northward I think you had better withdraw this side of the mountain to-morrow night, cross at

Shepherdstown next day (25th), and move over to Fredericktown. You will, however, be able to judge whether you can pass around their army without hindrance, doing them all the damage you can, and cross the river east of the mountains. In either case, after crossing the river you must move on and feel the right of Ewell's troops, collecting information, provisions, etc.

Mosby also pointed out that it would have been physically impossible for Stuart to have both watched Hooker's movements and maintain direct contact with Ewell (assuming he could even find him in a timely manner). Therefore, concluded Mosby, the route selected by Stuart was, militarily speaking, the correct one:

At this time Longstreet's Corps was the rear guard of the army, and Lee's instructions to Stuart were sent through him. On the day before Longstreet had forwarded a similar letter from General Lee, and urged Stuart to go to Ewell by the route around the rear of the enemy. So far from Stuart having been ordered to wait until the enemy moved northward, he was told to go immediately if they were not moving northward. At that time Hooker was waiting quietly on General Lee; all of his movements had been subordinate to Lee's. He had moved in a circle . . . so as to cover Washington. When Lee crossed the river, of course Hooker would cross and maintain the same relative position. General Lee knew that it was physically impossible for Stuart to pass the enemy's rear, and gave up communication with him; he knew that it would be equally impossible if he crossed the river west of the Blue Ridge at Shepherdstown . . . and moved on over the South Mountain, and joined the right of Ewell's column. How could Stuart be on the Susquehanna and at the same time watch and report Hooker's movements on the Potomac?

On June 22d General Lee had written Stuart, "one column of Ewell's army (under Early) will probably move toward the Susquehanna, by the Emmittsburg [*sic*] route—another by Chambersburg." So it was immaterial so far as giving information of Hooker's movements was concerned whether Stuart crossed the Potomac east or west of the Ridge. In either event after crossing he was required to go out of sight of Hooker, and to sever communication with General Lee. Stuart took the most direct route to join the right of Ewell's column, marching continuously day and night to do so. When he reached York he found that Early had been ordered back to Cashtown, the appointed rendezvous of the army. About all of this Colonel Marshall says nothing.

Mosby emphasized the point that Stuart did not have his entire division in tow, and that General Lee knew as early as June 26 the Federals were already north of the river:

> 3. Colonel Marshall leaves the impression on the reader that Stuart took the whole cavalry corps with him. He knew that Stuart left two brigades of cavalry with Longstreet.

> 4. Colonel Marshall says that General Lee, at Chambersburg, not having heard from Stuart since he left Virginia, thought that Hooker was still south of the Potomac, until on the night of the 28th he learned through a spy that Hooker was moving northward. This is equivalent to saying that General Lee had lost his head, for no rational being could have supposed that Hooker would remain on the south bank of the Potomac while the Confederates were foraging in Pennsylvania. He might as well have disbanded his army. When General Lee passed Hagerstown on the 26th he knew that the bulk of Hooker's army was north of the river and holding the South Mountain passes. If Hooker had still been in Virginia there would have been nothing to prevent General Lee from marching direct to Baltimore and Washington. If General Lee had supposed (as Colonel Marshall says he did) that the way was open to capture those cities, he would have marched east, and not north to Chambersburg. General Lee never committed any such military blunder. The spy, therefore, only told General Lee what he knew before.

> On the morning of June 28th, at Frederick, Hooker was superseded by Meade. His army remained there that day. Instead of threatening General Lee's communications, as Colonel Marshall says, Meade withdrew the two corps that were holding the mountain passes when General Lee passed through Maryland and moved his army the next day to the east, so as to cover Washington and Baltimore. There was never any interruption of Lee's communications.

Believing the aforementioned issues had been properly dealt with, Mosby turned his attention to Marshall's statements about the importance of Lee's communications:

> 5. Colonel Marshall says that General Lee took his army to Gettysburg simply to keep Meade east of the mountain and prevent a threatened movement against his communications. This statement is contradicted by the record. General Lee attached no such importance to his communications—if he had any. The road was

open to the Potomac, but it was not a line of supply; his army lived off the country, and took with it all the ammunition it expected to use. On June 25th, after crossing the river, he wrote Mr. Davis: "I have not sufficient troops to maintain my communications, and therefore have to abandon them."

According to Colonel Marshall he broke up his whole campaign trying to save them. The fact was they were not even threatened, and General Lee knew it. There was continual passing between the army and the river.

Mosby corrected Marshall's statement that Lee had planned to concentrate his army at Gettysburg prior to the battle, thereby returning the reader to the fact that a clash with the Federals on July 1 was unplanned. Mosby brought Henry Heth, who had spent years blaming Stuart for the loss at Gettysburg, into the argument and took him to task for his decision to pursue the fight on the first morning of the battle:

6. I deny that General Lee ever ordered his army to Gettysburg, as Colonel Marshall says, or had any intention of going there before the battle began. In an article published in Belford's Magazine (October and November, 1891) I demonstrated this fact from the records. Colonel Marshall ought to study them before he makes another speech.

On the morning of June 29th General Lee ordered a concentration of the army at Cashtown, a village at the eastern base of the mountain; Hill's Corps, was in advance; he reached Cashtown June 30th. That night Hill and Heth heard that there was a force of the enemy at Gettysburg; early the next morning Hill, without orders, with Heth's and Pender's divisions, started down the Gettysburg pike. General Lee was then west of the mountain with Longstreet. Buford's Cavalry was holding Gettysburg as an outpost. Heth was in advance, and soon ran against Buford. There was a pretty stiff fight with the cavalry until [Maj. Gen. John] Reynolds, who was camped some six miles back, came to his support. Heth says: "Archer and Davis were now directed to advance, the object being to feel the enemy; to make a forced reconnaissance, and determine in what force the enemy were – whether or not he was moving his forces on Gettysburg. Heavy columns of the enemy were soon encountered."

Davis's and Archer's brigades were soon smashed, and Archer, with a good many of his men, made prisoners. "The enemy," says

General Heth, "had now been felt and found to be in a heavy force. The division was now formed in line of battle," etc.

"The object of a reconnaissance is to get information," Mosby explained before continuing his attack against the former Third Corps division commander. "After getting the information the attacking force retires. It seems that General Heth ought now to have been satisfied that the enemy was in force, and should have returned to Cashtown—i.e., if he only went to make a reconnaissance." Mosby continued:

Hill now put in Pender's and Heth's divisions, and says they drove the enemy until they came upon the First and Eleventh corps that Reynolds had brought up. He says that he went to Gettysburg "to find out what was in my front." He had now found it. Hill would have been driven back to Cashtown if Ewell had not come to his support. With Rodes's and Early's divisions he had camped the night before a few miles north of Gettysburg, and had started to Cashtown, when he received a note from Hill telling him he was moving to Gettysburg. The battle had then begun. Ewell, not understanding Hill's object in going to Gettysburg, hearing the sound of battle, and no doubt supposing the army was assembling, there turned the head of his column and marched toward Gettysburg. He came up just in time to save Hill.

General Lee was still west of the mountain, when he heard the firing. He did not understand it, and rode forward at full speed to the battle. He arrived on the field just at the close. The battle had been brought on without his knowledge, and without his orders, and lasted from early in the morning until 4 o'clock in the evening. It is clear that Hill took the two divisions to Gettysburg just for an adventure. When General Lee arrived on the field he found about half of his army there. He had been so compromised that he was compelled to accept battle on those conditions, and ordered up the rest of his forces. That morning every division of the army was on the march, and converging on Cashtown. That night the whole army – infantry, cavalry, and artillery – would have been concentrated at Cashtown, or in supporting distance, if this rash movement on Gettysburg had not precipitated a battle. A British officer—Colonel [Arthur] Freemantle—was present as a spectator, and spent the night of July 1st at General Longstreet's headquarters. In his diary he says:

"I have the best reason for supposing that the fight came off prematurely, and that neither Lee nor Longstreet intended that it should have begun that day. I also think that their plans were deranged by the events of the 1st."

Mosby concluded by placing the blame for the outbreak of an unexpected battle on the pair he believed to be the most responsible: A. P. Hill and Henry Heth. As far as the former partisan raider was concerned, General Lee had been lured to Gettysburg by their actions entangled in a trap from which he could not easily extricate himself. Jeb Stuart, explained Mosby, had done nothing to either create or spring the July 1 trap. "The record shows who is responsible for the loss of the campaign, and that it was not Stuart. There were no orders to make a reconnaissance on July 1st, and no necessity for making one," concluded Mosby. "The success of the first day, due to the accident of Ewell's arrival on the field when he was not expected, was a misfortune to the southern army. It would have been far better if Ewell had let Hill and Heth be beaten. They had put the Confederates in the condition of a fish that has swallowed a bait with a hook to it."

As time passed, Mosby grew more agitated by the criticism heaped upon Stuart in newspapers, magazines, books, and in public addresses. He worked tirelessly on his manuscript over the next decade, honing his attacks as he came to Stuart's defense. Mosby frequently wrote to colleagues seeking their insight and opinions.[35] Before his work was completed, however, memoirs penned by one of Longstreet's former staff officers appeared. As was to be expected, the new book contained searing criticisms of Stuart's Gettysburg role.

Although he eventually became a brigadier general and commanded a brigade in Lee's army during the war's final days, G. Moxley Sorrel's claim to fame during the Civil War was his service as James Longstreet's chief of staff from 1861 to 1864. During the postwar years, Sorrel adamantly rejected the Lost Cause rhetoric and served proudly as one of Longstreet's staunchest apologists, to whom he owed all of his wartime promotions and opportunities. Sorrel's *Recollections of a Confederate Staff Officer* was published posthumously in 1905.[36] Full of personal anecdotes and candid observations of famous characters, his plainly written volume remains an underappreciated study of the Army of Northern Virginia.

Sorrel offered readers a glimpse of the criticism Stuart was in for as he set forth the preparations for the Pennsylvania campaign:

On the cavalry, special care was bestowed. It had been heavily strengthened and much improved by selections of men and horses. For some time, during inaction, they had been getting good forage and pasturage. Now, when the time was near for the use of this formidable arm under Stuart, its able and famous leader, it was ready for the Commander-in-Chief.

What irony of fate that the great approaching campaign should be fought and lost without that bold leader and his riders being at Lee's touch, when indeed he wanted them, bitterly missing having Stuart and his great body of unsurpassed horse near by him. . .

The operation now performed by General Lee was intricate, of much delicacy and hazard. It was to move from his position in front of Hooker without exposing any part of his forces, or Richmond, to be attacked in detail, and this important part of the grand maneuver was left to Longstreet and his corps, with the cavalry in communication.[37]

Having prepared the reader to assume that Stuart's subsequent performance was lacking, Sorrel asserted the campaign was thus doomed from the start:

Stuart's part with his cavalry was now most important. It is contended by some that Lee left it finally optional for him to decide upon his movements. Whether to follow the army by crossing the river in the west of the ridge or by one of the lower fords. In the latter event it was, as it proved, to lose Lee and leave him without his strong arm in an enemy's country. It has been attempted to show also that the order by which Stuart moved came from Longstreet. But this must be dismissed; positive information to the contrary being at hand. Surprising to say, it now appears that Stuart left the army with his fine command and started on his too fascinating raid, not only by his own preference, but actually in violation of Lee's orders, which failed to reach him. All doubt had passed from Lee's mind and he had ordered Stuart to keep with him. The latter was raiding, and Lee's campaign was lost.[38]

James Longstreet's former chief of staff addressed the fact that Lee had cavalry that remained with him, but uniquely asserts that it was useless to the army—as if to claim the two brigades of horse were all but invisible. He concluded by claiming Lee could have handily whipped the Federals, but for Stuart's excursion:

Major [Henry B.] McClellan, Stuart's A.A.G. and chief of staff, in his history of that cavalry (and excellent work) declares that in his opinion the absence of Stuart was the cause of Lee's trouble; and for myself I have never doubted it. It is not to be supposed that no cavalry whatever was left with the army. Stuart's defenders have taken pains to point that out. There was a squadron or two, here and there, a regiment at one place, and a brigade under an efficient commander left in the rear. But these separate little commands amounted to nothing. It was the great body of that splendid horse under their leader Stuart that Lee wanted. He was the eyes and ears and strong right arm of the commander, and well may he have missed him. All through the marches he showed it.

Stuart was on a useless, showy parade almost under the guns of the Washington forts, and his horse, laurel-wreathed, bore the gay rider on amid songs and stories. He met some opposition, of course, and had a share of fighting in Ashby's Gap and the plain on the east.

When he rejoined Lee it was with exhausted horses and half worn-out men in the closing hours of Gettysburg.

Had he been with Lee where would our commander have made his battle? Possibly, not on that unfavorable ground of Gettysburg. Lee with his personally weak opponent, and Stuart by him, could almost have chosen the spot where he would be sure to defeat the Union Army.[39]

Three years after Sorrel's book appeared Mosby finally published his own. *Stuart's Cavalry in the Gettysburg Campaign* appeared in 1908. It represented Mosby's primary contribution to the unending controversy. Believing that McClellan's defense of Stuart was not strong enough, Mosby took on all comers with his *tour de force* presentation.[40] The first half of his book addressed the Battle of Brandy Station. The second half staunchly defended both Stuart's and Mosby's roles in choosing the route taken by Stuart's cavalry. Mosby adopted the justifications for the ride set forth in Stuart's report. He repeated Stuart's contention that the wagon trains of Robert E. Lee's army were best protected by Stuart's attack on Union communications by drawing out the Federal cavalry to pursue him. His ride, argued Mosby, also diverted other Union resources: "One benefit of Stuart's crossing at Seneca was that it practically eliminated French's corps in the campaign, and put it on the defensive, to guard the line of the Potomac and the rear of Meade's army," postulated

Mosby. "It had been the garrison—11,000—at Harper's Ferry, but, when the place was abandoned, it was added to Meade's command. But Stuart's appearance created such a sensation that Meade sent 4000 to guard the canal, and 7000 were kept at Frederick. They were no more help to Meade in the battle than if they had stayed above the clouds on Maryland Heights."[41]

He continued by debunking the claim that Stuart's absence left Lee's army blind and without accurate intelligence. "Possibly if Stuart had burned the trains he captured on the march he might have arrived earlier and joined Early on the 30th," explained Mosby. "But none of Stuart's critics can show any bad results from his carrying the trains along with him. If he had arrived on the 30th, at York, he could not have communicated with General Lee. Lee was fifty-five miles away west of the South Mountain at Chambersburg." At that time, Mosby pointed out, "General Lee knew perfectly well . . . the direction in which Meade was heading his army, and that his cavalry occupied Gettysburg. Stuart could have told him no more. The instructions did not require him to report to General Lee but to Ewell. All the critics overlook that fact. But I have shown that while Early and Ewell had no need of more cavalry, Stuart's presence at Carlisle on the night of July 1 defeated a combination by which a heavy force would have been thrown on Lee's flank and rear when he was in the agony of combat."[42] Mosby's pen was sharp, as was his dismissal of the criticisms launched against his idol.

Perhaps the most striking contention offered by Mosby was that by moving toward the Potomac River on June 24 (the day before Stuart started), James Longstreet and A. P. Hill tipped the Confederates' hand to Joe Hooker, who in turn set his army in motion and blocked Stuart, thwarting his plan. "If Longstreet and Hill had stayed quiet a day longer, Stuart would have crossed the Potomac in advance of Hooker's army early in the morning of the 25th," hypothesized Mosby, "and the fate of the Confederate cause might have been different."[43] Mosby went on to add, with the benefit of hindsight, "Hooker, Meade, and the authorities at Washington all misunderstood the significance of Stuart's movement. They thought it was only a force detailed to harass their rear."[44]

Mosby effectively pointed out that Grumble Jones and Beverly Robertson—and not Jeb Stuart—were responsible for providing Lee with accurate intelligence on the movement of the Federal army. "On the morning of the 26th, Hooker's army moved across the front of Jones' and

Robertson's brigades to the pontoon bridges—and they retired to the Gaps. It is *literally* true that General Lee heard nothing from *Stuart* about it, and he had no right to expect to hear from *him*," continued Mosby, who added the interesting observation that Lee's report "*does not say that couriers from Jones and Robertson did not bring him any news.*"[45] All of these facts, at least according to Mosby, absolved Stuart of the duty to provide intelligence to Lee during this time because that duty had been delegated to the two cavalry brigades left behind to guard the mountain passes—a condition rarely if ever pointed out by the loudest of Stuart's detractors.

John Mosby was not through. He turned a page and went on the offensive again, this time attacking the manner in which Marshall and Taylor treated the former commander of the Army of Northern Virginia's cavalry division:

> [Lee's report's] partial and inaccurate statements that do so much injustice to the commander of the cavalry have been accepted as a judgment that estops all inquiry into the justice of the complaint. But in the Forum of History no judgment is final in the sense that it cannot be reviewed. After reading the report the public did not wait to hear the other side—it never does—but jumped to the conclusion that Stuart had gone off without authority with all the cavalry on a raid around Hooker's army; and that General Lee, having no cavalry, was left like a giant with his eyes put out. This is the illustration of his A.A.G., Colonel Walter Taylor. Stuart was thus made responsible for the loss of the battle and the charge has been re-echoed down the corridors of time. In the South a superstition prevailed that it was as sacred as an oracle that had been uttered from the Pythian Cave. A scapegoat was needed, and a scapegoat was found. It is said that in the days of the Exodus the goat was sent to the wilderness loaded with sins; but in this case that precedent was not followed. Stuart held his high command until he fell on the field and left a void that was never filled.
>
> He made no public defense against unjust criticism and was content to prove that his sword was still as potent as Arthur's "To lift his country's fame above the polar star."
>
> The report is understood to have been written by a staff officer, Colonel Charles Marshall, a great sophist—an able and astute lawyer. It is a fine example of special pleading, and the composition shows that the author possessed far more of the qualities of an

advocate than of a judge. It is unfair to Stuart as it says nothing about Ewell having gone several days in advance into Pennsylvania; and that Stuart was ordered to join him with three brigades of cavalry;—or that Stuart had authority to cross the Potomac in Hooker's rear—or that he left two brigades of cavalry with Longstreet and General Lee to watch the enemy and guard the flanks of the main army as it moved north. Yet Lee's letters to Ewell and Stuart, and Stuart's report, all prove these omissions of the report. In an elaborate address on General Lee's birthday on January 19, 1896, the writer of the report threw off all disguise and openly charged what had only been inferred from it, that the disaster was due to Stuart's disobedience.

The address was simply an extension of the report. That Lee's campaign was broken up by somebody's disobedience nobody can doubt who will study the records; but the name of the responsible person is not hinted at in the report, or in Marshall's address. Why it should have been kept a secret no one has explained. It may be that by remaining on the field and continuing a combat which a rash subordinate had begun, General Lee thought that he had condoned the deed, and given it a sanction which he could not recall. If Hill had been censured after the battle by General Lee, no doubt he would have pleaded an estoppel against him. It does not seem to have occurred to historians to compare Lee's two reports to each other, or with the contemporaneous correspondence, and to note the discrepancies on material points between them. The truth has been revealed by the publication of reports and dispatches which show that the story of Gettysburg that has come down to this generation is a fable.[46]

Mosby found it easy to tear apart Marshall's report, element by element, in an incisive, insightful, and instructive fashion. "The best evidence that [Marshall's] report is misleading is that all who read it were misled," wrote Mosby. "Nobody can reconcile the orders with the report; their publication was a revelation; the staff officers seem to have at least forgotten them although they appear in their handwriting in Lee's letter-book." He continued:

The gravamen of the complaint the report makes against Stuart is that the cavalry was absent, and that it was needed, not in the battle, but to make preliminary reconnaissances before the battle. If such was the case, General Lee was responsible for the absence of the cavalry with Stuart; but no one has shown that any harm resulted from it. He and Longstreet were responsible for the use of the cavalry left with them. Nor does the report explain why, if the cavalry was needed in Pennsylvania, the two brigades of Robertson and Jones were kept in Virginia after the enemy had gone; General Lee's second report says they were guarding the gaps; and that after the spy came in he ordered them to join the army. This shows that he knew he had this cavalry at his call to use when he needed it. If Robertson and Jones remained to guard the gaps it must have been by Lee's or Longstreet's orders. Stuart's orders to them were to cross the river when the enemy crossed; and to move on Longstreet's flank, and to watch and report to him.[47]

Mosby blamed Beverly Robertson for failing to take the initiative to bring Jones forward and join the army until ordered to do so by General Lee.[48]

Mosby concluded his legal brief with a flourish:

> Stuart was absent on the first day under orders; in my opinion the orders were right. I now repeat what I said in the *Richmond Times* in April, 1898, in reply to the strictures of Colonel Marshall in his address: "How could Stuart join Ewell on the Susquehanna, guard the gaps of the Blue Ridge Mountains in Virginia, watch and impede Hooker's crossing the Potomac, and then place himself on the right of the column as it advanced with Lee into Pennsylvania unless he was inspired with ubiquity. Even Hercules could not perform all of his twelve labors at the same time. This is the Age of Reason; the Age of Faith has passed. We wonder how a people as intellectual as the Athenians could believe that Thesus appeared at Marathon and led the last onset against the Persians; and yet we are now asked to believe that General Lee expected Stuart to surpass all the heroes of Greek mythology." And I might have added, how could Stuart pass around Hooker and at the same time keep between Hooker and Lee?[49]

As it turned out, Mosby was Stuart's most ardent defender for nearly a century. While writing his personal memoir, published in 1917,[50] Mosby couldn't resist again addressing at considerable length what he considered the foolishness of laying blame on Stuart for the results of Gettysburg:

> So it seems that General Lee suggested, and Longstreet urged, Stuart to pass by the enemy's rear. . . . After the war Longstreet wrote an account of Gettysburg, in which he forgot his own orders to Stuart and charged him with disobeying his instructions. He said

he ordered Stuart to march on his flank and to keep between him and the enemy; Lee's staff officers and biographers repeat the absurd story. They do not explain how Stuart could be with Ewell and the Susquehanna and, at the same time, on Longstreet's flank in Virginia. No precedent can be found for such a performance, except in the Arabian Nights . . .

Lee seemed to be more intent about [Stuart] gathering rations than anything else. There is not a word in either of his dispatches to Stuart about reporting the enemy's movements to him. Lee's biographers say there was. He would neither order Stuart to do an impossible thing, but he told him what instructions to give the commanders of the two cavalry brigades he would leave behind . . .

The plan for Stuart to pass through Hooker's army was really a copy of the campaign of Marengo, when Bonaparte crossed the Alps and cut the Austrian communications with Italy. It was a bold enterprise—its safety lay in its audacity—the enemy would be caught unprepared, and at the same time it would protect Lee's communications by drawing off Hooker's cavalry in pursuit. It was known that the camps of the different corps were so far apart that a column of cavalry could easily pass between them . . .

The staff officers knew perfectly well how the battle was precipitated, but they concealed it. They intentionally misrepresented it. Their animus toward Stuart is manifest . . .

Stuart's march of a column of cavalry around the Union army will be regarded, in the light of the record, as one of the greatest achievements in war, viewed either as an independent operation or raid, or in its strategic relation to the campaign.[51]

And so the controversy that began smoldering soon after the Confederate defeat at Gettysburg spread through the ranks of men who participated in the battle on both sides of the firing line, and across the decades that followed. The passing from the stage of these participants, however, did not bring the controversy to an end. If anything, the intensity of the argument increased during the balance of the 20th Century and continues to rage today. Few who have studied the issue disagree that Jeb Stuart's ride has become one of the most divisive modern debates over the how's and why's of the battle of Gettysburg.

Chapter 11

The Controversy Rages

"Regardless of what men will say *someday*, there are orders to follow and duty *today*.
Sometimes that is all a man can do. Sometimes that is all he needs to do.
Certainly it is all anyone can ask him to do."

— Mark Nesbitt, *Saber and Scapegoat: J. E. B. Stuart and the Gettysburg Controversy*

W ith the passing of the last of the veterans, 20th Century historians took up the debate. The controversy that is Stuart's Ride has been the beneficiary of multiple treatments over the years, but the vast majority of them have appeared during the last fifty years. If anything can be concluded by the amount of ink spilled over this issue, it is this: the controversy has grown more intense with the passage of time as historians and buffs alike wrestle with the question of whether Stuart violated his orders and, in turn, took action that directly led to the Confederate defeat at Gettysburg.

In this chapter we survey some of the voluminous literature addressing the controversy in order to provide a sampling of how modern historians have treated this debate. These treatments are presented in the order of their publication. Our analysis appears in the Conclusion to this book.

Captain John W. Thomason, Jr. was a career Marine who gained respect for his work as an historian in the years following World War I. Thomason was a great admirer of Jeb Stuart, and wrote the first full-length biography of Stuart to be published.[1] Not surprisingly, Thomason defended Stuart's conduct during the Gettysburg Campaign. After quoting the June 23 orders, Thomason began his analysis of the ride this way:

The fatal sentence is: "You will, however, be able to judge whether you can pass around their army without hindrance, doing them all the damage you can, and cross the river *east of the Mountains*." Probably Lee meant: *Immediately* east of the Mountains. But, at the time this order was sent, no passage immediately east was practicable. From Harpers Ferry down to Edward's Ferry the enemy concentration commanded approaches to the Potomac from the south. Stuart's first movements made it appear that he thought he could get through to this stretch of the river, but there are no direct statements bearing on this matter.[2]

Thomason proceeded to mount his defense of the gray cavalier from the perspective of an experienced military officer:

It is said, after the event: Stuart was the chief of cavalry, and he should have known better than to take any of the cavalry away. One of the people who says this loudest is Longstreet, that solemnly approved the detachment and the project of passing by the enemy's rear. And Lee authorized it, as Commanding General, and Stuart's subsequent course, although modified by circumstances which he could not control—notably the movement of Hooker's army—was well within the discretion extended by his instructions.

It is a principle of the military art, that orders should be clear, direct, and open to that interpretation, only, which the commander desires. Lee's instructions to Stuart do not conform to the principle. They fall outside, even, of that latitude which a general may with propriety extend to a trusted subordinate. Questions affecting vitally the operations of the army are the affair of the commander-in-chief—not any lieutenant, no matter how able. Whatever Stuart's error in judgment, the responsibility lay with Lee, nor, let us add, did Lee in his final report evade it.

And consider another thing: the Gettysburg Campaign failed. No one cause broke it down: Lee was poorly served by all his corps commanders, and full credit must be given to General Meade, and seventy-odd thousand Yankee soldiers. If—as he might well have done, and came breathlessly near doing—Lee had won his battle, Stuart's conduct of the cavalry force would certainly stand in the annals as a great and daring operation. Success justifies itself. Failure is wrong in the first place![3]

Thomason continued:

Had Stuart been up, and not the width of Hooker's army away, it is unlikely that the battle would have fought at Gettysburg: Meade's scattered corps might well have been crushed in detail before he could concentrate his army. On the other hand, if Stuart had been on Lee's front, Pleasonton would have been there, too, and Meade would have had his own information. It is idle to speculate at Gettysburg. Maybe it is as I have heard pious old men say who think much on these things, seen and unseen, in the quiet South: there was a current in the universe that set against the Confederacy. God did not mean for it to win the war. In the event, they shocked together on the iron-ribbed hills by the little town and fought as fiercely as men have ever fought—Hancock, Doubleday, and Sykes—Gordon—Hood—Garnett—Pettigrew—George Pickett. The armies, attacking and attacked, saw fall, or led off as prisoners in that three days, nearly a third of the strength of each. In the words of Froissart, "They were very noble: they did not value their lives."[4]

The author's deft closing argument in his defense of Jeb Stuart reads as follows:

The collision at Gettysburg was brought on by A. P. Hill and Heth, who provoked an action where Lee did not desire, nor expect one. In their reports, Hill and Heth say then were on reconnaissance looking for the enemy. Lee knew Buford was there, if they did not. In his post-war memoirs, Heth says he was looking for shoes. Early had been through Gettysburg on the 29th. If Heth expected to find any such gleanings behind Early, he was silly. He went looking for a fight. That contact was not brought on by the absence of cavalry.

Lee had already selected a position, in case he had to fight: Cashtown, four miles west of Gettysburg. Meade had selected a line: Pipe creek, ten miles east.

The engagement between Heth and Buford drew in Heth's support—A. P. Hill—and Buford's—Reynolds. The main armies were then drawn in.

None of the foregoing argues that it would not have been better for Stuart to be up: his presence would, at least, have removed the excuse for irresponsible wanderings on the part of Heth and Hill.

To repeat: It was within Stuart's discretion to cross the Potomac east or west of the Blue Ridge. He chose to cross east—approved specifically by Longstreet, Senior Officer Present. When the decision was made, it was then his mission to harass and intercept the Federal army lines of supply and communications. He did this so effectively that he drew after him two cavalry divisions, and caused Meade to retain a corps of infantry on the line of communications. He took an army supply train of one hundred and twenty-five wagons, and brought it off safely. He captured nearly 1,000 prisoners. He rode two hundred and fifty miles, lived off the country, whipped Kilpatrick, burnt Carlisle and immobilized 15,000 men in that region who were under orders that would have brought them upon Ewell's flank and rear, and he rejoined the main army—this with a loss of 89 men, killed, wounded, and missing.

The cavalry failure in the campaign was not Stuart's. Ewell made good use of Jenkins. He does not complain of lack of cavalry. Buford was too weak to do anything on Longstreet's flank, so Longstreet did not suffer for lack of cavalry.

Hill went outside his orders to pick a fight with Buford. And Robertson received no orders to come forward until 29 June, three days after Hooker had crossed, and one day before the scout Harrison reported. Then, although Robertson rode fast, he was one hundred and fifty miles behind the army, and took nearly three days to reach the zone of operations. Lee seems to have forgotten Robertson, whose usefulness south of the river ceased with the withdrawal of Hooker from his front, and wasted Robertson during the next four days.

What Lee missed at Gettysburg was not cavalry: he had plenty of cavalry. He missed Jeb Stuart.[5]

Thomason's status as a professional soldier lent credence to his lonely voice in the defense of Stuart's conduct during the Gettysburg Campaign.

With the passing of Jubal Early, Richmond newspaperman Douglas Southall Freeman became the keeper of the flame of the Lost Cause. Freeman devoted much of his life to telling the stories of heroic Southerners, and left behind a prodigious volume of material on the lives of George Washington, Robert E. Lee, and Lee's primary lieutenants. In 1934, Freeman published his Pulitzer Prize winning four-volume biography of Robert E. Lee.[6] In it, he devoted an entire chapter to the causes of the Confederate defeat at Gettysburg. "The invasion was, of course, a daring move, but, in the circumstances that Lee faced, politically and in a military sense, it probably was justified," began Freeman. He continued:

> The first mistake was in connection with Stuart's operations. To recapitulate this point, Lee intended to allow his cavalry commander latitude as to where he should enter Maryland. He is not to be blamed for giving Stuart discretion, nor is Stuart justly subject to censure for exercising it. But the *Beau Sabreur* of the South, by pushing on after he had encountered resistance east of the Bull Run Mountains, violated orders and deprived Lee of his services when most needed. He should have turned back then, as Lee had directed him to do should he find his advance hindered by the Federal columns. Stuart erred, likewise, in taking with him all the cavalry brigades that had been accustomed to doing the reconnaissance work of the Army of Northern Virginia. General Lee, for his part, was at fault in handling the cavalry left at his disposal. He overestimated the fighting value of Jenkins' and of Imboden's brigades, which had little previous experience except in raids, and he failed to keep in close touch with Robertson and Jones, who remained behind in Virginia. Once in Pennsylvania, Lee's operations were handicapped not only because he lacked sufficient cavalry, but also because he did not have Stuart at hand. He had become dependent upon that officer for information of the enemy's position and plans and, in Stuart's absence, he had no satisfactory form of military intelligence. It is not enough to say with General Early, in exculpation of Stuart, that Lee found the enemy in spite of the absence of his cavalry. Had "Jeb" Stuart been at hand, Lee would have had early information of the advance of the Federals and either would have outfooted them to Gettysburg or would have known enough about their great strength to refrain from attacking as he did. The injudicious employment of the Confederate horse during the Gettysburg campaign was responsible for most of the other mistakes on the Southern side and must always remain a warning of the danger of permitting the cavalry to lose contact with an army when the enemy's positions are unknown. In its consequence, the blunder was more serious than that which Hooker made at Chancellorsville in sending Stoneman on a raid when he should have had his mounted forces in front and on the flank of the XI Corps.[7]

That Freeman idolized Lee is obvious from his writings. To his credit, Freeman at least strove to be balanced in his presentation and fair in his critique. However, it is also clear he held Stuart entirely accountable for the Confederate defeat at Gettysburg.

Freeman followed his biography of Lee with an equally ambitious and similarly monumental three-volume study of the Army of Northern Virginia's subordinate commanders. *Lee's Lieutenants: A Study in Command* was published in 1942-1944, one installment each year.[8] Freeman analyzed the successes and failures of the Army of Northern Virginia by examining the strengths and weaknesses of Lee's subordinates. He produced a lengthy description of Stuart's ride, and summed up his findings with a quote from Stuart's report describing the condition of his command on the night of June 30:

> Such was the night of June 30 for "Jeb" Stuart, third of the men whose state of mind was making history for America while the Confederate Army converged on Gettysburg. He had gone on and on in the exercise of the discretion Lee had given. Almost six days Stuart had been on his raid. Not a single time had he heard from any of the infantry commanders with whom he was directed to co-operate. One dispatch only had he sent, and that on the 25th. Other adventure was to be his, but nothing he had achieved and nothing he could hope to accomplish with his exhausted men could offset the harm which the events of coming days were to show he already had done his chief and his cause.[9]

Later, after describing Stuart's return to the army, Freeman wrote, "Stuart may have been disappointed that no applause greeted his return from his longest raid, which he was to persuade himself was his greatest; but of his thoughts he said nothing to any of his lieutenants who left memoirs."[10] Freeman never left any room for doubt that Stuart's ride was the primary cause of the Confederate defeat at Gettysburg. He would not be the last historian to level similar blame.

General Edward Stackpole was a prolific military historian who wrote numerous books over a lengthy career. In 1956, Stackpole published an account of the Gettysburg Campaign entitled *They Met at Gettysburg*.[11] As a career soldier, Stackpole was well-acquainted with the difficulties faced by commanders in the field. His study offered a generally balanced and fair assessment of the pluses and minuses of Stuart's ride:

> And so we come to the question—was Stuart a major cause of Lee's failure to win the Battle of Gettysburg? There is no clean-cut answer nor unanimity of opinion among historians. The

controversy still rages, although not so caustically as between the critics and defenders of Custer, who are still writing books and digging into the unyielding Montana soil in which the remnants of the Battle of the Little Big Horn lie buried eighty years after the event.

In defense of Stuart, the fact must be recognized that Brandy Station and subsequent skirmishes in northern Virginia had a notable effect in taking the starch out of the Confederate cavalry. It wore them down in hard riding and fighting when they needed to conserve their strength and that of their irreplaceable horses for the long march into Pennsylvania, and it convinced them that they were up against a vastly improved Federal cavalry corps which had recently demonstrated its fighting capabilities.

It seems just as clear that Lee's orders to Stuart allowed entirely too much distraction, at a critical juncture, to the man who was smarting under public disapproval and who must, like Custer, have pictured the chance to restore by a bold stroke the prestige which he had so greatly enjoyed before Brandy Station. In this case Lee would have been well advised to issue more precise orders to insure strict conformity by his subordinate with his overall plan. So far as Stuart had been informed, Lee's strategic plans were rather vague and incomplete, with no specific geographic objective to tie Stuart to a fixed course or deadline date. Beside which Lee had at his disposal plenty of cavalry in addition to Stuart's brigades, had he properly employed them.

On the other hand, those who place the blame on Stuart maintain that he lagged badly in following Lee's time schedule and, either through misadventure or faulty judgment, failed miserably both in catching up to and covering Ewell's right and in keeping his commanding general informed, through Ewell, of the movements and actions of the Army of the Potomac.

He was certainly guilty of poor judgment in further delaying his own already retarded advance by burdening his column and slowing his pace through Maryland and Pennsylvania to that of the slow-moving Federal wagon train which he captured in his unprofitable side-adventure at Rockville and carried with him to Gettysburg.

Finally, his decision to move around Hooker's rear rather than cross the Potomac at Shepherdstown, as Lee had strongly suggested, had the effect of interposing Hooker between Lee's main body and himself, thus making it a practical impossibility for him to carry out either one of his two major missions.

The conclusion must therefore be that it is a fielder's choice as to whether Stuart was the villain of that piece.[12]

Stackpole's analysis is probably the most evenhanded of the many published since the ride concluded, and certainly the most fair-minded to appear during the 20th Century.

In 1958, historian Clifford Dowdey published his history of the Gettysburg Campaign.[13] Dowdey, a Richmond, Virginia native and devoted follower of General Lee, focused on the Confederate command structure and its failures. Much like Freeman before him, Dowdey placed the principal blame for Lee's defeat on Stuart and James Longstreet. Discussing the beginning of the ride, Dowdey wrote:

> Even this early in the campaign Jeb Stuart was failing in his mission, with apparent unawareness of his failure. Judging from his reports, his mind was sharp and his conscience was clear.
>
> In the details of his actions Stuart showed his usual vigor and initiative. He seems never to have considered that his success in details was totally unrelated to his major assignment: to screen Lee's infantry and to provide the general with information about the enemy.
>
> Somewhere between June 9, when he had been hard pressed at Brandy Station, and June 24, when communications with the northward-advancing infantry were severed, Stuart the man superseded Major General Stuart the cavalry leader.[14]

Dowdey continued:

> Lee left to Stuart's discretion only the place to cross the river and whether to move northward by the Valley or by circling Hooker's army if he could "without hindrance." Stuart was given no leeway regarding the purpose of the cavalry's movement. In fact, the repetitive instructions reflected Lee's anxiety over Stuart's big risk, and in the second letter he showed that he urgently wanted Stuart to follow the army quickly: "I think the sooner you cross into Maryland, after tomorrow [June 24], the better."[15]

"The personal behavior of the burly Dutchman revealed anything except the collaborative strategist of the memoirs," continued Dowdey, who was tying the threads of his argument together by bringing Stuart into his indictment of Longstreet's conduct during the Gettysburg Campaign:

> The fact that he [Longstreet] was opposed to the attack—to all or any attacks—even before the army left Virginia cannot properly be cited in debating the question of his rightness on the third day. The third day occurred because of Ewell's failure on the first and Longstreet's on the second, within the pattern made necessary by Stuart's failure to provide reconnaissance. Longstreet had been opposed to the offensive even before anyone could have conceived of their cavalry leader's disappearance, and he held to it when Ewell's victory needed only to be grasped. Because the final attack did fail—with various assists from him along the way—he was able to make out a case for his opposition.[16]

In Dowdey's mind, Longstreet was primarily responsible, but Stuart and Richard Ewell also shared a heavy burden of the responsibility for the defeat in Pennsylvania.

There was much of interest for readers of Civil War history in 1958. Newspaperman Glenn Tucker's account of the battle of Gettysburg also appeared that year.[17] Tucker's colorful and readable book offers one of the more detailed treatments of the specifics of Stuart's ride. Although he did not approve of Stuart's conduct, Tucker also criticized Charles Marshall for his contribution to these events:

> The engagement at Hanover, while minor, is of interest to those who believe that either destiny or chance control great events. While Stuart was trying to free himself and find the right flank of Lee's army, Early's division was passing across his front on the roads leading from York to Gettysburg and from York to Heidlersburg. Gordon's brigade and White's cavalry battalion were on the York-Gettysburg pike, which at Abbotstown is six miles north of Hanover and at the crossing of the Yellow Springs road five miles from New Oxford. As the Confederate infantry passed along the road they heard the firing five and six miles to the south, but did not suspect it was Stuart. Here Lee's staff had been at fault. After having written Stuart orders—lacking in sharpness—telling him to get in touch with Ewell's right, Colonel Marshall did not emphasize to Early the need of keeping a sharp lookout for the

cavalry. In complete ignorance that he might be approaching, Early moved across Stuart's front.

Possibly the fate of the Confederacy rested on a gap of five or six miles.

At York Stuart found that time had run out. Early had gone. The York residents who had fraternized with Extra Billy Smith were chary with their information about the direction Early had taken. Stuart was still gambling on the whereabouts of Lee's army. He guessed Carlisle, and again guessed wrong. On the verge of exhaustion he moved west through the night, his mounts jaded and mules famished and some of his men asleep in their saddles.

As he started toward Carlisle Stuart sent two staff officers, Major Andrew W. Venable and Captain Henry Lee, to look for army headquarters somewhere to the west, the direction in which Early had vanished. When he approached Carlisle on the evening of July, he found it occupied not by Lee, but by Major General William F. ("Baldy") Smith with Federal militia forces. He had ridden 125 miles since the previous morning and was not in good spirits. When his demand for surrender was rejected, he dropped some shells into the Carlisle barracks and set them on fire. At last, after a long, difficult and almost futile ride—which had given the enemy only minor inconveniences and had severely impeded the movements of his own army—Stuart learned, from one of Lee's messengers instead of his own, the whereabouts of the Confederate army. Instead of bringing intelligence, it was he who received it.

Colonel Marshall later tried to have Stuart court-martialed; he even declared, at a small dinner party, that Stuart should have been shot. He did not recognize that the lack of positive statement in his own composition of orders was perhaps more responsible for the absence of the cavalry than any other factor.[18]

Tucker laid out his analysis of the factors that caused the Confederate defeat at Gettysburg. To his way of thinking, inadequate staff work was the primary cause of the loss, and all other reasons flowed from that cause. The absence of cavalry, he declared, "led to the battle in circumstances that were not of Lee's choosing, deprived him of intelligence about Meade's concentration, and severely handicapped him at every turn both in the campaign and on the battlefield. A typical instance of the latter was Longstreet's groping flank march of July 2 without cavalry guide and over terrain no cavalry had reconnoitered."[19]

Tucker was one of the few critics to note the interplay of Lee's poor staff work and the resulting confusion about the precise meaning of the operational orders.

In 1965, Wilbur Sturtevant Nye, a former artillery officer who developed a sterling reputation as a Civil War historian, published *Here Come the Rebels!*, the work for which he is best known. This account of the invasion of Pennsylvania ends with the beginning of the battle.[20] Nye devoted a lengthy chapter to Stuart's Ride. "Many followers of Civil War history have felt, perhaps rightly so, that Stuart made the wrong choice in going east of the Federal army," began Nye . . .

> However, there were grave disadvantages in going by way of Shepherdstown. Stuart would have to cross the Blue Ridge once before getting to Shepherdstown and a second time later. The routes were filled with marching infantry and the crossings were in use by troops going north and wagons coming back with loot. To follow that route would take Stuart instantly and completely out of contact with the Federals and keep him in a state of ignorance for several days. Though the Rebels did not know it at the time, he would never have reached the Frederick area unless he defeated single-handedly several Federal corps. Likewise, he might have experienced great difficulty in getting through any of the passes west of Frederick, because Hooker had already issued orders for them to be seized and held. It was unlikely that he could reach the Waynesboro-Emmitsburg pass before the Federals. It was more likely that on June 30 he would still be in Cumberland Valley tagging along behind Longstreet's lengthy wagon train.

> In taking the route he chose, east of the Federals, he would have reached his assigned position on Ewell's right flank without encountering resistance of any consequence, provided he had started a day or two sooner and had not been delayed en route. But, having enjoyed such success, he would have been of little use to Lee. He would have been creeping along with Early from York to Wrightsville, several days' march ahead of the Federal army. He would, of course, have reached Gettysburg as soon as Lee.

> What should Stuart have done? The wisdom of hindsight suggests that he might have stayed where he was, in contact with the Federals. By making vigorous probes, employing more scouts like Mosby, he could have kept Lee supplied with reasonable, complete,

and up-to-date information on Federal movements. Then, when they started north, he might have dogged their heels, discovering where they were and what direction they were taking. This was information Lee desperately needed and that he never had. Lee shares the blame for not using the cavalry in its vital role of reconnaissance.[21]

Nye's analysis is fair and balanced, which may explain why it has survived the test of time.

The next major entrant into the arena was Edwin B. Coddington, whose 1968 epic work *The Gettysburg Campaign: A Study in Command*, published posthumously, is still considered by many to be the best single volume of the campaign—the "bible" for those truly serious about Gettysburg.[22] Coddington described the raid in some detail. He pointed out that Stuart filed the longest and most detailed report of any of Lee's subordinate officers, an effort by Stuart (according to Coddington) to defend his actions. The writer launched into a lengthy dissection of Stuart's report and an analysis of the merits of the ride that remains one of the most comprehensive and well-considered analyses written:

> General Stuart may have convinced himself and his friends that the military advantages gained in attacking the communications and supply lines of the Army of the Potomac were worth the delay in joining Lee, but no one else in either army believed it. The Union General Henry Hunt neatly summed up Stuart's exploit by saying: "It is a good lesson on cavalry raids around armies, a thing easily done but of no particular use."

> Although it was natural and understandable for a proud man such as Stuart to try to exalt his accomplishments and minimize his shortcomings, it was poor grace and unforgivable for him to try to find excuses at the expense of others. His complaint about the army not being where he thought it would be seemed to imply that all its movements should have been conditioned by what he chose to do. When near Hanover he had learned of the arrival of Meade's army at Taneytown. From this information he came to the unwarranted conclusion that Lee's army was already in York or Harrisburg. Annoyed that his own presuppositions had misled him, he accused two of his colleagues of tardiness and in so doing unwittingly questioned the soundness of Lee's strategy. "It is believed," he wrote, "that, had the corps of Hill and Longstreet moved on instead of halting near Chambersburg, York could have been the place of concentration instead of Gettysburg." After Hill and Longstreet,

Stuart's next culprit was Early, who had had the effrontery to depart from York without leaving word or a guide to direct Stuart to him. Early, Stuart charged, had "reason to expect me, and had been directed to look out for me. He heard my guns at Hanover, and correctly conjectured whose they were, but left me with no clue to his destination on leaving York, which would have saved me a long and tedious march to Carlisle and thence back to Gettysburg." Now who was derelict in the performance of his duties? Certainly not "Jeb" Stuart! By a neat sleight of hand he shifted the blame. Early's reaction when confronted with the charge after the war was surprisingly mild, though he emphatically denied having received instructions to "co-operate" with Stuart or "to send out scouts to endeavor to establish communications with him. Early had discussed the matter, he said, with Colonel Charles S. Venable, formerly of Lee's staff, who had agreed it was "absurd to suppose that I was to look out for the Cavalry and keep it informed of the movements of the army—that, in fact I was to play the part of a sort of wet-nurse for the cavalry." Beyond Stuart's report and the recollections of Major Henry B. McClellan there is no evidence to indicate that Lee or Ewell told Early to watch for Stuart.

In answer to his critics who complained of the lack of cavalry on July 1 Stuart rightly pointed to the availability of Jenkins' forces. He then observed that if the army had still felt the absence of his three brigades, Jenkins' cavalry had not been "as efficient as it ought to have been." Though this was a just criticism, Stuart forgot to mention that Lee had long worried about Jenkins' effectiveness as a cavalry leader and had wanted Stuart to direct him once he got to Pennsylvania.

If Stuart had been willing to arrive empty-handed, he could have joined Early before the battle and weakened the adverse comments of his critics. He had learned of Hooker's whereabouts in Maryland just after crossing his cavalry at Rowser's Ford early on June 28. Between then and late afternoon of June 29 his force had marched about forty-five miles to Westminster, and part of it had gone to Union Mills five miles farther north. They had spent many hours and gone many extra miles wrecking and seizing enemy property. If Stuart had decided to head straight north for Ewell's right wing without loitering along the way, he could have made Hanover instead of Westminster at a reasonable hour on June 29 without unduly taxing the energies of his men. There they could have obtained food and rest before an early start the next morning for a march of no more than fifteen miles to meet Early's column on its way from York to a point near Heidlersburg. There was a chance too that before coming up to Early, Stuart might have encountered Colonel White's troopers riding southwest on the York-Gettysburg Pike on the lookout for the enemy. But instead of this happy ending Stuart finally returned to the army at Gettysburg on the afternoon of July 2, over sixty hours late, and found himself, rightly or wrongly, in the position of a person who had betrayed a sacred trust.

Stuart's personal enemies never let him forget his performance, and over the years they made him the scapegoat for Confederate failure at Gettysburg. As a result his role in the campaign became an object of scorn and derision, as well as the most generally accepted explanation for what went wrong for the rebels. To say that Stuart's late arrival was a major cause of Lee's defeat is a little too pat an answer to the question of why the Confederates lost the battle. There was no doubt that when he was riding around Meade's army he was of little help to his commander. Who can say though what difference it might have made if he had met Early on June 30? He might have discovered the composition of the Federal force at Gettysburg, and Heth with his strong infantry division might have pushed boldly ahead to sweep Buford out of town before Reynolds could arrive with his corps, thus depriving this Pennsylvania community of its claim to fame. With Stuart there at the opening of the battle Lee might have decided upon a turning movement on July 2 to force Meade out of his position, instead of ordering Longstreet to attack the Federal left flank and Ewell the right. Such speculations are needed in appraising historical situations, but unless used with restraint they can lead to fruitless controversy.

Coddington continued:

One thing is sure. On the eve of July 1 Lee had his forces in splendid shape to carry out his strategy of defeating the Army of the Potomac "in detail," that is, one part of it at a time. If, as Stuart's accusers insisted, the absence of cavalry permitted Lee to be surprised into an unfortunate encounter of major proportions at Gettysburg, they overlooked two important elements in the situation. Meade was just as surprised, and the initial advantage lay with Lee.[23]

Lee's favorable position was largely due to his good judgment aided somewhat by luck. On June 28, the day of decision for three generals, he became convinced that the Union army was following him and made on the whole skillful arrangements to meet it. Stuart on that day received the same warnings of the approaching conflict, but he failed to see his duty clearly enough to prepare for it and thus lost the chance to redeem himself. General Fitz Lee raised the question of "whether Stuart exercised the discretion *undoubtedly given to him, judiciously*," and the answer is no. Therein lies the tragedy of "Jeb" Stuart in the Gettysburg Campaign.[24]

With that scathing indictment ringing, Coddington designated Stuart as one of the primary causes of the Confederate defeat.

Two important books appeared in 1986, a landmark year for the study of cavalry operations in the Gettysburg Campaign. Respected academic historian Emory M. Thomas penned a full-length biography of Stuart entitled *Bold Dragoon: The Life of J.E.B. Stuart*.[25] Thomas's treatment of Stuart's life is scholarly but highly critical at the same time; many students refer to it as revisionist history. One of the primary themes of Thomas's book is his use of *ex post facto* psychoanalysis of Stuart and his actions, a methodology that does not sit well with many students of the war who prefer a more traditional military interpretation. After addressing Stuart's role in the entire campaign, and reviewing the contents of Stuart's after-action report, Thomas offered his own opinion:

> Stuart's report/apologia was indeed unfortunate; it contained even more fantasy than his account of Brandy Station. Stuart's pretension and prevarication compounded his errors in the Gettysburg campaign. In fact Lee did grant him the discretion to take the route he did and to raid enemy lines of supply and communication on his way to join the army. Had his raiding not been so successful, Stuart might have joined the army in time to contribute to the ensuing battle. But Stuart moved too slowly, even before he captured the Federal wagon train. And once he had the wagons, he refused to give up his prize. He was greedy. He clearly underestimated the need for speed, and he gravely miscalculated the effect of his tardiness upon the campaign. And as he rode through enemy country, he seemed to see only the road on which he was, when he should have been seeing a map of Pennsylvania.[26]

Thomas went on to quote from Coddington's analysis, and called the assessment "fair." He continued:

> But compare Stuart's actions on this expedition with his conduct on the Dumfries or Chambersburg or Catlett's Station raids. In contrast to the rare brand of prudent audacity Stuart had displayed on former occasions, this time he had been both timid and careless. The man who had all but defined the art of reconnaissance had managed to lose two very large armies, his friends and his foes, within a

relatively small area (about fifty by thirty-five miles). Something was dreadfully wrong.

Stuart's critics, then and later, have erred when they accuse him of conducting his prolonged raid only in order to "do some great thing" to absolve himself for Brandy Station. He undertook this raid, not to atone for anything, but to confirm his vision of himself. And the difference is more than semantic.

Stuart had a serious problem with failure. Perhaps because he had failed so seldom at anything he deemed important, he never learned to confront failure. He feared failure perhaps more than anything else in life and certainly more than death. He dealt with failure not by dealing with it, by denying it. Stuart's reports on Brandy Station and Gettysburg, and more so, his letters to Flora, reveal him incapable of acknowledging shortcomings, much less failure. Stuart was an ironic victim of his own success; he had so often won that he became incapable of coping with defeat.[27]

The obvious problem with Thomas's approach is that it is extremely difficult (some would say utterly impossible) to accurately psychoanalyze someone more than a century after his death. The underlying thesis of Thomas's analysis remains in question.

The second major work to appear on this subject in 1986 was *The Cavalry at Gettysburg: A Tactical Study of Mounted Operations during the Civil War's Pivotal Campaign, 9 June-14 July, 1863*, by prominent cavalry historian Edward G. Longacre.[28] This award-winning book is the first full-length study of the critical role played by horse soldiers during the Gettysburg Campaign. Naturally, Longacre spent considerable energy addressing the Stuart controversy. Here is his take on Stuart's ride:

The lost time had worn away much of the gloss Stuart's reputation had accumulated over the past two years. In the weeks following his expedition, a chorus of critics would indict him for a number of crimes relating to his long absence. Soldiers and civilians alike— even members of the Confederate hierarchy—would accuse him of leaving General Lee sightless and vulnerable ("like unto the blind Samson feeling for the pillars of the temple of Dagon," in the words of one historian), causing him to stumble into battle on terms favorable to his enemy. Among Stuart's colleagues, criticism of his expedition ranged from "a useless, showy parade," to blame for every subsequent misfortune suffered by the Army of Northern

Virginia. One of Lee's staff officers even suggested that Stuart be shot for flagrant disobedience of orders.

Perhaps the most balanced assessment of Stuart's expedition was rendered forty years afterward by a veteran of the 9th Virginia Cavalry. "The man is a fool," he wrote, "that contends that Stuart disobeyed orders in riding around the Federal army. General Lee's orders to him plainly permitted him to do this, but the point is that Stuart ought not to have exercised the discretion conferred upon him. His hard horse sense ought to have told him to stick to Lee. That was the place where he was wanted. But...the criticism of Stuart is really not criticism. It is a lamentation that so great and powerful a man as he was not at Lee's right hand to counsel and advise with him about what was best to be done." In short, Lee missed Stuart's cavalry less than he missed Stuart.

Curiously, the man he had failed so deeply wrote little about Stuart's long absence. In his reports of the campaign, Lee confined his criticism to remarks that "the march toward Gettysburg was conducted more slowly than it would have been had the movements of the Federal Army been known," and that prior to the battle the army's operations were "much embarrassed by the absence of the cavalry."

Lee criticized his subordinates so infrequently that when he did he needed few words to drive home his feelings. This trait was evident during his belated rendezvous with Stuart late on 2 July. At first, the army commander regarded his cavalry leader with silence that was itself a rebuke. Finally he asked a quiet question: "General Stuart, where have you been?"

Flustered, Stuart attempted an explanation too long, too involved, and too vague for his superior's patience. Lee cut him short with a voice that smoldered: "I have not heard a word from you for days, and you the eyes and ears of my army!"

Embarrassed staff officers averted their eyes as Stuart struggled to reply. The cavalry leader looked like a man who had just taken a blow in the face.[29]

The prolific Longacre also addressed the controversy in a subsequent book called *Lee's Cavalrymen: A History of the Mounted Forces of the Army of Northern Virginia*, though he did not go into substantially more detail than he had in his previous work.[30]

The next major entrant into the arena was Mark Nesbitt's *Saber and Scapegoat: J. E. B. Stuart and the Gettysburg Controversy.*[31] Nesbitt, a Vietnam veteran, former park ranger, and historian at the Gettysburg National Military Park, penned the first book-length study devoted to Stuart's ride and the resulting controversy. It reached print in 1994. "I must admit that at one time, I too blamed Stuart for a major role in the Confederate defeat at Gettysburg," he observed. "I was not alone. It is truly amazing what careful study and a few eye-opening observations of fact will do in changing one's opinion." Nesbitt enumerated the primary criticisms of Stuart's ride, and concluded, "All those statements were patently false."[32] Nesbitt took up Mosby's cudgel and offered a stout defense of Stuart that, in most respects, parrots Mosby's effort.

Nesbitt's treatment of the tactical aspects of the ride and the controversy that followed are not examined in as much detail as they are in this book. However, following his tactical treatment he examined the 19th Century debates of Stuart's conduct. Nesbitt concluded with a cogent analysis that remains pertinent today:

> Perhaps the most remarkable thing about such studies is that historians have the advantage of hindsight as well as plenty of time in which to analyze and decide, to weigh and ponder, to propose and condemn. Stuart had none of that. He made life-and-death decisions from the saddle, with the same aching back, empty stomach, and blurry, sleepy mind as the rest of his troopers, and he had to do it quickly.
>
> It was easy for Coddington or Early to say that Stuart should have turned west upon crossing Early's track near Dover, but who knows what was going through Stuart's mind, what clutter or burden was occupying him at the moment? It is simple for Freeman to condemn him for not following orders, though even at his desk in his study, Freeman misunderstood Marshall's complicated, unclear directives. Stuart has been belittled for making immediate decisions, but had he not been the type to make them, and had he not made the correct ones so very often, he would never have attained his position before the Gettysburg campaign.
>
> Decisions can only be made once, with the knowledge, experience, and limited foresight that is available at the time, then acted upon with iron resolve. Regardless of what men will say *someday*, there are orders to follow and duty *today*. Sometimes that is all a man can

do. Sometimes that is all he needs to do. Certainly it is all anyone can ask him to do.[33]

And with that especially insightful analysis and well-written turn of phrase, Nesbitt ended his book. It did not, however, end the controversy. The coming of a new millennium did little to dampen the dispute. If anything, a bevy of new treatments released near the 140th anniversary of the battle provide additional fodder for the student of the controversy.

In 2001, Scott Bowden and Bill Ward published a controversial revisionist study of the Gettysburg Campaign entitled *Last Chance for Victory: Robert E. Lee and the Gettysburg Campaign*.[34] This book, the recipient of many major awards, tackles and dissects virtually every sacred belief about the Confederate defeat at Gettysburg. It contains much original thought, and no one who studies the battle can afford to leave it unread. Stuart's ride features prominently in this study. Like so many writers, Bowden and Ward believe Stuart's role played a large part in how the campaign unfolded and why Lee lost Gettysburg.

They offer an interesting interpretation of some of the language in Lee's orders to Stuart. For example, they believe Lee's use of the phrase "pass around their army" has been "almost universally misunderstood." The confusion is because of the false assumption that "pass around" meant Stuart should "ride around" the enemy army before moving north similar to what Stuart had done earlier in the war in his "Ride Around McClellan" in 1862. Mosby, continue Bowden and War, "whom Lee knew to be a reliable scout, had reported to Stuart that the widely scattered Federal corps bivouacked on the northern and northwestern ends of the Army of the Potomac could be cut right through without difficulty, and the Potomac crossed ten miles west of Rockville, Maryland, at Seneca Ford." As these authors emphasize, Mosby did not suggest that Southern cavalry should pass entirely around the Army of the Potomac. Such an attempt would drive the cavalry far to the south and east just to get into a position to enable a ride around the eastern flank of the Federals, at which time the Southern horse would have to turn back to the west in order to reach Seneca Ford.

Lee's use of the words "pass around" was understood by the principals involved as meaning to bypass the various Federal corps (Henry Slocum's Twelfth, Oliver Howard's Eleventh, and John Reynolds' First) that formed the northern and northwest flanks of the Army of the Potomac. This, after all, was the general route scouted by Mosby and reported by Stuart as being available for such a maneuver. Lee's words to Stuart, as well as his dispatches heretofore discussed regarding Stuart's mission in the campaign, leave no doubt that the phrase "pass around their army" meant move around and through the yawning gaps between the idle enemy corps.[35]

Unfortunately, Bowden and Ward fail to cite any original sources to support their contention that the principals involved, including Stuart, understood Lee's order to mean he was to pass *through* the Army of the Potomac's component pieces, and not around the entire army. The authors claim several events support their conclusion that Stuart did not do what Lee expected. They contend both Lee and Longstreet believed Stuart's ride across the Potomac was to be conducted quickly, at which time Stuart would find Ewell's corps and deploy on its right flank. This was all to be done before Hooker's army could react to Lee's move north. "Stuart's movement, therefore, was part of Lee's overall plan to steal a march on his enemy."

They next ask why an experienced cavalry leader like Stuart would ride northeast away from the Warrenton Turnpike to reach Haymarket if his intention all along was to ride around the Federal host. "In other words, Stuart would have never turned north to go to Haymarket, but would instead have taken a different road angling southeast in order to avoid Dan Sickles' Third Corps encamped at Centreville."

Bowden and Ward note that Mosby was both an outstanding scout and an attorney, and so knew the difference between riding through (between) the various enemy infantry corps and riding *around* the entire Federal army. Yet, according to Mosby, the idea was to "pass through" the idle Federals, which would "also result in the Federal army's transportation [being] destroyed and communications broken," which might seriously derange Hooker's effort to race after The Army of Northern Virginia. Mosby, claim the authors, "never suggested, advised, or intimated that Stuart undertake a ride around the entirety of the Federal host." Mosby had orders to meet up with Stuart's column at the junction formed by the Haymarket to Gum Springs Road and Little River Turnpike. According to the scout, when he arrived there he discovered the "head of Hancock's column . . . heading toward the Potomac." Mosby backtracked and rode north down the Shenandoah Valley.

"All of this evidence considered in its totality—Lee's letters, Longstreet's correspondence, Mosby's scouting reports and memoirs, and Jeb Stuart's attempt to turn his command northward at Haymarket," continue Bowden and Ward, "presents clear and unmistakable proof that Stuart, in attempting to 'pass by the rear' of the Federal troops on the eastern slopes of Bull Run Mountain, was an attempt to 'pass through' the widely separated Federal corps. Thus, when Lee used the term 'pass around their army' and Longstreet penned the phrase 'passing by the rear,' both generals were referring to the path scouted by Mosby which was to 'pass through' the idle Federal corps nearest the Confederates." Lee nor Longstreet, conclude these authors, "ordered, or gave Stuart permission to embark on a route that would carry his command around the southern, eastern, and northeastern extremities of the Army of the Potomac."[37]

Although articulately presented, and with much originality of thought, Bowden and Ward offer little in the way of corroboration for their vehement condemnation of Stuart's actions. They continued their indictment of Stuart by describing the state of his command at the end of the ride as "worn out," which indeed it was. Worse, the cavalier had exhausted his trio of brigades "on an unauthorized raid that violated his orders. With the enemy close at hand and the whereabouts of his own army still a mystery, one wonders when Stuart anticipated he would be able to give his command the rest it so desperately needed."[38]

According to Bowden and Ward, Stuart's poor decisions, combined with poor staff work, led to the debacle in Pennsylvania. To their way of thinking, Stuart's conduct of his ride was one of the four most important factors that led to the Confederate defeat at Gettysburg and triggered many of the subsequent errors that plagued the Army of Northern Virginia during its three days of fighting in Pennsylvania. "One of the most controversial aspects of the Gettysburg drama is the idea that General Lee gave Jeb Stuart permission to go on a raid near the beginning of the campaign," explain the authors. They had more to say on this always fascinating issue:

> Virtually every influential writer on the subject advances the notion that Lee's written orders to Stuart were either so ambiguous that Stuart could interpret his instructions any way he saw fit, or that the commanding general's orders gave Stuart permission to perform

the raid he actually undertook. *Neither view is correct* [emphasis in the original]."

Stuart, claim Bowden and Ward, was given clear-cut orders. He had the discretion "framed by certain restrictions to choose the route he would take across the Potomac." Once across, however, his primary mission was to "move on & feel the right of Ewell's troops." After Stuart joined up with Ewell's infantry, he would have the opportunity to collect information and provisions "while retaining the latitude to cause the enemy as much damage as possible within his primary task. Lee's parameters for Stuart's movements, including the all-important restraining orders directing Stuart to 'withdraw' and retrace his steps westward before turning northward to the Potomac should the cavalry general encounter 'hindrance,' came out of Lee's realistic analysis of the operational situation." As far as Bowden and Ward are concerned, the written instructions Stuart received were easily understood "if analyzed in the historical context within which they were written (i.e., the location of the respective elements of each army, the author of each piece of correspondence, and so on).

Bowden and Ward conclude as follows:

> A close and dispassionate examination demonstrates that Jeb Stuart, a gallant and exceptional military officer, made a critical error in judgment after he approached Haymarket on June 25 that resulted in his disobeying Lee's orders. The result was that Stuart and his three finest brigades of cavalry were not available when Lee needed them most. The ramifications of his act limited Lee's options, especially once the enemy was found and engaged. Stuart's actions seriously impacted Confederate chances for victory in Pennsylvania.[39]

It should again be pointed out that this condemnation depends entirely on an interpretation of the operating orders, as opposed to any support found in primary source material. Thus, while their indictment is well-reasoned and quite fascinating to read and ponder, they offer nothing new in the way of firsthand accounts that directly support their position.

*   *   *

The approach of the 140th anniversary of the battle of Gettysburg in 2003 unleashed a flurry of new books on the conflict in Pennsylvania, including three treatments of the entire battle written by three respected historians. The first to appear was Noah Andre Trudeau's fine work *Gettysburg: A Testing of Courage*, which sought to update Coddington's landmark campaign study.[40] Trudeau correctly points out that Lee and Stuart had planned similar moves to those anticipated during the Gettysburg Campaign, and that neither had any reason to expect difficulties as a consequence.[41] After discussing the operational orders for Stuart's expedition, Trudeau penned the following:

> Stuart made his first mistake in this operation on June 24. Faced with the task of deciding which two brigades would remain behind and which three would undertake the movement, Stuart chose the best to accompany him. Left with the army were the brigades of Brigadier Generals Beverly H. Robertson and William E. ("Grumble") Jones. Robertson had muffed an important assignment at Brandy Station on June 9, and Jones and Lee were barely on speaking terms. Neither was well known to Lee, nor did either enjoy his confidence or comprehend his expectations. Although he was following his instructions to the letter, Stuart had badly misread the degree of personal connection his superior required. Longstreet understood this about Lee, and so had specifically requested that Stuart select an officer whom Lee knew and trusted, Brigadier General Wade Hampton, to coordinate the cavalry remaining with the army. Stuart's failure to comply embittered Longstreet. The infantryman's later recollections would roundly condemn the cavalryman's vainglorious ride, and not always fairly so.

> Stuart had valid reasons for being where he was on the morning of June 25, and he had Lee's sanction to "judge whether you can pass around their army without hindrance, doing them all the damage you can, and cross the [Potomac] river east of the [Blue Ridge] mountains." Once his scouts had cleared the way through Glasscock Gap, his riders continued toward Centreville, where John Mosby's information suggested they might find easy passage through Hooker's rear echelon.[42]

Although Trudeau did not come right out and condemn Stuart's actions with language as strong as that employed by many other historians, his use of the word "vainglorious" to describe the ride signifies his position on the matter.

Two significant works were published in 2003, 140th anniversary of the battle. Steven E. Woodworth of Texas Christian University published a short narrative history of the Gettysburg Campaign.[43] At only 240 pages, this work does not purport to be a definitive account of the battle, but it is a readable overview on the subject. Consequently, Woodworth's account does not go into minute detail when dealing with Stuart. However, like most other historians, Woodworth accuses Stuart of disobeying Lee's orders and contributing to the Confederate defeat at Gettysburg:

> For the year that Lee had now commanded the Army of Northern Virginia, his main reliance for intelligence had been on his cavalry chief, Major General Jeb Stuart, a master of cavalry scouting. Stuart, however, was having a bad month. Surprised at Brandy Station on the 9th, he now had made highly questionable use of the discretion Lee had given him and had taken himself and half of his cavalry corps—including the best troops and commanders—on an attempt to ride completely around the Army of the Potomac, as he had done twice before at earlier stages of the war. While Lee was moving northward on the west side of the Army of the Potomac, Stuart would stay east of it, get well north of it, and then cross in front of it to join Lee to the west of the enemy, presumably bringing lots of good information about just where every Federal unit was located.
>
> Unfortunately for Stuart, about the time he launched this effort, Hooker had put the Union army into rapid northward movement, and subsequently Meade had continued that march to the north. Taking the long outside arc and trying to move past the hard-marching blue-coat foot soldiers, Stuart certainly had his information about where the enemy's main body lay. It was right between his own command and the rest of Lee's army, but he could not share that discovery with Lee. Stuart's gray-clad cavaliers had to ride a great deal farther than he had planned to get around the Army of the Potomac, and they were out of contact with Lee at a time when they were supposed to be doing the army's scouting. Although Stuart had left Lee with half the army's cavalry, the brigade commanders he had left behind were not particularly enterprising, and in any case it was Stuart on whom Lee depended to conduct reconnaissance.
>
> The absence of Stuart was a problem but not necessarily a fatal development. Lee had gotten the information he needed, though not

from the source he would have preferred. As for the Army of the Potomac, Lee was surprised to hear that it was that close, assuming that Stuart would have informed him as soon as it crossed the river. Nonetheless, it was natural for the Yankees to be where they were. Lee had promised Jefferson Davis that his own northward move would pull the Federals after him, bringing them out of Virginia, and that is what had happened. The silence from Stuart had led Lee to believe that the showdown battle he had come north to seek might be delayed longer than he had initially thought. Harrison's report told him that it was at hand after all. Lee respected Meade, but no general could be expected to have his army full in hand and responding efficiently to his orders within the space of a few days. That suited Lee well, for he intended to meet the Army of the Potomac, still adjusting to its new commander, just as soon as he could get his own army concentrated. Until that time, perhaps another four or five days hence, he would wait.[44]

With that, Woodworth condemned Stuart for being away from the Army of Northern Virginia while it advanced into Pennsylvania.

Historian Stephen W. Sears also addressed the Gettysburg Campaign in a lengthy treatment published in 2003.[45] According to Sears, Stuart's decisions and conduct were a primary reason for the Confederate defeat. After discussing the operating orders in great detail, which included a discussion of the various ambiguities and inconsistencies contained therein, he pointed out the following:

> At 1 o'clock on the morning of Thursday, June 25, at the head of the brigades of Wade Hampton, Fitz Lee, and John Chambliss (commanding in place of the wounded Rooney Lee), Jeb Stuart set off for Pennsylvania. Events over the next eight days would demonstrate that, whatever else occurred, Stuart faithfully carried out General Lee's orders. He rode around the enemy's army (although not without hindrance) and confused it and broke its communications, he gathered military intelligence, he collected ample supplies, and he tried his best to "feel the right" of Ewell's corps. In doing all this he also rode into a torrent of controversy.[46]

In his final chapter, where he addressed the reasons for the Southern loss, Sears wrote:

> This explanation [that the Army of the Potomac was ready to meet a threat while the Army of Northern Virginia was not], in obvious reference to the second day's fighting, suggested that a cause

beyond General Lee's control contributed to the defeat—that is, a lack of intelligence about the Federal army. As early as July 18, Charles M. Blackford of Longstreet's staff was writing his wife, "General Stuart is much criticized for his part in our late campaign....In his anxiety to 'do some great thing' General Stuart carried his men beyond the range of usefulness and Lee was not thereafter kept fully informed as to the enemy's movements as he should have been...." Lee in his report was uncharacteristically blunt: "The movements of the army preceding the battle of Gettysburg had been much embarrassed by the absence of the cavalry."

In going on to note that Stuart had exercised "the discretion given him," Lee appeared to accept a share of the blame for that embarrassment. Yet his serious misjudgment in permitting Stuart to go off on his improbable adventure in the first place largely escaped notice. Stuart's dereliction in many eyes (including Lee's) was his utter failure to communicate with the army during his long sweep around Hooker's (and then Meade's) army. When Major Andrew Venable found Lee on the July 1 battlefield, he brought with him the first news of the cavalry in a week. Apparently it never occurred to Stuart during that eventful week that cavalry scouting reports on the Yankee army would be a great deal more valuable to General Lee than the 125 captured Yankee wagons he was dragging along with his column.

If Stuart in fact expected the brigades of Beverly Robertson and Grumble Jones, left behind with the army, to do Lee's scouting for him, that was a point he and Lee failed to settle in advance. Lee ignored the two and just waited for Stuart to appear; he seemed only to trust Stuart to bring him usable intelligence. As a consequence, when the Confederates stumbled into battle on July 1, they not only knew nothing of the opposing army but nothing of the battlefield either. Lee was guilty of mishandling his cavalry during the campaign, but Jeb Stuart's failing was the more grave. His lack of reconnaissance deprived Lee of one of the cornerstones on which his campaign was based—the choice of battlefield.[47]

Sears places the primary responsibility for the loss squarely on Stuart's shoulders.

In addition to all of the books discussed in this chapter, many magazine articles have addressed the controversy surrounding Stuart's actions, some taking the cavalrymen's side[48] and others not.[49]

We have reviewed the major treatments of the Confederate cavalier's ride and a few trends stand out: most writers either side for Stuart or against him. There is no middle ground. They either condemn the cavalier or praise him by failing to find fault in his conduct. Most writers are critical of Stuart; indeed, few openly defend his actions. Most focus exclusively on his decisions, and not on the issue of whether Stuart obeyed Lee's orders. Even fewer examine all of the circumstances surrounding Stuart's ride.

Having surveyed the writings of both the contemporaries of Stuart and of modern historians, we will now present our analysis of these events in the Conclusion that follows.

Chapter 12

Conclusion

"The ranks of our cavalry were much reduced by its long and arduous march, repeated conflicts, and insufficient supplies of food and forage, but the day after its arrival at Gettysburg it engaged the enemy's cavalry with unabated spirit, and effectually protected our left."

— Robert E. Lee, Official report of the Gettysburg Campaign

T he debate over whether Jeb Stuart's long journey into Pennsylvania contributed to, or directly caused, the Confederate defeat at Gettysburg is as old as the battle itself. The argument caused further subdivisions among an already divided group of veterans. Because the battle of Gettysburg was touted soon after the war as the "turning point" of the conflict—that point beyond which the Confederacy, it was claimed, could not have hoped to win the war with major battlefield victories—debate over the causes of its loss took on a relentless intensity.

Discussions of Gettysburg are full of such debates. In addition to the question of Stuart's role, several other major disputes provided fodder for the veterans' heated discussions over "responsibility" for the battle's loss. Should Richard Ewell have assaulted Cemetery Hill on the first day while the Federals were rallying on the high ground? Was James Longstreet too slow in attacking the Union left on the battle's second day? Was Pickett's Charge on the third day properly planned, executed, and supported? The list is nearly endless; definitive answers, however, remain elusive. Wrap all of it within the shroud of the "Lost Cause" environment (amid concerted efforts to absolve Robert E. Lee of personal blame) and it is easy to understand the vitriol veterans harbored on one side or the other of each question.

When examining these controversies, it is important to keep in mind that the vast majority of these participants had elevated their former commanders to hero status—leaders under whom they had marched, fought, and bled (in many cases), often for the duration of the war. These "heroes" were men they knew and loved, even if they never had the privilege of commanding a moment's attention from any of them. For example, articles, speeches, letters, and books written by General Lee's foot soldiers are replete with admiration for their leader, one in whom they expressed complete confidence and for whom no effort would have failed if, for instance, his lieutenants would have only done as he ordered.

In Stuart's case, such an assumption formed the basis of argument for his detractors. As has been demonstrated in the previous three chapters, the foundation of the conflict over Stuart's role in the campaign rests almost entirely on his success or failure in following Lee's orders. Historians have since joined heartily in this dialogue. Several points must be fully considered when discussing this most basic and underlying facet of the debate.

* * *

Most of Stuart's detractors claim his failure to provide the Army of Northern Virginia with adequate intelligence of Federal movements caused Lee to blunder into a battle he did not desire, upon ground he did not choose. Sufficient evidence exists to demonstrate this criticism may not be justified. An important dispatch that was <u>not</u> reproduced in the *Official Records* of the Civil War has wallowed in obscurity since 1866, when it was published in John B. Jones's diary kept during his years spent working in the Confederate War Department. In this dispatch, composed by Stuart and forwarded to Lee, is a report that the Army of the Potomac was marching after Lee's army.

The dispatch reads as follows:

> Headquarters, Cavalry Division,
> June 27, 1863.
>
> General:—I took possession of Fairfax C.H. this morning at nine o'clock, together with a large quantity of stores. The main body of Hooker's army has gone toward Leesburg, except the garrison of

Alexandria and Washington, which has retreated within the fortifications.

Very respectfully, Your obedient servant,

J.E.B. Stuart, Major-General.[1]

Whether Stuart can be blamed because the courier never made it to Lee is a separate question (indeed, there is no evidence he only sent one messenger). However, the evidence plainly demonstrates he passed on intelligence critical to both the Southern army and the authorities in Richmond. Complicating matters is the fact that the Confederate War Department received a copy of Stuart's dispatch but made no effort to determine whether it had reached General Lee. As best as we can determine today, Lee never saw this information despite Stuart's efforts to place it in his hands. The fact that the dispatch was not reproduced in the *Official Records* provided Stuart's critics with grounds to claim the cavalier failed to inform Lee of the whereabouts of the enemy, leaving the Army of Northern Virginia to its fate and vulnerable to attack as it groped blindly across the Pennsylvania countryside. One can imagine how the debate over Stuart's efforts to forward intelligence would have been different had this dispatch been included in the *Official Records*. We do not believe Stuart can properly or accurately be blamed for failing to report to Lee that Joe Hooker's Army of the Potomac was marching northward when evidence exists that he attempted to do just that.

During the winter of 1863-1864, Lee's aide Charles Marshall gathered all available reports and materials to prepare Lee's report on the Gettysburg Campaign. Marshall sent several times for Stuart to complete his own accounting. Although this episode was discussed in an earlier chapter outlining the controversy that raged in the years following the battle, we think it bears repeating. "At last General Stuart brought his report," Marshall recounted, "and asked me to read it carefully, and to tell him what I thought of his conduct." According to the aide, he gave numerous reasons to Stuart why he believed the cavalier had not obeyed Lee's orders in maintaining contact with the army as he moved north, and that he [Stuart] had not provided information on the movements of the enemy.[2]

"Stuart said that when he crossed at Rowser's Ferry, and found that Hooker had crossed the day before above him, he had sent a dispatch to

General Lee back by way of Ashby's Gap [referring to the June 27 dispatch that appears only in the Jones diary and quoted above]," explained Marshall. "We never got that dispatch, and, as I showed him, if we had, still we had no cavalry to get information for us."[3] Although his explanation clearly admits that Stuart defended himself by bringing up the dispatch, the existence of which is verified by its appearance in the Jones diary, Marshall's account is disingenuous. Had such critical information about the Federal pursuit reached Lee, the events would have almost certainly played out much differently during the four days leading up to July 1. Marshall's failure to mention the June 27 dispatch during subsequent decades of criticizing Stuart's role in the campaign speaks loudly in favor of the dispatch's importance. Despite a plethora of speeches and broad body of written work, Marshall never mentioned its existence or that Stuart had claimed to have sent just such a report on enemy movements. Since he did not personally see it, Marshall dismissed its possible existence altogether.

From available primary sources, it is clear Lee began to worry about the whereabouts of his trusted cavalry chief and his command soon after the Southern army began marching north. When Lee arrived at Cashtown, just six miles west of Gettysburg, on the morning of July 1, he could plainly hear the distant field pieces signaling the beginning of a battle. "General Lee exhibited a degree of anxiety and impatience and expressed his regret at the absence of the cavalry," recalled a staff officer. Lee lamented "that he had been kept in the dark ever since crossing the Potomac and intimated that Stuart's disappearance had materially hampered his movements and disorganized the plans" for the invasion of Pennsylvania.[4]

Although obviously distressed, Lee was trying to determine just how large an enemy force was in front of him at Gettysburg. "Have you heard anything about my cavalry? Any news to give me about General Stuart?" he inquired of his corps and division commanders. Major General Henry Heth overheard the anxious Lee say, "I hope no disaster has overtaken my cavalry."[5] One of his staff officers recounted that Lee "repeatedly stated that in consequence of the absence of Stuart with the cavalry he was unaware of the near proximity of the Federal army, and when [A. P.] Hill reported a large force of infantry in his front on July 1st, he did not believe it."[6]

Major Campbell Brown, an aide to General Ewell, claims to have overheard a similar discussion later that same day. Lee, "with a peculiar searching, almost querulous, impatience, which I had never seen in him before [asked] whether Gen'l Ewell had heard anything from Gen'l Jeb Stuart, & on my replying in the negative, said that he had heard nothing from or of him for three days, & that Gen'l Stuart had not complied with his instructions. 'I told him to cross one of the upper fords of the Potomac, keeping along the Eastern base of the [Blue] Ridge, & constantly in communication with me, & rather than abandon communications to fall back into the Gaps of the mountain, but he has gone off clear around Gen'l Meade's army & I see by a paper that he is near Washington,'" explained the general. According to Brown, the Confederate commander concluded, "Tell Gen'l Ewell to send out to his left & try to open communications with Gen'l Stuart. I am told that firing was heard last night near Hanover Junction, [and] that may be his command." Lee's comments took Brown aback. "This from a man of Lee's habitual reserve surprised me at the time, I being a young staff officer of a subordinate commander. I now appreciate that he was really uneasy and irritated by Stuart's conduct & had no objection to his hearing of it. If no ill consequences had happened, I suppose Lee would have passed the matter over lightly in his report. But as the battle was lost, it became necessary to enlarge on this among other consequences—and his talk to me before his Staff passed unnoticed & forgotten except by me & one or two others."[7]

Because he was a reserved and very circumspect man, Lee never stated his opinion on the issue in writing during, or more importantly *after*, the war. Some have argued that because Lee barely addressed Stuart's role in the campaign, he must have been furious with his cavalry chief. In other words, Lee's was a condemnation by omission. "The movements of the army preceding the battle of Gettysburg had been much embarrassed by the absence of the cavalry," stated Lee's after-action report of the campaign.[8] Here again, however, must be noted the 19th Century definition of "embarrassed" as used in the report. Lee was admitting that his movements were hindered by a lack of information; he was *not* claiming that Stuart's actions were shameful, which is, unfortunately, the traditional argument or "spin" some modern commentators have applied to Lee's verbiage.

After relating the movements of Stuart and his cavalry, Lee's official report continues: "The ranks of our cavalry were much reduced by its long and arduous march, repeated conflicts, and insufficient supplies of food and forage, but the day after its arrival at Gettysburg it engaged the enemy's cavalry with unabated spirit, and effectually protected our left."[9] Lee, however, did not personally write this report. His aide, Col. Charles Marshall, penned it and Lee read and signed it. As previously demonstrated, Marshall blamed Stuart for Lee's defeat at Gettysburg. "I then concluded my report for General Lee," Marshall admitted. "In doing so I dealt with Stuart in the plainest language, in fact, I have told him [General Lee] before, I thought he ought to be shot," for going on his ride just prior to a major battle. Marshall's admission is nothing if not revealing.[10]

Many of Stuart's critics argue these sparse references, such as those included in Lee's report, were intended to demonstrate the great commander's displeasure with his cavalry chief. Major Henry B. McClellan observed, perhaps rightly, "It was not the want of cavalry that General Lee bewailed, for he had enough of it had it been properly used. It was the absence of Stuart himself that he felt so keenly; for on him he had learned to rely to such an extent that it seemed as if his cavalry were concentrated in his person, and from him alone could information be expected."[11]

McClellan's opinion warrants more attention than it has heretofore received. As one of Stuart's staff officers and a man in whom the cavalier confided frequently, McClellan was in a position to observe what Stuart became, in time, to Lee. By June 1863 Stuart was more than a trusted corps commander—more than just a capable subordinate officer. Lee's affection for Stuart pervades his official correspondence, but is especially conspicuous in his letters to his wife. It is no stretch to conclude that Lee was deeply concerned about the personal safety of his cavalry chief.

Others claim Lee's failure to promote Stuart to lieutenant general in the fall of 1863, when Wade Hampton and Fitz Lee received promotions to major general and assumed command of divisions, also reflected Lee's displeasure with Stuart. This claim is baseless. The Army of Northern Virginia's mounted arm had just been formed into a corps for the first time, and while lieutenant generals usually held corps command, it was not uncommon for a major general to lead a corps in a Confederate army.

Further, such promotions had to be approved by the Confederate Senate, and that argumentative body often withheld promotions. During the fall of 1863, there were no openings for lieutenant generals, and only two cavalry officers—Hampton and Nathan Bedford Forrest—ever received promotion to that coveted rank, and then only during the war's final days in 1865.[12]

If it were true that Lee was displeased with Stuart, he never said so publicly during or after the war, and he never took steps to remove his cavalry chief from command or to censure him for as long as Stuart lived. Had Lee been miffed at Stuart, the proud and sensitive cavalier would almost certainly have reported that fact (or at the very least alluded to it) to his wife Flora, with whom he corresponded frequently and candidly. On July 10, he swaggered, "My Cavalry has nobly sustained its reputation and done better and harder fighting than it ever has since the war." A few days later, when he had more time to write, he offered her more detail. "I had a grand time in Pennsylvania," he declared, "and we returned without defeat, to recuperate and reinforce, when no doubt the role will be re-enacted. I shelled Carlisle and burnt the barracks. I crossed near Dranesville and went close to Georgetown and Washington, cutting four important railroads, joining our army in time for the battle of Gettysburg, with 900 prisoners and 200 wagons and splendid teams." He concluded, "I have been blessed with great success on this campaign and the accidents and losses in the way of captives are in no way chargeable to my command."[13] Stuart's private correspondence is devoid of any suggestion that Lee was unhappy with his performance.

Stuart's detractors often overlook a statement by Lee in his official report that concedes Stuart acted within the scope of his orders in making his ride. Lee wrote that his cavalry chief's route and activities were an "exercise of the discretion given him."[14] When he penned his own after-action report, Stuart confirmed it. "It was deemed practicable to move entirely in the enemy's rear, intercepting his communications with his base (Washington)," he claimed, "and, inflicting damage upon his rear, to rejoin the army in Pennsylvania in time to participate in its actual conflicts." He correctly, albeit a bit melodramatically, pointed out that his raid "involved serious loss to the enemy in men and materiel (over 1,000 prisoners having been captured), and spread terror and consternation to the very gates of the capital."[15] Most of the 1,000 prisoners, however, were wagon teamsters or detached cavalry, and were hardly a "serious loss" to the Union army. The loss of the wagon train only temporarily inconvenienced Meade. But the fact remains that Stuart pounced on the opportunity to carry out his orders—to collect provisions for the use of the army—when it presented itself. If blame is to be leveled as to whether Stuart followed orders, the culpability probably rests with Col. Charles Marshall. After all, it was Marshall who drafted the original orders for the ride on June 22. Those orders—recounted for the reader in the Introduction to this volume—were vaguely worded and created the very problems set forth herein. We shall now examine them in more detail.

When James Longstreet, the commander of Lee's First Corps, initially responded to Stuart's request for orders, he advised the cavalryman, "You had better not leave us, therefore, unless you can take the route in rear of the enemy." This injunction was the first of several mixed messages the cavalry chief received. Lee's own note, sent the same day, gave Stuart permission to move north, guard the mountain passes, keep contact with Ewell's right, and "collect all the supplies you can for the use of the army." Both missives were more vague than they were specific, but with them in hand Stuart formulated his plan. Based on John Mosby's advice that Hooker's thinly stretched line (nearly 25 miles long) could be easily pierced, Stuart finalized his design and sought Lee's approval.

Stuart received the army commander's reply on June 23, and it pleased him. However, it too was vague and ambiguous. Lee granted Stuart wide discretion. The horseman would have to judge "whether you can pass around [Hooker's] army without hindrance, doing them all the damage you can," and to "move on and feel the right of Ewell's troops, collecting information, provisions, etc." The wording of this message was nothing short of illogical—especially in light of Lee's earlier instructions, where he expressed concern that Hooker "might steal a march on us" and make for the Potomac ahead of the Southerners.

In addition to providing Stuart two different routes of march, Lee's second letter downplayed his desire that Stuart maintain constant and direct contact with Ewell by allowing him to "move on and feel the right of Ewell's troops." This stands in stark contrast to Lee's earlier demand that Stuart "*take position* on General Ewell's right, *place yourself* in communication with him, *guard* his flank, *keep him informed* of the enemy's movements . . . [emphasis added]." Further, the tone of the

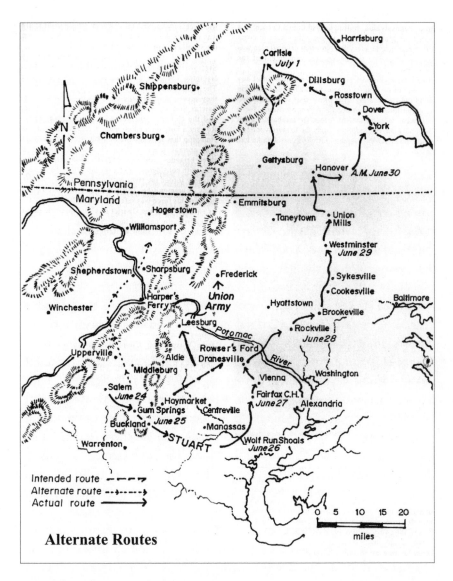

Intended route - - - →
Alternate route - -→ - - - →
Actual route ——————→

Alternate Routes

missive, when taken in its entirety, smacks more of permission to allow a classic mounted raid behind enemy lines than it does of ordering a simple flank-guarding mission. In all likelihood Stuart read it the same way. Veterans and historians, seeking to contrast Stuart's activities with Lee's supposedly specific orders, failed then and now to evaluate the raid in light of Lee's more recent—and more discretionary—commands.

*   *   *

Another school of thought claims that Stuart undertook the ride (some label or denigrate his expedition by calling it little more than a "joy ride") while still smarting from the surprise he suffered at Brandy Station on June 9, as well as the public fallout from that action that followed. This, compounded by the defeat of his horsemen at Upperville, prompted Stuart to attempt something spectacular in an effort to reassert the dominance of his troopers and polish his own tarnished image at the same time. Another sneaky "ride around the Union Army" would be just the thing to pitch embarrassment upon the Federal cavalry and the commander *du jour*, and once again throw Washington into a panic—all while Lee's foot soldiers tramped deeper into enemy territory. Given his competitive warrior spirit, Stuart certainly would have relished the laurels that would have been heaped upon him with another ride around the Army of the Potomac. He was also acutely aware, however— especially after Brandy Station and Upperville—that the past was no longer the present; the enemy cavalry had evolved since the previous year. The Eastern Theater Federal horsemen had finally been brought together under the blanket of their own cohesive cavalry corps. They fought Stuart to a standstill at Brandy Station and steadfastly slugged it out against his vaunted riders during the weeks that followed. As Major McClellan candidly observed in the wake of the battle for Fleetwood Hill at Brandy Station, the Federals "gained on this day that confidence in themselves and in their commanders which enabled them to contest so fiercely the subsequent battle-fields of June, July, and October."[16] Given this, it is more likely Stuart was on the same page as both Lee and Longstreet regarding how best to use his cavalrymen in the campaign to come.

Fortunately for Stuart, and contrary to what many historians have written, reasonably good luck followed him for the entire expedition. Most obvious is the fact that his enemy fumbled several opportunities to interrupt, cut off his ride, or capture and destroy his command altogether. The confusion over who had authority over the forces assigned to picket the Potomac River fords meant Col. Charles Russell Lowell's 2nd Massachusetts Cavalry was not at Rowser's Ford when Wade Hampton's Brigade approached the river. Stuart managed an unlikely personal escape from Elon Farnsworth's troopers at Hanover, when many others in his position would have been killed, wounded, or captured. Finally, Judson Kilpatrick's failure to pursue Stuart aggressively after the

Hanover combat provided Stuart with the breathing room he so desperately needed to prevent a command breakdown, or even the capture or scattering of his column that might have occurred had the Union cavalry been more aggressively handled. Moreover, the capture of the 125 wagons provided desperately needed fodder for Stuart's horses. It is difficult to argue that good luck did not ride with Jeb Stuart throughout much of his expedition.

*   *   *

Bitter recriminations inevitably followed the Confederate defeat at Gettysburg, and a scapegoat was needed in order to rationalize the stunning loss. The passage of Stuart's column so close to the national capital caused a great deal of fear and consternation in Washington, and the Southern troopers succeeded in damaging Union lines of communication and supply. However, the minimal damage inflicted did not justify the absence of the cavalry from Lee's army for so lengthy a period. Although most observers point to the wagon train captured in Maryland as the critical factor that delayed Stuart's arrival at Gettysburg, not everyone saw it that way. "Here was a godsend for our poor horses," recalled Capt. William Blackford, Stuart's engineering officer, "for every wagon was loaded with oats intended for Meade's army and it did one's heart good to see the way the poor brutes got on the outside of those oats."[17]

For all of their size and strength, horses are fragile beasts. They require a tremendous amount of rest, fodder, fresh water, and personal care and attention in order to keep them in decent physical condition. A cavalry column on the move offers few opportunities to keep the animals in good health. Stuart had served as the regimental quartermaster of the 1st U.S. Cavalry in the years prior to the Civil War, and he keenly understood the importance of making sure cavalrymen had adequate supplies to feed and maintain both men and horses. Stuart understood the importance of the cargo carried in those wagons, and without those tons of fodder it is difficult to conclude how his starving horses could have carried on much longer—or ever reached Gettysburg in a condition to fight a major engagement the day after their arrival. The wagons also carried fodder and provisions that were used by other elements of Lee's army. These supplies helped the Confederates carry on with the fighting around Gettysburg and assisted the Southerners during their long retreat into Virginia.[18]

Without those wagons, Stuart would not have been able to carry off the provisions stripped from the farmers in Pennsylvania. Therefore, the wagons provided the means necessary for Stuart to fulfill that portion of Lee's order directing him to collect all the provisions he could for the use of the army. In addition to the skirmishing and fighting conducted by the Southerners along the road to Gettysburg, much of their time was consumed loading tons of captured cargo into the wagons for their own use and to present to Lee's army once they found it. Therefore, a full understanding of the totality of the activities conducted by Stuart's troopers—marching, skirmishing, fighting, confiscating and loading tons of provisions, and the consequent exhaustion that resulted—makes the common characterization of Stuart's expedition as a simple "joy ride" all the more unreasonable. This much should be obvious from even a general understanding of the events of the ride.

There is a further point to consider regarding the wagons and their contents. Without the large constant supply of fodder, which was replenished along the way, Stuart would have been forced to regularly turn out his horses to graze, consuming a great deal of time spreading the animals and brigades across a wide swath of terrain. The availability of high-grade fodder in the wagons allowed Stuart to maintain a more compact column, and one able to respond to an enemy threat more quickly. Thus, the speed with which he was able to move across Maryland and Pennsylvania could not have been equaled had the horses required more grazing. The grueling pace Stuart maintained, which has been amply demonstrated in this study, is unmistakably evident in the writings left by the ride's participants.

Stuart was always cognizant that speed was essential. According to Pvt. J. A. Buxton (reproduced in Chapter 2), in order to both keep up a brisk pace and shorten the wagon train's length, before leaving Rockville Stuart ordered that two mules be disconnected from each wagon. This decision left the burden of pulling the wagon to the remaining pair of mules, shortened the train (the four-mule teams were harnessed two abreast), and permitted the Confederates to regularly substitute the harnessed mules for fresh ones. The participants agreed the mules were stubborn, starving, and a constant headache. Stuart's strategy, however, extended and enhanced their performance, made the train's length more manageable, and the wagons more defensible.

In addition to the provisions the wagons carried, once the battle ended the rolling stock was put to good use as ambulances. They comprised part of a train stretching seventeen miles long carrying thousands of Lee's wounded soldiers away from the field.[19] In many ways, the wagons allowed many of Lee's soldiers and animals to continue fighting in Pennsylvania as long as they did, and many made it back home only because of the wagons Stuart seized along the way. Contrary to what so many have written, Stuart's 125 wagons assisted as much and perhaps more than they hindered his expedition and the army's campaign in Pennsylvania.

*   *   *

Another popular argument that arose immediately after the fighting ended was that Stuart should have taken an alternate route in his ride north. Mosby vigorously defended Stuart against this criticism, a defense due at least in part to Mosby's involvement in mapping the course. Primarily, however, the partisan recognized that under the circumstances as they unfolded, the route Stuart selected was the best route he could have chosen. Still, Stuart made two poor tactical decisions in the early phases of the raid. First, he chose the Glasscock's Gap route instead of the Hopewell Gap route proposed by Mosby. Had he used Hopewell Gap, Stuart would have missed Hancock's Second Corps and the heavily traveled Warrenton Road, and would have avoided the skirmish with the enemy infantry that delayed his advance. Stuart compounded this error by waiting for Mosby at Buckland Mills for nearly ten hours. This delay broke apart the ride's timetable. Even Mosby, Stuart's most staunch defender, admitted, "Had Stuart started twelve hours sooner or General Lee delayed that long the march of his two army corps to the Potomac, there would have been nothing to prevent the accomplishment of the undertaking; for, as I have stated, it was the unexpected movement of Hancock's Corps that delayed Stuart two days in crossing the river."[20]

Major McClellan also deftly refuted the argument that an alternative route would have been better. "On the evening of [June] 25th, when Stuart drew back to Buckland out of the way of Hancock's Corps, at least sixty miles of a mountainous road lay between him and Shepherdstown, the nearest ford on the Potomac west of the mountains," McClellan correctly observed. "He could not hope to reach Shepherdstown with his artillery earlier than the evening of the 27th; and he would have been more than fortunate could he have occupied the passes of South Mountain on the 28th."

McClellan also rightly pointed out that Stuart "would even then have been at least thirty miles from Gettysburg, and twice that distance from York. It should not therefore be wondered at if this consideration alone decided Stuart to persist in the movement already begun, especially when there was also the hope of damaging the enemy in his rear and thus delaying his movement. Moreover," concluded McClellan with a final noteworthy observation, Stuart "had a right to expect that the information he had forwarded concerning the movement of Hancock's corps would cause Robertson and Jones to be active on their front, and would put General Lee himself on the alert in the same direction."[21]

*   *   *

Eight days of nearly non-stop marching, skirmishes at Thoroughfare Gap, Rockville, Cooksville, and Westminster, major battles at Hanover and Hunterstown, and the shelling of Carlisle wore out men and beasts. One of Stuart's troopers, Pvt. G. N. Saussy of the 6th Virginia Cavalry, recalled that the ride was "the most strenuous and exhausting in [my] experience. Men and horses did not average above four hours' rest in each twenty-four in that terrible strain. When Stuart's three brigades at last came in contact with the main army, it may be said it came limping."[22]

During any lengthy ride, even under ideal conditions, the shoes of a mount had to be replaced and maintained. According to various contemporary accounts, most horseshoes were replaced every 100 miles. Stuart's expedition covered about 200 miles before reaching Gettysburg. One can easily surmise the farriers and blacksmiths of Stuart's command stayed constantly busy during this time. The conditions encountered on this ride, much like any mounted raid conducted during the Civil War, were hardly ideal; inclement weather, difficult road conditions, hilly terrain, a quickened pace, and the demands of battle caused horseshoes to wear out even more quickly. It must also be kept in mind that just like a person's shoes, horseshoes are not always interchangeable. Different sizes and breeds of horses require different sizes and styles of shoes—a fact that only increased the demands made upon Stuart's farriers. The blacksmiths and farriers attempted to keep an adequate supply of different sizes of horseshoes on hand, and the troopers also carried extra sets of shoes, all of which had to be modified to fit their particular mounts. The result of improperly worked or ill-fitted shoes was usually a lame horse. This fact alone—more than the combination of constant riding and inadequate forage and rest, contributed to the breakdown of the cavalry and artillery horses. Few people consider that something as simple as an ill-fitted horseshoe could break a horse as quickly as overburdening it or failing to provide it with adequate rest or fodder.

Horseshoes of all types, therefore, were constantly in demand and worth their weight in gold to every trooper riding with Stuart. This helps explain why any available horses were confiscated by both sides during the war, and it was not uncommon to see entire hooves cut off dead horses on a battlefield. The heavier draft horse, commonly found on farms, was ideally suited to pulling wagons and artillery. Lighter, swifter breeds were better suited to carry cavalrymen, and troopers were always on the lookout to swap a worn-out mount for a fresher one. Confiscated horses that were not in immediate need were pressed into the column and for later use. It took a great deal of time for squadrons, which typically marched along roads parallel and perpendicular to the main column, to capture, round up, and bring in confiscated mounts.

Even with the available fodder and all the steps taken to maintain the horses, the long ride took its toll on Stuart's mounts. The 1st Maryland Cavalry (CSA), part of Grumble Jones's Brigade, was detached on June 13 and assigned to escort Albert Jenkins's command. Company A of the 1st Maryland was detached to serve as General Ewell's personal escort. The balance of the regiment joined up with Brig. Gen. Beverly H. Robertson's Brigade when the North Carolinians entered Pennsylvania on July 3.[23] Consequently, Confederate troopers, either without mounts or who had been separated from their commands, were scattered across the countryside, which reduced the effective strength of Stuart's command. "The country on the Virginia side . . . was filled with straggling cavalrymen who had not been able to accompany their commands by reason of being on detached service when they had moved, or had remained behind to have their horses shod, and, like us, were trying to rejoin their commands," observed the 1st Maryland's Capt.

George Booth.[24] It is not difficult to imagine what the toll on Stuart's horses might have been if the 125 wagons of fodder and transport had not been captured and utilized during the expedition.

* * *

A cavalryman is really two entities: man and horse. The impact the ride had on the men cannot be overlooked. Not even the nearly indefatigable Stuart was immune to the effects of the exhaustion created by so many hours in the saddle. Everyone requires adequate rest and food in order to function properly and remain mentally alert. As sleep and nourishment diminish, so does the ability to make sound decisions. The ride wore Stuart down, and as the days passed his judgment flagged. By the time he and his three brigades arrived at Gettysburg on July 2, they were in no condition to fight another major battle; yet, they were asked to do just that the following day.

"For more than three weeks previous to the battle of Gettysburg, the [2nd Virginia Cavalry] had been constantly if not continuously on active duty, marching, scouting, picketing, and fighting almost daily until they arrived upon the historic field of Gettysburg," recounted a 2nd Virginia trooper of Fitz Lee's Brigade. "From the time it left Virginia and crossed the Potomac during its long and arduous march through Maryland into Pennsylvania around by Carlisle down to the left flank of the Army of Northern Virginia, the regt had not at any one time taken more than an hour or two to rest. Consequently it was worn out with hard service, and for the want of sleep," the Old Dominion horseman concluded. "When the morning of the 3d of July dawned it found our command in a poor condition to undergo the hardship of a battle with credit either to themselves or their country, but the deep thunder of the artillery and long continuous roll of musketry that began to be heard early in the day, seemed to revive in a measure the exhausted troopers and to nerve them for the part they were soon to take in the great drama then being enacted in their hearing but out of sight."[25]

These men were fortunate that on June 30, after the fighting ended at Hanover, Kilpatrick broke off the pursuit of Stuart's column. That evening, Kilpatrick informed Alfred Pleasonton that the stubborn resistance put up by Stuart meant that Lee and his army must be near. General Meade's adjutant general, Seth Williams, emphasized to

Pleasonton that same day that the cavalry must turn over every stone to find Lee's main body: "People in the country are so frightened that he [Meade] must depend solely upon the cavalry for all the information he can gain. . . . The duty you have to perform is of a most important and sacred character. Cavalry battles must be secondary to this object."[26]

Had Kilpatrick been aggressive in his pursuit, or if Pleasonton had devoted additional resources to chasing down Stuart's horsemen, the Confederate column might well have been destroyed. Encumbered as it was with the wagon train, the troopers and animals near the outer limits of their endurance, the destruction of Stuart's three brigades was a real possibility. However, Jeb Stuart was nothing if not lucky, and good fortune smiled upon him more than once during his ride to Pennsylvania.

Once back with the army at Gettysburg, Stuart and his men did not have an opportunity to recover from their ordeal before riding out beyond the army's left flank and fighting on East Cavalry Field the next afternoon in one of the most important cavalry battles of the entire war.[27] Although the Federal cavalry got the best of them that day, the Southern horsemen offered a surprisingly good account of themselves in what turned out to be a long and hard-fought combat. Even more hard riding and fighting lay ahead during the retreat from Gettysburg. Stuart and his horsemen bore the burden of keeping the Army of the Potomac's vigilant and aggressive cavalry away from the wounded army until General Lee was able to prepare a strong defensive position near Falling Waters.

*   *   *

In order to place the balance of this discourse in its proper context, some discussion regarding the whereabouts of the infantry of the Army of the Potomac during the days leading up to the fighting at Gettysburg is necessary. While a detailed description of the advance of the Union army goes far beyond the scope of this book, it is important to know where its elements were, and when they got there, in order to permit an understanding of how the absence of Stuart's cavalry impacted Lee's movements in Pennsylvania.

The Army of the Potomac moved out of its lines near Fredericksburg on June 11. It headed first to Dumfries, and then to Fairfax Court House, where General Hooker established his headquarters on June 15. By June 17, most of the Federal infantry had concentrated between Fairfax Court

House and the Potomac River. Hooker decided to cross the Potomac in the vicinity of Edwards Ferry, not far from the town of Leesburg. A pontoon bridge was laid across the river and the Yankees began crossing in the pre-dawn hours of June 25. This was the same time Stuart encountered the head of Hancock's advancing column at Glasscock's Gap. By the next day (June 26), all of the Army of Northern Virginia's infantry was north of the Potomac River, and most of Richard Ewell's Second Corps was already in Pennsylvania.

The balance of the Army of the Potomac was across the river by June 27, which meant that all of Hooker's Federals were north of the Potomac River and in Maryland. That night, Hooker established his headquarters at Poolesville, with the advance elements of his army occupying the South Mountain passes near Frederick. The army converged on Frederick and was in the process of concentrating there on June 27. During the early morning hours of June 28, Hooker was relieved of command at his own request, and Maj. Gen. George G. Meade, the commander of the Fifth Corps, assumed leadership of the Army of Potomac at Lincoln's order. The First, Fifth, Eleventh, and Twelfth Corps were in Frederick, the Second Corps was just south of Frederick at Hyattsville, and the Third Corps was north of Frederick at Woodsboro. Most of the Federal infantry was within two days' march of Gettysburg.

By the 29th of June, the bulk of the Army of the Potomac had begun arriving in the area between Emmitsburg and Taneytown, just a few miles south of the Mason-Dixon Line. By June 30, Meade had established his headquarters at Taneytown, while the rest of the army took up position along the Pipe Creek Line, just south of the Mason-Dixon Line. The entire Army of the Potomac, nearly 75,000 men strong, had made its way to a position just a few miles south of Gettysburg virtually undetected.[28]

During this time frame, Stuart's ride was pinning down significant Federal resources that would have otherwise been available to pursue Lee's army to Gettysburg. "In his report of the battle, General Meade says that General French was ordered to guard the Baltimore and Ohio railroad with seven thousand men, and that an escort of four thousand men had been sent with the public property to Washington," claimed Mosby in 1877. "The alarm produced by Stuart's movement around the rear of the Union army with three brigades of cavalry, had thus neutralized all this force and kept it on the defensive."[29] The impact the presence of an additional 11,000 Federal infantry might have had on the outcome of the fighting at Gettysburg will never be known.

*   *   *

Another major criticism leveled at Stuart is that his ride left Robert E. Lee blind, without any cavalry to screen the advance of the army. If Stuart had been available when Lee received Harrison's June 29 report that the Army of the Potomac was on the move, the cavalier's active and diligent cavalry could have searched for the Federals instead of the infantry and staff scouts who actually did so. The cavalry brigades left behind in Virginia could have—indeed should have—performed this critical duty. A wider net of cavalry scouts probably would have detected the approach of Brig. Gen. John Buford's Union cavalry and perhaps given Lee an opportunity to seize and hold Gettysburg before Buford's arrival late on the morning of June 30. However, many people overlook the fact that Union cavalry under Brig. Gen. Joseph T. Copeland occupied Gettysburg as early as June 28, and could have remained there if necessary.

This entire argument that Stuart's ride left Lee and the army blind ignores one critical fact: Stuart only took three of the seven available brigades of cavalry with him on his ride. This means he left four full brigades to screen the Army of Northern Virginia's advance. Let us examine each in turn.

One of these brigades was led by Brig. Gen. Albert G. Jenkins, augmented by Lt. Col. Elijah V. White's 35th Battalion of Virginia Cavalry. Jenkins's troopers rode with Richard Ewell all the way to the west shore of the Susquehanna River and fought skirmishes with Federal troops at Oyster Point and Sporting Hill in Camp Hill on June 29 and 30, respectively. Jenkins's men conducted themselves well, and his 17th Virginia Cavalry, commanded by Col. William H. French, led Ewell's advance to Gettysburg early on the morning of July 1. It is entirely possible that one of French's men fired the first shot of the battle of Gettysburg while leading the infantry forward that morning.[30] The contention made by some observers that there was no Confederate cavalry present on the battlefield on July 1 is simply untrue.

Before examining the remaining three brigades, we will take up the issue of the lack of Stuart's presence at Gettysburg on July 1 in the context of French's availability. Some critics contend Stuart's troopers could have reconnoitered the field and possibly taken and held Culp's Hill before the Army of the Potomac seized the critical high ground for the remainder of the fighting. While true as far as it goes, this statement overlooks the fact that Jenkins and his men (as discussed above) were present on the battlefield on July1 and could have performed the same duty. Colonel French's men arrived near the field as early as 7:00 a.m. that morning, but spent the rest of the day performing provost duty.[31] The balance of Jenkins's command arrived by 5:00 p.m. that afternoon. These troopers could also have assisted in this duty. Other than rounding up and guarding prisoners, however, Jenkins and his large brigade played no role in the first day's fighting other than the desultory skirmishing engaged in by French's men during the morning's opening phase.[32] Jenkins was specifically assigned to serve with the Second Corps, so Ewell could have ordered these horsemen to seize and hold Culp's Hill. For reasons never fully explained, he chose not to do so. This seems to suggest Ewell never intended to assault Culp's Hill on July 1. Whatever his intent, the fact that Ewell decided not to make effective use of Jenkins cannot be attributed to—or held against— Jeb Stuart. The responsibility for this decision lies solely with Ewell.

Brigadier Generals William E. "Grumble" Jones, Beverly H. Robertson, and John D. Imboden commanded the other three brigades of Confederate cavalry. It is worth spending a few paragraphs of background material to get to know these men. Robertson was the most senior of the three officers. An 1849 graduate of West Point, he spent his entire Regular Army career in the 2nd Dragoons on the western frontier. Robertson served under Turner Ashby in the Shenandoah Valley and assumed command of Ashby's Brigade after the legendary cavalier was killed during Jackson's 1862 Valley Campaign. He did well in that position, besting John Buford in the final engagement at Second Bull Run, but butted heads with Stuart, who sent Robertson packing shortly thereafter. "Robertson has been relieved and sent to North Carolina," he announced to Flora in October 1862. "'Joy's mine.' My command is now okay."[33] Stuart once described Robertson as the "most troublesome man in the Army."[34] Stuart thought he had rid himself of Robertson by banishing him to North Carolina, where he spent the next six months raising and training new regiments of cavalry.

Brigadier General William E. "Grumble" Jones, a superb outpost officer who was unable to get along with Jeb Stuart. The two men respected each other's talents, but despised each other personally.

USAMHI

After receiving Lee's request for more cavalry, however, Robertson and two regiments of his green brigade received orders to transfer back to Virginia for the forthcoming movement north. Robertson's fresh start under Stuart proved disappointing. Neither Robertson nor his troopers did well in their first combat at Brandy Station. When a Federal cavalry division crossed the Rappahannock River at Kelly's Ford, Robertson idly stood by and permitted the Yankees to pass largely unmolested. The North Carolinians barely fired a shot during the largest cavalry battle of the Civil War, and Stuart was greatly displeased with their performance.[35] Robertson was an excellent organizer, trainer, and administrator, but on the battlefield he was cautious to a fault and undependable—and Stuart was painfully aware of it. Robertson's Brigade, the smallest in Stuart's division, consisted of two large but inexperienced regiments and numbered about 966 sabers.[36]

Grumble Jones, a member of the West Point class of 1848 (he was Buford's classmate) commanded a fine veteran brigade consisting entirely of Virginia horsemen from the Shenandoah Valley. Jones, described by one of his men as "that stern old warrior," richly deserved his nickname.[37] He "was an eccentric officer, who seemed to take pleasure in self-torture, as if doing penance," observed a Kentucky horse soldier who served under Jones after the close of the Gettysburg

Campaign. "He was a small man, beyond middle life, exceedingly plain in dress, brave to a fault, cool and imperturbable."[38]

The 39-year-old Jones graduated from Emory and Henry College in Virginia in 1844 before matriculating at West Point, where he graduated twelfth out of 48. Jones spent his entire Regular Army career in the mounted arm, riding the frontier in the Regiment of Mounted Rifles fighting Indians and serving garrison duty in the Pacific Northwest. He resigned his commission in 1857 and spent the next several years as a reclusive farmer. It proved a lonely and bitter life. But Jones had not always been so short-tempered. His young wife was washed from his arms in a shipwreck shortly after their marriage, a loss from which he never fully recovered. Jones grew "embittered, complaining and suspicious" as a result, and frequently quarreled with his fellow officers.[39]

At the outbreak of the Civil War, Jones formed a cavalry company and was elected its captain, serving under Jeb Stuart in the First Manassas (Bull Run) Campaign. He became colonel of the 1st and later 7th Virginia Cavalry and was promoted to brigadier general on September 19, 1862. Shortly thereafter, Jones assumed command of Robertson's former brigade, consisting of the 6th, 7th, 11th, and 12th Virginia Cavalry. Jones was a plain dresser with a legendary gift for profanity. He was also a martinet who was "brave as a lion and . . . was known as a hard fighter. He was a man, however, of high temper, morose and fretful," as John D. Imboden, a fellow Confederate general, described him. "He held the fighting qualities of the enemy in great contempt, and never would admit the possibility of defeat where the odds against him were not much over two to one."[40]

With such different personalities, it is not surprising that Jones and Stuart did not take a liking to one another. In the fall of 1862, when Jones came up for promotion, Stuart wrote to his wife Flora, "I hope he will be assigned to the Infantry, I don't want him in the Cavalry, and I have made a formal statement to that effect."[41] Stuart also wrote a scathing condemnation letter to the Confederate War Department: "I have the honor to state further that I do not regard Brigadier General Jones as deserving this command or as a fit person to command a Brigade of Cavalry. I say this from a thorough acquaintance with him in every grade from Lieutenant up. . . . With Brigadier General Jones I feel sure of opposition, insubordination, and inefficiency to an extent that would in a short time ruin discipline and subvert authority in that brigade."[42] Jones returned the sentiment, referring to Stuart as "that young whippersnapper." Despite Stuart's pleas, Jones was assigned to command the same brigade from which Robertson had just been relieved.[43]

Although Stuart personally disliked Jones, he respected his abilities in the field. Stuart even went so far as to praise his "marked courage and determination," and often referred to him as "the best outpost officer in the army."[44] Jones's Brigade did splendidly at Brandy Station, where it carried the brunt of that difficult day's fighting. Jones's troopers also performed most of the fighting in the defeat at Upperville on June 21, and acquitted themselves well there under adverse circumstances. Jones's veteran command, which consisted entirely of men from the Shenandoah Valley, was, like its leader, always itching for a fight. Jones counted 1,743 sabers when the campaign began.[45]

The fourth brigade of cavalry left behind with Lee's army was led by John Daniel Imboden, a 40-year-old Virginian born near Staunton. He attended, but did not graduate from, Washington College in Lexington (today known as Washington & Lee University). After teaching at the Virginia Institute for the Education of the Deaf, Dumb and Blind in Staunton, Imboden studied law, practiced in his hometown, and was elected twice as a representative to the Virginia Legislature.[46] He won high acclaim as the commander of

Brigadier General John D. Imboden. His untried cavalry brigade played virtually no role during the early phases of the Gettysburg Campaign.

the Staunton Artillery at Harpers Ferry, and was wounded at First Manassas in July 1861. In 1862, Imboden resigned from the artillery to raise companies of partisan rangers and fought at Cross Keys and Port Republic during Stonewall Jackson's Valley Campaign. By January 1863, his First Virginia Partisan Rangers was reorganized into two regular cavalry regiments, the 18th Virginia Cavalry and the 62nd Virginia Mounted Infantry, and a battery of horse artillery. Imboden was promoted to brigadier general.

Imboden's Northwestern Brigade, as it was known, operated independently of division command, receiving orders directly from General Lee. Until the opening of the Gettysburg Campaign, it had performed mostly partisan ranger service. With Grumble Jones, Imboden led what came to be known as the "Jones-Imboden Raid" into northwestern Virginia in April and May 1863, severing the Baltimore & Ohio Railroad and capturing thousands of horses and cattle for the Confederacy.[47] The movement into Pennsylvania marked the Northwestern Brigade's first foray into "regular" cavalry service, meaning that it was largely untested in any capacity but as partisan rangers and raiders. During the campaign, Imboden's command included the 18th Virginia Cavalry, led by his brother Col. George H. Imboden; the 62nd Virginia Mounted Infantry under Col. George H. Smith; the Virginia Partisan Rangers under Capt. John H. "Hanse" McNeill; and the Staunton Horse Artillery, Virginia Battery, under Capt. James H. McClanahan. All told, Imboden's command numbered 2,245 troopers.[48]

It is evident from the above information that, in addition to Jenkins's Brigade, General Lee had available 5,000 horse soldiers capable of scouting the countryside and screening the army's advance. Many were veterans extremely well-suited for these tasks. Lee, however, did not use them in this manner. He was unsure whether Imboden's command was reliable, and Robertson's troopers performed poorly at Brandy Station. Consequently, Imboden's command operated well west of Gettysburg. As late as June 30, Imboden's men skirmished with troopers from the 1st New York (Lincoln) Cavalry in the streets of McConnellsburg, nearly sixty miles west of Gettysburg. Imboden did not arrive in Gettysburg until July 3. His men performed magnificently during the retreat to Virginia, which suggests they were capable of more than General Lee was willing to ask of them.

Library of Congress

Brigadier General Beverly H. Robertson, the senior cavalry officer left behind by Jeb Stuart. Did he violate Stuart's orders and contribute to the Confederate defeat in Pennsylvania?

While Lee marched his army north Robertson and Jones remained in Virginia, three or four days' ride distant. There was no good reason not to make use of Jones's veteran command. The fact that Jones and Stuart were unable to get along should not have precluded Lee from using Jones's horsemen in roles for which they were clearly qualified. Robertson and Jones have long been roundly criticized for not forwarding intelligence to Lee regarding the dispositions of the Federals as they marched themselves north toward Gettysburg. In Robertson's case the criticism seems justified. Not surprisingly, Robertson vehemently disagreed.

In an 1877 letter to Henry Heth, Robertson defended his actions by writing the following:

> On the 29th of June I received orders from General Lee to leave one regiment of my command to picket south of the Potomac and report to him forthwith. I left Ashby's Gap the same day in the evening (as soon as I could collect my command), and reached Gettysburg on the morning of July 3rd, a distance which could not have been traveled except by rapid marching. *During the separation of my command from General Lee's army there was constant communication between us* [emphasis added]. He was fully aware of my position and the specific duty I was then performing. That it met his entire approbation is proven by the fact that no complaint on his part or from any other source, was ever made against me or my command.[49]

Robertson's claim of "constant communication" between his command and Lee omits the fact that he did not inform Lee of Hooker's movement across the river on June 27. In fact, there is no evidence to suggest Robertson was in communication with Lee's headquarters in any substantive form, even though his orders from Stuart instructed him to do so. In a subsequent newspaper interview, Robertson expanded on this defense of his actions:

> Correspondent: Could it have been possible for you to have acquainted General Lee on the first of July of the movements of the enemy then in his front?
>
> General Robertson: No, because my instructions compelled me to remain where I was left by Stuart for a certain time during which General Lee's army was marching toward Gettysburg; and from the time when I left Snicker's and Ashby's gaps, on the twenty-ninth of June, it would have been impossible to have made the distance to Gettysburg.[50]
>
> Correspondent: Suppose you had followed up the enemy instead of going to the valley and after Lee, what would have been the result?

General Robertson: With the Federal army between me and General Lee, communication with him would have been impossible.[51]

Correspondent: Was your route prescribed in these orders?

General Robertson: Distinctly. I recall particularly this sentence: "To sweep through the valley, picking up deserters and stragglers."

Correspondent: Then, by your orders, you could not have crossed the river at Harpers Ferry?

General Robertson: I think not. I crossed at Williamsport, and marched directly to Chambersburg.

Correspondent: What would have been the consequences had you not arrived in rear of General Lee's army on the third?

General Robertson: The unquestionable capture of all the baggage and supply trains of the army, as Pleasanton [sic] was marching unmolested on them. Immediately upon my arrival at Castletown [Cashtown], a letter of instruction from General Lee directed me to meet and drive back this force, which was done promptly, and as before stated, with heavy loss to the enemy.

Correspondent: Had you, as Colonel Mosby says you ought to have done, moved on to join Lee's army on a route parallel with his and Hooker's, so as to observe the latter and keep Lee acquainted with his movements, would you not have disobeyed your instructions?

General Robertson: Yes. I was ordered as I have said, to march through the Shenandoah Valley, and there had the specific duty to perform of picking up deserters and stragglers, after holding the gaps for a certain time, which I presume was to mislead Hooker as to General Lee's designs, or for some other purpose not communicated to me.[52]

When asked whether he or Stuart were ever censured or court-martialed for their conduct during the Gettysburg Campaign, Robertson declared, "No. There were no grounds for such charges. I never heard that I was in the least to be blamed until I read the statement of Colonel Mosby, upon which you base your interview."[53]

Robertson spent the rest of his life defending his actions during the Gettysburg Campaign. He reiterated his claims in a letter to a prominent magazine in response to another of John Mosby's effective salvoes.

Robertson's response triggered another acid exchange with the pugnacious Mosby, who remained determined to defend Stuart. "Colonel Mosby knows very little of Stuart's character if he supposes that so true a soldier would have silently passed over such disobedience of orders as Colonel Mosby imputes to me," Robertson lashed out. "The orders left with me by General Stuart, dated June 24th, were exactly obeyed by me, to his entire satisfaction as well as to that of General R. E. Lee. These orders embraced the duty of holding Ashby's and Snicker's gaps, to prevent Hooker from interrupting the march of Lee's army; and 'in case of a move by the enemy on Warrenton, to counteract it if possible,'" continued Robertson. "I was also ordered when I withdrew from the gaps to 'withdraw to the west side of the Shenandoah,' to cross the Potomac where Lee crossed, and to 'follow the army, keeping on its right and rear.'"

Robertson continued: "The only road by which the orders (which particularly specified the avoidance of 'turnpikes' on account of the difficulty and delay of shoeing horses) could be complied with, carried my command to Martinsburg; at which place, and not in the gaps of the mountains, as Colonel Mosby insinuates, a courier from General Lee met me. If there existed the least ground for Colonel Mosby's statements," contended Robertson, "there would be found among the reports of general officers some reference to the imputed dereliction of duty on my part. As no such reference is made, and no imputation of disobedience to orders intimated, it may be assumed that neither Stuart nor Lee had any reason to complain of my command."[54] In other words, Robertson tried to spin the lack of an affirmative condemnation as active approval on the part of the Confederate high command.

Mosby's quick response pointed out the flaws in this argument. "The complaint against Robertson is, that having been placed with a large force of cavalry in observation, with orders to follow on the *right* of the army *next to the enemy*, he gave General Lee no information of their movements, but followed on the *left*, and never reached the battlefield." Mosby also pointed out the lack of urgency in Robertson's movements. "He had marched from Berryville to Chambersburg in *three* days— which is exactly the time that it took Longstreet's infantry to march the same distance. But then Longstreet did not pretend to be in a hurry," he observed. "If keeping behind the *left* wing is the same thing as being the *right* flank of the army, then there can be no doubt that General

Robertson obeyed orders."[55] Though sarcastic, Mosby's retort raised valid points: Robertson's argument was filled with holes and did little to mitigate the fact that he showed no initiative and no urgency in carrying out his orders. Mosby also effectively pointed out that there was a big difference between damning with faint praise and explicit condemnation.

Robertson was not asked and so never specifically answered the important question of why he failed to inform Lee that Hooker's army had already crossed the Potomac by June 27th, nor why he waited until June 29th to begin his own move northward. There was no reason why Stuart or Jones should have been censured—they obeyed their operative orders to the letter. Both officers did precisely what they were ordered to do by Robert E. Lee, so it is extremely difficult to conceive of a scenario wherein court-martial charges could have been preferred against either of them. Robertson's claim that he was in regular communication with Lee regarding the dispositions of the enemy is difficult to accept at face value. There is no evidence in the *Official Records*, correspondence files, or writings or statements of any of the participants that Robertson made any attempt to inform Lee of Hooker's movements. Robertson insisted he was in "constant contact," but offered no proof to support his claim, and none to date has been found. The upshot is that the blame for General Lee's lack of accurate intelligence cannot be deposited at Stuart's feet.

Although Robertson was correct in that he was not directly criticized for his performance during the Gettysburg Campaign, the cavalryman was indirectly censured for his failure during the campaign. Shortly after Lee's army returned to Virginia, Robertson requested either assignment to a larger command (casualties and detachments had reduced his brigade to less than 300), or a transfer away from the Army of Northern Virginia so he could return to the regiments he had raised in North Carolina.[56] Stuart gladly endorsed his request on the day he received it. Lee, however, ordered Robertson to report to Richmond for reassignment to a contemplated cavalry recruitment camp.[57] Stuart, without regret, heartily bid his "most troublesome" subordinate adieu. Robertson never again led horse soldiers in the Army of Northern Virginia. Lee often resorted to transfers as a means of ridding himself of failed commanders.

As historian David Powell notes, by ordering John Imboden to operate to the west, Robertson and Jones to the south, and Jenkins to the north and east, Lee surrounded his army with cavalry. This ring of horse soldiers was certainly capable of providing the necessary intelligence for

Lee to learn and understand the location and dispositions of the Army of the Potomac.[58] It also makes sense that Lee would have wanted to leave a substantial force of cavalry in Virginia in order to protect his lines of supply and communication. Since Jones was considered the army's best outpost officer, he was the logical choice for this role, even though his large and dependable brigade could have provided even more useful service elsewhere.

A related criticism is that Stuart should have left Wade Hampton's reliable command with James Longstreet's First Corps infantry and taken only two brigades on his ride, or that he should have substituted either Jones or Robertson for Hampton. While Stuart and Wade Hampton were not close in a personal sense, each respected the other's abilities. Hampton was a determined fighter who could be depended upon in a crisis, so it is not surprising Stuart preferred the South Carolinian to either Jones or Robertson. Hindsight makes it easy to contend that Stuart erred by not leaving Hampton with Longstreet, and perhaps using Robertson in that role was a mistake. However, retrospect cannot be used to determine whether a particular decision was the correct one; we must instead look at the circumstances under which a decision was made. Stuart knew a cavalry ride deep into enemy territory would be highly dangerous, and so he took with him his best and most reliable officers. Stuart also did not expect the Federals to block his route in such force, and therein lies the basic problem associated with the successful completion of the mission.

*   *   *

Finally, we must examine the question of what impact, if any, Stuart's absence from the Army of Northern Virginia had upon the outcome of the battle at Gettysburg. There is little doubt that even if Stuart had been with the army, a large scale battle would have been waged in Pennsylvania. Lee's options were limited: fight or retreat. He could not remain in Pennsylvania indefinitely because his supply lines were too attenuated, and leaving the Confederate capital undefended for an extended period of time was politically and militarily inexpedient. Likewise, President Abraham Lincoln would not have permitted Lee to march at will across Pennsylvania unchecked for an extended period of time. Eventually, inevitably, sooner rather than later, the resources at

Lincoln's disposal would have been concentrated against Lee. Given his naturally aggressive temperament as a field commander, it is unlikely Lee would have simply retreated south of the Potomac without seeking a decisive engagement—with or without Stuart. The only real question is where that fight would have occurred.

Once Lee committed his army to fighting in Pennsylvania, the issue boils down to whether Stuart's presence on the battlefield would have made a difference. Of course, this line of inquiry is speculative at best because Stuart was not present on July 1 or for much of July 2. We can examine how Lee fought the battle with the cavalry that was available, however, and in doing so find it difficult to see how the presence or absence of the brigades that rode with Stuart would have made any difference at all in the outcome of the fighting once Lee committed his army at Gettysburg. Let's examine why.

As already pointed out, Jenkins's troopers operated with General Ewell's Second Corps since the beginning of the movement toward Pennsylvania. They screened Ewell's advance up the Cumberland Valley and performed that role competently. They may well have fired the opening shots of the battle of Gettysburg on the morning of July 1. On July 2, they were supposed to be screening Ewell's left flank. Jenkins received orders to ride to the extreme left flank and relieve the infantry brigades of Brig. Gens. William "Extra Billy" Smith and John B. Gordon. Jenkins, however, was badly wounded by an artillery shell fragment while standing on Blocher's (Barlow's) Knoll, leaving Col. Milton J. Ferguson to assume command. For reasons that remain unclear, the horsemen never arrived to relieve the waiting infantry. Their failure in that task left two brigades of veteran infantry to perform the traditional role of cavalry—screening the army's flanks.[59] The failure of Jenkins's Brigade to reach its assigned position also forced Brig. Gen. James Walker's Stonewall Brigade to perform picket duty on the Confederate far left flank on Brinkerhoff's Ridge near Culp's Hill.

When Union cavalry under command of Brig. Gen. David M. Gregg attacked Walker's infantry on Brinkerhoff's Ridge, the Confederate foot soldiers were pinned down and unable to participate in the assaults against Culp's Hill on the evening of July 2.[60] In addition, the presence of active and diligent Federal cavalry on the Southern army's left flank prevented "Extra Billy" Smith's Brigade from taking part in Jubal Early's dusk attack against East Cemetery Hill that same evening. Both assaults came within a whisker of success. Although we will never know, the presence of these veteran Confederate infantry brigades might have tipped the balance in one or perhaps both of these actions. Therefore, the only tangible effect of Stuart's absence from the battlefield on the second day was that two critical brigades of Second Corps infantry were kept out of the fighting on the Confederate left that evening. Rather inexplicably, Lee did not employ any of his available cavalry to scout those positions or the Federal left flank prior to James Longstreet's afternoon assault that same day. Lee had available horsemen on July 1 and 2 but did not use them to scout the enemy army. Nothing in the historical record suggests he would have acted differently if Stuart's three brigades had been present.

*   *   *

Many Confederate officers share the blame for the defeat at Gettysburg. As the commander of the Army of Northern Virginia, Robert E. Lee bears the primary responsibility for the loss. It was Lee who ordered Stuart's expedition in the first place. Lee did not oversee the issuance of clear and unambiguous orders that would have made speculation or interpretation by Stuart unnecessary. Had Lee written unequivocal orders, the dispute that has raged over their meaning (or whether Stuart violated them) for more than a century would not have erupted. Lee must also shoulder the primary fault for not using his available cavalry to screen his movements once he received word from Longstreet's spy that the Federal army was marching north after him. The army commander also failed to use the horsemen riding with the army on the morning of July 1 to scout the ground ahead while Heth's Division tramped blindly toward Gettysburg.

Although we believe many of the accusations leveled against Jeb Stuart have been either grossly exaggerated or factually wrong, the cavalier nevertheless bears some of the blame for the way events transpired and for the pair of tactical misjudgments he made early in the ride. Stuart, by his very nature, took liberties with the vague and ambiguous orders presented to him. He interpreted them in the fashion most favorable to his desire to lead an expedition into the Union rear. He could have selected a different lineup of brigades to accompany him, leaving Lee and the main army with more tested and reliable cavalry and commanders. He should have taken the Hopewell Gap route. Had he done so, he would have missed running into Hancock's Corps altogether. He also could have pressed on instead of wasting ten precious hours waiting for Mosby at Buckland Mills. These two delays set the schedule for his march irretrievably behind. Stuart could have ignored the temptation to capture the wagon train, though as we have shown, its presence almost certainly helped him rather than hindered his expedition as so many writers have claimed. That same train could easily have been abandoned along the way once the need for speed became critical and negated any benefits the wagons may have provided his column. Because establishing contact with Ewell in Pennsylvania was one of Stuart's primary objectives, he could have made more exhaustive attempts to find the Second Corps, or some other portion of the Army of Northern Virginia once his initial efforts to locate Ewell failed. However, as we have already demonstrated, there were valid reasons why Stuart followed the course he did.

We believe Beverly Robertson deserves a large share of the blame for failing to communicate to Longstreet or Lee the critical intelligence that Hooker's army had crossed north of the Potomac between June 25 and June 27. The cavalry leader compounded his omission by violating Stuart's direct order to follow the army immediately if the enemy moved north. Instead, Robertson waited two full days before advancing his cavalry command. His inactivity beginning on June 25 resembled his inactivity at Brandy Station on June 9. His late June sluggishness, however, left Lee's army without its eyes and ears, even though Stuart made careful dispositions to make certain Robertson had full and complete (and easy to follow) orders. Had Robertson performed as ordered, Lee would have had plenty of cavalry available to perform the usual role he expected of his mounted arm. Instead, Robertson demonstrated his penchant for idleness, which in turn left Lee without the cavalry screen Stuart had carefully planned for him to have. Robertson's lack of diligence deprived Lee of the benefit of both his own small brigade and the larger, more reliable brigade of Grumble Jones until the third day of July. These two brigades could have led the Army of Northern Virginia's advance toward Gettysburg if Robertson had obeyed his orders and marched immediately when he learned the Army of the Potomac was in full pursuit of the Confederates. Perhaps John S. Mosby summed it up best when he stated, "General Stuart had passed around

Hooker's army, while General Robertson had passed around General Lee's."[61]

Jubal Early also must bear some of the responsibility for the way events played out. Early clearly heard the guns booming at Hanover on June 30, yet did absolutely nothing to discover who was doing the shooting and why. Even a cursory investigation would have revealed to Early that Stuart's command was only a handful of miles away. The reverse is also true, for a courier from Early would have informed Stuart that one of Ewell's divisions was close at hand. Had Early taken simple, prudent steps that should have been second nature to someone with his experience and command responsibilities, he could have brought Stuart's three brigades with him and the entire command would have reached Gettysburg on July 1—in time to participate in the critical fighting that day. Jubal Early, one of Stuart's most vociferous critics, played a tragically significant role in triggering the chain of events that resulted in Stuart's absence from Gettysburg until late in the day on July 2.

The Confederate War Department must be held accountable for its failure to ensure that Stuart's critical intelligence dispatch of June 27 reached Robert E. Lee. This was the dispatch reporting that Hooker's army had abandoned its camps at Fairfax Court House and was already across the Potomac in pursuit of the Army of Northern Virginia. Stuart knew that this information was so essential he sent it to Lee through Ashby's Gap by courier, and a second copy to Richmond. When this critical intelligence arrived, the War Department should have taken steps to verify Lee had received the report. There is no evidence anyone in Richmond made any such attempt.

John Singleton Mosby, Stuart's most vocal defender, is not immune from criticism for the role he played in the drama. Mosby scouted the route for the ride, and Stuart relied heavily upon the work of his favorite and most dependable scout. However, Mosby does not appear to have been particularly aggressive or diligent in his efforts to link up with Stuart, and never reconnected with Stuart's command once the ride was under way. Further, Frank Stringfellow, another of Stuart's favorite scouts, had been captured, which in turn left the Southern cavaliers without accurate intelligence and without their usual complement of diligent scouts to lead their advance. Instead of providing Stuart with accurate intelligence, Mosby and his men made their way to Mercersburg, Pennsylvania, on July 1, nearly sixty miles from

Gettysburg, and were disappointed to find that Lee's army had already departed. Mosby and his rangers returned to Virginia with only one herd of rustled cattle to show for their efforts.[62] Had Mosby linked up with Stuart, his scouting and intelligence might have made it possible for Stuart to connect with either Early or Ewell quickly and in a more effective fashion. It is unlikely Mosby died unaware of the fact that he failed his patron, although he never alluded to it. Thus, his own foibles may explain the ferocity of Mosby's defense of Stuart in the years following the end of the war.

The plucky Federal cavalry deserves a significant portion of the credit for the delays that befell Stuart's expedition. The brave, desperate, and hopeless charge of the 11th New York Cavalry at Fairfax Court House hindered Stuart for half a day. "So, as the old saying is, 'A little always helps,' and to Major Remington and his gallant little band of Scott's 900 belongs the honor of causing the delay," noted an Empire State horseman.[63]

Likewise, the desperately heroic but hopeless charge of the 1st Delaware Cavalry at Westminster cost Stuart yet another half-day of riding. "Several of the officers and many of the Delaware cavalrymen claim that Stuart lost at Westminster or near it from ten to twelve hours, or to be more precise from five or six o'clock when they halted that afternoon, till four or five o'clock the next morning when they resumed the march," observed General Wilson some years after the war. "Of course this was in the night and half of it at least was necessary for rest and sleep for both men and horses, though if they had pushed on till even nine or ten o'clock, fifteen to twenty miles more might have been easily covered before they went into bivouac." Stuart, concluded Wilson, "could easily have reached Hanover less than thirty miles to the northward, before the Federal cavalry could have barred the road to the west from that point. This accomplished he could have passed on through Hunterstown, to a junction with Lee in a single day's march instead of taking three days, and thus giving effective support to Lee."[64]

Finally, Judson Kilpatrick's division cost Stuart a full day at Hanover, both by engaging him in battle and by forcing Stuart to take an unplanned, longer route that prevented him from linking up with Early's Division before the Virginian headed for Gettysburg. The feisty Federal cavalry cost Stuart two full days of riding. But for those two days, Stuart would have linked up with Early at York, and his entire command would have reached Gettysburg no later than the morning of July 1. Perhaps the largest portion of the credit, or blame as it were, for Stuart's untimely arrival at Gettysburg falls on the Union horse soldiers who blocked his way.

If Stuart disappointed anyone at Gettysburg, he more than redeemed himself during the retreat to Virginia. His performance during those difficult days, as well as that of his vaunted cavaliers, to whom the previous few weeks must have seemed a lifetime, was nothing short of magnificent. Stuart's handling of General Lee's mounted arm was a major reason the Army of Northern Virginia was even able to safely cross the Potomac River.

*   *   *

As we hope this study has demonstrated, no single person or condition can or should be made to shoulder the blame for the crippling Southern loss at Gettysburg. Rather, a combination of circumstances led to the Confederate disaster. We believe the Army of Northern Virginia would have lost the battle of Gettysburg whether Jeb Stuart and his cavalry were present earlier or not. Their absence simply provides more fodder for the endless debates that continue to swirl nearly a century and a half after he finally rode up and reported his presence to Robert E. Lee.

There was plenty of blame to go around.

Stuart's Command in the Ride to Pennsylvania

Rosters as of June 30, 1863 as reported at Union Mills, Maryland

Army of Northern Virginia
Cavalry Division

Maj. Gen. James Ewell Brown Stuart, Commanding

Staff
Maj. Henry Brainerd McClellan – Asst. Adj. Gen.
Maj. Andrew Reid Venable – Asst. Adj. Gen.
Capt. J.L. Clarke – Aide-de-Camp
1st Lt. Chiswell Dabney – Aide-de-Camp
Lt. Theodore Stanford Garnett – Aide-de-Camp
Capt. William Willis Blackford – Chief Engineer
Capt. Richard Edgar Frayser – Chief Signal Officer
Maj. Norman R. Fitzhugh – Quartermaster
Capt. J.M. Hanger – Asst. Quartermaster
Tacott Eliason – Chief Surgeon
Capt. John Esten Cooke – Chief of Ordnance
Maj. W.J. Johnson – Chief Commissary

Orderlies
Acting Sgt. Samuel A. Nelson (Co. B, 4th Virginia)
Pvt. E.D. Cole (Co. H, 15th Virginia)
Pvt. Francis Henry Deane (Co. E, 4th Virginia)
Pvt. Augustine Henry Ellis (Co. H, 13th Virginia)
Pvt. Robert William Goode (Co. G, 1st Virginia)
Pvt. William P. Jones (Co. E, 9th Virginia)

Pvt. William T. Thompson (Co. G, 13th Virginia)
Pvt. Benjamin Franklin Weller (Co. E, 1st Virginia)
Pvt. George N. Woodbridge (Co. E, 4th Virginia)

Hampton's Brigade
Brig. Gen. Wade Hampton III, Commanding

Staff
Capt. Theodore C. Barker – Asst. Adj. Gen.
Lt. Wade Hampton IV – Aide-de-Camp
Lt. William Preston Hampton – Aide-de-Camp
Benjamin Walter Taylor – Chief Surgeon

1st North Carolina Cavalry – Col. Laurence Simmons Baker
29 officers, 437 enlisted
1st South Carolina Cavalry – Lt. Col. John David Twiggs
34 officers, 349 enlisted
2nd South Carolina Cavalry – Maj. Thomas Jefferson Lipscomb
34 officers, 178 enlisted
Cobb's Legion – Col. Pierce Manning Butler Young
30 officers, 347 enlisted men
Jeff Davis Legion – Lt. Col. Joseph Frederick Waring
21 officers, 260 enlisted
Phillips's Legion Battalion – Lt. Col. William W. Rich
17 officers, 252 enlisted

Fitzhugh Lee's Brigade
Brig. Gen. Fitzhugh Lee, Commanding

Staff
Capt. James D. Ferguson – Asst. Adj. Gen.
Capt. James Breckinridge – Asst. Adj. Gen.
Capt. C.T. Litchfield – Asst. Adj. Gen.
Capt. Julius G. Tucker – Aide-de-Camp (Co. E, 10th Virginia)
1st Lt. Henry C. Lee – Aide-de-Camp
Lt. Charles Minnegerode – Aide-de-Camp
J.B. Fontaine – Chief Surgeon

1st Virginia Cavalry – Col. James Henry Drake
25 officers, 339 enlisted
2nd Virginia Cavalry – Col. Thomas Taylor Munford

28 officers, 420 enlisted
3rd Virginia Cavalry – Col. Thomas Howerton Owen
26 officers, 221 enlisted
4th Virginia Cavalry – Col. Williams Carter Wickham
34 officers, 594 enlisted
5th Virginia Cavalry – Col. Thomas Lafayette Rosser
7 officers, 163 enlisted

W. H. F. Lee's (Chambliss's) Brigade
Col. John Randolph Chambliss, Jr., Commanding

Staff
Lt. Walter B. Chambliss – Aide-de-Camp
Lt. Junius B. Jones – Aide-de-Camp
Maj. Albert Gallatin Dade – Commissary of Subsistence

2nd North Carolina Cavalry – Lt. Col. William Henry Fitzhugh Payne
19 officers, 144 enlisted
9th Virginia Cavalry – Col. Richard Lee Turberville Beale
14 officers, 560 enlisted
10th Virginia Cavalry – Col. James Lucius Davis
26 officers, 243 enlisted
13th Virginia Cavalry – Maj. Joseph Ezra Gillette
14 officers, 341 enlisted

Breathed's Battery (1st Stuart Horse Artillery)
(2) 3-inch Ordnance Rifles

Capt. James W. Breathed, Commanding
2 officers, 50 enlisted

McGregor's Battery (2nd Stuart Horse Artillery)
(2) 3-inch Ordnance Rifles, (2) 12-pounder Napoleons

Capt. William Morrell McGregor, Commanding
5 officers, 100 enlisted

Note: "officers" denotes commissioned officers; "enlisted" denotes non-commissioned officers and enlisted men.

Orders of Battle

Hanover, Pennsylvania
June 30, 1863

Army of Northern Virginia
Cavalry Division

Maj. Gen. James Ewell Brown Stuart, Commanding

W. H. F. Lee's (Chambliss's) Brigade
Col. John Randolph Chambliss, Jr., Commanding

2nd North Carolina Cavalry – Lt. Col. William Henry Fitzhugh Payne
(captured); Capt. William A. Graham, Jr.
9th Virginia Cavalry – Col. Richard Lee Turberville Beale
10th Virginia Cavalry – Col. James Lucius Davis
13thVirginia Cavalry – Maj. Joseph Ezra Gillette (wounded)
Capt. Benjamin F. Winfield

Fitzhugh Lee's Brigade
Brig. Gen. Fitzhugh Lee, Commanding

1st Virginia Cavalry – Col. James Henry Drake
2nd Virginia Cavalry – Col. Thomas Taylor Munford
3rd Virginia Cavalry – Col. Thomas Howerton Owen
4th Virginia Cavalry – Col. Williams Carter Wickham
5th Virginia Cavalry – Col. Thomas Lafayette Rosser

Hampton's Brigade
Brig. Gen. Wade Hampton III, Commanding

1st North Carolina Cavalry – Col. Laurence Simmons Baker
1st South Carolina Cavalry – Lt. Col. John David Twiggs
2nd South Carolina Cavalry – Maj. Thomas Jefferson Lipscomb
Cobb's Legion – Col. Pierce Manning Butler Young
Jeff Davis Legion – Lt. Col. Joseph Frederick Waring
Phillips's Legion Battalion – Lt. Col. William W. Rich

Breathed's Battery (1st Stuart Horse Artillery)
Capt. James W. Breathed, Commanding

McGregor's Battery (2nd Stuart Horse Artillery)
Capt. William Morrell McGregor, Commanding

Total Strength: 5,363 officers and enlisted men.

Total Losses: approximately 125 officers and men,
representing 2% of the number engaged.

Army of the Potomac
Third Cavalry Division

Brig. Gen. Hugh Judson Kilpatrick, Commanding

Headquarters Guard – 1st Ohio Cavalry, Companies A and C
Company A – Capt. Noah Jones, Commanding
Company C – Capt. Samuel N. Stanford, Commanding

First Brigade
Brig. Gen. Elon John Farnsworth, Commanding

5th New York Cavalry – Maj. John Hammond
1st Vermont Cavalry – Lt. Col. Addison Webster Preston
1st West Virginia Cavalry – Col. Nathaniel Pendleton Richmond
18th Pennsylvania Cavalry – Lt. Col. William Penn Brinton

Second Brigade
Brig. Gen. George Armstrong Custer, Commanding

1st Michigan Cavalry – Col. Charles Henry Town
5th Michigan Cavalry – Col. Russell Alexander Alger
6th Michigan Cavalry – Col. George Gray
7th Michigan Cavalry – Col. William D'Alton Mann

Battery M, 2nd United States Artillery
Lt. Alexander Cummings McWhorter Pennington, Jr., Commanding

Battery E, 4th United States Artillery
Lt. Samuel Sherer Elder, Commanding

Total Strength: 3,500 officers and enlisted men

Total Losses: 183 officers and men, representing 5% of the number engaged.

*   *   *

Hunterstown, Pennsylvania
July 2, 1863

Army of Northern Virginia

Hampton's Brigade
Brig. Gen. Wade Hampton III, Commanding

1st North Carolina Cavalry – Col. Laurence Simmons Baker
1st South Carolina Cavalry – Lt. Col. John David Twiggs
2nd South Carolina Cavalry – Maj. Thomas Jefferson Lipscomb
Cobb's Legion – Col. Pierce Manning Butler Young
Jeff Davis Legion – Lt. Col. Joseph Frederick Waring
Phillips' Legion Battalion – Lt. Col. William W. Rich

Louisiana Guard Artillery (One Section)*
Capt. Charles A. Green, Commanding
(2 10-lb. Parrott guns)

Total Strength: 2,008 officers and enlisted men.

Total Losses: 21 officers and men,
representing less than 1% of the numbers engaged

Army of the Potomac
Third Cavalry Division

Brig. Gen. Hugh Judson Kilpatrick, Commanding

Headquarters Guard – 1st Ohio Cavalry, Companies A and C
Company A – Capt. Noah Jones, Commanding
Company C – Capt. Samuel N. Stanford, Commanding

First Brigade
Brig. Gen. Elon John Farnsworth, Commanding

5th New York Cavalry – Maj. John Hammond
1st Vermont Cavalry – Lt. Col. Addison Webster Preston
1st West Virginia Cavalry – Col. Nathaniel Pendleton Richmond
18th Pennsylvania Cavalry – Lt. Col. William Penn Brinton

Second Brigade
Brig. Gen. George Armstrong Custer, Commanding

1st Michigan Cavalry – Col. Charles Henry Town
5th Michigan Cavalry – Col. Russell Alexander Alger
6th Michigan Cavalry – Col. George Gray
7th Michigan Cavalry – Col. William D'Alton Mann

* The Louisiana Guard Artillery Battery, Captain Green Commanding, was attached to Ewell's Corps but one section was sent to Hunterstown at Hampton's request.

Battery M, 2nd United States Artillery
Lt. Alexander Cummings McWhorter Pennington, Jr., Commanding

Battery E, 4th United States Artillery
Lt. Samuel Sherer Elder, Commanding

Total Strength: 3,350 officers and enlisted men.

Total Losses: 33 officers and men, representing 1% of the number engaged.

Major General Jeb Stuart's
Official Report of the Gettysburg Campaign

Below is the full text of the report Jeb Stuart filed for the Gettysburg Campaign:

HDQRS. CAVALRY DIVISION, *ARMY OF NORTHERN VIRGINIA,*
August 20, 1863.

GENERAL: I have the honor to make the following report of the operations of the Cavalry Division, Army of Northern Virginia, from the time of crossing the Rappahannock on June 16, to July 24, when, having recrossed the Blue Ridge after the Pennsylvania campaign, our pickets were re-established on the south bank of the Rappahannock:

After holding in check a cavalry force at least double our own for months, with a command stretched on the outposts from the Blue Ridge to the Chesapeake, engaging in numerous hand-to-hand encounters, illustrating the superiority of southern cavalry, it was with joy that the order of the commanding general to advance was received by the cavalry. I was instructed by the commanding general to leave a sufficient force on the Rappahannock to watch the enemy in front, and move the main body parallel to the Blue Ridge and on Longstreet's right flank, who was to move near the base of the mountains, through Fauquier and Loudoun Counties.

The position of the enemy as far as known was as follows: His cavalry massed in Fauquier, principally from Warrenton Springs to Catlett's Station, with the Twelfth Corps and other infantry supports, the main body of Hooker's army being in Stafford and Lower Fauquier, hastening to interpose itself between our main body and Washington, with a corps or two confronting A. P. Hill's corps at Fredericksburg, having made a lodgment on the south side of the river there, near the mouth of Deep Run.

I accordingly left the Fifteenth Virginia Cavalry (Major [C. R.] Collins), W. H. F. Lee's brigade, on the Lower Rappahannock, cooperating with A. P. Hill, and directed Brigadier-General Hampton to remain with his brigade on the

Rappahannock, in observation of the enemy during the movement of our forces, and directed also Fitz. Lee's brigade (Col. T. T. Munford temporarily in command) to cross on the morning of the 15th at Rockford, and take the advance of Longstreet's column, via Barbee's Cross-Roads, and put Robertson's and W. H. F. Lee's brigades *en route* to cross the Rappahannock lower down (at Hinson's Mills), while Jones' brigade followed, with orders to picket the Aestham River the first day.

The movement was not interrupted the enemy having disappeared from our front during the night, and our march continued to within a few miles of Salem, to bivouac for the night. Scouting parties were sent to Warrenton, where it was ascertained the enemy had withdrawn his forces to Centreville the day previous.

General Fitz. Lee's brigade, having encamped near Piedmont, moved on the morning of the 17th (Wednesday), by my direction, toward Aldie, via Middleburg, with the view, if possible, to hold the gap in Bull Run Mountain as a screen to Longstreet's movements. W. H. F. Lee's brigade was kept near the plains, reconnoitering to Thoroughfare Gap, while Robertson's brigade was halted near Rectortown, to move to the support of either.

I accompanied Fitz. Lee's brigade as far as Middleburg, where I remained to close up the command, and keep in more ready communication with the rear.

The brigade, moving to Aldie, being much worn and the horses having had very little food, was halted by its commander near Dover, to close up, and pickets sent forward to the Aldie Gap. These pickets were soon attacked by the enemy's cavalry, advancing from the direction of Fairfax, and were driven back on the main body, which took a position just west of Aldie, on a hill commanding the Snickersville road, but which was liable to be turned by the road to Middleburg.

Simultaneously with this attack, I was informed that a large force of the enemy's cavalry was advancing on Middleburg from the direction of Hopewell. Having only a few pickets and my staff here, I sent orders to Munford to look out for the road to Middleburg, as by the time my dispatch reached him the enemy would be in the place, and retiring myself toward Rector's Cross-Roads, I sent orders for Robertson to march without delay for Middleburg, and Chambliss to take the Salem road to the same place.

At Aldie ensued one of the most sanguinary cavalry battles of the war, and at the same time most creditable to our arms and glorious to the veteran brigade of Brig. Gen. Fitz. Lee. They fought most successfully, punishing the enemy with great severity, and maintaining their position till the dispatch received from me made it necessary to move farther back, on account of the threatening attitude of the force at Middleburg.

This brigade captured 134 prisoners, among whom were a colonel and captain, several stand of colors, together with horses, arms, and equipments. A large number of the enemy's dead, including a colonel, were left on the field.

Brigadier-General Robertson arrived at Middleburg just at dark. I ordered him to attack the enemy at once, and, with his two regiments, he drove him handsomely out of the place, and pursued him miles on the Hopewell road, the force appearing to scatter. He captured a standard and 70 prisoners.

Chambliss' brigade, approaching from that direction, caught that night and early next morning 160 and several guidons, the colonel and a small detachment only escaping. It was the First Rhode Island Cavalry. Horses, arms, and equipments were captured in proportion. Among the captured were included a number of officers.

Our own loss in Robertson's brigade was slight, excepting Major [James H.] McNeill, Sixty-third [Fifth] North Carolina Cavalry, whose wound deprived us of the services of a most valuable officer, and Lieutenant-Colonel [Edward] Cantwell, Fifty-ninth North Carolina troops [Fourth North Carolina Cavalry], captured.

Major Heros von Borcke, of my staff, being sent by me with the attacking column, behaved with his usual fine judgment and distinguished gallantry.

Our loss in Fitz. Lee's brigade was heavier, as the fighting was more desperate and continued. His report, which I hope to forward with this, will state the casualties.

We occupied Middleburg that night, and on the 18th took position around the place with Robertson's and W. H. F. Lee's brigades, and directed Fitz. Lee's brigade to take position at Union, on my left, while Jones' brigade was expected to arrive that day.

The enemy soon made such encroachments on our left that I deemed it requisite to leave Middleburg out of my line of battle, keeping pickets, however, close to the enemy. Slight skirmishing continued.

A general engagement of cavalry was not sought by me, because I preferred waiting for the arrival of the cavalry still in rear (Jones' and Hampton's brigades), and I confined my attention to procuring, through scouts and reconnoitering parties, information of the enemy's movements.

In one of these, Major Mosby, with his usual daring, penetrated the enemy's lines, and caught a staff officer of General Hooker, bearer of dispatches to General Pleasonton, commanding United States cavalry near Aldie. These dispatches disclosed the fact that Hooker was looking to Aldie with solicitude; that Pleasonton, with infantry and cavalry, occupied the place, and that a reconnaissance in force, of cavalry, was meditated toward Warrenton and Culpeper.

I immediately dispatched to General Hampton, who was coming by way of Warrenton from the direction of Beverly Ford, this intelligence, and directed him to meet this advance at Warrenton. The captured dispatches also gave the entire number of divisions, from which we could estimate the approximate strength of the enemy's army. I therefore concluded in no event to attack with cavalry alone the enemy at Aldie. As long as he kept within supporting distance of his infantry at that point, my operations became necessarily defensive, but masking thereby the movement of our main body by checking the enemy's reconnaissance and by continually threatening attack. Hampton met the enemy's advance toward Culpeper, at Warrenten, and drove him back without difficulty, a heavy storm and night intervening to aid the enemy's retreat.

On the 19th, the enemy showed signs of an advance, and our pickets beyond Middleburg were driven back upon the main body, composed of Robertson's and W. H. F. Lee's brigades, posted far enough west of the place not to bring it under fire. The enemy, with a large force of cavalry, advanced, attacking with dismounted men deployed as infantry. This attack was met in the most determined manner by these two brigades, which rough roads had already decimated for want of adequate shoeing facilities, Chambliss commanding Lee's brigade upon the left and Robertson's on the right. Brig. Gen. Fitz. Lee's brigade in the meantime was occupied with the enemy on the Snickersville turnpike, opposite us. The enemy finally gained possession of a woodland in front of our line of battle, and while our brave men met and repelled every attempt to advance from it, yet our charges invariably brought us under a severe carbine fire from these woods, as well as a fire from the artillery beyond.

Appreciating this difficulty, I withdrew my command to a more commanding position a half mile to the rear, where we possessed every advantage, and could more readily debouch for attack. In withdrawing, while riding at my side, the brave and heroic Major von Borcke received a very severe, and it was thought fatal, wound in the neck from one of the enemy's sharpshooters, who, from a stone fence a few hundred yards off, poured a tempest of bullets over us. I will not pause here to record the praise due this distinguished Prussian.

The enemy did not attack our new position on the 19th. Jones' brigade came up on the evening of the 19th, and was ordered to the left, near Union, General Fitz. Lee's brigade being farther to the left, looking out for Snicker's Gap and the Snickersville pike.

Hampton's brigade arrived on the 20th, too late to attack the enemy, still in possession of Middleburg. A continuous rain was also an obstacle to military operations. Skirmishing, however, continued principally on our left, beyond Goose Creek, where Colonel Rosser, with his regiment (Fifth Virginia Cavalry), attacked and drove the enemy's force across the stream in handsome style. He was supported by Brigadier-General Jones with a portion of his brigade.

I was extremely anxious now to attack the enemy as early as possible, having, since Hampton's arrival, received sufficient re-enforcement to attack the enemy's cavalry, but the next morning (21st) being the Sabbath, I recognized my obligation to do no duty other than what was absolutely necessary, and determined, so far as was in my power, to devote it to rest. Not so the enemy, whose guns about 8 a.m. showed that he would not observe it. Had I attacked the enemy, I would have encountered, besides his cavalry, a heavy force of infantry and artillery, and the result would have been disastrous, no doubt.

Hampton's and Robertson's brigades were moved to the front to a position previously chosen, of great strength against a force of ordinary size, or against cavalry alone; but although the enemy's advance was held in check gallantly and decidedly for a long time, it soon became evident that the enemy, utterly foiled for days in his attempt to force our lines, had, as usual, brought a heavy infantry force—part of the Fifth Corps, under General Vincent—to his support, and its advance was already engaged in conjunction with the cavalry.

I therefore directed General Hampton to withdraw to the next height whenever his position was hard pressed, and sent orders at once to Colonel Chambliss and General Jones—the former having informed me that the enemy was advancing in heavy force in his front—to afford all the resistance possible, and General Jones to join to his left, and, retiring apace with the main body, to effect a junction with it at Upperville, where I proposed to make a more determined stand than was compatible with our forces divided. The commands were from 4 to 6 miles apart.

In retiring from the first position before Middleburg, one of the pieces of Captain [J. F.] Hart's battery of horse artillery had the axle broken by one of the enemy's shot, and the piece had to be abandoned, *which is the first piece of my horse artillery which has ever fallen into the enemy's hands.* Its full value was paid in the slaughter it made in the enemy's ranks, and it was well sold.

The next position was on the west bank of Goose Creek, whence, after receiving the enemy's attack, and after repulsing him with slaughter, I again withdrew *en échelon* of regiments in plain view, and under fire of the enemy's guns. Nothing could exceed the coolness and self-possession of officers and men in these movements, performing evolutions with a precision under fire that must have wrung the tribute of admiration from the enemy, even, who dared not trust his cavalry unsupported to the sabers of such men.

In the meantime, Jones' and W. H. F. Lee's brigades were hotly engaged with another column of the enemy moving parallel to this, and were gradually retiring toward Upperville, before reaching which point, however, the enemy had pressed closely up, so as to render an attempt to effect a junction at Upperville hazardous to those brigades, and also made it necessary for Hampton's and Robertson's brigades to move at once to the west side of Upperville, on account of the number of roads concentrating at that point, so as to favor the enemy's flank movements.

I was anxious on account of the women and children to avoid a conflict in the village, but the enemy, true to those reckless and inhuman instincts, sought to take advantage of this disinclination on our part, by attacking furiously our rear guard. In an instant, the same men who had with so much coolness retired before the enemy, wheeled about, and with admirable spirit drove back the enemy, killing, wounding, and capturing a large number. In this, General Hampton's brigade participated largely and in a brilliant manner. His report, not yet sent in, will no doubt give full particulars.

After this repulse, which was not followed up, as the enemy's infantry was known to be in close supporting distance, I withdrew the command leisurely to the mountain gap west of Upperville.

The enemy attacked Brigadier-General Robertson, bringing up the rear in this movement, and was handsomely repulsed. The brave and efficient Colonel [P. G.] Evans, of the Sixty-third North Carolina troops, was, however, severely, and it was feared fatally, wounded, his body falling into the hands of the enemy.

Jones' and W. H. F. Lee's brigades joined the main body near the gap, and positions were taken to dispute any farther advance. The day was far spent. The enemy did not attack the gap, but appeared to go into camp at Upperville. In the conflicts on the left, the enemy was roughly handled. Lieutenant-Colonel [M.] Lewis, Ninth Virginia Cavalry, was very severely, and it was believed fatally, wounded, and left in the hands of the enemy. The reports of brigade commanders will show further details of these encounters.

Fitz. Lee's brigade being before Snicker's Gap, did not participate in these operations. By night, part of Longstreet's corps occupied the mountain pass, and the cavalry was ordered farther back for rest and refreshment, of which it was sorely in need, leaving ample pickets in front and on either flank.

When the mist had sufficiently cleared away next morning, it was evident the enemy was retiring, and the cavalry was ordered up immediately to the front, to follow. The enemy was pursued to within a short distance of Aldie, and a number captured. Colonel Rosser, Fifth Virginia Cavalry, having been sent across from Snickersville early to reconnoiter, contributed very materially to the vigor of this pursuit. Major [John] Eells, of his regiment, a gallant and meritorious officer, was killed in a charge upon the enemy near Goose Creek Bridge. Our lines were much farther advanced than before, and Monday, the 22d, was consumed in their re-establishment.

Our loss in these operations was 65 killed, 279 wounded, and 166 missing. I resumed my own position at Rector's Cross-Roads, and, being in constant communication with the commanding general, had scouts busily engaged watching and reporting the enemy's movements, and reporting the same to the commanding general. In this difficult search, the fearless and indefatigable

Major Mosby was particularly active and efficient. His information was always accurate and reliable.

The enemy retained one army corps (Fifth) at Aldie, and kept his cavalry near enough to make attack upon the latter productive of no solid benefits, and I began to look for some other point at which to direct an effective blow. I submitted to the commanding general the plan of leaving a brigade or so in my present front, and passing through Hopewell or some other gap in Bull Run Mountains, attain the enemy's rear, passing between his main body and Washington, and cross into Maryland, joining our army north of the Potomac. The commanding general wrote me, authorizing this move if I deemed it practicable,-and also what instructions should be given the officer in command of the two brigades left in front of the enemy. He also notified me that one column should move via Gettysburg and the other via Carlisle, toward the Susquehanna, and directed me, after crossing, to proceed with all dispatch to join the right (Early) of the army in Pennsylvania.

Accordingly, three days' rations were prepared, and, on the night of the 24th, the following brigades, Hampton's, Fitz. Lee's, and W. H. F. Lee's, rendezvoused secretly near Salem Depot. We had no wagons or vehicles excepting six pieces of artillery and caissons and ambulances. Robertson's and Jones' brigades, under command of the former, were left in observation of the enemy on the usual front, with full instructions as to following up the enemy in case of withdrawal, and rejoining our main army. Brig. Gen. Fitz. Lee's brigade had to march from north of Snicker's Gap to the place of rendezvous. This brigade was now for the first time for a month under the command of its noble brigadier, who, writhing under a painful attack of inflammatory rheumatism, nevertheless kept with his command until now.

At 1 o'clock at night, the brigades with noiseless march moved out. This precaution was necessary on account of the enemy's having possession of Bull Run Mountains, which in the daytime commanded a view of every movement of consequence in that region. Hancock's corps occupied Thoroughfare Gap.

Moving to the right, we passed through Glasscock's Gap without serious difficulty, and marched for Hay Market. I had previously sent Major Mosby with some picked men through, to gain the vicinity of Dranesville, find where a crossing was practicable, and bring intelligence to me near Gum Springs to-day (25th).

As we neared Hay Market, we found that Hancock's corps was *en route* through Hay Market for Gum Springs, his infantry well distributed through his trains. I chose a good position, and opened with artillery on his passing column with effect, scattering men, wagons, and horses in wild confusion; disabled one of the enemy's caissons, which he abandoned, and compelled him to advance in order of battle to compel us to desist.

As Hancock had the right of way on my road, I sent Fitz. Lee's brigade to Gainesville to reconnoiter, and devoted the remainder of the day to grazing our horses, the only forage procurable in the country. The best of our information represented the enemy still at Centreville, Union Mills, and Wolf Run Shoals. I sent a dispatch to General Lee concerning Hancock's movement, and moved back to Buckland, to deceive the enemy. It rained heavily that night. To carry out my original design of passing west of Centreville, would have involved so much detention, on account of the presence of the enemy, that I determined to cross Bull Run lower down, and strike through Fairfax for the Potomac the next day. The sequel shows this to have been the only practicable course. We marched through Brentsville to the vicinity of Wolf Run Shoals, and had to halt again in order to graze our horses, which hard marching without grain was fast breaking down. We met no enemy to-day (26th).

On the following morning (27th), having ascertained that on the night previous the enemy had disappeared entirely from Wolf Run Shoals, a strongly fortified position on the Occoquan, I marched to that point, and thence directly for Fairfax Station, sending General Fitz. Lee to the right, to cross by Burke's Station and effect a junction at Fairfax Court-House, or farther on, according to circumstances. Fairfax Station had been evacuated the previous day, but near this point General Hampton's advance regiment had a spirited encounter with and chase after a detachment of Federal cavalry denominated Scott's Nine Hundred, killing, wounding, and capturing the greater portion, among them several officers; also horses, arms, and equipments. The First North Carolina Cavalry lost its major in the first onset—Major [John H.] Whitaker—an officer of distinction and great value to us.

Reaching Fairfax Court-House, a communication was received from Brig. Gen. Fitz. Lee at Annandale. At these two points, there were evidences of very recent occupation, but the information was conclusive that the enemy had left this front entirely, the mobilized army having the day previous moved over toward Leesburg, while the local had retired to the fortifications near Washington. I had not heard yet from Major Mosby, but the indications favored my successful passage in rear of the enemy's army. After a halt of a few hours to rest and refresh the command, which regaled itself on the stores left by the enemy in the place, the march was resumed for Dranesville, which point was reached late in the afternoon. The camp-fires of Sedgwick's (Sixth) corps, just west of the town, were still burning, it having left that morning, and several of his stragglers were caught. General Hampton's brigade was still in advance, and was ordered to move directly for Rowser's Ford, on the Potomac, Chambliss' brigade being held at Dranesville till Brig. Gen. Fitz. Lee could close up.

As General Hampton approached the river, he fortunately met a citizen who had just forded the river, who informed us there were no pickets on the other side, and that the river was fordable, though 2 feet higher than usual. Hampton's brigade crossed early in the night, but reported to me that it would be utterly impossible to cross the artillery at that ford. In this the residents were also very positive, that vehicles could not cross. A ford lower down was examined, and found quite as impracticable from quicksand, rocks, and rugged banks. I, however, determined not to give it up without trial, and before 12 o'clock that night, in spite of the difficulties, to all appearances insuperable, indomitable energy and resolute determination triumphed; every piece was brought safely over, and the entire command in bivouac on Maryland soil. In this success the horse artillery displayed the same untiring zeal in their laborious toil through mud and water which has distinguished its members in battle.

The canal, which was now the supplying medium of Hooker's army, soon received our attention. A lock-gate was broken, and steps taken to intercept boats. At least a dozen were intercepted, and the next morning several loaded with troops, negroes, and stores were captured by Colonel Wickham, Fourth Virginia Cavalry, commanding rear guard. I ascertained that Hooker was on the day previous at Poolesville, and his army in motion for Frederick.

I realized the importance of joining our army in Pennsylvania, and resumed the march northward early on the 28th. General Hampton was sent by Darnestown to Rockville, and the other brigades took the direct route to the same place. General Hampton encountered small parties of the enemy, which, with a number of wagons and teams, he captured, and reached Rockville in advance of the main body. The advance guard of W. H. F. Lee's brigade had a running fight with the Second New York Cavalry, but the speed of their horses deprived us of the usual results in captures. At Rockville, General Hampton encountered what he believed to be a large force of the enemy, and, moving up W. H. F. Lee's brigade quickly to his assistance, I found that the enemy had already disappeared, having retreated toward the Great Falls.

Rockville was speedily taken possession of. This place is situated on the direct wagon road from Washington City to Hooker's army, and, consequently, on his route of communication with Washington after crossing the Potomac. The telegraph line along it was torn down for miles.

Soon after taking possession, a long train of wagons approached from the direction of Washington, apparently but slightly guarded. As soon as our presence was known to those in charge, they attempted to turn the wagons, and at full speed to escape, but the leading brigade (W. H. F. Lee's) was sent in pursuit. The farthest wagon was within only 3 or 4 miles of Washington City, the train being about 8 miles long. Not one escaped, though many were upset and broken, so as to require their being burned. More than one hundred and twenty-five best United States model wagons and splendid teams with gay caparisons were secured and driven off. The mules and harness of the broken wagons were also secured.

The capture and securing of this train had for the time scattered the leading brigade. I calculated that before the next brigade could march this distance and reach the defenses of Washington, it would be after dark; the troops there would have had time to march to position to meet attack on this road. To attack at night with cavalry, particularly unless certain of surprise, would have been extremely hazardous; to wait till morning, would have lost much time from my march to join General Lee, without the probability of compensating results. I therefore determined, after getting the wagons under way, to proceed directly north, so as to cut the Baltimore and Ohio Railroad (now becoming the enemy's main war artery) that night. I found myself now encumbered by about 400 prisoners, many of whom were officers. I paroled nearly all at Brookeville that night, and the remainder next day at Cooksville. Among the number, were Major [James C.] Duane and Captain [Nathaniel] Michler, Engineers, U.S. Army.

At Cooksville, our advance encountered and put to flight a small party of the enemy, and among the prisoners taken there were some who said they belonged to the "Seven Hundred Loyal Eastern Shoremen."

Brig. Gen. Fitz. Lee reached the railroad soon after daylight, the march having continued all night. The bridge at Sykesville was burned, and the track torn up at Hood's Mills, where the main body crossed it. Measures were taken to intercept trains, but trains ran to the vicinity of the obstruction, took the alarm, and ran back. The various telegraph lines were likewise cut, and communications of the enemy with Washington City thus cut off at every point, and Baltimore threatened. We remained in possession of the Baltimore and Ohio Railroad nearly all day.

The enemy was ascertained to be moving through Frederick City northward, and it was important for me to reach our column with as little delay as possible, to acquaint the commanding general with the nature of the enemy's movements, as well as to place with his column my cavalry force. The head of the column, following a ridge road, reached Westminster about 5 p.m. At this place, our advance was obstinately disputed for a short time by a squadron of the First Delaware Cavalry, but what were not killed were either captured or saved themselves by precipitate flight. In this brief engagement, 2 officers of the Fourth Virginia Cavalry (Lieuts. Pierre Gibson and [John W.] Murray) were killed. Gallant and meritorious, they were noble sacrifices to the cause. *The ladies of the place begged to be allowed to superintend their interment, and, in accordance with their wishes, the bodies of these young heroes were left in their charge.(*)* The fugitives were pursued a long distance on the Baltimore road, and I afterward heard created a great panic in that city, impressing the authorities with the belief that we were just at their heels. Here, for the first time since leaving Rector's Cross-Roads, we obtained a full supply of forage, but the delay and difficulty of procuring it kept many of the men up all night. Several flags and one piece of artillery without a carriage were captured here. The latter was spiked and left behind. We encamped for the night a few miles beyond the town (Fitz. Lee's brigade in advance), halting the head of the column at Union Mills, midway between Westminster and Littlestown, on the Gettysburg road. It was ascertained here that night by scouts that the enemy's cavalry had reached Littlestown during the night, and encamped.

Early next morning (June 30), we resumed the march direct by a cross route for Hanover, Pa., W. H. F. Lee's brigade in advance, Hampton in rear of the wagon train, and Fitz. Lee's brigade moving on the left flank, between Littlestown and our road.

About 10 a.m. the head of the column reached Hanover, and found a large column of cavalry passing through, going toward the gap of the mountains which I intended using. The enemy soon discovered our approach, and made a demonstration toward attacking us, which was promptly met by a gallant charge by Chambliss' leading regiment, which not only repulsed the enemy, but drove him pell-mell through the town with half his numbers, capturing his ambulances and a large number of prisoners, all of which were brought, safely through to our train, but were closely followed by the enemy's fresh troops. If my command had been well closed now, this cavalry column, which we had struck near its rear, would have been at our mercy; but, owing to the great elongation of the column by reason of the 200 wagons and hilly roads, Hampton was a long way behind, and Lee was not yet heard from on the left.

In retiring with the prisoners and ambulances, Lieut. Col. W. H. Payne, Fourth Virginia Cavalry, temporarily in command of the Second North Carolina Cavalry, was taken prisoner, in a gallant attempt to cut off a body of the enemy by a flank movement on the town.

The delay in getting up re-enforcements enabled the enemy to regain possession of the town, by no means desirable for us to hold, as it was in a valley completely commanded by the heights in our possession, which were soon crowned by our artillery. Our position was impregnable to cavalry even with so small a force. We cut the enemy's column in twain. General Fitz. Lee in the meantime fell upon the rear portion, driving it handsomely, and capturing one of Kilpatrick's staff and many other prisoners.

Our wagon train was now a subject of serious embarrassment, but I thought, by making a détour to the right by Jefferson, I could save it. I therefore determined to try it, particularly as I was satisfied, from every accessible source of information, as well as from the lapse of time, that the Army of Northern Virginia must be near the Susquehanna. My numerous skirmishers had greatly diminished—almost exhausted—my supply of ammunition. I had this immense train in an enemy's country, very near a hostile army, and, besides, about 400 prisoners, which had accumulated since the paroling at Cooksville. I therefore had the train closed up in park, and Hampton, arriving in the meantime, engaged the enemy farther to the right, and finally, with his sharpshooters, dislodged the enemy from the town, the enemy moving toward our left apparently to reunite his broken column, but pressing us with dismounted men on our left flank. General Fitz. Lee's brigade was put at the head of the column, and he was instructed to push on with the train through Jefferson for York, Pa. and communicate as soon as practicable with our forces. Hampton's brigade brought up the rear.

We were not molested in our march, which, on account of the very exposed situation of our flank and the enemy's knowledge of it, was continued during the night. The night's march over a very dark road was one of peculiar hardship, owing to loss of rest to both man and horse. After a series of exciting combats and night marches, it was a severe tax to their endurance. Whole regiments slept in the saddle, their faithful animals keeping the road unguided. In some instances they fell from their horses, overcome with physical fatigue and sleepiness.

Reaching Dover, Pa., on the morning of July 1, I was unable to find our forces. The most I could learn was that General Early had marched his division in the direction of Shippensburg, which the best information I could get seemed to indicate as the point of concentration of our troops. After as little rest as was compatible with the exhausted condition of the command, we pushed on for Carlisle, where we hoped to find a portion of the army. I arrived before that village, by way of Dillsburg, in the afternoon. Our rations were entirely out. I desired to levy a contribution on the inhabitants for rations, but was informed before reaching it that it was held by a considerable force of militia (infantry and artillery), who were concealed in the buildings, with the view to entrap me upon my entrance into the town. They were frustrated in their intention, and although very peaceable in external aspect, I soon found the information I had received was correct. I disliked to subject the town to the consequences of attack; at the same time it was essential to us to procure rations. I therefore directed General Lee to send in a flag of truce, demanding unconditional surrender or bombardment. This was refused. I placed artillery in position commanding the town, took possession of the main avenues to the place, and repeated the demand. It was again refused, and I was forced to the alternative of shelling the place.

Although the houses were used by their sharpshooters while firing on our men, not a building was fired excepting the United States cavalry barracks, which were burned by my order, the place having resisted my advance instead of peaceable surrender, as in the case of General Ewell. General Fitz. Lee's brigade was charged with the duty of investing the place, the remaining brigades following at considerable intervals from Dover. Maj. Gen. W. F. Smith was in command of the forces in Carlisle. The only obstacle to the enforcement of my threat was the scarcity of artillery ammunition.

The whereabouts of our army was still a mystery; but, during the night, I received a dispatch from General Lee (in answer to one sent by Major Venable from Dover, on Early's trail), that the army was at Gettysburg, and had been engaged on this day (July 1) with the enemy's advance. I instantly dispatched to Hampton to move 10 miles that night on the road to Gettysburg, and gave orders to the other brigades, with a view to reaching Gettysburg early the next day, and started myself that night.

My advance reached Gettysburg July 2, just in time to thwart a move of the enemy's cavalry upon our rear by way of Hunterstown, after a fierce engagement, in which Hampton's brigade performed gallant service, a series of charges compelling the enemy to leave the field and abandon his purpose. I took my position that day on the York and Heidlersburg roads, on the left wing of the Army of Northern Virginia.

On the morning of July 3, pursuant to instructions from the commanding general (the ground along our line of battle being totally impracticable for cavalry operations), I moved forward to a position to the left of General Ewell's left, and in advance of it, where a commanding ridge completely controlled a wide plain of cultivated fields stretching toward Hanover, on the left, and reaching to the base of the mountain spurs, among which the enemy held position. My command was increased by the addition of Jenkins' brigade, who here in the presence of the enemy allowed themselves to be supplied with but 10 rounds of ammunition, although armed with the most approved Enfield musket. I moved this command and W. H. F. Lee's secretly through the woods to a position, and hoped to effect a surprise upon the enemy's rear, but Hampton's and Fitz. Lee's brigades, which had been ordered to follow me, unfortunately debouched into the open ground, disclosing the movement, and causing a corresponding movement of a large force of the enemy's cavalry.

Having been informed that Generals Hampton and Lee were up, I sent for them to come forward, so that I could show them the situation at a glance from the elevated ground I held, and arrange for further operations. My message was so long in finding General Hampton that he never reached me, and General Lee remained, as it was deemed inadvisable at the time the message was delivered for both to leave their commands.

Before General Hampton had reached where I was, the enemy had deployed a heavy line of sharpshooters, and were advancing toward our position, which was very strong. Our artillery had, however, left the crest, which it was essential for it to occupy on account of being of too short range to compete with the longer range guns of the enemy, but I sent orders for its return. Jenkins' brigade was chiefly employed dismounted, and fought with decided effect until the 10 rounds were expended, and then retreated, under circumstances of difficulty and exposure which entailed the loss of valuable men.

The left, where Hampton's and Lee's brigades were, by this time became heavily engaged as dismounted skirmishers. My plan was to employ the enemy in front with sharpshooters, and move a command of cavalry upon their left flank from the position lately held by me, but the falling back of Jenkins' men (that officer was wounded the day previous, before reporting to me, and his brigade was now commanded by Colonel [M. J.] Ferguson, Sixteenth Virginia Cavalry) caused a like movement of those on the left, and the enemy, sending forward a squadron or two, were about to cut off and capture a portion of our dismounted sharpshooters.

To prevent this, I ordered forward the nearest cavalry regiment (one of W. H. F. Lee's) quickly to charge this force of cavalry. It was gallantly done, and about the same time a portion of General Fitz. Lee's command charged on the left, the First Virginia Cavalry being most conspicuous. In these charges, the impetuosity of those gallant fellows, after two weeks of hard marching and hard fighting on short rations, was not only extraordinary, but irresistible. The enemy's masses vanished before them like grain before the scythe, and that regiment elicited the admiration of every beholder, and eclipsed the many laurels already won by its gallant veterans. Their impetuosity carried them too far, and the charge being very much prolonged, their horses, already jaded by hard marching, failed under it. Their movement was too rapid to be stopped by couriers, and the enemy perceiving it, were turning upon them with fresh horses. The First North Carolina Cavalry and Jeff. Davis Legion were sent to their support, and gradually this hand-to-hand fighting involved the greater portion of the command till the enemy were driven from the field, which was now raked by their artillery, posted about three-quarters of a mile off, our officers and men behaving with the greatest heroism throughout. Our own artillery commanding the same ground, no more hand-to-hand fighting occurred, but the wounded were removed and the prisoners (a large number) taken to the rear.

The enemy's loss was unmistakably heavy; numbers not known. Many of his killed and wounded fell into our hands.

That brave and distinguished officer, Brigadier-General Hampton, was seriously wounded twice in this engagement.

Among the killed was Major [W. G.] Conner, a gallant and efficient officer of the Jeff. Davis Legion. Several officers and many valuable men were killed and wounded whose names it is not now in my power to furnish, but which, it is hoped, will be ultimately furnished in the reports of regimental and brigade commanders.

Notwithstanding the favorable results obtained, I would have preferred a different method of attack, as already indicated; but I soon saw that entanglement by the force of circumstances narrated was unavoidable, and determined to make the best fight possible. General Fitz. Lee was always in the right place, and contributed his usual conspicuous share to the success of the day. Both he and the gallant First Virginia begged me (after the hot encounter) to allow them to take the enemy's battery, but I doubted the practicability of the ground for such a purpose.

During this day's operations, I held such a position as not only to render Ewell's left entirely secure, where the firing of my command, mistaken for that of the enemy, caused some apprehension, but commanded a view of the routes leading to the enemy's rear. Had the enemy's main body been dislodged, as was confidently hoped and expected, I was in precisely the right position to discover it and improve the opportunity. I watched keenly and anxiously the indications in his rear for that purpose, while in the attack which I intended (which was forestalled by our troops being exposed to view), his cavalry would have separated from the main body, and gave promise of solid results and advantages.

After dark, I directed a withdrawal to the York road, as our position was so far advanced as to make it hazardous at night, on account of the proximity of the enemy's infantry.

During the night of July 3, the commanding general withdrew the main body to the ridges west of Gettysburg, and sent word to me to that effect, but his messenger missed me. I repaired to his headquarters during the latter part of the night, and received instructions as to the new line, and sent, in compliance therewith, a brigade (Fitz. Lee's) to Cashtown, to protect our trains congregated there. My cavalry and artillery were somewhat jeopardized before I got back to my command by the enemy having occupied our late ground before my command could be notified of the change. None, however, were either lost or captured.

During the 4th, which was quite rainy, written instructions were received from the commanding general as to the order of march back to the Potomac, to be undertaken at nightfall. In this order two brigades of cavalry (Baker's and Hampton's) were ordered to move, as heretofore stated, by way of Cashtown, guarding that flank, bringing up the rear on the road, via Greenwood, to Williamsport, which was the route designated for the main portion of the wagon trains and ambulances, under the special charge of Brigadier-General Imboden, who had a mixed command of artillery, infantry, and cavalry (his own).

Previous to these instructions, I had, at the instance of the commanding general, instructed Brigadier-General Robertson, whose two brigades (his own and Jones') were now on the right, near Fairfield, Pa., that it was essentially necessary for him to hold the Jack Mountain passes. These included two prominent roads-the one north and the other south of Jack Mountain, which is a sort of peak in the Blue Ridge chain.

In the order of march (retrograde), one corps (Hill's) preceded everything through the mountain; the baggage and prisoners of war escorted by another corps. Longstreet's occupied the center, and the third (Ewell's) brought up the rear. The cavalry was disposed of as follows Two brigades on the Cashtown road, under General Fitz. Lee, and the remainder (Jenkins' and Chambliss'), under my immediate command, was directed to proceed by way of Emmitsburg, Md., so as to guard the other flank.

I dispatched Captain [W. W.] Blackford, Corps of Engineers, to General Robertson, to inform him of my movement, and direct his co-operation, as Emmitsburg was in his immediate front, and was probably occupied by the enemy's cavalry. It was dark before I had passed the extreme right of our line, and, having to pass through very dense woods, taking by-roads, it soon became so dark that it was impossible to proceed. We were in danger of losing the command as well as the road. It was raining, also.

We halted for several hours, when, having received a good guide, and it becoming more light, the march was resumed, and just at dawn we entered Emmitsburg. We there learned that a large body of the enemy's cavalry (the citizens said 15,000, which I knew, of course, was exaggerated) had passed through that point the afternoon previous, going toward Monterey, one of the passes designated in my instructions to Brigadier-General Robertson.

I halted for a short time to procure some rations, and, examining my map, I saw that this force could either attempt to force one of those gaps, or, foiled in that (as I supposed they would be), it would either turn to the right and bear off toward Fairfield, where it would meet with like repulse from Hill's or Longstreet's corps, or, turning to the left before reaching Monterey, would strike across by Eyler's Gap, toward Hagerstown, and thus seriously threaten that portion of our trains which, under Imboden, would be passing down the Greencastle pike the next day, and interpose itself between the main body and its baggage. I did not consider that this force could seriously annoy any other portion of the command under the order of march prescribed, particularly as it was believed that those gaps would be held by General Robertson till he could be re-enforced by the main body. I therefore determined to adhere to my instructions, and proceed by way of Cavetown, by which I might intercept the enemy should he pass through Eyler's Gap.

In and around Emmitsburg we captured 60 or 70 prisoners of war, and some valuable hospital stores *en route* from Frederick to the army.

The march was resumed on the road to Frederick till we reached a small village called Cooperstown, where our route turned short to the right. Here I halted the column to feed, as the horses were much fatigued and famished. The column, after an hour's halt, continued through Harbaugh's Valley, by Zion Church, to pass the Catoctin Mountain. The road separated before debouching from the mountain, one fork leading to the left by Smithtown, and the other to the right, bearing more toward Leitersburg.

I divided my command, in order to make the passage more certain, Colonel Ferguson, commanding Jenkins' brigade, taking the left road, and Chambliss' brigade, which I accompanied, the other. Before reaching the western entrance to this pass, I found it held by the enemy, and had to dismount a large portion of the command, and fight from crag to crag of the mountains to dislodge the enemy, already posted.

Our passage was finally forced, and, as my column emerged from the mountains, it received the fire of the enemy's battery, posted to the left, on the road to Boonsborough. I ascertained, too, about this time by the firing that the party on the other route had met with resistance, and sent at once to apprise Colonel Ferguson of our passage, and directed him, if not already through, to withdraw, and come by the same route I had followed. Our artillery was soon in position, and a few fires drove the enemy from his position.

I was told by a citizen that the party I had just attacked was the cavalry of Kilpatrick, who had claimed to have captured several thousand prisoners and 400 or 500 wagons from our forces near Monterey; but I was further informed that not more than 40 wagons accompanied them, and other facts I heard led me to believe the success was far overrated. About this time, Captain [G. M.] Emack, Maryland cavalry, with his arm in a sling, came to us, and reported that he had been in the fight of the night before, and partially confirmed the statement of the citizen, and informed me, to my surprise, that a large portion of Ewell's corps trains had preceded the army through the mountains.

It was nearly night, and I felt it of the first importance to open communication with the main army, particularly as I was led to believe that a portion of this force might still be hovering on its flanks. I sent a trusty and intelligent soldier (Private Robert W. Goode, First Virginia Cavalry) to reach the commanding general by a route across the country, and relate to him what I knew, as well as what he might discover *en route*, and moved toward Leitersburg as soon as Colonel Ferguson came up, who, although his advance had forced the passage of the gap, upon the receipt of my dispatch turned back and came by the same route I had taken, thus making an unnecessary circuit of several miles, and not reaching me till after dark.

Having heard from the commanding general at Leitersburg about daylight (6 o'clock) next morning, and being satisfied that all of Kilpatrick's force had gone toward Boonsborough, I immediately, notwithstanding the march of a greater portion of both the preceding nights, set out toward Boonsborough. Jones' brigade had now arrived by the route from Fairfield. Soon after night,

Brigadier-General Jones, whose capture had been reported by Captain Emack, came from the direction of Williamsport, whither he had gone with the portion of the train which escaped. The enemy's movements had separated him from his command, and he had made a very narrow escape. He informed me of Imboden's arrival at Williamsport.

Having reached Cavetown, I directed General Jones to proceed on the Boonsborough road a few miles, and thence proceed to Funkstown, which point I desired him to hold, covering the eastern front of Hagerstown. Chambliss' brigade proceeded direct from Leitersburg to Hagerstown, and Robertson's took the same route, both together a very small command.

Diverging from Jones' line of march at Cavetown, I proceeded with Jenkins' brigade, by way of Chewsville, toward Hagerstown. Upon arriving at the former place, it was ascertained that the enemy was nearing Hagerstown with a large force of cavalry from the direction of Boonsborough, and that Colonel Chambliss needed reenforcements. Jenkins' brigade was pushed forward, and, arriving before Hagerstown, found the enemy in possession, and made an attack in flank by this road, Jones coming up farther to the left, and opening with a few shots of artillery. A small body of infantry, under Brigadier-General Iverson, also held the north edge of the town, aided by the cavalry of Robertson and Chambliss. Our operations were here much embarrassed by our great difficulty in preventing this latter force from mistaking us for the enemy, several shots striking very near our column. I felt sure that the enemy's designs were directed against Williamsport, where, I was informed by General Jones, our wagons were congregated in a narrow space at the foot of the hill, near the river, which was too much swollen to admit their passage to the south bank. I therefore urged on all side the most vigorous attack to save our trains at Williamsport. Our force was very perceptibly much smaller than the enemy's, but by bold front and determined attack, with a reliance on that help which has never failed me, I hoped to raise the siege of Williamsport, if, as I believed, that was the real object of the enemy's designs. Hagerstown is 6 miles from Williamsport, the country between being almost entirely cleared, but intersected by innumerable fences and ditches. The two places are connected by a lane and perfectly straight macadamized road. The enemy's dismounted skirmishers fought from street to street, and some time elapsed before the town was entirely clear, the enemy taking the road first toward Sharpsburg, but afterward turned to the Williamsport road. Just as the town was cleared, I heard the sound of artillery at Williamsport.

The cavalry, excepting the two brigades with General Fitz. Lee, were now pretty well concentrated at Hagerstown, and one column, under Colonel Chambliss, was pushed directly down the road after the enemy, while Robertson's two regiments and Jenkins' brigade kept to the left of the road, moving in a parallel direction with Chambliss. A portion of the Stuart Horse

Artillery also accompanied the movement. The first charge was gallantly executed by the leading brigade (Chambliss'), now numbering only a few hundred men, the Ninth and Thirteenth Virginia Cavalry participating with marked gallantry. The column on the flank was now hurried up to attack the enemy in flank, but the obstacles, such as post and rail fences, delayed its progress so long that the enemy had time to rally along a crest of rocks and fences, from which he opened with artillery, raking the road.

Jenkins' brigade was ordered to dismount and deploy over the difficult ground. This was done with marked effect and boldness, Lieutenant-Colonel Witcher, as usual, distinguishing himself by his courage and conduct. The enemy, thus dislodged, was closely pressed by the mounted cavalry, but made one effort at a counter-charge, which was gallantly met and repulsed by Col. James B. Gordon, commanding a fragment of the Fifth North Carolina Cavalry, that officer exhibiting under my eye individual prowess deserving special commendation. The repulse was soon after converted into a rout by Colonel Lomax's regiment (Eleventh Virginia Cavalry), Jones' brigade, which now took the road, under the gallant leadership of its colonel, with drawn sabers, and charged down the turnpike under a fearful fire of artillery.

Lieutenant-Colonel Funsten behaved with conspicuous gallantry in this charge, and Captain [S.] Winthrop, a volunteer aide of Lieutenant-General Longstreet, also bore himself most gallantly.

The enemy was now very near Williamsport, and this determined and vigorous attack in rear soon compelled him to raise the siege of that place, and leave in hasty discomfiture by the Downsville road. His withdrawal was favored by night, which set in just as we reached the ridge overlooking Williamsport. An important auxiliary to this attack was rendered by Brig. Gen. Fitz. Lee, who reached the vicinity of Williamsport by the Greencastle road very opportunely, and participated in the attack with his accustomed spirit.

Great credit is due the command for the fearless and determined manner in which they rushed upon the enemy and compelled him to loose his hold upon the main portion of the transportation of the army. Without this attack, it is certain that our trains would have fallen into the hands of the enemy, for, while some resistance was made by General Imboden, still, the size and nature of his command, the peculiar conformation of the ground, overlooked by hills and approached by six plain roads, go to show conclusively that not even a display of Spartan heroism on the part of his command could have saved those wagons from the torch of the enemy. I communicated with him after opening the road, by a lieutenant, whom I met but a short distance from the town. Officers present with General Imboden during the attack assure me I am right in the foregoing opinion. I was apprised when about midway that Lieutenant-General Longstreet had arrived at Hagerstown.

As a part of the operations of this period, I will here report that about 60 of the wagons belonging to Lee's brigade, while in the special charge of General Imboden, *en route* to Williamsport, near Mercersburg, were captured by the enemy. A court of inquiry has been convened to inquire into the circumstances of this capture. I therefore forbear animadversion on the subject.

My command bivouacked near Hagerstown, and I took position that night on the road leading from Hagerstown to Boonsborough.

The next day (July 7), I proceeded to Downsville, establishing there a portion of Wofford's brigade, sent me for the purpose by General Longstreet, and posted Jenkins' cavalry brigade on that portion of our front in advance of the infantry. Robertson's brigade, being small, and the enemy being least threatening from that direction, was assigned to the north front of Hagerstown, connecting with General Jones, on the right, on the Cavetown road. The Maryland cavalry was ordered on the National road and toward Greencastle, on a scout.

On the 8th, the cavalry was thrown forward toward Boonsborough, advancing on the different roads, in order, by a bold demonstration, to threaten an advance upon the enemy, and thus cover the retrograde of the main body. The move was successful, the advance under General Jones encountering the enemy on the Boonsborough road, at Beaver Creek Bridge, from which point to the verge of Boonsborough an animated fight ensued, principally on foot, the ground being entirely too soft from recent rains to operate successfully with cavalry. This contest was participated in in a very handsome manner by the other brigades (Fitz. Lee's, Hampton's, now commanded by Baker, and W. H. F. Lee's, commanded by Chambliss) and the Stuart Horse Artillery. Prisoners taken assured us the main cavalry force of the enemy was in our front, which, notwithstanding their known superiority in numbers and range of fire-arms, was driven steadily before us, our brave men, nothing daunted or dispirited by the reverses of the army, maintaining a predominance of pluck over the enemy calculated to excite the pride and admiration of beholders. Just as we neared the village, Jenkins' brigade, under Ferguson, moved up on the Williamsport road, driving the enemy on that flank in such a manner as to cause him to begin his withdrawal from the village to the mountain pass. His batteries had been driven away from the hill by the Napoleons of McGregor's battery, which, for close fighting, evinced this day their great superiority over rifled guns of greater number.

About this time, I was informed that the enemy was heavily re-enforced, and that our ammunition, by this protracted engagement, was nearly exhausted; and, despairing of getting possession of the town, which was completely commanded by artillery in the mountain gap, and believing that, in compelling the enemy to act upon the defensive (all that day retreating before us) the desired object had been fully attained, I began to retire toward Funkstown, excepting Jenkins' brigade, which was ordered to its former position on the Williamsport road. The enemy, observing this from his mountain perch, tried to profit by it with a vigorous movement on our heels, but was foiled. As the last regiment was crossing the bridge over Beaver Creek, a squadron of the enemy more bold than its comrades galloped forward as if to charge. Steadily a portion of the First North Carolina Cavalry awaited their arrival within striking distance, but, before reaching their vicinity, the enemy veered off across the fields, when a Blakely gun of Chew's battery, advantageously posted on a point, marked their movement, and, although the squadron moved at a gallop, never did sportsman bring down his bird with more unerring shot than did that Blakely tell upon that squadron. In vain did it turn to the right and left. Each shot seemed drawn to the flying target with fatal accuracy, until the enemy, driven by the shots of the Blakely and followed by shouts of derision of our cavalry, escaped at full speed over the plain.

The command moved leisurely to the vicinity of Funkstown, and bivouacked for the night.

The fight of the 8th administered a *quietus* to the enemy on the 9th, and my command kept the position in front of Funkstown assigned to it the night before.

The left of our main line of battle now rested just in rear of Funkstown, on the Antietam, and some infantry and artillery were thrown forward as a support to the cavalry beyond.

The enemy advanced on the 10th on the Boonsborough road, and our cavalry was engaged dismounted nearly all day. General Jones was farther to the left, on the Cavetown road, and the infantry was placed in position covering Funkstown, with dismounted cavalry on each flank. The enemy's advance was handsomely repulsed, in which Lieutenant-Colonel Witcher's cavalry, on foot, behind a stone fence immediately on the left of the turnpike, performed a very gallant part, standing their ground with unflinching tenacity. On the left, a portion of Fitz. Lee's brigade, under Captain Wooldridge, Fourth Virginia Cavalry, who handled his skirmishers with great skill and effect, compelled the enemy's infantry to seek cover in a body of woods at some distance from our lines.

In this day's operations, the infantry before mentioned participated very creditably, indeed, in the center, and I regret exceedingly that I have not the means of knowing the regiments and commanders, so as to mention them with that particularity to which by their gallantry they are entitled; but their conduct has no doubt been duly chronicled by their commanders, and laid before the commanding general, a part of which was under his own eye.

Owing to the great ease with which the position at Funkstown could be flanked on the right, and, by a secret movement at night, the troops there cut off, it was deemed prudent to withdraw at night to the west side of the Antietam, which was accordingly done.

July 11 was not characterized by any general engagement, excepting that General Fitz. Lee, now on the right, toward Downsville, was compelled to retire upon the main body; and the main body having assumed a shorter line, with its left resting on the National road, just west of Hagerstown, Chambliss' brigade was sent to that flank, and General Fitz. Lee's, also. The enemy made no movement on Jones' front, embracing the Funkstown and Cavetown roads.

On the 12th, firing began early, and the enemy having advanced on several roads on Hagerstown, our cavalry forces retired without serious resistance, and massed on the left of the main body, reaching with heavy outposts the Conococheague, on the National road. The infantry having already had time to intrench themselves, it was no longer desirable to defer the enemy's attack.

The 13th was spent in reconnoitering on the left, Rodes' division occupying the extreme left of our infantry, very near Hagerstown, a little north of the National road. Cavalry pickets were extended beyond the railroad leading to Chambersburg, and everything put in readiness to resist the enemy's attack. The situation of our communications south of the Potomac caused the commanding general to desire more cavalry on that side, and, accordingly, Brigadier-General Jones' brigade (one of whose regiments, Twelfth Virginia Cavalry, had been left in Jefferson) was detached, and sent to cover our communication with Winchester. The cavalry on the left consisted now of Fitz. Lee's, W. H. F. Lee's, Baker's, and Robertson's brigades, the latter being a mere handful.

On the 13th, skirmishing continued at intervals, but it appeared that the enemy, instead of attacking, was intrenching himself in our front, and the commanding general determined to cross the Potomac. The night of the 13th was chosen for this move, and the arduous and difficult task of bringing up the rear was, as usual, assigned to the cavalry. Just before night (which was unusually rainy), the cavalry was disposed from right to left, to occupy, dismounted, the trenches of the infantry at dark, Fitz. Lee's brigade holding the line of Longstreet's corps, Baker's of Hill's corps, and the remainder of Ewell's corps. A pontoon bridge had been constructed at Falling Waters, some miles below Williamsport, where Longstreet's and Hill's corps were to cross, and Ewell's corps was to ford the river at Williamsport, in rear of which last, after daylight, the cavalry was also to cross, excepting that Fitz. Lee's brigade, should he find the pontoon bridge clear in time, was to cross at the bridge; otherwise to cross at the ford at Williamsport.

The operation was successfully performed by the cavalry. General Fitz. Lee, finding the bridge would not be clear in time for his command, moved after daylight to the ford, sending two squadrons to cross in rear of the infantry at the bridge. These squadrons, mistaking Longstreet's rear for the rear of the army on that route, crossed over in rear of it. General Hill's troops being notified that these squadrons would follow in his rear, were deceived by some of the enemy's cavalry, who approached very near, in consequence of their belief that they were our cavalry. Although this unfortunate mistake deprived us of the lamented General Pettigrew, whom they mortally wounded, they paid the penalty of their temerity by losing most of their number in killed or wounded, if the accounts of those who witnessed it are to be credited. The cavalry crossed at the fords without serious molestation, bringing up the rear on that route by 8 a.m. on the 14th.

To Baker's (late Hampton's) brigade was assigned the duty of picketing the Potomac from Falling Waters to Hedgesville. The other brigades were moved back toward Leetown, Robertson's being sent to the fords of the Shenandoah, where he already had a picket, which, under Captain [L. A.] Johnson, of the North Carolina cavalry, had handsomely repulsed the enemy in their advance on Ashby's Gap, inflicting severe loss, with great disparity in numbers.

Harper's Ferry was again in possession of the enemy, and Colonel Harman, Twelfth Virginia Cavalry, had in an engagement with the enemy gained a decided success, but was himself captured by his horse falling.

Upon my arrival at the Bower that afternoon (15th), I learned that a large force of the enemy's cavalry was between Shepherdstown and Leetown, and determined at once to attack him in order to defeat any designs he might have in the direction of Martinsburg.

I made disposition accordingly, concentrating cavalry in his front, and early on the 16th moved Fitz. Lee's brigade down the turnpike, toward Shepherdstown, supported by Chambliss, who, though quite ill, with that commendable spirit which has always distinguished him, remained at the head of his brigade. Jenkins' brigade was ordered to advance on the road from Martinsburg toward Shepherdstown, so as by this combination to expose one of the enemy's flanks, while Jones, now near Charlestown, was notified of the attack, in order that he might co-operate. No positive orders were sent him, as his precise locality was not known.

These dispositions having been arranged, I was about to attack when I received a very urgent message from the commanding general to repair at once to his headquarters. I therefore committed to Brig. Gen. Fitz. Lee the consummation of my plans, and reported at once to the commanding general, whom I found at Bunker Hill. Returning in the afternoon, I proceeded to the scene of conflict on the turnpike, and found that General Fitz. Lee had, with his own and Chambliss' brigades, driven the enemy steadily to within a mile of Shepherdstown, Jenkins' brigade not having yet appeared on the left. However, it soon after arrived in Fitz. Lee's rear, and moved up to his support. The ground was not practicable for cavalry, and the main body was dismounted, and advanced in line of battle. The enemy retired to a strong position behind stone fences and barricades, near Colonel [A. R.] Boteler's residence, and it being nearly dark, obstinately maintained his ground at this last point until dark, to cover his withdrawal.

Preparations were made to renew the attack vigorously next morning, but daybreak revealed that the enemy had retired toward Harper's Ferry.

The enemy's loss in killed and wounded was heavy. We had several killed and wounded, and among the latter Col. James H. Drake, First Virginia Cavalry, was mortally wounded, dying that night (16th), depriving his regiment of a brave and zealous leader, and his country of one of her most patriotic defenders.

The commanding general was very desirous of my moving a large portion of my command at once into Loudoun, but the recent rains had so swollen the Shenandoah that it was impossible to ford it, and cavalry scouting parties had to swim their horses over.

In the interval of time from July 16 to the 22d, the enemy made a demonstration on Hedgesville, forcing back Baker's brigade. Desultory skirmishing was kept up on that front for several days with the enemy, while our infantry was engaged in tearing up the Baltimore and Ohio Railroad near Martinsburg. Parts of Jones' brigade were also engaged with the enemy in spirited conflicts not herein referred to, resulting very creditably to our arms, near Fairfield, Pa., and on the Cavetown road from Hagerstown, the Sixth and Seventh Virginia Cavalry being particularly distinguished. Accounts of these will be found in the reports of Brigadier-General Jones and Colonel Baker.

It soon became apparent that the enemy was moving upon our right flank, availing himself of the swollen condition of the Shenandoah to interpose his army, by a march along the east side of the Blue Ridge, between our present position and Richmond. Longstreet's corps having already moved to counteract this effort, enough cavalry was sent, under Brigadier-General Robertson, for his advance guard through Front Royal and Chester Gap, while Baker's brigade was ordered to bring up the rear of Ewell's corps, which was in rear, and Jones' brigade was ordered to picket the Lower Shenandoah as long as necessary for the safety of that flank, and then follow the movement of the army. Fitz. Lee's, W. H. F. Lee's, and Jenkins' brigades, by a forced march from the vicinity of Leetown, through Millwood, endeavored to reach Manassas Gap, so as to hold it on the flank of the army, but it was already in possession of the enemy, and the Shenandoah, still high, in order to be crossed without interfering with the march of the main army, had to be forded below Front Royal.

The cavalry already mentioned, early on the 23d reached Chester Gap by a by-path, passing on the army's left, and, with great difficulty and a forced march, that night bivouacked below Gaines' Cross-Roads, holding the Rockford road and Warrenton turnpike, on which, near Amissville, the enemy had accumulated a large force of cavalry.

On the 24th, while moving forward to find the locality of the enemy, firing was heard toward Newby's Cross-Roads, which was afterward ascertained to be a portion of the enemy's artillery firing on Hill's column, marching on the Richmond road. Before the cavalry could reach the scene of action, the enemy had been driven off by the infantry, and on the 25th the march was continued, and the line of the Rappahannock resumed.

In taking a retrospect of this campaign, it is necessary, in order to appreciate the value of the services of the cavalry, to correctly estimate the amount of labor to be performed, the difficulties to be encountered, and the very extended sphere of operations, mainly in the enemy's country. In the exercise of the discretion vested in me by the commanding general, it was deemed practicable to move entirely in the enemy's rear, intercepting his communications with his base (Washington), and, inflicting damage upon his rear, to rejoin the army in Pennsylvania in time to participate in its actual conflicts.

The result abundantly confirms my judgment as to the practicability as well as utility of the move. The main army, I was advised by the commanding general, would move in two columns for the Susquehanna. Early commanded the advance of that one of these columns to the eastward, and I was directed to communicate with him as early as practicable after crossing the Potomac, and place my command on his right flank. It was expected I would find him in York. The newspapers of the enemy, my only source of information, chronicled his arrival there and at Wrightsville, on the Susquehanna, with great particularity. I therefore moved to join him in that vicinity. The enemy's army was moving in a direction parallel with me. I was apprised of its arrival at Taneytown when I was near Hanover, Pa.; but believing, from the lapse of time, that our army was already in York or at Harrisburg, where it could choose its battle-ground with the enemy, I hastened to place my command with it. It is believed that, had the corps of Hill and Longstreet moved on instead of halting near Chambersburg, York could have been the place of concentration instead of Gettysburg.

This move of my command between the enemy's seat of government and the army charged with its defense involved serious loss to the enemy in men and *matériel* (over 1,000 prisoners having been captured), and spread terror and consternation to the very gates of the capital. The streets were barricaded for defense, as also was done in Baltimore on the day following. This move drew the enemy's overweening force of cavalry, from its aggressive attitude toward our flank near Williamsport and Hagerstown, to the defense of its own communications, now at my mercy. The entire Sixth Army Corps, in addition, was sent to intercept me at Westminster, arriving there the morning I left, which in the result prevented its participation in the first two days' fight at Gettysburg.

Our trains in transit were thus not only secured, but it was done in a way that at the same time seriously injured the enemy. General Meade also detached 4,000 troops, under General French, to escort public property to Washington from Frederick, a step which certainly would have been unnecessary but for my presence in his rear, thus weakening his army to that extent. In fact, although in his own country, he had to make large detachments to protect his rear and baggage. General Meade also complains that his movements were delayed by the detention of his cavalry in his rear. He might truthfully have added, by the movement in his rear of a large force of Confederate cavalry, capturing his trains and cutting all his communications with Washington.

It is not to be supposed such delay in his operations could have been so effectually caused by any other disposition of the cavalry. Moreover, considering York as the point of junction, as I had every reason to believe it would be, the route I took was quite as direct and more expeditious than the alternate one proposed, and there is reason to believe on that route that my command would have been divided up in the different gaps of South Mountain covering our flank, while the enemy, by concentration upon any one, could have greatly endangered our baggage and ordnance trains without exposing his own.

It was thought by many that my command could have rendered more service had it been in advance of the army the first day at Gettysburg, and the commanding general complains of a want of cavalry on the occasion; but it must be remembered that the cavalry (Jenkins' brigade) specially selected for advance guard to the army by the commanding general on account of its geographical location at the time, was available for this purpose, and had two batteries of horse artillery serving with it. If therefore, the peculiar functions of cavalry with the army were not satisfactorily performed in the absence of my command, it should rather be attributed to the fact that Jenkins' brigade was not as efficient as it ought to have been, and as its numbers (3,800) on leaving Virginia warranted us in expecting. Even at that time, by its reduction incident to campaign, it numbered far more than the cavalry which successfully covered Jackson's flank movement at Chancellorsville, turned back Stoneman from the James, and drove 3,500 cavalry under Averell across the Rappahannock. Properly handled, such a command should have done everything requisite, and left nothing to detract by the remotest implication from the brilliant exploits of their comrades, achieved under circumstances of great hardship and danger.

Arriving at York, I found that General Early had gone, and it is to be regretted that this officer failed to take any measures by leaving an intelligent scout to watch for my coming or a patrol to meet me, to acquaint me with his destination. He had reason to expect me, and had been directed to look out for me. He heard my guns at Hanover, and correctly conjectured whose they were, but left me no clew to his destination on leaving York, which would have saved me a long and tedious march to Carlisle and thence back to Gettysburg. I was informed by citizens that he was going to Shippensburg.

I still believed that most of our army was before Harrisburg, and justly regarded a march to Carlisle as the most likely to place me in communication with the main army. Besides, as a place for rationing my command, now entirely out, I believed it desirable. The cavalry suffered much in this march, day and night, from loss of sleep, and the horses from fatigue, and, while in Fairfax, for want of forage, not even grass being attainable.

In Fauquier, the rough character of the roads and lack of facilities for shoeing, added to the casualties of every day's battle and constant wear and tear of man and horse, reduced the command very much in numbers. In this way some regiments were reduced to less than 100 men; yet, when my command arrived at Gettysburg, from the accessions which it received from the weak horses left to follow the command, it took its place in line of battle with a stoutness of heart and firmness of tread impressing one with the confidence of victory which was astounding, considering the hardness of the march lately endured.

With an aggregate loss of about 2,200 killed, wounded, and missing, including the battle of Fleetwood, June 9, we inflicted a loss on the enemy's cavalry confessedly near 5,000.

Some of the reports of subordinate commanders are herewith forwarded; others will follow; and it is hoped they will do justice to that individual prowess for which Confederate soldiery is most noted, and which the limits of personal observation and this report deprive me of the power of doing.

Appended will be found a statement of casualties and a map; also a list of non-commissioned officers and privates whose conduct as bearers of dispatches and otherwise entitle them to favorable mention.

The bravery, heroism, fortitude, and devotion of my command are commended to the special attention of the commanding general, and are worthy the gratitude of their countrymen.

I desire to mention among the brigadier-generals one whose enlarged comprehensions of the functions of cavalry, whose diligent attention to the preservation of its efficiency, and intelligent appreciation and faithful performance of the duties confided to him, point to as one of the first cavalry leaders on the continent, and richly entitle him to promotion. I allude to Brig. Gen. Fitz. Lee.

I cannot here particularize the conduct of the many officers who deserve special mention of less rank than brigadier-general without extending my remarks more than would be proper. To my staff collectively, however, I feel at liberty to express thus officially my grateful appreciation of the zeal, fidelity, and ability with which they discharged their several duties, and labored to promote the success of the command.

Maj. Heros von Borcke, assistant adjutant and inspector general (that gallant officer from Prussia, who so early espoused our cause), was disabled in Fauquier, so as to deprive me of his valuable services on the expedition, but it is hoped that the command will not long be deprived of his inspiring presence on the field.

Maj. Henry B. McClellan, my adjutant-general, was constantly at my side, and with his intelligence, ready pen, and quick comprehension, greatly facilitated the discharge of my duties.

The untiring energy, force of character, and devotion to duty of Maj. A. R. Venable, my inspector-general, and Lieut. G. M. Ryals, C. S. Army, provost-marshal, deserve my special gratitude and praise.

The same qualities, united to a thorough knowledge of much of the country, are ascribable to Capt. B. S. White, C. S. Army, who, though still suffering from a severe wound received at Fleetwood, accompanied the command, and his services proclaim him an officer of merit and distinction.

Chief Surgeon Eliason; Captain Blackford, engineer; Captain [John Esten] Cooke, ordnance officer; Lieutenant [Chiswell] Dabney, aide-de-camp; Asst. Engineer F. S. Robertson; Cadet [W. Q.] Hullihen. C. S. Army, and Lieut. H. Hagan, Virginia Provisional Army, all performed their duties with commendable zeal and credit.

Major [Norman R.] Fitzhugh, chief, and Capt. J. M. Hanger, assistant quartermaster, and Maj. W. J. Johnson, chief commissary, discharged their arduous duties in their usual highly creditable manner.

First Lieut. R. B. Kennon, Provisional Army Confederate States, temporarily attached, on two different occasions was intrusted with duties attended with great peril, which he performed in a highly successful and satisfactory manner—once in testing experimentally at night an unknown ford on the Potomac, and again in bearing a dispatch to the commanding general from Emmitsburg.

Grateful to the Giver of all good for the attainment of such results with such small comparative losses, I have the honor to be, most respectfully, your obedient servant,

J. E. B. STUART,
Major-General

A Driving Tour of
Jeb Stuart's Ride to Gettysburg

T he mileage between each stop is given, so you can easily reset your trip odometer at any of the stops in case you make any detours or lose track of your mileage. At several of the stops we suggest you reset your odometer in order to assist you with various turns and points of interest. Note that the mileage given may vary slightly.

We begin and end this tour in Gettysburg, Pennsylvania. You may, however, begin the tour in Westminster, Maryland, if that is more convenient for you. It is important to note this tour does not address that portion of the raid that occurred in Virginia or near Washington, D. C.

The tour presented below will take about one full day to complete, but we suggest setting aside two days in order to fully enjoy each stop. It is our hope you will more fully appreciate the distance Stuart and his command covered in less than three days, as well as the numerous skirmishes and battles they waged.

Please do not trespass onto private property, and be aware of traffic as you conduct this tour.

*   *   *

Begin your tour in Gettysburg, Pennsylvania

* Start by driving south on the Baltimore Pike, which is Rt. 97.
*Drive 3.8 miles and enter the town of Two Taverns, Pennsylvania. Brig. Gens. George A. Custer and Elon J. Farnsworth of Kilpatrick's Federal cavalry division left here for Hunterstown on the morning of July 2. The two old taverns are on opposite sides of the road just before you cross Little's Run. Continue on Rt. 97.

* Drive another 4.8 miles and enter the town of Littlestown. Note the high ground behind the McDonalds fast food restaurant on your right, which is now covered by a new housing development. The 5th and 6th Michigan Cavalry of Custer's brigade camped here on June 29, with Farnsworth's brigade in the surrounding area. Continue on Rt. 97.

* Drive .2 miles, in the center of the town, you will see the "Hanover Road" to your left (do not turn, but continue straight). Hanover is seven miles away. Kilpatrick took this road to Hanover with Farnsworth's brigade early on the morning of June 30, after Custer did the same with the 1st and 7th Michigan regiments a few hours earlier. Here, also, the Union 12th Corps concentrated later on June 30 before the Gettysburg battle. Continue on Rt. 97.

* Drive 2.2 miles and you come to the Mason-Dixon Line, the boundary between Maryland and Pennsylvania. Continue on Rt. 97.

* Drive 4.1 miles and enter the historic settlement of Union Mills. Stuart's column arrived here late on the afternoon of June 29 after the fight at Westminster, Maryland, and spent the night on the Shriver Farms. Continue on Rt. 97, because we will be returning here after following Stuart's column chronologically.

* Drive .6 miles and you will come to Big Pipe Creek. Continue on Rt. 97.

* Drive .9 miles. To your front is the high ground that General Meade desired to hold along the Pipe Creek Line. This strong defensive terrain was nearly adopted as a position from which to give battle to General Lee's Confederate army. Continue on Rt. 97.

* Drive 4.6 miles. Be sure to continue straight and enter downtown Westminster; do not bear right onto Rt. 97, as this is a bypass that will take you to a commercial district.

WESTMINSTER, MARYLAND

* Drive another .2 miles and enter the town of Westminster. You are entering town on Pennsylvania Avenue. It merges into West Main Street after another .4 miles, where you will bear slightly left.

* Drive another .2 miles and cross a set of railroad tracks. Those railroad tracks are part of what in 1863 was called the Western Maryland Railroad. The Western Maryland connected Westminster with Baltimore, and was a major supply artery for the Union army. This was the reason why Union troops were in the town when Stuart's command arrived on June 29. The railroad had just been extended to Westminster in the spring of 1863.

* Drive .5 miles from the railroad tracks and pull over at 206 Main Street on your right. This is the Shellman House, built circa 1807. Mary Shellman lived here in 1863. She called Jeb Stuart a "Johnny Reb Coat" when he entered the town after the fight with the Delaware Cavalry, and received a kiss from the plumed cavalier as "punishment." The home today houses the Carroll County Historical Society.

The next building up the street, to the left of the Shellman House, is the Westminster Visitor Information Center in the Kimmey House (210 Main Street). Park in front and enter if you would like additional information. Continue on Main Street.

* Drive .3 miles and you will come to the intersection of Main Street and Washington Road. Park in the Sheetz convenience store parking lot just ahead of you. This intersection was the scene of "Corbit's Charge." A historic wayside is located at the intersection, placed there by the Delaware Civil War Centennial Commission. The 1st Delaware Cavalry charged up Main Street toward where you are standing and met Stuart's advance in the block ahead of you.

Also at this intersection, at 297 Main Street, is the Trumbo-Chrest home. Walk carefully across the intersection. On the right side of the home you will plainly see marks of Confederate bullet damage suffered during the fight. This home is on the National Register of Historic Places.

* Exit the Sheetz parking lot and turn left onto the Washington Road. Reset your odometer.

* Drive .2 miles. At the curve in the road, 45 Washington Road, is the scene where the first encounter took place. Lt. D. W. C. Clark of Co. C of the 1st Delaware Cavalry and his 12-man advance, dispatched by Capt. Corbit, were captured here by Fitz Lee's advance troopers (The "Summerville Assisted Living" home is on left).

Authors

Scene of Capt. Charles Corbit's Charge, looking down Main Street in Westminster, Maryland. Corbit and his Delawareans charged toward the camera. After routing Corbit's troopers, Stuart pursued them a few hundreds yards down Main Street as far as the railroad tracks.

Side of the Trumbo-Chrest home on Main Street, Westminster, Maryland, showing small arms fire damage from Corbit's Charge. The home is on the National Register of Historic Places.

* **Turn around in the Pritts Funeral Home lot on your right (or any convenient and safe place nearby). Turn left onto Washington Road and turn left back onto Main Street. Reset your odometer.**

* **At the next intersection, where Bishop Street crosses Main Street, was the Michael Baughman Blacksmith Shop.** The shop was located on the right side, on the north corner of the intersection. Fitz Lee's advance, upon entering the town, captured five troopers of the 1st Delaware Cavalry whose horses were being shod here. They were taken back to the column. Shortly afterward, Lt. Clark and his detail clashed with Lee's troopers on the Washington Road.

* **Drive .3 miles from when you turned back onto Main Street, and turn right onto North Court Street.** To your right on this corner stood the Westminster Hotel and Tavern, where Maj. Napoleon B. Knight of the 1st Delaware Cavalry was imbibing local spirits prior to the engagement.

* **Drive .1 miles. On your right is the Ascension Episcopal Church**, built in 1844. Park in front of the church, if possible. In the small cemetery behind the church under the large tree on the right side is the grave of Lt. John Murray of the 4th Virginia Cavalry, who was killed in the fighting with Corbit's men. The original headstone is the taller of the pair. His newer headstone reads: JOHN WILLIAM MURRAY, 1st Lt. Co. E 4th VA Cav., June 29, 1863.

Authors

The grave of Lt. John W. Murray of the 4th Virginia Cavalry in the graveyard of
the Ascension Episcopal Church, Westminster, Maryland.

Lt. St. Pierre Gibson of the 4th Virginia Cavalry was also killed in the
fighting with Corbit's men. He was laid to rest beside Murray, but his body was
later reclaimed and returned to Virginia.

The old County Courthouse, built circa 1838, is at the end of North Court
Street. Walk up to the Courthouse and you will see wayside markers at the front
of the building. This is the location where some of Stuart's troopers attempted to
tear down the US flag that flew from the cupola. Thirteen ladies of Westminster
had sewn the flag and signed their names on the stars. One of the wayside
markers recounts the story.

*** Return to your vehicle. Turn left onto Court Place, then take the first
right. Turn left at the stop sign. Reset your odometer and drive .1 miles,
turn left onto North Center Street. Proceed another .1 miles, turn left back
onto Main Street, and drive .2 miles, turning left onto Church Street.** The
Westminster Cemetery is directly ahead of you. You may pull into the entrance
of the cemetery and park where convenient. The cemetery was established in
1790. Just to the right inside the entrance is the grave of William Winchester,
Revolutionary War soldier (170-1790), for whom the town of Winchester,
Virginia, was named. At the center of the circle to your left is a large urn. This
urn is actually a monument that marks the location of the Federal field hospital
established during the Battle of Winchester.

The Old Carroll County Courthouse, Westminster, Maryland.

* **Drive around the circle to turn around and exit the cemetery the same way you entered. Continue driving .1 miles, turn right to get back on to Main Street.**

* **Drive .1 miles.** At 71 East Main Street on your right side (now the Westminster Union Bank) was the Abner Neal home. Two of Abner's sons, Henry and Francis, served in James Breathed's horse artillery battery, part of Stuart's cavalry column. They were in the advance and fought against Corbit and his Delawareans. As the Federals retreated, pursued by Fitz Lee's troopers down Main Street, the Neal brothers worked their guns almost directly in front of their old family homestead. There is a plaque on the side of the building recounting their participation in the fight. Because of their Southern sentiments, this was the last time Henry and Francis returned home to Westminster.

* **Drive .5 miles and cross over the railroad tracks again.** These railroad tracks mark the farthest point of the Confederate pursuit of the fleeing Delaware Cavalry.

* **Drive .2 miles and bear to your right back onto Pennsylvania Avenue.**

* **Drive .5 miles. Note the high ground on your left.** This is the campus of McDaniel (formerly known as Western Maryland) College, which was the campsite of the 1st Delaware Cavalry. For many years prior to the war, this area was used by local residents for picnics, political rallies, and Fourth of July celebrations. It was selected as the campsite because of its commanding view of the town and surrounding roads. Reset your odometer while passing the college.

* Drive back to Union Mills on 97 North. You are now following the same route Stuart took from Westminster to Union Mills. Remember that Stuart's column, in addition to nearly 4,000 cavalrymen and their associated baggage, also had with them the 125 wagons and 800 mules captured at Rockville, Maryland. The long train slowed down the pace of the column considerably. Each brigade took turns guarding the train, following in the rear.

UNION MILLS

* Drive 6.1 miles from McDaniel College. Note the wayside marker on the right. If it is safe to do so, pull over to read the marker. You are back in Union Mills. You will see a sign for the "Union Mills Homestead" and a Civil War Trails marker. Drive forward and pull into the Union Mills park site.

Slightly ahead on the left is the white William Shriver house (William sympathized with the Confederates). On your right is the home of his brother, Andrew (who sympathized with the Union). Andrew's home is the original homestead of the Shriver family. Stuart's command camped throughout this area on the night of June 29. That night, Stuart entertained the Shrivers by playing the piano and singing for them, including performing his signature song, "If you want to have some fun, jine the cav'ry." The next morning, Stuart and his brigade commanders and their staff enjoyed a sumptuous breakfast in William's

The Westminster Cemetery. The urn at the center marks the site of a Union hospital during the Battle of Winchester.

home before departing for Pennsylvania with William's sixteen-year-old son Herbert leading the way.

The following day, June 30, the Federal 12th Corps camped here during its march to the Gettysburg battlefield. The Union Mills Homestead Foundation owns and operates the property, and guided tours are available. There is a gift shop and several informative wayside markers on the property.

The front balcony of the homestead was copied after Thomas Jefferson's Monticello. Politicians such as Roger Brooke Taney gave speeches from the home's front porch. Francis Scott Key also spoke from the porch. On the property was a post office, general store, and a stagecoach inn. Both John James Audobon and Washington Irving were guests at the Inn. Stuart intended to go straight to Littlestown from here. However, on the night of June 29, his scouts informed him that Federal cavalry occupied Littlestown, so Stuart ordered a detour around the town and guided his column, with the wagons in tow, 10 miles east to Hanover.

* Exit the parking lot and turn right to proceed on 97 North. Reset your odometer. Drive .1 miles from Union Mills and turn right onto the Old Hanover Road. You will cross Big Pipe Creek, for which Meade's proposed defensive line was named. The Old Hanover Road is the route Stuart chose to try and reach Hanover without running into Kilpatrick's troopers. On the morning of June 30, however, two cavalry divisions—Stuart's and Kilpatrick's—were riding nearly parallel to one another, each heading for Hanover. Stuart's distance to Hanover was 10 miles, while Kilpatrick's was seven miles.

Authors

The Andrew Shriver home. Stuart's men camped here on June 29 after the fight at Westminster. Fitz Lee slept under an apple tree in the orchard behind the house.

As you head east on the Old Hanover Road, note once again the prominent high ground on your right, which played an integral part of Meade's Pipe Creek Plan.

* Drive 3.9 miles and reenter Pennsylvania (Adams County). Drive another .5 miles and turn right at the stop sign onto the Old Westminster Road. Continue another 1.5 miles and you will see the waters of a reservoir and large earthen dam ahead of you. In 1863, the original road continued straight (the gravel road you see ahead). Because the original road trace is now flooded, you must bear left and continue around the lake on the new road.

* Drive another .8 miles and you will come to a stop sign. To your right, where the original road ran, was the Gitt farm. It was here the 18th Pennsylvania Cavalry's Thaddeus Freeland skirmished with some of Stuart's Confederates, signifying the first encounter of the Hanover battle. Much of the Gitt farm is now under water.

* Turn left at this stop sign onto Grand Valley Road and drive .1 miles until you cross Conewago Creek. It was in this area that Lt. Henry C. Potter, commanding the rear guard of the 18th Pennsylvania Cavalry, stopped to water his horses. Potter was met by a local farmer who told him of Confederates scouring the area for food and horses.

* Drive 1 mile from the creek. Take note of the fields to your right and left (South Hills Golf Course is on the left). During the Hanover battle, Stuart parked the captured wagons here. They were guarded by some of Hampton's troopers, who had orders to burn the wagons to keep them out of Federal hands.

* Drive another .1 miles and turn left onto Little Bridge Road, which is at the end of the golf course. The high ground on your right is Rice's Hill, which became one of the two positions where Stuart placed his batteries of horse artillery once the Hanover fighting commenced.

* Drive another .3 miles and you will reach a cul-de-sac in a housing development. Park at the white fence ahead of you on the right. Make sure you can safely do so. If you have permission to do so, walk up the slight rise along this fence while angling to your left to the point where the fence ends at the line of woods. Please keep in mind you are on private property. From the top of the rise you will have a nice vantage point. The Samuel Keller Farm was located just ahead of you down the hill—the farm is gone and the area completely covered with townhouses. Stuart's guns were deployed there, and also on the farm to your right, which was the Jesse Rice farm.

* If you left your car return to it, leave the cul-de-sac, and turn left back onto Westminster Road. Reset your odometer. You will again see Rice's Hill, where the Jesse Rice farm was located, directly in front of you at the intersection. Continue on Westminster Road.

* Drive .5 miles and on your right you will see the Rest Haven Cemetery and the high ground from which Stuart watched the opening of the Hanover fight. This was the location of Stuart's Headquarters during the battle. If you wish, you may enter the cemetery to look around. When you leave the cemetery, we will continue driving north on Westminster Road.

* Reset your odometer and drive .4 miles. Turn right onto Frederick Street at the stop sign. Pull off to the right as soon as you can safely do so and park. You will see a Gettysburg Campaign marker on the right, along with one of the new wayside markers placed in and around Hanover in 2005 through a cooperative effort of local and county groups. There are also two more wayside markers across the street.

You are now standing where the main battle of Hanover began. Lt. Potter and the 18th Pennsylvania Cavalry rearguard initially clashed here with men of Col. John R. Chambliss's 13th Virginia Cavalry, while the rest of Brig. Gen. Elon J. Farnsworth's brigade was strung out ahead of you in the town of Hanover. In 1863, this hamlet of homes, farms, and open cultivated and grazing fields was called "Mudtown." When Potter and his men were pushed into the rear of their brigade, Farnsworth ordered his men to about-face in your direction and counterattack. Reset your odometer.

* Pull back onto Frederick Street and drive eastbound. Note that the first two streets to the right are named Stuart Avenue and Kilpatrick Avenue, respectively.

* Drive another .6 miles and you will reach the Hanover Town Square.

HANOVER TOWN Square

* Park in any available space. Depending on the season and time of day, it may be difficult to find parking on the Square. You may need to look for space along one of the side streets. When walking across intersections in the Square, please exercise caution as traffic can be very heavy.

Two cannons are located here on the Square. Note the gun tube marked #1, which was personally inspected by Robert P. Parrott, and has the date of 1861 engraved on the trunion. The gun was manufactured at the West Point Armory in Cold Spring, New York. The other gun tube is marked #6.

Kilpatrick's Headquarters, the Central Hotel, is at 1 Frederick Street. Kilpatrick's headquarters were located in the room at the front of the hotel on the second floor, affording him a clear view of the Town Square. A flag often flies beneath the window of the room. Custer's Headquarters was the old theater building, which is the next building down Frederick Street to the west of the hotel. Farnsworth's Headquarters were in the building (a jewelry store as of the time of this writing), located at 11 Frederick Street.

The location of the so-called "Custer Maple," where George Custer was said to have tied his horse upon arriving in the town, is marked on the sidewalk in the Square, and there is also a nearby plaque with the story.

The impressive Picket Monument, which originally (1903) sat in the center of the Square, was moved to its present location between Carlisle and Broadway streets in 1967. It was sculpted by Cyrus Dallin of Boston, Massachusetts. The statue does not represent any one soldier, but instead commemorates all of the Federal Cavalry that fought in the battle. Note the small iron statue of a dog near the Picket Monument. It is named "Iron Mike," and originally stood in the lawn of resident George Welsh. When Welsh died, the statue was placed near his grave in Mt. Olivet Cemetery. The dog frightened horses that passed by, so the statue was given to the town and placed next to the Picket Monument, and remains standing guard to this day. (Iron Mike has no significance to the Battle of Hanover.)

There are a number of new wayside markers about the battle and the history of the town positioned around the Square, including several in a kiosk. They contain very interesting information and are worth visiting.

Other Sites to See in Hanover

* From the location you parked, start your car and drive through the Square. Turn right onto Rt. 94 North, which is Carlisle Street. There is no

Authors

The Central Hotel on the Square in Hanover, Pennsylvania. Brig. Gen. Judson Kilpatrick made his headquarters here during the battle on June 30. He commandeered room number 4, which is on the second story.

need to reset your odometer. **Turn right at the second light onto Park Street. At the stop sign where Park Street intersects Railroad Street, drive a short distance and park near the chain link fence.** You will note an abandoned set of railroad tracks on your immediate left. The railroad junction and depot were located here in 1863; this was the industrial center of Hanover.

It was at this location that President Abraham Lincoln addressed citizens of Hanover on November 18, 1863, on his way to the dedication of the Gettysburg National Cemetery. This area of town was called "The Commons." During the Hanover battle, the 5th New York Cavalry rallied here for a counterattack. Note the blue towers ahead of you. That was where the 18th Pennsylvania Cavalry rallied after the initial attack. The high ground behind this position, known locally as Bunker Hill, served as the location of Elder's and Pennington's batteries of Federal horse artillery, which engaged in counter-battery fire with the Confederate batteries unlimbered south of the town.

* Turn your vehicle around and turn left onto Railroad Street, then turn right onto East Chestnut Street. Drive .1 miles and turn left onto Baltimore Street, which is Rt. 94 South. Drive halfway around the Square to continue straight. Drive .9 miles from the Square and turn right into Mt. Olivet Cemetery. There are three roads in the cemetery; stay on the road heading straight. Some of Kilpatrick's artillery deployed here early in the battle. The cemetery was founded in 1859, and in the center circle is a monument to Civil War veterans as well as two field pieces.

The Picket Monument, dedicated in 1903 to all of the
Federal cavalry that fought at Hanover.

Authors

The ditch near Westminster Street in Hanover, Pennsylvania, where Jeb Stuart made his famous jump to safety from pursuing Federals. Shallow today, it was much deeper and wider in 1863.

* **Drive around the small circle and exit the cemetery the way you came in, turn left onto Baltimore Street, and drive back toward the Town Square. Once you reach the Square, turn left onto Frederick Street. Reset your odometer. Drive .3 miles and turn left onto Fleming Street. Continue a short distance up Fleming Street and turn right onto West Walnut Street at the stop sign.** About 30 yards up on West Walnut Street on the right side is a paved vacant lot where the Winebrenner Tannery was located during the battle. It was here Lt. Col. William Payne, the commander of the 2nd North Carolina Cavalry, fell into a tanning vat and was captured by the Federals.

* **Drive forward and after a short distance turn right at the stop sign onto Forney Street. Take an immediate left back onto Frederick Street and drive another .3 miles before turning left onto Westminster Street.** You are now heading back to the spot at "Mudtown" where the main battle began. Drive another .2 miles and you will come to a shallow drainage ditch (just past Hartman Avenue) that runs perpendicular to the road. You will see a small bridge where it runs under the road. This is where Jeb Stuart and several of his staff jumped their horses to escape pursuing Federals of the 5th New York Cavalry. Stuart jumped the ditch on your left. At the time of the battle, the ditch was much deeper and wider.

* **Continue driving south on Westminster Road .8 miles from the ditch and turn left onto Cooper Road.** You are now heading up Rice's Hill, the location of the Jesse Rice farm that you saw earlier. At the summit, the highest point on your right, is where Chambliss deployed two sections of guns aimed at the town. Continue driving on Cooper Road. This is a very narrow and unimproved road, so drive with extreme caution.

* **Drive .6 miles and you will come to a stop sign at the intersection of Cooper Road and Beck Mill Road.** Pause here, traffic permitting. Across the road to your right is a brick home. Along the right side of this home was a road that no longer exists (although you can see traces of it near the home's driveway). This road connected to the Baltimore Pike, and was the route along which Wade Hampton led the 125 wagons out of Hanover after the battle.

* **Turn left onto Beck Mill Road and drive another .4 miles.** On your right is Mt. Olivet Cemetery, where you previously stopped. This marked Stuart's right flank during the battle.

* **Drive another .4 miles from the cemetery and on your left you will see the two-story brick Forney home.** This is one of the homes through which one of Stuart's shells, fired from the hill behind you, passed early in the fight. The shell is now part of the collection of the Hanover Historical Society.

* **Drive a short distance, bear left at the fork in the road, and you will come to a stop sign.** Directly in front of you is the ground (now a residential area covered with homes) over which Custer's dismounted troopers fought that afternoon. This dismounted fighting marked one of the first instances where Confederate troops faced the firepower of the new Spencer repeating rifles carried by men of the 5th and 6th Michigan Cavalry.

* **At the stop sign, turn left onto Boundary Avenue and drive another .4 miles. Turn right onto Forney Avenue and drive .1 miles.** You will notice the crest of the hill where Hartman Road crosses Forney Avenue. This hill marks the farthest advance by Custer's 6th Michigan Cavalry before the troopers were driven off the hill late in the fight.

* **Continue driving straight on Forney Avenue and after .2 miles turn right onto Frederick Street to drive back to the Town Square.**

PIGEON HILLS

* **From the Town Square, drive east until you turn right onto Broadway Street.** This is the wartime "Abbottsown Road." Reset your odometer.

* **Drive approximately three miles and you will see the Pigeon Hills** ahead of you, where Kilpatrick and the van of his column (Farnsworth's brigade) were located when the 18th Pennsylvania Cavalry at the rear of this long column was attacked back in town behind you.

* When you reach the top of the summit, turn left onto Hershey Heights Road and park where convenient and safe to do so. From here, you will have a commanding view back toward the town of Hanover. When he heard the firing in the town, Kilpatrick rode his horse back (to the right of the road) from this area, through fields and over fences. When he reached the Town Square, his horse died of exhaustion and was later buried at Bunker Hill three miles away.

* Turn your vehicle around and go back down Broadway Street into town to the Square. Turn onto Baltimore Street (Rt. 94 South) to leave the Square heading south. Reset your odometer and drive approximately 1.5 miles. On your right was the spot where Stuart's captured wagon train came out onto the Baltimore Road on the now non-existent road. Stuart's cavalry and the wagon train turned to the right from that road and trotted and rolled over the route you are now following.

* Drive .9 miles and turn left at Grandview Road, heading toward Jefferson, Pennsylvania. This route was known as the "Jefferson Road."

* Drive 6 miles, turn left onto Fuhrman Mill Road, reset your odometer, and drive just under two miles. Note how hilly and narrow this road becomes. The Simon Barnhart Farm is on the left side of the road. A Confederate casualty of the Hanover battle was buried near the red barn, and Stuart's men took forty bushels of corn from Barnhart. Another .2 miles ahead is the William Allbright farm, where four horses were taken.

* At the first stop sign, turn right onto Black Rock Road and reset your odometer. In front of you was the John M. Wildasin farm. One horse was taken from his farm.

* Drive another .2 miles, turn left onto Dubs Church Road, and drive another 1.6 miles before bearing right onto Baumgardner Road. With the building of the 1,275-acre Lake Marburg in Codorus State Park, several roads used by Stuart and various detachments have been covered by water. At this point we must leave the original route for a time to circumvent the lake. There were actually several farms on the land, now under water, from which Stuart's men appropriated many items.

* Drive .3 miles and turn right onto Blooming Grove Road at the stop sign. Drive another 1.2 miles and turn left onto Sinsheim Road. The historic route joins this road from your left after about two miles. You're now once again on the historical route. When you come to a set of railroad tracks just ahead, bear left and reset your odometer.

JEFFERSON

* Drive 1.1 miles and enter the town of Jefferson. Drive another .4 miles and you will reach Jefferson's Town Square. Proceed halfway around and

continue straight on York Street, heading for Spring Grove. Continue another 3.4 miles and turn left onto Panther Hill Road. If traffic permits, pause just after turning onto this road. Near this intersection (historians debate the actual location) stood the John Zeigler home and farm buildings. It was in Zeigler's home that Stuart held a council of war late on the night of June 30. Probably the wealthiest man in this area, Zeigler lost an enormous amount of hay, oats, and corn to the Confederates, as well as six fine horses. Continue driving on Panther Hill Road. It becomes a narrow dirt road, and so offers a good idea of what this road might have looked like in 1863. Drive with caution.

   * **Drive .4 miles and you will see the Henry Hoff farm in the valley on your left.** Eight of Stuart's troopers left the main column, rode up to the house, and confiscasted horses, food, and clothing. Hoff also operated a distillery, and the Confederates helped themselves to several barrels of whiskey. The troopers rode back up to Panther Hill Road, but began a drinking binge and passed out. Hoff's wife, Rosanna, quietly retrieved her favorite horse after dusk. The troopers left later that night, apparently none the wiser.

   * **Continue driving another .6 miles and you will come to a stop sign. Proceed straight through for another .5 miles and you will see the cemetery of Ziegler's Church.** A burial was taking place when Stuart's column passed this point, and the terrified locals hurried to their homes to hide their horses. It is widely believed the man being buried when the head of Stuart's column appeared was a local Union soldier who had been killed at Chancellorsville in early May 1863.

   * **Drive another .1 miles and turn left onto Cemetery Road. Drive another mile and turn left at the stop sign onto Seven Valleys Road, which is Rt. 616 North. From this point drive 4.2 miles and turn right onto Rt. 30 East.** Because of the relocation and modernization of the roads in this area, we are forced to leave the historic route for a few minutes.

   * **Continue on Rt. 30 East for 4.3 miles and take the exit for Rt. 74 North toward Dover.** You are now once again on the historic route. Reset your odometer at the stoplight.

   * **Pass under Rt. 30 and stay in the right lane for 4.8 miles to Dover.** As you proceed, note the hilly terrain of this area and imagine riding horses and wagons up and down this undulating geography.

DOVER

Stuart stopped his column in Dover to rest. He also scoured Northern newspapers for any information on the whereabouts of Lee's army. Note also the creek that runs through town, where many of the horses and mules were watered.

ROSSVILLE

* Continue driving on 74 North to Rossville for six miles, and then turn left to stay on 74 North (the Carlisle Road), heading toward the old town of Wellsville. Note the winding and often steep terrain and imagine how it would have worn out horses, mules, and men.

WELLSVILLE

* Drive another 1.1 miles and you will reach Wellsville. On your left is the old stone Quaker Meeting House building with cemetery. Wellsville was founded in 1737. Many of the buildings on Main Street are from the era of the town's founding.

* Proceed another .3 miles to the stop sign and turn right, staying on Rt. 74 North. Drive 1.3 miles and make another right turn at the stop sign, staying on Rt. 74 North. Proceed 1.9 miles and you will pass through a crossroads called Mount Top. Drive another 3.1 miles, turn right at the stop sign (you are still on Rt. 74). You are heading toward Dillsburg. There is a beautiful view of South Mountain from this point. Reset your odometer.

DILLSBURG

* Drive 1.5 miles and stop at the County Historical marker on the right. This marker notes that Stuart's column stopped here on July 1, and that "local stores and the U.S. Post Office were vandalized." As you proceed north, the area to the right of the road is where Wade Hampton parked the captured wagon train.

* Proceed a short distance (.1 miles) beyond the historical marker and turn right to remain on Rt. 74 North. The roads here have been changed, so we are forced to detour slightly off the historical route for a short time.

* Ease into the left lane to make a left turn onto 74 North after driving 1.9 miles to proceed to Carlisle. You are back on the historical route. Note how much this road winds, and also note the many old farms you will see along the way. You are about 11 miles from Carlisle. After driving for about 9 miles you will see a Gettysburg Campaign marker on the right side of the road.

CARLISLE

* After you enter Carlisle (about 11 miles from Dillsburg), you will see the Carlisle Plaza Mall on your right. Get into the left lane and turn left at the light to remain on 74 North (East High Street). Ahead is a postwar gray brick building on the site of the gasworks Stuart burned during his attempts to capture the town. Flame and smoke from this site could be seen for miles around.

* **Drive .1 miles and turn right at the stop light onto Spring Garden Street, then turn left into the Weis Market parking lot to view the location of the gasworks.** Here you will see the large postwar brick building on the site.

* **Drive back out of the parking lot and turn left back onto Spring Garden Street. Stay straight through the first stop sign to the next stop sign. Here, turn right onto East North Street to head for the Carlisle Barracks, which you will reach after .7 miles.** Since this is still a military base, security at the front gate will likely prohibit you from stopping here for any length of time or from taking any pictures. Stuart ordered many of the buildings burned.

* **Turn around wherever it is permissible and safe to do so and drive back down North Street for .7 miles before turning left back onto Spring Garden Street. Drive another .2 miles and turn right onto East High Street at the stop light. Reset your odometer.**

* **Drive .1 miles and you will cross Letort Creek.** Stuart unlimbered his guns here to shell the town.

* **Get into the left lane and turn left onto Hanover Street, which is Rt. 34. Park in the first available parking spot on your right.** Walk back up to the intersection, where the old Cumberland County Court House is on the left of the corner. Damage from one of Stuart's shells can still be seen on one of the pillars. The original court house was built in 1766. It burned down and was rebuilt in 1845.

There is much to see in the historic town of Carlisle, and you are encouraged to avail yourself of its historic sites. If you choose to do so, head west on High Street for several blocks and you will come to the campus of Dickinson College, founded in 1773 by Dr. Benjamin Rush, a signer of the Declaration of Independence. Col. Richard L. T. Beale, commander of the 9th Virginia Cavalry, Chambliss's Brigade, was an alumnus of this college (as is co-author Eric Wittenberg). Shells from Stuart's horse artillery struck buildings on the Dickinson campus, slightly damaging several. The handsome fieldstone building on your right with the cupola is called Old West, which was constructed in 1805. Old West suffered some damage from the Confederate shelling on the night of July 1, 1863. There are several historical markers at the front of the building, including one that mentions the occupation of the campus by Lt. Gen. Richard S. Ewell's Second Corps on June 27, 1863, and the shelling by Stuart. Ewell's men passed through the town again on the way to Gettysburg on June 30. After your optional side trip to the Dickinson campus, return to the court house and resume the tour.

* **When you are ready to leave Carlisle, continue south on Rt. 34 to Mt. Holly Springs, approximately seven miles away.** As you head south on Route 34 from Carlisle, you will see a walled cemetery on your left. That is the Carlisle town cemetery, the resting place of Mary "Molly Pitcher" Ludwig of the battle of Monmouth fame (1778), a Revolutionary War general, and other notable residents. William "Baldy" Smith's New York infantry used these stone walls as natural breastworks during Stuart's shelling of the town. The cemetery is worth a visit if you have time to stop.

MT. HOLLY SPRINGS

As you drive through the hamlet, note the heights of South Mountain rising in front of you. Stuart's troopers foraged widely here, as they did all along their route of march. As they passed through the town, the exhausted column was ordered to "close up."

* **Drive through Mt. Holly Springs and proceed another 1.5 miles, leave Rt. 34 and follow Rt. 94 South up South Mountain.** Reset your odometer. In this area Stuart's column halted for a brief rest before beginning the climb up the mountain. The burning Carlisle Gas Works could still be seen as Stuart's column ascended South Mountain. Many of the troopers dropped from their saddles and slept in the road and on the rocks on both sides. You are also following General Ewell's route of march to Gettysburg on July 1. Note the many hills and steep inclines.

* **Drive seven miles and you will reach the town of York Springs. At the far end of town, watch carefully for the Harrisburg Road on your right. Turn right onto this road (this is old Rt. 15). Reset your odometer. Drive another 3.9 miles.** On the right side of the road you will see a boulder with a plaque on it. Carefully pull over if you wish to examine it. Martin L. Wade of Alabama deeded this piece of land to his home state in 1966. It mentions that Confederate Maj. Gen. Robert Rodes's Division camped here on the night of June 30 before its march to Gettysburg, as does the wayside marker located along the road nearby. Rodes was a native of Alabama.

* **Proceed south on the Harrisburg Road and after a short distance you come into the town of Heidlersburg. Continue straight after stopping at the stop sign.** You are entering Hunterstown on the route that Kilpatrick used on July 2.

* **Drive about three miles from Heidlersburg. Continue straight after stopping at the stop sign, staying on 15 South (Business Route). Reset your odometer. Drive another 2.9 miles and turn left onto Shaeler Road, proceeding another .4 miles to a stop sign. Keep heading straight, crossing over the Hunterstown Road, and drive another .5 miles, turn left onto the**

The site of the Carlisle Gasworks, which Jeb Stuart shelled during
his occupation of the town on July 1, 1863.

**York Road (Rt. 30 East) at the stop light. Stay on Rt. 30 East and after one
mile you will see a sign for the East Cavalry Field segment of the Gettysburg
National Military Park on your right. Do not turn. Remain on Rt. 30 East.**
The cavalry battlefield is about two miles down that road. There, on the Rummel
Farm and land surrounding it, Jeb Stuart battled David Gregg's Federal Cavalry
Division on July 3. If you haven't already, you may wish to visit this battlefield
at another time.

    *** Remain on Rt. 30 and turn left onto Coleman Road after another 2.7
miles (Coleman Road was known as the York Pike).** There is a sign here that
points to Hunterstown. Reset your odometer.

    * Drive another 1.4 miles, noting the open fields to your left. In the road
and in these fields is where the opening skirmish of the Battle of Hunterstown
began. Kilpatrick's advance, led by Capt. Llewellyn Estes, chased Col. Pierce
M. B. Young's rearguard. Samuel McCreary's farm was in the field to your left,
and that was the first position of Pennington's Federal battery.

    *** Drive another .2 miles and turn left onto Swift Run Road at the stop
sign.** There was skirmishing in the road and fields here all the way into town.

    * Drive .6 miles and you will enter Hunterstown on Main Street.

Authors

The Grass Hotel in Hunterstown, Pennsylvania, served as Kilpatrick's headquarters during the battle on July 2. It was used as a hospital after the fighting ended.

HUNTERSTOWN

Watch for the War Department marker in a small field to your right where Red Bridge Road meets Main Street. Turn right onto Red Bridge Road and pull over where safe to do so. There may be parking available to the left, but note that this is private property. This small grassy area was the town Square in 1863. Note the Grass Hotel on the other side of Main Street, which was Kilpatrick's headquarters during the battle. It, like many buildings here, was used as a hospital after the fighting.

* **Turn around and then turn right onto Main Street. After .1 miles, turn left onto the Hunterstown Road.** The ridge just ahead of you is Felty Ridge, the primary Union position during the main fighting. After passing over the ridge, pause at the bottom, traffic allowing (exercise extreme caution). The large red barn ahead of you to the right is the Felty barn, with the wartime brick home just beyond it. Kilpatrick's artillery was posted on the ridge behind you to the right.

* **Continue to the Felty Farm.** You may pull briefly into the driveway to examine the property, keeping in mind that the land is private. Do not trespass.

* **Drive another .2 miles.** The curve to the right in the road is where Pierce Young deployed his skirmish line. On the left side of the road is the entrance to

Authors

View from Felty's Ridge at Hunterstown, Pennsylvania. This was the Federal position during the battle. Custer made his famous first mounted charge as a brigadier from this position, down the road toward Wade Hampton's position. The Felty farm and barn are shown here on the right side of the road.

the large utility plant here, which has unfortunately altered this section of the battlefield. You may pull into the entrance and park if you wish to exit your vehicle to examine the battlefield.

＊ Drive another .3 miles beyond the curve and you will see the wooden Gilbert Farm home on the right. After a short distance you will come to the Gilbert Ridge and Gilbert's Woods, which was Hampton's primary position during the battle. Briefly pause here, traffic allowing. It was in the curve behind you where Custer and his horse went down in a heap during his charge up this road. This ridge marks the position where Greene's artillery was deployed later in the fight. Greene kept up an artillery duel with Kilpatrick's gunners on the opposite ridge until well after dark.

This concludes the driving tour.

＊   ＊   ＊

To return to Gettysburg, continue on the Hunterstown Road. After traveling 3.5 miles beyond Gilbert Ridge you will come to Rt. 30. As you are driving, note the old wooden farmhouse on the right of the road 1.9 miles beyond Gilbert Ridge. This is the house where the wounded Henry Kyd Douglas (formerly of

Authors

View from Gilbert's Ridge at Hunterstown, Pennsylvania. This was the Confederate position during the battle. The Gilbert house is shown here, on the left side of the road. After making his charge, Custer and his horse went down in a heap at the curve in the road.

Stonewall Jackson's staff) was taken after Gettysburg to recuperate from his injury.

    * When you reach Rt. 30, turn right at the stop sign to head west and you will reach the Gettysburg Square after 1.2 miles.

Notes

Introduction

1. Adele H. Mitchell, ed., *The Letters of Major General James E. B. Stuart* (Richmond: Stuart-Mosby Historical Society, 1990), 326.

2. The specifics of the Battle of Upperville go well beyond the scope of this book. For more about the Battle of Upperville and the other fierce fights that took place in the Loudoun Valley in June 1863, see Robert F. O'Neill, Jr., *The Cavalry Battles of Aldie, Middleburg and Upperville, Small but Important Riots, June 10-27, 1863* (Lynchburg, Va.: H. E. Howard Co., 1993).

3. *Charleston Mercury*, July 6, 1863.

4. William B. Styple, ed., *Writing & Fighting the Confederate War: The Letters of Peter Wellington Alexander, Confederate War Correspondent* (Kearny, N. J.: Belle Grove Publishing Co., 2002), 153.

5. For a detailed discussion of Stuart's role in the Battle of Chancellorsville, see Ernest B. Furgurson, *Chancellorsville 1863: The Souls of the Brave* (New York: Alfred A. Knopf, 1992), 221-253.

6. Emory N. Thomas, *Bold Dragoon: The Life of J. E. B. Stuart* (New York: Harper & Row, 1986), 31.

7. Ezra J. Warner, *Generals in Gray: The Lives of the Confederate Commanders* (Baton Rouge: Louisiana State University Press, 1959), 296-97.

8. Historian Emory N. Thomas is the primary advocate of this theory. See Thomas, *Bold Dragoon*, for his version of these events.

9. William W. Hassler, ed., *The General to His Lady: The Civil War Letters of William Dorsey Pender to Fanny Pender* (Chapel Hill: University of North Carolina Press, 1965), 239.

10. Mitchell, *The Letters of Major General James E. B. Stuart*, 324.

11. Thomas, *Bold Dragoon*, 233.

12. Thomas L. Rosser, *Addresses of Gen'l T. L. Rosser, at the Seventh Annual Reunion of the Association of the Maryland Line, Academy of Music, Baltimore, Md., February 22, 1889 and on Memorial Day, Staunton, Va., June 8, 1889* (New York: The L. A. Williams Printing Co., 1889), 41.

13. United States War Department, *The War of the Rebellion: A Compilation of the Official Records of the Union and Confederate Armies,* 70 vols. in 128 parts

(Washington: Government Printing Office, 1880-1901), series 1, vol. 27, pt. 2, 692. Hereafter cited as *OR*. All references are from series 1 unless noted.

14. Edward Porter Alexander, *Military Memoirs of a Confederate* (New York: Charles Scribner's Sons, 1907), 374.

15. *OR* 27, pt. 2, 316.

16. Stephen W. Sears, *Gettysburg* (Boston: Houghton-Mifflin Co., 2003), 104.

17. R. Shepard Brown, *Stringfellow of the Fourth: The Amazing Career of the Most Successful Confederate Spy* (New York: Crown Publishers, 1960), 1-15 and 206-8.

18. *OR* 27, pt. 3, 913.

19. Charles Marshall, *An Aide-de-Camp of Lee*, Sir Frederick Maurice, ed. (Boston: Little, Brown & Co., 1927), 207.

20. *OR* 27, pt. 3, 915.

21. *Ibid.*

22. Ibid., 914-915.

23. *OR* 27, pt. 3, 923. Stuart's adjutant, Maj. Henry B. McClellan, claimed that there was yet a third order from Lee, delivered on the night of June 23, and that no copy of that order survived. McClellan claimed that it discussed at considerable length the plan of passing around the enemy's rear, and informed Stuart that Maj. Gen. Jubal A. Early would move upon York, Pennsylvania. According to McClellan, the letter suggested that since the roads leading northward from Shepherdstown and Williamsport were already clogged with the passage of the Army of Northern Virginia, Stuart should instead pass around the enemy's rear in order to avoid the delay that would result if Stuart waited for the balance of Lee's army to cross the river and head north. There is no record of this third communication; McClellan's memoirs are the sole source for it. "It is much to be regretted that a copy of this letter cannot now be produced," he wrote. "A diligent search has failed to find it, and as General Stuart did not forward a copy of it with his report, I presume it was destroyed during our subsequent march. But I have many times had occasion to recall its contents, and I find that my recollection of it is confirmed by several passages of General Stuart's report." Henry B. McClellan, *The Life and Campaigns of Major General J. E. B. Stuart* (Boston: Houghton-Mifflin, 1895), 317.

24. *Ibid.*, 317-318.

25. *Ibid.*, 318.

26. James Robbins Jewell, ed., "Theodore S. Garnett Recalls Cavalry Service With General Stuart, June 16-28, 1863," *The Gettysburg Magazine* 20 (June 1999), 48.

27. John S. Mosby, *Stuart's Cavalry in the Gettysburg Campaign* (New York: Moffatt, Yard & Co., 1908), 77-81, 91-92, and 169.

28. *Ibid.*, 26

29. "The part assigned to me was to cross the Bull Run at night with my small force by a bridle path, and uniting with Stuart near Gum Spring in Loudoun take command of his advance guard," wrote Mosby in an article that appeared in the *Philadelphia Weekly Times*. John S. Mosby, "General Stuart at Gettysburg," *Philadelphia Weekly Times*, December 15, 1877.

30. Mosby, *Stuart's Cavalry in the Gettysburg Campaign*, 174.

31. *OR* 27, pt. 3, 927-28; McClellan, *The Life and Campaigns*, 318.

32. *Ibid.*, pt. 2, 692; Warner, *Generals in Gray,* 178.

33. Donald A. Hopkins, *The Little Jeff: The Jeff Davis Legion Cavalry, Army of Northern Virginia* (Shippensburg, Pa.: White Mane Books, 1999), 144.

34. William R. Carter, *Sabres, Saddles, and Spurs*, Walbrook D. Swank, ed. (Shippensburg, Pa.: Burd Street Press, 1998), 71.

35. William W. Blackford, *War Years with Jeb Stuart* (New York: Charles Scribner's Sons, 1945), 221.

36. John W. Peake, "Recollections of a Boy Cavalryman," *Confederate Veteran*, 34 (1926), 261.

Chapter 1

1. Robert J. Trout, ed., *In the Saddle With Stuart: The Story of Frank Smith Robertson of Jeb Stuart's Staff* (Gettysburg, PA.: Thomas Publications, 1998), 74.

2. *OR* 27, pt. 2, 692.

3. Hopkins, *The Little Jeff*, 144.

4. Blackford, *War Years with Jeb Stuart*, 222.

5. *Ibid.*, 8.

6. *Ibid.*, 11-14.

7. *Ibid.*; Robert J. Driver Jr., *1st Virginia Cavalry* (Lynchburg Va: H.E. Howard Inc., 1991), 210.

8. Blackford, *War Years with Jeb Stuart*, 63 and 69.

9. *Ibid.*, 223.

10. John Esten Cooke, *Wearing of the Gray, Being Personal Portraits, Scenes & Adventures of the War* (New York: E. B. Treat & Co., 1867), 230.

11. Jewell, "Theodore Garnett Recalls," 48.

12. *OR* 27, pt. 2, 692.

13. Jewell, "Theodore Garnett Recalls," 48.

14. Cooke, *Wearing of the Gray*, 230-31.

15. H. H. Matthews, "The Pelham-Breathed Battery, Part XII: The Raid into Maryland, Hanover and Carlisle Pa., up to and including Gettysburg," *St. Mary's Beacon*, April 20, 1905.

16. Hazel C. Wolf, ed., "Campaigning with the First Minnesota: A Civil War Diary," *Minnesota History* 25, No. 4 (December 1944), 358.

17. William Lochren, "The First Minnesota at Gettysburg," in *Glimpses of the Nation's Struggle: A Series of Papers Read before the Minnesota Commandery of the Military Order of the Loyal Legion of the United States, 1889-1892* (1893), 44.

18. Return I. Holcombe, *History of the First Regiment Minnesota Volunteer Infantry* (Stillwater, Minn.: Easton & Masterman Printers, 1916), 314.

19. John Day Smith, The History of the Nineteenth Regiment of Maine Volunteer Infantry 1862-1865 (Minneapolis: Great Western Printing Co., 1909), 58.

20. Holcombe, *History of the First Regiment*, 314.

21. Cooke, *Wearing of the Gray*, 230-31.

22. Samuel Roberts to Alexander S. Webb, August 18, 1883, included in David L. Ladd and Audrey J., eds., *The Bachelder Papers: Gettysburg in Their Own Words*, 3 vols. (Dayton, Ohio: Morningside, 1995), 2:964-65.

23. Jewell, "Theodore Garnett Recalls," 48.

24. Diary of Jesse R. Sparkman, entry for June 25, 1863, Archives, Fredericksburg and Spotsylvania National Military Park, Fredericksburg, Virginia.

25. George W. Beale, "A Soldier's Account of the Gettysburg Campaign." *Southern Historical Society Papers (SHSP)*, 11 (July 1883), 320.

26. Roberts to Webb, *The Bachelder Papers*, 2:969.

27. Statement of Col. Charles H. Morgan, *The Bachelder Papers*, 3:1347; Francis Amasa Walker, *History of the Second Army Corps in the Army of the Potomac* (New York: Charles Scribner's Sons, 1886), 259.

28. *OR* 27, pt. 3, 309.

29. *Ibid.*

30. *Ibid.*

31. *Ibid.*, 322.

32. Mosby, *Stuart's Cavalry*, 171.

33. *OR* 27, pt. 2, 692.

34. Mosby, *Stuart's Cavalry*, 177.

35. McClellan, *The Life and Campaigns*, 321.

36. Thomas P. Nanzig, *3rd Virginia Cavalry* (Lynchburg, Va: H.E. Howard Inc., 1989), 118.

37. *Ibid.*; Heros Von Borcke, *Memoirs of the Confederate War for Independence,* 2 vols., (Edinburgh, 1866) 2:220-221.

38. *OR* 27, pt. 2, 681, 685.

39. *Ibid.,* 693.

40. McClellan, *The Life and Campaigns*, 322.

41. Beale, "A Soldier's Account," 320.

42. Cooke, *Wearing of the Gray*, 231.

43. *OR* 27, pt. 2, 693; Sparkman diary, entry for June 26, 1863 ("On our way down to Occoquon, very hard riding and a great many horses gave out," he wrote).

44. Carter, *Sabres, Saddles and Spurs*, 72.

45. Jewell, "Theodore Garnett Recalls," 48.

46. *OR* 27, pt. 2, 693.

47. Robert J. Trout, *They Followed the Plume: The Story of J.E.B. Stuart and His Staff* (Mechanicsburg, Pa.: Stackpole Books, 1993), 89-91; Cooke, *Wearing of the Gray*, 232-3.

48. Jewell, "Theodore Garnett Recalls," 48.

49. Cooke, *Wearing of the Gray*, 233.

50. Jewell, "Theodore Garnett Recalls," 48.

51. Thomas West Smith, *The Story of a Cavalry Regiment: "Scott's 900," Eleventh New York Cavalry From the St. Lawrence River to the Gulf of Mexico, 1861-1865* (Chicago: Veteran Assoc. of the Regiment, 1897), 77-78.

52. *Ibid.*, 81.

53. *Ibid.*, 78.

54. *Ibid.*, 79.

55. *Alexandria Gazette*, June 30, 1863.

56. *OR* 27, pt. 1, 1037.

57. Smith, *The Story of a Cavalry Regiment*, 84.

58. *Washington Evening Star*, June 29, 1863; Jewell, "Theodore Garnett Recalls," 48-49.

59. *Ibid.*, 49.

60. *OR* 27, pt. 1, 1037.

61. *Daily National Intelligencer*, June 29, 1863.

62. McClellan, *The Life and Campaigns*, 323.

63. *Daily National Intelligencer*, June 29, 1863.

64. Smith, *The Story of a Cavalry Regiment*, 86.

65. *OR* 27, pt. 2, 693.

66. Smith, *The Story of a Cavalry Regiment*, 83.

67. *Ibid.*, 84.

68. *Ibid.*, 85.

69. *OR* 27, pt. 1, 1037-8.

70. Smith, *The Story of a Cavalry Regiment*, 86.

71. *Ibid.*, 88-89.

72. Fortunately for Campbell, he escaped Stuart's wrath. However, Captain Campbell died of disease at Staten Island on March 15, 1864. *Ibid.* See entry for Campbell in regimental roster at end of book.

73. *Ibid.*, 98-99.

74. *Alexandria Gazette*, June 29, 1863.

75. *Daily National Intelligencer*, June 30, 1863.

76. *Alexandria Gazette*, June 29, 1863.

77. *Daily National Intelligencer*, June 30, 1863; *Daily Constitutional Union*, June 29, 1863.

78. *Alexandria Gazette*, June 29, 1863.

79. *Ibid.*, June 30, 1863.

80. *Ibid.*, June 29, 1863.

81. Matthews, "Pelham-Breathed Battery."

82. John B. Jones, *A Rebel War Clerk's Diary at the Confederate States Capital,* 2 vols. (Philadelphia: J. B. Lippincott, 1866), 1:366.

83. Apparently, this dramatically important dispatch never reached Lee via courier. The courier may have been captured before he could reach the army. Because it appears in Jones's diary, we do know that it was forwarded to—and received by—the Confederate War Department. Incredulously, there is no evidence to suggest that anyone in Richmond forwarded, confirmed, or otherwise even mentioned this intelligence to Lee.

84. Jewell, "Theodore Garnett Recalls," 49.

85. Sparkman diary, entry for June 27, 1863.

86. Cooke, *Wearing of the Gray*, 234.

87. Jewell, "Theodore Garnett Recalls," 49.

88. W. A. Graham, "From Brandy Station to the Heights of Gettysburg," *The News & Observer*, February 7, 1904.

89. Richard L. T. Beale, *History of the Ninth Virginia Cavalry in the War Between the States* (Richmond, Va.: B. F. Johnson Publishing Co., 1899), 77.

90. *Ibid.*, 78.

91. *OR* 27, pt. 2, 693.

92. Cooke, *Wearing of the Gray*, 235.

93. Carol Bundy, *The Nature of Sacrifice: A Biography of Charles Russell Lowell, Jr., 1835-64* (New York: Farrar, Straus & Giroux, 2005), 196.

94. Edward W. Emerson, ed., *Life and Letters of Charles Russell Lowell* (Boston: Houghton-Mifflin Co., 1907), 268-9. Lowell fully expected to be cashiered as a scapegoat for Stuart's breakthrough. "Of course I was troubled, expecting that I should be made the scapegoat, although I was only to blame for having been unmilitary enough to express a wish to General Hooker to serve in a more active place and to leave the 'all quiet along the Potomac' to some poorer regiment," he wrote to his fiancée on July 1. Fortunately for Lowell, he was not sanctioned for this chaos, and it did not harm his career, which was stellar. *Ibid.*, 269.

Chapter 2

1. Walter Brian Cisco, *Wade Hampton: Confederate Warrior, Conservative, Statesman* (Washington, D.C.: Brassey's, Inc., 2004), 8.

2. *Ibid.*, 16.

3. *Ibid.*, 57-62.

4. George Baylor, *Bull Run to Bull Run; or, Four Years in the Army of Northern Virginia* (Richmond: B.F. Johnson Publishing Co., 1900), 149.

5. Cisco, *Wade Hampton*, 93.

6. Graham, "From Brandy Station to the Heights of Gettysburg."

7. *OR* 27, pt. 2, 693; McClellan, *The Life and Campaigns*, 323.

8. McClellan, *The Life and Campaigns*, 323.

9. Trout, *They Followed the Plume*, 188-89.

10. Kennon to his daughter, quoted in Trout, *They Followed the Plume*, 190. Stuart promised Kennon a promotion to major, and Stuart presented Kennon with the promotion certificate with his own hands. However, the promotion was never confirmed, and Kennon remained a captain until the end of the war.

11. Blackford, *War Years with Jeb Stuart*, 223.

12. William J. Campbell, "Stuart's Great Ride Around the Enemy," *Confederate Veteran*, 9 (1901), 222.

13. "The Thirteenth Regiment of Virginia Cavalry in Gen. J.E.B. Stuart's Raid Into Pennsylvania," *The Southern Bivouac*, 1 (1883), 205.

14. Matthews, "Pelham-Breathed Battery."

15. McClellan, *The Life and Campaigns*, 323-24.

16. *OR* 27, pt. 2, 693.

17. Blackford, *War Years with Jeb Stuart*, 223.

18. They narrowly missed capturing $20,000 in cash, which had been sent to Washington for safekeeping a day earlier. *Alexandria Gazette*, June 30, 1863.

19. D. B. Rea, *Sketches of Hampton's Cavalry, Embracing the Principal Exploits of the Cavalry in the Campaigns of 1862 and 1863* (Columbia, S.C.: South Carolinian Steam Press, 1864), 114.

20. Robert J. Driver, Jr., *1st Virginia Cavalry* (Lynchburg, Va.: H. E. Howard Co., 1991), 63.

21. Rufus H. Peck, *Reminiscences of a Confederate Soldier of Co. C, 2nd Va. Cavalry* (Fincastle, Va.: privately published, 1913), 32.

22. *OR* 27, pt. 2, 694.

23. Blackford, *War Years with Jeb Stuart*, 223-4.

24. *Ibid.*, 224.

25. Francis H. Wigfall to Miss Louise Wigfall, July 18, 1863, Louis T. Wigfall Papers, Manuscripts Division, Library of Congress, Washington, D. C.

26. Carter, *Sabres, Saddles, and Spurs*, 72.

27. Trout, *They Followed the Plume*, 232-38.

28. Trout, *In the Saddle with Stuart*, 74.

29. Jewell, "Theodore Garnett Recalls," 50.

30. Robert J. Driver, Jr., *5th Virginia Cavalry* (Lynchburg, Va.: H. E. Howard Co., 1997), 57.

31. Jewell, "Theodore Garnett Recalls," 50.

32. *OR* 27, pt. 2, 694.

33. McClellan, *The Life and Campaigns*, 324.

34. Rea, *Sketches of Hampton's Cavalry*, 114.

35. *OR* 27, pt. 2, 694.

36. *Alexandria Gazette*, June 29, 1863.

37. *Washington Evening Star*, June 29, 1863.

38. Campbell, "Stuart's Great Ride Around the Enemy," 222.

39. Cooke, *Wearing of the Gray*, 237.

40. Jewell, "Theodore Garnett Recalls," 50.

41. Trout, *In the Saddle with Stuart*, 76.

42. Beale, *History of the Ninth Virginia Cavalry*, 79.

43. Campbell, "Stuart's Great Ride Around the Enemy," 222.

44. *Washington Evening Star*, June 29, 1863.

45. *Brooklyn Daily Eagle*, June 29, 1863.

46. McClellan, *The Life and Campaigns*, 324; Blackford, *War Years with Jeb Stuart*, 24.

47. Blackford, *War Years with Jeb Stuart*, 224.

48. Beale, "Soldier's Account," 321.

49. Cooke, *Wearing of the Gray*, 238.

50. Jewell, "Theodore Garnett Recalls," 50.

51. Campbell, "Stuart's Great Ride Around the Enemy," 222.

52. Rea, *Sketches of Hampton's Cavalry*, 114.

53. *Brooklyn Daily Eagle*, June 29, 1863.

54. *Daily Intelligencer*, June 29, 1863.

55. Matthews, "Pelham-Breathed Battery."

56. Campbell, "Stuart's Great Ride Around the Enemy," 222.

57. *OR* 27, pt. 2, 694.

58. Blackford, *War Years with Jeb Stuart*, 225.

59. Beale, *History of the Ninth Virginia Cavalry*, 80.

60. Warner, *Generals in Gray*, 20-21. Beale also wrote a well-regarded history of the 9th Virginia Cavalry that was published posthumously by his son George, who also served as an officer in the 9th Virginia.

61. Beale, *History of the Ninth Virginia Cavalry*, 80.

62. Warner, *Generals in Gray*, 46-7.

63. Trout, *In the Saddle with Stuart*, 76.

64. Jewell, "Theodore Garnett Recalls," 50.

65. *OR* 27, pt. 2, 694.

66. J. Buxton, "One of Stuart's Couriers," *Confederate Veteran,* 30 (1922), 343- 44.

67. *OR* 27, pt. 3, 382.

68. *Ibid.*, 378.

69. *Ibid.*

70. *Ibid.* This vitriolic exchange continued. "The cavalry, some 300 in number, remounted and started out yesterday. Had two skirmishes with Fitzhugh Lee's brigade, one on the River road, the other near Rockville. They returned with a loss of about 16, saving their own baggage train, and are in camp at Tennallytown. Had this cavalry escorted the wagon train and behaved as well as they did with their own, they would have saved it," wrote Meigs at 10:30 that night. "A deserter reports that there are several brigades in all, including Fitzhugh Lee's, and that Stuart commands in person; 6,000 men and seven pieces of artillery," he concluded. Ingalls replied. "Your dispatch is received. I regret the misfortune, but do not understand that you hold me responsible for it. I gave orders for the teams just as I require other property. I had nothing to do with its escort. I only hope our losses may not be greater. Our trains here are not sufficiently guarded. We are deficient in cavalry now. All will be done that is possible." These recriminations continued. Nobody wanted to be blamed for the loss of 125 valuable wagons or their even more valuable cargo of oats. *Ibid.*

71. Thomas Nelson Conrad, *The Rebel Scout: A Thrilling History of Scouting Life in the Southern Army* (Washington, D.C: The National Publishing Co., 1904), 83-85.

72. *Brooklyn Daily Eagle*, June 29, 1863.

73. Conrad, *The Rebel Scout*, 83.

74. T. H. M., "Letter from the Californians in the Massachusetts Contingent," *Alta California*, August 2, 1863.

75. "The Thirteenth Regiment of Virginia Cavalry," 205-6.

76. Quoted in Hopkins, *The Little Jeff*, 146-7.

77. Beale, *History of the Ninth Virginia Cavalry*, 80.

78. Blackford, *War Years with Jeb Stuart*, 225.

79. Cooke, *Wearing of the Gray*, 236-37.

80. *Daily National Reporter*, June 29, 1863.

81. *Washington Evening Star*, June 29, 1863.

82. *Ibid.*

83. *Alexandria Gazette*, June 30, 1863.

84. Cooke, *Wearing of the Gray*, 238.

85. *Washington Evening Star*, June 30, 1863; *Baltimore American*, July 1, 1863.

86. Carter, *Sabres, Saddles and Spurs*, 72-3.

87. *OR* 27, pt. 2, 694.

88. McClellan, *The Life and Campaigns*, 326.

89. *Alexandria Gazette*, June 30, 1863.

90. Cooke, *Wearing of the Gray*, 239.

91. Matthews, "Pelham-Breathed Battery."

92. *OR* 27, pt. 2, 695.

93. McClellan, *The Life and Campaigns*, 326.

94. *Daily Constitutional Union*, June 30, 1863.

95. Carter, *Saddles, Sabres and Spurs*, 73.

96. *OR* 27, pt. 2, 695.

Chapter 3

1. *OR* 27, pt. 3. 913.

2. *Ibid.*, pt. 2, 201; A. H. Huber, "The Real Facts About the Fight at Westminster, Maryland, June 29, 1863," RG 1810.035, Box 390195, Public Archives of Delaware, Dover Delaware ("The Real Facts").

3. Frederic Shriver Klein, *Just South of Gettysburg: Carroll County, Maryland in the Civil War* (Westminster, Md.: The Newman Press, 1963), 43.

4. A. H. Huber, "Account of the 1st Del. Cavalry at Westminster, MD, 1863," Governor's Correspondence, RG 1801, Box 55510, Delaware Public Archives, Dover Delaware, 2 ("Huber Account").

5. Today, this area is known as College Hill. The campus of McDaniel College, formerly known as Western Maryland College, was built in 1866 and occupies a significant portion of this prominent piece of high ground. Western Maryland College was the first coeducational college south of the Mason-Dixon Line.

6. Huber Account, 3.

7. James H. Wilson, *Captain Charles Corbit's Charge at Westminster With a Squadron of the First Delaware Cavalry, June 29, 1863* (Wilmington: The Historical Society of Delaware, 1913), 11-12. According to General Wilson, Corbit and Churchman had a total of 130 men with them, but most accounts indicate that the total force of Delaware horse soldiers numbered less than 100 men.

8. *OR* 27, pt. 2, 201.

9. *Ibid.*, 201-202.

10. *Ibid.*, 202.

11. Account of Dr. Hering, included in Klein, *Just South of Gettysburg*, 63.

12. *OR* 27, pt. 2, 202.

13. Account of Dr. Hering, included in Klein, *Just South of Gettysburg*, 63.

14. *OR* 27, pt. 2, 202.

15. *Ibid.*, 695.

16. *Ibid.*

17. *Ibid.*, 202; Huber, "The Real Facts."

18. Klein, *Just South of Gettysburg*, 44.

19. Wilson, *Captain Charles Corbit's Charge*, 16.

20. Huber Account, 5.

21. Wilson, *Captain Charles Corbit's Charge*, 16.

22. Diary of Mary J. Shellman, entry for June 29, 1863, included in Klein, *Just South of Gettysburg*, 48.

23. *Baltimore American*, July 3, 1863.

24. Diary of Mary J. Shellman, entry for June 29, 1863, included in Klein, *Just South of Gettysburg*, 48.

25. Letter of Eugene W. LaMotte, February 10, 1862, included in *Ibid.*, 56.

26. *OR* 27, pt. 2, 202; Huber Account, 5. Huber referred to the Charge of the Light Brigade at the Battle of Balaklava during the Crimean War, where six hundred British cavalrymen charged into the teeth of a large force of Russian artillery, taking nearly four hundred casualties in just a few minutes.

27. Benjamin J. Haden, *Reminiscences of J. E. B. Stuart's Cavalry* (Charlottesville, Va.: Progress Publishing Co., 1912), 63.

28. Robert J. Driver, Jr. and Harold E. Howard, *2nd Virginia Cavalry* (Lynchburg, Va.: H. E. Howard Co., 1995), 90.

29. William R. Carter, *Sabres, Saddles, and Spurs*, Walbrook D. Swank, ed. (Shippensburg, Pa.: Burd Street Press, 1998), 73.

30. Huber, "The Real Facts."

31. Wilson, *Captain Charles Corbit's Charge*, 17.

32. *Ibid.*, 27-28; *Baltimore American*, June 30 and July 3, 1863.

33. Woodford B. Hackley, *The Little Fork Rangers: A Sketch of Company D Fourth Virginia Cavalry* (Richmond, Va.: Press of the Dietz Printing Co., 1927), 100.

34 *Ibid.*

35. Account of I. Everett Pearson, included in Klein, *Just South of Gettysburg*, 69.

36. Hackley, *Little Fork Rangers*, 100.

37. Pearson account, included in Klein, *Just South of Gettysburg*, 69.

38. McClellan, *The Life and Campaigns*, 326.

39. *OR* 27, pt. 2, 202.

40. Hackley, *The Little Fork Rangers*, 100.

41. *OR* 27, pt. 2, 202.

42. Huber Account, 6.

43. *OR* 27, pt. 2, 202.

44. Wilson, *Captain Charles Corbit's Charge*, 30.

45. McClellan, *The Life and Campaigns*, 326.

46. *OR* 27, pt. 2, 202.

47. Philip Fisher to Dear Nellie, July 16, 1863, included in Klein, *Just South of Gettysburg*, 60.

48. David Shriver Lovelace, *The Shrivers: Under Two Flags* (Westminster, Md.: Willow Bend Books, 2003), 15.

49. Huber Account, 8-9. Francis Shriver's gravestone calls him a "hero" and indicates he fought with the 1st Delaware Cavalry that day. See Lovelace, *The Shrivers*, 15. Shriver wounded Private John Allan Randolph of the 4th Virginia Cavalry.

50. *Baltimore American*, July 3, 1863.

51. Carroll County Visitor Center, "'Corbit's Charge': A Civil War Self-Guided Tour in Westminster, Maryland," n.d.

52. *Ibid.*

53. *OR* 27, pt. 2, 202.

54. *Ibid.*, 695.

55. *Baltimore American*, July 3, 1863. The names of the killed and wounded of the 1st Delaware Cavalry were as follows: Killed—Daniel Welsh and William Vandergraft. Wounded—Joseph Wilson, Samuel Bigler, James Newkirk, Frank Steward, Dickinson Meredith, Theodore Jones, and Robert Machin; the latter two died of their wounds.

56. *OR* 27, pt. 2, 202-203.

57. Hering account, included in Klein, *Just South of Gettysburg*, 64-65.

58. Carter, *Sabres, Saddles, and Spurs*, 73; *Baltimore American*, July 2, 1863.

59. Carroll County Visitor Center, "Corbit's Charge."

60. *OR* 27, pt. 2, 695.

61. Susan Cooke Soderberg, *A Guide to Civil War Sites in Maryland: Blue and Gray in a Border State* (Shippensburg, Pa.: White Mane, 1986), 45. The encounter apparently took place in front of the Shellman house at 206 East Main Street, which Confederate Gen. Bradley T. Johnson used as his headquarters in July 1864 on a raid into Maryland. The home, next door to the Carroll County Office of Tourism, is today a museum.

62. Hering account, included in Klein, *Just South of Gettysburg*, 64-65.

63. *Baltimore American*, July 2, 1863.

64. Pearson account, included in Klein, *Just South of Gettysburg*, 72.

65. *Ibid.*

66. *Baltimore American*, July 3, 1863.

67. *OR* 27, pt. 2, 695.

68. Fred L. Schultz, "A Cavalry Fight Was On," *Civil War Times Illustrated* 23, no. 10 (February 1985), 44.

69. *Ibid.*; *Baltimore American*, July 3, 1863.

70. Soderberg, *A Guide to Civil War Sites in Maryland*, 47; The Union Mills Homestead Foundation, *Union Mills Homestead: 200 Years of History* (Union Mills, Md.: privately published, 1997). In addition to the mills, the brothers also established a tannery, cooper shop, blacksmithing, and a post office on the property. Shriver descendants continuously occupied the house until the mid 1960's.

71. George Rummell, III, *Cavalry on the Roads to Gettysburg: Kilpatrick at Hanover and Hunterstown* (Shippensburg, Pa.: White Mane, 2000), 161.

72. Schultz, "A Cavalry Fight Was On," 44.

73. The Union Mills Homestead Foundation, *Union Mills Homestead*; Kate Shriver account, included in Klein, *Just South of Gettysburg*, 183 and 186.

74. Driver, *1st Virginia Cavalry,* 32.

75. Jeb Stuart letter to Fitzhugh Lee, July 28, 1862, Fitzhugh Lee Papers, Alderman Library, University of Virginia.

76. Kate Shriver account, included in Klein, *Just South of Gettysburg*, 197.

77. Twenty-six-year-old Elon J. Farnsworth was promoted from captain to brigadier general on June 28, 1863, along with Capt. Wesley Merritt and Lt. George A. Custer. These three young officers were jumped several grades over more senior officers through the efforts of Maj. Gen. Alfred Pleasonton, the Army of the Potomac Cavalry Corps commander. Farnsworth wore his general's star for five days. He was killed leading a heroic but fruitless attack after the repulse of Pickett's Charge at Gettysburg on July 3. For more on Elon Farnsworth's charge and death, see Eric J. Wittenberg, *Gettysburg's Forgotten Cavalry Actions* (Gettysburg, Pa.: Thomas Publications, 1998).

78. *OR* 27, pt. 2, 695; McClellan, *The Life and Campaigns*, 327.

79. Lovelace, *The Shrivers*, 28.

80. *Ibid.*

81. Herbert subsequently witnessed not only the June 30, 1863 Battle of Hanover, but accompanied Stuart to Gettysburg as well, and even joined with Company K of the 1st Virginia Cavalry for the balance of the campaign. He later enrolled at VMI as Stuart had

promised. Cadet Shriver was wounded during the Battle of New Market. See Historical Publication Committee of the Hanover Chamber of Commerce, *Prelude to Gettysburg: Encounter at Hanover* (Shippensburg, Pa.: Burd Street Press, 1962), 24.

82. Lovelace, *The Shrivers*, 30.

83. Shriver account, included in Klein, *Just South of Gettysburg*, 201-202.

84. Wilson, *Captain Charles Corbit's Charge*, 18-19.

85. Statement of Charles H. Morgan, *The Bachelder Papers*, 3:1348.

Chapter 4

1. Hanover Chamber of Commerce, *Prelude to Gettysburg*, 4. The 1860 census marked 1632 residents of the town.

2. *OR* 27, pt. 1, 991. Although Kilpatrick's new division rolled 4,000 troopers on paper, he reported its actual strength of effectives, upon taking command, to be 3,500.

3. Warner, *Generals in Blue,* 266. Kilpatrick was hit in the thigh by canister at the Big Bethel skirmish in June 1861.

4. Wittenberg, *The Union Cavalry Comes of Age*, 319.

5. Warner, *Generals in Blue*, 266.

6. *OR* 27, pt. 2, 695-96.

7. *Ibid.*

8. Beale, *History of the 9th Virginia Cavalry*, 81.

9. *Ibid.*

10. *Ibid.*

11. *Ibid.*

12. The most recent scholarship on Fitz Lee's possible routes toward Hanover has been done by John Krepps, Licensed Gettysburg Battlefield Guide, in his article "Before and After Hanover: Tracing Stuart's Cavalry Movements of June 30, 1863," *Blue & Gray,* Vol. 21, No. 1 (Holiday 2003), 48. Through an exhaustive analysis of local citizens' accounts and claims for damages done by Stuart's troopers, Krepps has determined that Lee likely used a road known today as Pine Grove Road, in addition to various other minor roads and farm lanes, to parallel Stuart's route. The most common claim involved horses taken by Lee's troopers, and many were filed to the Government by locals along many of the roads west of Stuart's main column. The text of the captured dispatch appears in the *New York Herald* of July 3, 1863. It is not known who captured the courier—apparently it was not one of Kilpatrick's men, or Kilpatrick would have been forewarned of Stuart's approach, which he was not. The dispatch instead made its way to the *Herald* offices a few days later, where it obviously did neither Stuart nor Kilpatrick any good, and allowed the battle of Hanover to erupt. The authors postulate that perhaps the courier was captured by the detachment of the 2nd U.S. Cavalry, led by Lt. Col. Andrew J. Alexander, which was scouting in the area of Littlestown.

13. James H. Kidd, *Personal Recollections of a Cavalryman with Custer's Michigan Brigade in the Civil War* (Ionia, Mich.: Sentinel Printing Co., 1980), 125. See also Asa B. Isham, *An Historical Sketch of the Seventh Regiment Michigan Volunteer Cavalry* (New York, NY: Town Topics Publishing Company, 1893), 20. Isham details the wide-ranging scouting done by his regiment up the Catoctin Valley and in the vicinity of Gettysburg.

14. *OR* 27, pt. 3, 400. Having erroneously assumed that Custer and his Michigan Brigade marched with Kilpatrick's column out of the Littlestown camp on the morning of June 30 toward Hanover, most historians have missed this order, which proves that neither Custer nor any of his Michigan regiments were with Kilpatrick. George Rummel makes the unfortunate error in Chapter 8 of *Cavalry on the Roads to Gettysburg.* See also Edward G. Longacre, *Custer and His Wolverines: The Michigan Cavalry Brigade 1861-1865* (Conshohocken, Pa: Combined Publishing, 1997), 132; and Thom Hatch, *Clashes of Cavalry: The Civil War Careers of George Armstrong Custer and Jeb Stuart* (Mechanicsburg, Pa: Stackpole Books, 2001), 98-99. A careful reading of the recollections of both Kidd and Isham confirm Custer and the 1st and 7th Michigan were already at Abbottstown early on the morning of June 30, having passed through Hanover about dawn. Curiously, Kilpatrick, in his official report of the campaign (*OR* 27, pt. 1, 991-92) wrote Custer's brigade and Pennington's Battery were in the column from Littlestown to Hanover—despite having ordered them elsewhere. Kilpatrick's recollection was in error. Custer's report, and those of his subordinates, are unclear on the matter. We wish to thank fellow cavalry historian Al Ovies for bringing these contradictions to light, which help explain why Custer was so far north of Farnsworth's brigade when the Hanover fight began.

15. Kidd, *Personal Recollections,* 124-25.

16. There are dozens of biographies of George A. Custer. There are so many, in fact, that it is a monumental task just keeping them straight. For a balanced but thorough treatment of Custer's life and career, see Jeffry D. Wert, *Custer: The Controversial Life of George Armstrong Custer* (New York: Simon & Schuster, 1996).

17. Henry C. Parsons, "Gettysburg: The Campaign was a Chapter of Accidents," *National Tribune*, August 7, 1890.

18. John P. Nicholson, comp., *Pennsylvania at Gettysburg: Ceremonies at the Dedication of the Monuments Erected by the Commonwealth of Pennsylvania to Mark the Positions of the Pennsylvania Commands Engaged in the Battle*, 4 vols. (Harrisburg: B. Singerly, 1893), 2:868.

19. Samuel L. Gillespie, *A History of Company A, First Ohio Cavalry, 1861-1865* (Washington Court House, Oh: Press of Ohio State Register, 1898), 147. Companies A and C of the 1st Ohio were detailed as Kilpatrick's guard, as they had been for Brig. Gen. Julius H. Stahel before him. Even though the Cavalry Corps' other two division chiefs, Buford and Gregg, had authority to appoint an escort, they never chose to do so.

20. Henry C. Parsons, "Gettysburg," *National Tribune*, August 7, 1890. Capt. Henry Parsons of the 1st Vermont Cavalry wrote, "Gen. Farnsworth wore . . . a blue coat—which had been presented to him by Gen. Pleasonton, who had divided his wardrobe between him and Kilpatrick when he made them Generals a few days before."

21. Wittenberg, *Gettysburg's Forgotten Cavalry Actions*, 9.

22. Abner N. Hard, *History of the Eighth Cavalry Regiment, Illinois Volunteers During the Great Rebellion* (Aurora, Ill.: privately published, 1868), 56.

23. Warner, *Generals in Blue,* 149.

24. For a good study of the role of the 18th Pennsylvania during the Gettysburg Campaign, see Harold A. Klingensmith, "A Cavalry Regiment's First Campaign: The 18th Pennsylvania at Gettysburg," *The Gettysburg Magazine* 20 (June 1999): 51-74.

25. Regimental Publication Committee, *History of the Eighteenth Regiment of Cavalry, Pennsylvania Volunteers, 1862-1865* (New York, N. Y.: published by the Committee, 1909), 77. It was not preferable to have a relatively inexperienced regiment such as the 18th Pennsylvania guarding the rear of the brigade's march, but the marching rotation placed them there this day. No one in the ranks, including Kilpatrick, expected to meet trouble on the march to Hanover. If so, it is more likely a more veteran regiment would have been in the rear. See Rummell, *Cavalry on the Roads to Gettysburg*, 172-73.

26. Kidd, *Personal Recollections*, 129.

27. John A. Bigelow, "Draw Saber, Charge!" *National Tribune*, May 27, 1886.

28. Kidd, *Personal Recollections*, 125.

29. Frank L. Klement, ed., "Edwin B. Bigelow: A Michigan Sergeant in the Civil War," *Michigan History* 38, no. 3 (September 1954), 220. Bigelow noted in his diary, reproduced and annotated in this article, that he was one of a small group of the 5th Michigan detailed to guard the Littlestown Road that day. He was to await the return of his company, "but they did not come so I remained all night." He rejoined his regiment the following day, where he learned of the Hanover fight.

30. D. H. Robbins, "Kilpatrick's Cavalry: The Lively Saber Fight at Hanover, Pa." *National Tribune*, May 20, 1915.

31. James A. Morgan III, *Always Ready, Always Willing: A History of Battery M, Second U.S. Artillery from its Organization Through the Civil War* (Gaithersburg, Md: Olde Soldier Books, Inc, n. d.), 19.

32. *Ibid.*, 1, 13. Born in New Jersey, Pennington finished the war in command of cavalry, first as colonel of the 3rd New Jersey in October 1864, and then in command of the brigade a few weeks later. He remained in the Army and retired as a brigadier general in 1899 after nearly 40 years of service.

33. Captain James Penfield, *The 1863-1864 Civil War Diary, 5th New York Volunteer Cavalry* (Ticonderoga, N. Y.: Press of America, Inc., 1999), 69. Penfield wrote in his diary the weather that morning of Kilpatrick's march to Hanover was "showery."

34. Rummell, *Cavalry on the Roads to Gettysburg*, 168.

35. Kidd, *Personal Recollections*, 124-25.

36. In various modern accounts of the battle, Mudtown is often referred to as "Pennville" or "Buttstown." Both names, however, are post-war, even though a John Butt resided in the hamlet during the battle. According to a Federal infantryman who marched through the area on July 1 on his unit's way to Gettysburg, the village was called "Mudtown" then. Krepps, "Before and After Hanover," 51.

37. Hanover *Record Herald*, July 1, 1905.

38. Hanover Area Historical Society, *History and Battle of Hanover* (Hanover, Pa.: privately published, 2002).

39. Louis N. Beaudry, *War Journal of Louis N. Beaudry, Fifth New York Cavalry*, Richard E. Beaudry, ed. (Jefferson, N. C.: McFarland & Co., Inc., 1996), 49.

40. Letter from an unidentified 5th New York Cavalry trooper in R.L. Murray, *Letters from Gettysburg: New York Soldiers' Correspondences from the Battlefield* (Wolcott, N. Y.: Benedum Books, 2005), 142.

41. *The Evening Sun (Baltimore)*, August 6, 2003.

42. *The Times* (Gettysburg), June 30, 1900.

43. J. P. Allum, "The Fight at Hanover," *National Tribune*, September 29, 1887.

44. Hanover Chamber of Commerce, *Prelude to Gettysburg*, 57.

45. Parsons, "Gettysburg."

46. *Hanover Spectator*, June 19, 1863.

47. John Gibson, ed., *History of York County, Pennsylvania* (Chicago, Ill.: F. A. Battey Publishing Co., 1886), 213.

48. Hanover Chamber of Commerce, *Prelude to Gettysburg*, 27.

49. Mosby, *Stuart's Cavalry in the Gettysburg Campaign*, 156.

50. *Ibid.*, 90.

51. Nye, *Here Come the Rebels!*, 279.

52. Gibson, *History of York County*, 213.

53. Hanover Spectator, letter to editor from "Ajax," July 17, 1863.

54. Nye, *Here Come the Rebels!*, 279; Hanover Chamber of Commerce, *Prelude to Gettysburg*, 35. Hanover Junction, often confused with the town of Hanover, was where the north-to-south Northern Central Railroad met the east-to-west Hanover Branch. The Junction was approximately equidistant between Hanover and York.

55. Gibson, *History of York County*, 213.

56. Hanover Chamber of Commerce, *Prelude to Gettysburg,* 43; William Anthony, *Anthony's History of the Battle of Hanover* (*York County, Pennsylvania*), *Tuesday, June 30, 1863* (Hanover, PA: privately published, 1945), 57. About 250 troopers were with White, but he had ordered two companies to fan out in the area to scout the roads for signs of Federals and secure much-needed horses.

57. *OR* 27, pt. 1, 1005.

58. Anthony, *Anthony's History of the Battle of Hanover*, 143.

59. Hanover Chamber of Commerce, *Prelude to Gettysburg*, 43-44.

60. Publication Committee, *History of the Eighteenth Pennsylvania Cavalry*, 77.

61. Rummell, *Cavalry on the Roads to Gettysburg*, 190; Publication Committee, *History of the Eighteenth Pennsylvania Cavalry*, 87. Interestingly, Freeland had recently been under arrest for, according to Potter's personal account of the battle, "being the worst forager I ever knew." Freeland apparently had a penchant for stealing private property, and is reported by Potter to have taken at least one detour from his duties that morning to rummage in a farmer's barn for booty. Hanover Chamber of Commerce, *Prelude to Gettysburg*, 253-54.

62. Hanover Chamber of Commerce, *Prelude to Gettysburg*, 42-43, 163-65. After the battle, locals buried the body of the Confederate on a nearby farm. According to the June 30, 1903, issue of *The Herald*, in 1869, "two well-dressed strangers," one of them claiming to be the victim's brother, appeared at Gitt's store in Hanover and asked for the whereabouts of the remains. William Gitt, Josiah's son, took the men to their farm and pointed out the grave near their barn. The remains were exhumed and shipped south.

63. Publication Committee, *History of the Eighteenth Pennsylvania Cavalry*, 217.

64. *Ibid.* Exchanged later that year, Freeland's health suffered greatly while imprisoned and he was unable to rejoin his regiment. He received a medical discharge from the service in December 1863.

65. Publication Committee, *History of the Eighteenth Pennsylvania Cavalry*, 87-88. In another of Potter's accounts, quoted in *Prelude to Gettysburg* (252-259 from the *Hanover Herald*), he wrote he immediately assumed it was Freeland who stole the farmer's animals. It should be noted that Potter made an error in identifying Frank A.

Street, who was actually a private at the time according to the June 30, 1863 regimental roll for the 18th Pennsylvania Cavalry.

66. *Ibid.*

67. *Ibid.*

68. Murray, *Letters from Gettysburg,* 142.

69. Robbins, "The Lively Saber Fight at Hanover, Pa."

70. Stephen A. Clark, "Hanover, Pa.," *National Tribune*, February 23, 1888.

71. *Record Herald*, July 1, 1905.

72. Kidd, *Personal Recollections*, 125.

73. Gillespie, *A History of Company A, First Ohio Cavalry*, 149.

74. Parsons, "Gettysburg."

75. *OR* 27, pt. 1, 1011. Darlington, on sick leave, was not present at Hanover. Because Colonel Brinton was absent when the official report of the Gettysburg Campaign was composed over a month later, Darlington signed it as ranking officer, but the information in it came from those present.

76. Publication Committee, *History of the Eighteenth Pennsylvania Cavalry,* 90-91.

77. E. A. Paul, "Operations of Our Cavalry—The Michigan Cavalry Brigade," *The New York Times*, August 6, 1863.

78. Louis N. Boudrye, *Historic Records of the Fifth New York Cavalry* (Albany, N. Y.: J. Munsell, 1868), 64; Ide, *History of the First Vermont Cavalry*, 107.

79. *In Memoriam: John Hammond* (Chicago: P. F. Pettibone & Co., 1890), 1-5.

80. *Ibid.*, 59.

81. Hanover Chamber of Commerce, *Prelude to Gettysburg*, 58; Gibson, *History of York County*, 213.

82. Trout, *Galloping Thunder,* 281.

83. *Hanover Citizen*, July 2, 1863.

84. *OR* 27, pt. 1, 992.

85. *Ibid.*, pt. 2, 695.

86. Cooke, *Wearing of the Gray*, 240.

87. Blackford, *War Years with Jeb Stuart*, 225.

88. Graham, "From Brandy Station."

89. Publication Committee, *History of the Eighteenth Pennsylvania Cavalry,* 88.

90. Cooke, *Wearing of the Gray*, 241.

91. Publication Committee, *History of the Eighteenth Pennsylvania Cavalry*, 90.

92. *Hanover Record Herald,* July 8, 1905.

93. Anthony, *Anthony's History of the Battle of Hanover*, 15.

94. *OR* 27, pt. 1, 1011.

95. Hanover Chamber of Commerce, *Prelude to Gettysburg*, 46.

96. Anthony, *Anthony's History of the Battle of Hanover*, 15.

97. Allum, "The Fight at Hanover."

98. Rummell, *Cavalry on the Roads to Gettysburg*, 237.

99. Boudrye, *Historic Records of the Fifth New York Cavalry*, 64-65.

100. Hanover *Record Herald*, July 2, 1913.

101. Anthony, *Anthony's History of the Battle of Hanover*, 15; Boudrye, *Historic Records of the Fifth New York Cavalry*, 65.

102. *In Memoriam: John Hammond,* 62.

103. Ide, *History of the First Vermont Cavalry*, 108.

104. Parsons, "Gettysburg."

105. F. M. Sawyer, Adj. 5th New York Cavalry, to Mrs. Bowen, Sept. 4, 1863 in B. Conrad Bush, comp., *Articles from Wyoming County Newspapers and Letters from Soldiers of the 5th New York Cavalry* (West Falls, N. Y.: Bush Research, 2000), 103-04. Bowen was Wales's sister. She wrote the regiment asking for the information on her brother. She didn't learn of his death at Hanover until reading Sawyer's letter nearly three months later.

106. Frederick Phisterer, *New York in the War of the Rebellion, 1861-1865,* 2 vols. (Albany, N. Y.: J. B. Lyon Co., 1912), 1:833, 839.

107. Boudrye, *Historic Records of the Fifth New York Cavalry,* 65-66. Later recovered by his comrades, the Catholic officer was first buried in St. Matthew's Lutheran Cemetery on Chestnut Street in Hanover that evening. Subsequently removed, Gall now rests in the Gettysburg National Cemetery, New York, Section E, Grave no. 94, alongside two other members of the regiment killed that day. Commonwealth of Pennsylvania: *Report of the Select Committee Relative to the Soldiers' National Cemetery* (Harrisburg, PA.: Singerly & Myers, State Printers, 1865), 82.

108. Rummell, *Cavalry on the Roads to Gettysburg*, 240-41. Wounded three times and twice captured during the war, White eventually rose to colonel and commanded the regiment to the end of the war. It took three months for him to recuperate from his Hanover wound before he could rejoin the 5th New York.

109. Hanover Chamber of Commerce, *Prelude to Gettysburg*, 255.

110. Publication Committee, *History of the Eighteenth Pennsylvania Cavalry*, 131. Parker, as the history relates, arrived at the regiment's organizational camp at Harrisburg in October 1862 and asked to go along with the unit since "he had no home." The men provided him with a uniform and a horse, and he served unofficially with the regiment until it mustered out three years later. Parker was captured once but escaped. After the war, the regimental officers attempted to secure a pension for the boy, but were unsuccessful. No one saw Parker again until a reunion nearly 30 years later when "a medium-sized man, plainly dressed" showed up at a meeting and informed the veterans that he was, indeed, "Little Ed." The veterans greeted him most heartily.

111. Hanover Chamber of Commerce, *Prelude to Gettysburg,* 63-5. Hoffacker's brother William was killed the following year at the Battle of Spottsylvania Court House.

112. Allum, "The Fight at Hanover."

113. *Ibid.*

114. Balfour, *13th Virginia Cavalry,* 21. Balfour notes that upon Gillette's wounding, command of the 13th for the rest of the Gettysburg Campaign likely passed to Capt. Benjamin F. Winfield (of Company D). Gillette recuperated at his home in Virginia and rejoined the regiment in August. He was wounded again at the second battle at Brandy Station in October and died shortly after.

115. Boudrye, *Historic Records of the Fifth New York Cavalry,* 65.

116. Ide, *History of the First Vermont Cavalry,* 108.

117. Boudrye, *Historic Records of the Fifth New York Cavalry,* 65.

118. *OR* 27, pt. 1, 1008.

119. Beale, *History of the 9th Virginia Cavalry,* 83.

120. Hanover Chamber of Commerce, *Prelude to Gettysburg,* 47.

121. Hanover Area Historical Society, *History and Battle of Hanover*. The flag now rests in the Society's collection at the Neas House Museum on West Chestnut Street.

122. Clark, "Hanover, Pa."

123. *Ibid.*

124. *OR* 27, pt. 1, 1008.

125. Diary of Sgt. Atchinson Blinn, 1st Vermont Cavalry, entry for June 30, 1863, copy in files, GNMP.

126. Stephen A. Clark, "Farnsworth's Death," *National Tribune,* December 3, 1891.

127. *OR* 27, pt. 1, 1008-09; Balfour, *13th Virginia Cavalry,* 21. The Irish-born Burke was awarded the Medal of Honor in 1878 for capture of the flag, the first such awarded for heroism displayed on Northern soil. The location today of Burke's action was near the intersection of Boundary and Westminster Avenues. The flag now rests in the Confederate Museum in Richmond.

128. Clark, "Hanover, Pa."

129. Allum, "The Fight at Hanover."

130. Anthony, *Anthony's History of the Battle of Hanover,* 16.

131. Hanover Chamber of Commerce, *Prelude to Gettysburg,* 48; Rummell, *Cavalry on the Roads to Gettysburg,* 223. Hanover citizens loaded Kilpatrick's horse on a wagon and buried the animal on Bunker Hill, an elevation north of town just southwest of the Pigeon Hills, near the intersection of Ridge Avenue and Broadway Street. Local legend states that the animal's bones were unearthed some years later when the Borough was installing water pipes in the area. Meckley, "Reminiscences of the Civil War."

132. Cooke, *Wearing of the Gray*, 241.

133. Rummell, *Cavalry on the Roads to Gettysburg,* 232-33.

134. Blackford, *War Years with Jeb Stuart,* 226.

135. Anthony, *Anthony's History of the Battle of Hanover,* 77.

136. *Hanover Spectator,* August 4, 1937.

137. Hanover Chamber of Commerce, *Prelude to Gettysburg,* 113.

138. Warner, *Generals in Gray,* 230.

139. John H. Eicher and David J. Eicher, *Civil War High Commands* (Stanford, CA: Stanford University Press, 2001), 420.

140. Hanover Chamber of Commerce, *Prelude to Gettysburg,* 93. In his story, Folger claimed to have first been captured by Payne, and while being marched off, picked up a carbine and shot Payne's horse, tumbling the Southerner in the vat. However, some of Folger's claim is suspect, because a regimental commander likely would not take responsibility for one prisoner during the heat of battle.

141. D. H. Robbins, "Stuart at Hanover," *National Tribune,* July 30, 1908. Payne, 33 years old at Hanover, was wounded several times and captured thrice during the war, and spent over a year in Federal prisons.

142. Hanover Chamber of Commerce, *Prelude to Gettysburg,* 94.

143. William H. Payne to Joseph R. Anderson, December 13, 1903 in John Coski, "Forgotten Warrior," *North & South* 2, No. 7 (September 1999), 81.

144. William A. Graham, "Nineteenth Regiment (Second Cavalry)," in Walter Clark, ed., *Histories of the Several Regiments and Battalions from North Carolina in the Great War, 1861-1865.* (Goldsboro, N.C.: Nash Bros., 1901): 2:79-98.

145. Blackford, *War Years with Jeb Stuart,* 226.

146. Anthony, *Anthony's History of the Battle of Hanover,* 15. Although the officer, a "Captain Cabell," was reported to have been on Stuart's staff at the time, no one by that name ever served in that capacity.

147. Blackford, *War Years with Jeb Stuart,* 226.

148. Beale, *History of the 9th Virginia Cavalry,* 83.

149. Blackford, *War Years with Jeb Stuart,* 226.

150. Hanover Chamber of Commerce, *Prelude to Gettysburg,* 71.

151. Blackford, *War Years with Jeb Stuart,* 227.

152. *Ibid.,* 227-28.

153. Beale, *History of the 9th Virginia Cavalry,* 83.

154. Trout, *Galloping Thunder,* 281.

155. Gillespie, *A History of Company A, First Ohio Cavalry,* 149-50.

156. Boudrye, *Historic Records of the Fifth New York Cavalry,* 65.

157. *OR* 27, pt. 1, 992; Hanover Chamber of Commerce, *Prelude to Gettysburg,* 50.

158. Rummell, *Cavalry on the Roads to Gettysburg,* 255; Trout, *Galloping Thunder,* 281.

159. *Hanover Herald,* July 1, 1905.

160. *OR* 27, pt. 1, 992; Moore, *The 1st and 2nd Stuart Horse Artillery,* 69.

161. Hanover Chamber of Commerce, *Prelude to Gettysburg,* 50-51. Winebrenner found the projectile and threw it out into the yard. The shell and damaged bureau were later preserved by the family as mementos of the fight.

162. Hanover Area Historical Society, *History and Battle of Hanover.*

163. *OR* 27, pt. 1, 1009. Undoubtedly, the safer duty of supporting Elder's artillery was in recognition of the hard fighting and high casualties borne by Hammond's men that morning. However, as the reader will soon see, Kilpatrick had others plans for the 5th New York.

164. *Ibid.*

165. Rummell, *Cavalry on the Roads to Gettysburg,* 270.

166. *Ibid.,* 271.

Chapter 5

1. Asa B. Isham, *An Historical Sketch of the Seventh Regiment Michigan Volunteer Cavalry* (New York, NY: Town Topics Publishing Company, 1893), 21.

2. Anthony, *Anthony's History of the Battle of Hanover,* 70. Cut down in the 1940s, the "Custer Maple" was long a prize attraction in the town square. Today, a star in the pavement and plaque featuring a relief of Custer mark where it stood.

3. Isham, *Seventh Regiment Michigan Volunteer Cavalry,* 21; John Robertson, comp., *Michigan in the War* (Lansing, Mich.: W.S. George & Co., 1882), 581.

4. Anthony, *Anthony's History of the Battle of Hanover,* 18.

5. Kidd, *Personal Recollections,* 125-26.

6. *Ibid.,* 127.

7. Rummell, *Cavalry on the Roads to Gettysburg,* 276-77.

8. Kidd, *Personal Recollections,* 127.

9. Robertson, *Michigan in the War,* 580.

10. Rummell, *Cavalry on the Roads to Gettysburg,* 277.

11. Haden, *Reminiscences of J. E. B. Stuart's Cavalry*, 28.

12. Robertson, *Michigan in the War,* 580.

13. Allen D. Pease to his mother, July 18, 1863, Allen D. Pease Letters, Eloise A. Haven Collection, Kentwood, Michigan. The inclusion of Pease's account in this book is due to last-minute good fortune, as well as considerable detective work. The book was literally in the final stages of production when Haven contacted us to offer Pease's letter collection for our use. This particular account was described by Pease as having taken place at "Hanover, Pennsylvania." The owner of the collection was under the impression that her ancestor was describing a fight at Littlestown, Pennsylvania, and not Hanover, since another soldier from Company B wrote of the same episode occurring at "Littlestown." However, we knew there was no fighting at Littlestown at any time during the campaign, and certainly not between Michigan troopers and "two brigades" of Stuart's cavalry. It was readily apparent the account was detailing something that happened at Hanover, of which precious little detail has ever been found. After coordinating accounts and investigating all known facts, and "under the gun" of publishing deadlines, we determined that Pease's account is the first detailed contemporary description of Colonel Gray's unexpected clash with Stuart's troopers at Keller's Hill, outside Hanover. Had this account arrived just one day later, we could not have included it in this book. We are very grateful to Haven for offering the letter for our use, and to Theodore P. Savas for "stopping the presses" so we could include it.

14. *OR* 27, pt. 1, 825.

15. *Ibid,* 835-36.

16. Rummell, *Cavalry on the Roads to Gettysburg,* 283.

17. Robertson, *Michigan in the War,* 578.

18. All of the 5th Michigan and companies A, D, E, and H of the 6th Michigan are known to have been supplied with this new and deadly weapon. Contrary to some accounts, ordnance returns show that not a single trooper in the cavalry corps of the Army of the Potomac was armed with the shorter Spencer repeating *carbine* at any time during the campaign. The Spencer carbine, in fact, was only in prototype model in July 1863 and very few existed at that time. That weapon would not be mass produced until after the Gettysburg Campaign.

19. William H. Rockwell to My Dear wife, July 27, 1863, William H. Rockwell Letters, Western Michigan University Archives and Regional History Center, Kalamazoo, Michigan. Rockwell was killed in action at Brandy Station, VA, on October 12, 1863.

20. Karla J. Husby and Eric J. Wittenberg, eds., *Under Custer's Command: The Civil War Journal of James Henry Avery* (Dulles, Va.: Brassey's, Inc., 2000), 31-32.

21. Kidd, *Personal Recollections,* 128.

22. Gillespie, *A History of Company A, First Ohio Cavalry,* 150.

23. Robertson, *Michigan in the War,* 580.

24. Paul, "Operations of Our Cavalry – The Michigan Cavalry Brigade."

25. *OR* 27, pt. 2, 695.

26. McClellan, *The Life and Campaigns,* 329.

27. Anthony, *Anthony's History of the Battle of Hanover,* 146. The clearing in which the wagons were parked is now occupied in part by a golf course.

28. *Ibid,* 15.

29. Haden, *Reminiscences of J. E. B. Stuart's Cavalry*, 24.

30. Peck, *Reminiscences*, 32.

31. Rummell, *Cavalry on the Roads to Gettysburg*, 288.

32. Kidd, *Personal Recollections*, 125-28.

33. Rummell, *Cavalry on the Roads to Gettysburg*, 289.

34. *Record Herald*, July 1, 1905.

35. *Ibid.*

36. *OR* 27, pt. 1, 987-88.

37. James Harrison Wilson, *The Life and Services of Brevet Brigadier-General Andrew Jonathan Alexander, United States Army* (New York: privately published, 1887), 37-8.

38. McClellan, *The Life and Campaigns*, 329.

39. *Ibid.*

40. Rummell, *Cavalry on the Roads to Gettysburg*, 290.

41. Hanover Area Historical Society, *History and Battle of Hanover*. The Market House, built in 1815 and 60 feet long, was dismantled in 1872.

42. Beaudrye, *War Journal*, 49.

43. *OR* 27, pt. 1, 986-87.

44. *Ibid.*, 992.

45. *Ibid.*, pt. 2, 696.

46. McClellan, *The Life and Campaigns*, 329.

47. Meckley, "Reminiscences of the Civil War;" Krepps, "Before and After Hanover," 54-55.

48. *OR* 27, pt. 2, 696.

49. *Ibid.*; McClellan, *The Life and Campaigns*, 329-330.

50. Cooke, *Wearing of the Gray*, 242.

51. *OR* 27, pt. 1, 987. After the battle, not all the citizens were so pleased with the behavior of the Federal troopers. Rudisill later complained directly to Kilpatrick that his entire wheat crop, as well as all his fences, had been destroyed, and all his corn taken out of his barn and consumed by the hungry Federals and their horses. Early the next day, Kilpatrick convened a hearing with all complainants and finally made out a bill to be sent to the Federal government to reimburse the farmers, but no reimbursement ever came.

52. *Ibid.*, 992; New York Monuments Commission, *New York at Gettysburg*, 3 vols. (Albany, N. Y.: J. B. Lyon Co., 1902), 3:992; Parsons, "Gettysburg."

53. *Ibid.*, 987.

54. For a discussion of Pleasonton's dismal intelligence-gathering failures during the war, see J. David Petruzzi, "The Fleeting Fame of Alfred Pleasonton," *America's Civil War* 18, no. 1 (March 2005), 22-28.

55. Warner, *Generals in Blue*, 373.

56. Petruzzi, "The Fleeting Fame of Alfred Pleasonton," 22-28.

57. *OR* 27, pt. 1., 987-88.

Chapter 6

1. Carter, *Sabres, Saddles and Spurs*, 73.

2. James McClure, *East of Gettysburg: A Gray Shadow Crosses York County, Pa.* (York, Pa.: York Daily Record, 2003), 88.

3. William Swallow, "From Fredericksburg to Gettysburg," *Gettysburg Sources*, James L. McLean, Jr. and Judy W. McLean, eds., 3 vols. (Baltimore: Butternut & Blue, 1897), 2, 15.

4. Marcellus M. French, "Southern Scout Cavalry Alert at Gettysburg," *Richmond Times-Dispatch*, June 19, 1910.

5. See The American Heritage Dictionary of the English Language, Fourth Edition (Boston: Houghton Mifflin Co., 2000), 117.

6. *OR* 27, pt. 2, 696.

7. *Ibid.*

8. Matthews, "Pelham-Breathed Battery."

9. "The Thirteenth Regiment of Virginia Cavalry," 206.

10. Meckley, "Reminiscences of the Civil War."

11. "The Thirteenth Regiment of Virginia Cavalry," 206-7.

12. Krepps, "Before and After Hanover," 55-56.

13. James McClure, *Almost Forgotten: A Glimpse of Black History in York County, Pa.*, (York, PA.: York Daily Record, 2002), 29.

14. John Esten Cooke, *Wearing of the Gray*, 243-4.

15. McClure, *East of Gettysburg*, 98.

16. Prowell, *A History of York County*, 887.

17. *OR* 27, pt. 2, 696.

18. Hackley, *The Little Fork Rangers*, 86.

19. Krepps, "Before and After Hanover," 57.

20. Prowell, *A History of York County*, 887.

21. McClure, *East of Gettysburg*, 99.

22. McClellan, *The Life and Campaigns of Major General J. E. B. Stuart*, 329-30. See, also, Blackford, *War Years With Jeb Stuart*, 228.

23. Today, the area is known as Seven Valleys. However, we use the contemporary name, Seven Valley, in this narrative.

24. Krepps, "Before and After Hanover," 57. This discussion lays out Stuart's route in great detail and was a tremendous help to us. See, also, Armand Gladfelter, *The Flowering of the Codorus Palatine: A History of North Codorus Township, PA 1838-1988 York, PA.* (York, PA.: Sesquicentennial Commission, 1988), 264. We are deeply grateful to Scott Mingus, Sr., for his superb detective work in identifying Private Miller and in providing this information to us.

25. Elanine King, William L. Ziegler, and H. Alvin Jones, *History of New Oxford: Looking at the Past, 1874-1974, 100th Anniversary* (New Oxford, PA.: privately published, 1974), 128-29.

26. McClure, *East of Gettysburg*, 104.

27. *OR* 27, part 1, 987.

28. Wilson, *Andrew Jonathan Alexander*, 38.

29. *OR* 27, pt. 2, 709.

30. Cassandra Small to Lizzie Lattimer, July 8, 1863, Cassandra Small Letters, York Heritage Trust, York, Pennsylvania.

31. McClellan, *The Life and Campaigns of Major General J. E. B. Stuart*, 330.

32. Trout, *They Followed the Plume*, 268-71; Gordon W. McCabe, "Major Andrew Reid Venable, Jr.," *SHSP*, 37 (January-December 1909), 62.

33. Venable to Mosby, March 8, 1907, included in Mosby, *Stuart's Cavalry*, 183-84. The "regiment" mentioned by Venable was probably Colonel Alexander's detachment of Regulars, which was following and harassing Stuart's column.

34. Terry L. Jones, ed., *Campbell Brown's Civil War: With Ewell and the Army of Northern Virginia* (Baton Rouge: Louisiana State University Press, 2001), 204-5.

35. Mosby, *Stuart's Cavalry*, 184; Robert J. Driver, Jr., *39th Battalion Virginia Cavalry* (Lynchburg, VA: H.E. Howard, Inc., 1996), 51. During the Gettysburg Campaign, Companies A and C of the 39th Battalion served Lee as couriers, escorts, and scouts.

36. Trout, *Galloping Thunder*, 283.

37. Carter, *Sabres, Saddles and Spurs*, 76.

38. *OR* 27, pt. 2, 709.

39. Beale, *A Lieutenant of Cavalry*, 114.

40. Robert W. Hunter, "An Address Delivered on Fitzhugh Lee Day at the Jamestown Exposition," *SHSP*, 35 (January-December 1907), 143.

41. Rummel, *Cavalry on the Roads to Gettysburg*, 304-5.

42. Prowell, *History of York County*, 870.

43. Fitzhugh Lee to J. T. Zug, August 25, 1882, Civil War File Collection, CCHS.

44. Henry B. McClellan to John B. Bachelder, included in Ladd and Ladd, *The Bachelder Papers*, 2,1204.

45. *OR* 27, pt. 2, 696.

46. Garland C. Hudgins and Richard B. Kleese, eds., *Recollections of an Old Dominion Dragoon: The Civil War Experiences of Sgt. Robert S. Hudgins II, Co. B, 3rd Virginia Cavalry* (Orange, VA.: Publisher's Press, Inc., 1993), 81-82.

47. McClure, *East of Gettysburg*, 104.

48. Trout, *In the Saddle With Stuart*, 77.

49. Buxton, *"One of Stuart's Couriers,"* 343-44.

50. William F. Smith to Joseph F. Knipe, July 1, 1863, RG 393, Department of the Susquehanna and Pennsylvania, 1862-1865, Collection No. 4612, The National Archives, Washington, D. C.

51. A detailed discussion of the history of the Carlisle Barracks strays far beyond the scope of this discussion. For those readers interested in the history of the Barracks, see Thomas G. Tousey, *Military History of Carlisle and Carlisle Barracks* (Richmond: The Dietz Press, 1939).

52. *Ibid.*, 419, 421, and 424.

53. Beale, *History of the Ninth Virginia Cavalry*, 84.

54. *OR* 27, pt. 3, 696.

55. The superb work done by Boyd and his troopers during the Gettysburg Campaign has received scant attention from historians. Recognition of their service is long overdue. One of Boyd's men, Cpl. William Rihl, was the first Union soldier killed north of the Mason-Dixon Line during the Gettysburg Campaign. He received a fatal wound in a skirmish with Albert Jenkins's men at Greencastle, Pennsylvania, on June 22. The thirty-eight year old Captain Boyd received a promotion to colonel and appointment to command a newly formed regiment of Pennsylvania cavalry as a reward for his fine

service during the campaign. For more information about their service in the campaign, see William H. Beach, *The First New York (Lincoln) Cavalry, From April 19, 1862 to July 7, 1865* (New York: The Lincoln Cavalry Assoc., 1902), 246-53 and James H. Stevenson, *"Boots and Saddles": A History of the First Volunteer Cavalry of the War, Known as the First New York (Lincoln) Cavalry and also as the Sabre Regiment, Its Organization, Campaigns and Battles* (Harrisburg, PA.: Patriot Publishing Co., 1879), 199-217.

56. Stevenson, *"Boots and Saddles,"* 212. They never got near Robert E. Lee. Instead, they ran into a force of Southern cavalry (probably John D. Imboden's Brigade) near Fayetteville, which prevented them from reaching their objective.

57. *Carlisle Herald*, July 10, 1863.

58. Warner, *Generals in Blue*, 462-63; D. W. Thompson, "Salute to Baldy Smith", *Essays on the Confederate Invasion, Occupation, and Bombardment of Carlisle During the Gettysburg Campaign of 1863* (Carlisle, PA.: Cumberland County Historical Society, 1963), 33.

59. Francis B. Heitman, *Historical Register and Dictionary of the United States Army*, 2 vols. (Washington, D.C.: U.S. Government Printing Office, 1903), 1, 600. Lieutenant King's father, Brig. Gen. Rufus King, Sr., organized the legendary Iron Brigade and commanded a division in Maj. Gen. Irvin McDowell's corps during the Second Bull Run Campaign of 1862. King's poor performance was one of the primary factors that led to the Union debacle at Second Bull Run. He was reprimanded for dereliction of duty as a consequence, which ended his active military career. General King resigned his commission in 1863, ostensibly because of poor health. Warner, *Generals in Blue*, 270.

60. Interestingly, Landis, a prominent Philadelphia attorney, was married to a sister of Maj. Gen. John F. Reynolds, who was killed at Gettysburg on that day (July 1).

61. Robert V. Vaughn, "The Pennsylvania Militia: They Rendered Important Service During the Gettysburg Campaign," *The National Tribune*, April 1, 1915.

62. John Gunmere diary, entry for July 1, 1863, Henry D. Landis Papers, Historical Society of Pennsylvania, Philadelphia.

63. *OR* 27, pt. 2, 221.

64. *Carlisle Herald*, July 10, 1863.

65. Thomas H. C. Kinkaid, "Thirty Days with the Militia," *The National Tribune*, April25, 1895.

66. Gunmere diary, entry for July 1, 1863.

67. Trout, *In the Saddle with Stuart*, 77.

Chapter 7

1. *Carlisle Herald*, July 10, 1863.
2. *OR* 27, pt. 2, 221.
3. Kinkaid, "Thirty Days with the Militia."
4. Hudgins and Kleese, *Recollections of an Old Dominion Dragoon*, 82.
5. McClellan, *The Life and Campaigns of Major General J. E. B. Stuart*, 331.
6. *Carlisle Herald*, July 31, 1863.
7. *Ibid.*, July 10, 1863; Rummel, *Cavalry on the Roads to Gettysburg*, 308-9.

8. James W. Sullivan, "Boyhood Memories of the Civil War, 1861-1865," typescript, CCHS, 51.

9. *OR* 27, pt. 2, 696-7; Robert E. L. Krick, *Staff Officers in Gray: A Biographical Register of the Staff Officers in the Army of Northern Virginia* (Chapel Hill: University of North Carolina Press, 2003), 199.

10. *Carlisle Herald*, July 10, 1863.

11. Conway Hillman to Dear Morgan, September 9, 1930, Conway Hillman Letters, Special Collections, Boyd Lee Spahr Library, Dickinson College, Carlisle, Pennsylvania ("DC").

12. *OR* 27, pt. 2, 221.

13. *Ibid.*, pt. 3, 473.

14. *Ibid.*, pt. 2, 697.

15. Gunmere diary, entry for July 1, 1863.

16. *Carlisle Herald*, July 31, 1863.

17. Trout, *In the Saddle With Stuart*, 78.

18. Margaret Fleming Murray to Harmar Denny Murray, July 3, 1863, Civil War File Collection, CCHS.

19. *Ibid.*

20. Hillman to Dear Morgan, September 9, 1930.

21. B. J. Haden, *Reminiscences of J. E. B. Stuart's Cavalry* (Charlottesville, Va.: Progress Publishing Co., 1912), 24.

22. Cassandra Small to Lizzie Lattimer, July 20, 1863, Small Letters.

23. *OR* 27, pt. 2, 221.

24. Hillman to Dear Morgan, September 9, 1930.

25. Christian P. Humerich account of the shelling of Carlisle, January 3, 1903, Civil War File Collection, CCHS.

26. Hillman to Dear Morgan, September 9, 1930. Some of those marks, such as the one on a column in front of the old Cumberland County Courthouse building, still exist, and can still be seen today.

27. *OR* 27, pt. 2, 221.

28. Thomas Griffith to L. B. and M. A. Griffith, July 3, 1863, Thomas Griffith letters, DC. Griffith's claim that the shelling lasted until 3 am is later than most accounts, which place the cessation shortly after midnight.

29. Trout, *In the Saddle With Stuart*, 78.

30. *Carlisle Herald*, July 10, 1863.

31. *OR* 27, pt. 2, 697.

32. *The Carlisle Volunteer*, July 9, 1863.

33. *Carlisle Herald*, July 31, 1863.

34. *Ibid.*, July 10, 1863.

35. Sullivan, "Boyhood Memories," 56.

36. Beale, *A Lieutenant of Cavalry*, 114.

37. Carter, *Sabres, Saddles and Spurs*, 76.

38. *Carlisle Herald*, July 10, 1863.

39. *OR* 27, pt. 2, 221 and 697.

40. Sullivan, "Boyhood Memories," 55.

41. Thomas Herbert Shriver to his mother, August 11, 1863, copy in files, GNMP. Herbert Shriver penned an interesting letter to his mother on August 10, 1863, describing his great adventure in detail. Herbert participated in the great melee on East Cavalry Field at Gettysburg on July 3, and then accompanied his new command, the 1st Virginia Cavalry, on the Confederate retreat from Gettysburg.

42. Blackford, *War Years With Jeb Stuart*, 228.

43. Edwin Selvage, "Reunited at Gettysburg," *Confederate Veteran*, 30 (1922), 445-46.

44. *Ibid.*

45. *Ibid.;* Milton E. Flower, "Wednesday, July 1st, 1863," *Essays on the Confederate Invasion, Occupation, and Bombardment of Carlisle During the Gettysburg Campaign of 1863* (Carlisle, Pa.: Cumberland County Historical Society, 1963), 18.

46. *OR* 27, pt. 2, 697; Henry B. McClellan to John B. Bachelder, included in Ladd and Ladd, *The Bachelder Papers*, 2:1204.

47. Cooke, *Wearing of the Gray*, 245-46.

48. Haden, *Reminiscences of J.E.B Stuart's Cavalry*, 24.

49. Carter, *Sabres, Saddles and Spurs*, 76.

50. *Carlisle Herald*, July 10, 1863; Lee to Zug, August 25, 1882.

51. Gunmere diary, entry for July 1, 1863.

52. *Carlisle Herald*, July 10, 1863..

53. John K. Stayman to Dear Edgar, undated letter of July 1863, DC.

54. Mary Penny Murray to Harmar Denny Murray, July 23, 1863, Civil War File Collection, CCHS.

55. Stayman to Dear Edgar, undated letter of July 1863.

56. Tousey, *Military History of Carlisle*, 242-3. Capt. Daniel H. Hastings, who commanded the garrison, proudly wrote, "I have the honor to report that I re-established the depot here yesterday. On my return I found the buildings burned by the rebels. The brick walls are standing and many of them can be repaired and made available in reconstructing the Barracks. Two frame buildings are but slightly injured, one of which was used as a Quartermaster storehouse and the other for officers."

57. *Carlisle American*, July 15, 1863.

58. Sullivan, "Boyhood Memories," 57.

59. *OR* 27, pt. 2, 221 and 697.

60. That proud legacy included its founders, John Dickinson and Dr. Benjamin Rush of Philadelphia, a patriot who signed the Declaration of Independence. Its alumni included Supreme Court chief justice Roger B. Taney and the fifteenth President of the United States, James Buchanan.

61. *Carlisle Herald*, July 10, 1863.

62. Margaret Fleming Murray to Harmar Denny Murray, July 3, 1863.

63. Lee to Zug, August 25, 1882.

64. Sarah E. Motts, *Personal Experiences of a House That Stood on the Road* (Carlisle, Pa.: privately published, 1941), 10.

65. Hillman to Dear Morgan, September 9, 1930.

66. *Carlisle American*, November 4, 1863.

67. *Ibid.*

68. Small to Lattimer, July 20, 1863.

69. Hudgins and Kleese, *Recollections of an Old Dominion Dragoon*, 82.

70. Beale, *History of the Ninth Virginia Cavalry*, 84.

71. Beale, *A Lieutenant of Cavalry*, 115.

72. Cooke, *Wearing of the Gray*, 245-6; "Reunited at Gettysburg," *Confederate Veteran*, 30 (1922), 445.

73. Trout, *In the Saddle With Stuart*, 29.

74. Hackley, *The Little Fork Rangers*, 86.

75. Carter, *Sabres, Saddles and Spurs*, 76.

76. Beale, *A Lieutenant of Cavalry*, 115.

77. *First Troop Philadelphia City Cavalry* (Philadelphia: published by the Troop, 1991), 1.

78. *Ibid.*

79. *Ibid.*, 8.

80. *OR* 27, pt. 2, 697.

81. James W. Biggs to Thomas T. Munford, April 16, 1886, *The Bachelder Papers*, 3:1343.

82. Burke Davis, *J.E.B Stuart: The Last Cavalier* (New York: The Fairfax Press, 1988), 334.

83. *Ibid.*

84. Beale, *History of the Ninth Virginia Cavalry*, 85-6.

85. Peck, *Reminiscences*, 32-3.

86. Carter, *Sabres, Saddles and Spurs*, 76.

87. McClellan, *The Life and Campaigns of Major General J. E. B. Stuart*, 332.

88. Driver, *5th Virginia Cavalry*, 57-8.

89. Hackley, *The Little Fork Rangers*, 86.

90. Turner Holley to his wife, July 10, 1863, copy in files, GNMP.

91. Diary of S. A. J. Creekmore, entry for July 14, 1863, Mississippi Department of Archives and History, Jackson, Mississippi.

92. Matthews, "Pelham-Breathed Battery."

Chapter 8

1. Rummel, *Cavalry on the Roads to Gettysburg,* p. 320; Samuel J. Martin, *Kill-Cavalry: The Life of Union General Hugh Judson Kilpatrick* (Mechanicsburg, Pa.: Stackpole Books, 2000), 110. The same problem with Kilpatrick's kidneys had occurred after the battles near Aldie the previous month, early symptoms of Bright's disease, caused by his years on horseback during the war and which eventually ended his life at the age of 45.

2. Boudrye, *Historic Records of the Fifth New York Cavalry,* 66.

3. *OR* 27, pt. 1, 992.

4. *Ibid.*

5. Blinn diary, entry for July 2, 1863.

6. Kidd, *Recollections of a Cavalryman,* 134. As Kidd relates, Colonel Gray and the 6th Michigan Cavalry had the place of honor that day, leading the division.

7. *OR* 27, pt. 1, 992.

8. Publication Committee, *History of the Eighteenth Pennsylvania Cavalry,* 78.

9. *OR* 27, pt. 1, 992. According to Kilpatrick, Pleasonton's staff officer directed him to report to Gregg for orders. Brigadier General Gregg was Kilpatrick's senior by nearly seven months. Gregg evidently concurred with Kilpatrick's choice of position, which would allow the junior brigadier's division to probe the area around nearby Hunterstown.

10. "History of Hunterstown," unpublished and undated manuscript in the GNMP files; *The Gettysburg Times,* September 15, 1933.

11. C.E.G., "The Hunterstown Fight," *The Philadelphia Record,* September 15, 1901.

12. *The Gettysburg Times,* December 8, 1948.

13. Paul M. Shevchuk, "The Battle of Hunterstown, Pennsylvania, July 2, 1863," *The Gettysburg Magazine* 1 (July 1989), 96.

14. C.E.G., "The Hunterstown Fight."

15. Wilbur Sturtevant Nye, "The Affair at Hunterstown," *Civil War Times Illustrated* (February 1971), 29; *The Gettysburg Times*, September 15, 1933.

16. The legend of "Hampton's Duel" at Hunterstown, in which Hampton is supposed to have carried on a tété-a-tété with an upstart of the 6th Michigan Cavalry at about this time in the narrative stems from an article by T.J. Mackey in volume 22 of the *SHSP* (1894) and a recounting of the tale in Wellman's biography of the general, *Giant in Gray.* See T. J. Mackey, "Duel of General Wade Hampton on the Battle-Field at Gettysburg with a Federal Soldier," *SHSP,* 22 (1894), 122-26.

The story has, however, no hard evidence for its basis. For one, his antagonist, identified as either Frank Pearson or James Parsons of the 6th Michigan, is a mystery. There is no Frank Pearson listed on any Michigan cavalry unit rolls, and Pvt. James Parsons of Company I was on detached service at Washington DC at the time. For another, no medical records of any wound that Hampton is supposed to have suffered at Hunterstown exist, nor is there any mention of such a wound by Hampton or anyone else in the Official Records or any other extant recollections. Hampton or another officer most assuredly would have made note of it. If the reader is interested in accounts of the "duel," see Mackey's story in SHSP pages 125-26, and Wellman's on pages 115-16. More recently, despite the evidence against its veracity, author Edward G. Longacre has repeated the legend as fact in his biography of Hampton in *Gentleman and Soldier: The Extraordinary Life of General Wade Hampton* (Nashville, Tenn.: Rutledge Hill Press, 2003), 147-48.

17. Shevchuk, "The Battle of Hunterstown," 98; *OR* 27, pt. 2, 724.

18. Rummell, *Cavalry on the Roads to Gettysburg,* 338.

19. *OR* 27, pt. 2, 724.

20. Rummell, *Cavalry on the Roads to Gettysburg*, 338; Henry E. Jackson letter (untitled), *Confederate Veteran,* 7 (1899), 415. Rarely did regimental commanders lead small, detached patrols of their men. In this instance, however, Colonel Young chose the dangerous position instead of remaining behind with his party in the town.

21. Rummell, *Cavalry on the Roads to Gettysburg*, 339; Harold A. Klingensmith, "A Cavalry Regiment's First Campaign: The 18th Pennsylvania Cavalry at Gettysburg," *The Gettysburg Magazine,* 20 (January 1999), 59-60. A native of Oldtown, Maine, the 19-year-old Estes began his career with the 1st Maine Cavalry in October 1861. He joined Kilpatrick's staff in March 1863 and continued to serve with the general until the end of the war. In September 1865, Estes was brevetted brigadier general and received the

Medal of Honor in 1894 for gallantry in August 1864. See Edward P. Tobie, *History of the First Maine Cavalry 1861-1865* (Boston, Mass.: Press of Emery & Hughes, 1887), 465.

22. T. W. Herbert, "In Occupied Pennsylvania," *The Georgia Review*, vol. IV, No. 2 (1950), 109.

23. Jackson letter to *Confederate Veteran,* 415.

24. *Ibid.*

25. Murray, *Letters from Gettysburg,* 143.

26. Nye, "The Affair at Hunterstown," 30; Shevchuk, "The Battle of Hunterstown," 98.

27. Paul, "Operations of our Cavalry – The Michigan Cavalry Brigade."

28. CEG, "The Hunterstown Fight," *The National Tribune,* October 10, 1901.

29. Rummell, *Cavalry on the Roads to Gettysburg,* 343.

30. The Hunterstown battlefield is, today, relatively untouched by modern intrusions, except for one large utility plant that has unfortunately altered its eastern side dramatically. The modern Gettysburg-Hunterstown road follows the original road trace, several of the farmhouses are extant, and the opposing ridges offer a wonderful interpretation of the fight. In the town of Hunterstown itself, several of the 1863 buildings important to the battle still exist and can be visited today. Hunterstown today remains a small, rural borough much as it was in 1863, and efforts to protect what remains of the battlefield continue.

31. Editorial, "The Hunterstown Fight," *Philadelphia Record,* September 15, 1901.

32. N. H. Green, "Cavalry Fight at Hunterstown," *National Tribune,* July 5, 1923.

33. Lynwood M. Holland, *Pierce Young: The Warwick of the South* (Athens, Ga.: University of Georgia Press, 1964), 48-9. When Young resigned, Custer wrote his close friend a sorrowful letter lamenting the broken bonds: "We all miss you very much. . . . When you write do not fail to remember me, and I know that because we happened to be born and raised on different sides of the Mason's and Dixon's line you will still consider me as your true friend." *Ibid.,* 52. Despite the war, their friendship remained close until Custer's death at Little Big Horn in 1876, a loss Young deeply lamented. See also Ralph Kirshner, *The Class of 1861: Custer, Ames, and Their Classmates after West Point* (Carbondale, Ill.: Southern Illinois University Press, 1999), 62-3.

34. Frederick Whittaker, *A Popular Life of Gen. George A. Custer* (New York: Sheldon & Co., 1876), 173.

35. *Ibid.*

36. Kidd, *Personal Recollections of a Cavalryman,* 134; Robertson, *Michigan in the War,* 580.

37. Robertson, *Michigan in the War,* 581.

38. Shevchuk, "The Battle of Hunterstown," 99.

39. Whittaker, *A Popular Life,* 173.

40. *OR* 27, pt. 2, 724.

41. Shevchuk, "The Battle of Hunterstown," 100.

42. Holland, *Pierce Young,* 73.

43. Wiley C. Howard, *Sketch of Cobb Legion Cavalry and Some Scenes and Incidents Remembered* (Atlanta: Atlanta Camp 159, S.C.V., 1901), 9.

44. Tammy Harden Galloway, ed., *Dear Old Roswell: The Civil Letters of the King Family of Roswell, Georgia* (Macon, Ga.: Mercer University Press, 2004), 29.

45. William G. Delony to My Dear Rosa, July 7, 1863. Copy in the GNMP files.

46. Jackson letter to *Confederate Veteran,* 415.

47. Howard, *Sketch of Cobb Legion Cavalry*, 9.

48. Shevchuk, "The Battle of Hunterstown," 100

49. Delony letter, July 7, 1863.

50. William G. Delony to My Dear Rosa, July 4, 1863. Copy in the GNMP files.

51. Delony letter, July 7, 1863.

52. Holland, *Pierce Young,* 73; Delony letter, July 4, 1863.

53. Howard, *Sketch of Cobb Legion Cavalry*, 9. The badly wounded Delony rose from his sick bed to help lead the defense of the Potomac River crossings at Williamsport, Maryland on July 6 during the retreat from Gettysburg.

54. Delony letter, July 4, 1863.

55. *Ibid.* Lts. Nathan S. Pugh and J. W. Cheesboro were actually mortally wounded in the charge. Lt. Thomas Houze, commanding Company C, was shot in the head and toppled from his horse near the Felty farm, dying instantly. Cheesboro, his second in command, was also shot near the Felty Farm and was captured along with Pugh. Both were taken to a Union hospital established in the Grass Hotel, where the pair died later that night.

56. Jackson letter to *Confederate Veteran,* 415.

57. Sparkman diary, entry for July 2, 1863.

58. Whittaker, *A Popular Life,* 173. Thompson, suffering a severe gunshot wound, was carried back to safety by one of his men. He eventually recovered from his wounds, but was discharged due to medical disability after a year's recuperation and received a brevet colonelcy for his service. Rummell, *Cavalry on the Roads to Gettysburg,* 359.

59. Whittaker, *A Popular Life,* 174.

60. *Ibid.* Churchill had only been detailed to Custer's staff from Company L of the 1st Michigan Cavalry three days earlier. He had served in the regiment since its formation in September 1861. The ordeal at Hunterstown would be only the first of many experiences in which he would ride with a commander who repeatedly laughed at death. Rummell, *Cavalry on the Roads to Gettysburg,* 358; Shevchuk, "The Battle of Hunterstown," 100.

61. *OR* 27, pt. 2, 724.

62. Green, "Cavalry Fight at Hunterstown."

63. Rummell, *Cavalry on the Roads to Gettysburg,* 359; Penfield, *Civil War Diary,* 70. Ballard, slightly wounded during the charge, was thrown from his horse and was unable to remount. He was taken prisoner and later marched south to Libby Prison, where he spent nearly the balance of the war. He was released and returned to the 6th Michigan in March 1865.

64. Gershon W. Matoon, "Custer's Fight at Hunterstown," *National Tribune,* November 21, 1901.

65. *OR* 27, pt. 1, 999.

66. Editorial, "The Hunterstown Fight," *Philadelphia Record,* September 15, 1901.

67. Green, "Cavalry Fight at Hunterstown."

68. *Ibid.*

69. *Ibid.*

70. Kidd, *Personal Recollections of a Cavalryman,* 134-35. It should be noted that Kidd made an error here in that the 6th was armed with the Spencer *rifle*, not the shorter carbine model.

71. Murray, *Letters from Gettysburg,* 143.

72. Green, "Cavalry Fight at Hunterstown."

73. Jackson letter to *Confederate Veteran,* 415.

74. *OR* 27, pt. 2, 724.

75. Ide, *History of the First Vermont Cavalry,* 112.

76. The only casualty in Farnsworth's brigade was a member of the 18th Pennsylvania who was wounded during the artillery duel that followed. *OR* 27, pt. 1, 1011.

77. *Ibid.*

78. *Ibid.*

79. *Ibid.*, 497.

80. Green, "Cavalry Fight at Hunterstown." Unfortunately, one of Green's comrades was killed by friendly fire as they vacated the Felty buildings. In the gathering darkness, as he notes, "some of our men on the hill thought we were rebs and fired into us and killed a man in Co. C, and shot Liet. Shipman through the left lung." Lt. Seymour Shipman of Company D recovered from the ghastly wound but it caused his discharge the following year. Rummell, *Cavalry on the Roads to Gettysburg,* 367-68.

81. One unidentified Hunterstown local, in the *Philadelphia Record* editorial of September 15, 1901, gives these times for the cessation of the duel. In the November 2 issue of that year, Pvt. Gershon Mattoon of the 6th Michigan agrees. In a December 3, 1891 article, Lt. Stephen Clark of the 1st Vermont states that Kilpatrick remained in position at Hunterstown, with Clark's regiment supporting the cannons, "until 11 o'clock at night." Additionally, Horace K. Ide in his *History of the First Vermont Cavalry*, page 112, states that the artillery fired "for an hour or so, and then we remained quiet for some time till about 11 P.M., when the troops began retiring."

82. *OR* 27, pt. 1, 1000.

83. *Ibid,* pt. 2, 495.

84. Murray, *Letters from Gettysburg,* 143.

85. *Ibid.,* 697.

86. *Ibid.,* pt. 1, 992. The numbers include the one casualty of the 18th Pennsylvania Cavalry.

87. Robert K. Krick, *The Gettysburg Death Roster: The Confederate Dead at Gettysburg* (Dayton, OH: Morningside Press, 1985), 16. Krick's volume is of great assistance in determining southern casualties, as reliable reported numbers are too often nonexistent. In his report, Hampton acknowledged that "The Cobb Legion . . . suffered quite severely, Lieutenant-Colonel Delony and several other officers being wounded, while the regiment lost in killed quite a number of brave officers and men." *OR* 27, pt. 2, 724.

88. Rea, *Sketches of Hampton's Cavalry*, 115.

89. *OR* 27, pt. 2, 497.

90. *Ibid.*, 724.

91. Jackson letter to *The Confederate Veteran,* 415.

92. Graham, "From Brandy Station."

Chapter 9

1. Mobile *Daily Advertiser and Register*, August 11, 1863.

2. Susan Leigh Blackford, comp., *Letters From Lee's Army* (New York: Charles Scribner's Sons, 1947), 195.

3. *OR* 27, pt. 2, 707-9.

4. Hampton's letter quoted in Emory M. Thomas, *Bold Dragoon*, 253.

5. Unpublished manuscript by David Gregg McIntosh regarding a dinner party held February 24, 1887, David Gregg McIntosh Papers, Virginia Historical Society. Richmond.

6. *Ibid.*

7. *OR* 27, pt. 2, 306.

8. *Ibid.*, 307.

9. *Ibid.*, 316.

10. *Ibid.*, 321-22.

11. Interestingly, John S. Mosby later stated "I do not believe General Lee ever read [the report penned by Marshall], simply signed it mechanically. It is full of errors and contradictions." Adele H. Mitchell, ed., *The Letters of John S. Mosby*, 2nd ed. (Richmond: Stuart-Mosby Historical Society, 1986), 86.

12. Charles Marshall, *An Aide-de-Camp of Lee*, Sir Frederick Maurice, ed. (Boston: Little, Brown & Co., 1927), 180-81.

13. *The Richmond Dispatch,* January 26 and February 16, 1896.

14. *Ibid.*, January 26, 1896.

15. *Ibid.*, February 16, 1896.

16. *Ibid.*

17. *Ibid.*

18. *Ibid.*

19. For the most recent scholarship on the elusive Harrison, see Bernie Becker, "A Man Called Harrison," *America's Civil War,* November 2004, 46-52.

20. *The Richmond Dispatch,* February 16, 1896.

21. *Ibid.*

22. *Ibid.*

23. *Ibid.*

24. Marshall, *An Aide-de-Camp of Lee*, 201-2.

25. *Ibid.*, 205.

26. *Ibid.*, 206-7.

27. *Ibid.*, 209-10.

28. *Ibid.*, 214-16.

29. *Ibid.*, 224.

30. John S. Mosby to Lunsford L. Lomax, February 19, 1896, included in Mitchell, *The Letters of John S. Mosby*, 85.

31. Walter H. Taylor, *Four Years With General Lee* (New York: D. Appleton, 1877), 92.

32. *Ibid.*, 93.

33. Walter H. Taylor, *General Lee: His Campaigns in Virginia 1861 to 1865* (Norfolk, Va.: Nusbaum Book and News Co., 1906).

34. *Ibid.*, 184-85.

35. *Ibid.*, 187.

36. Memorandum dated April 15, 1868, written by Col. William Allen, Southern Historical Collection, Wilson Library, University of North Carolina at Chapel Hill.

37. Henry Heth, "Why Lee Lost at Gettysburg," included in Peter Cozzens, ed., *Battles and Leaders of the Civil War*, vol. 5 (Urbana: University of Illinois Press, 2001), 367-68, 373.

38. Jubal A. Early, "Causes of Lee's Defeat at Gettysburg," *SHSP*, 4 (1877), 56-7.

39. James Longstreet, *From Manassas to Appomattox: Memoirs of the Civil War in America* (Philadelphia: J. B. Lippincott Co., 1896), 343.

40. Fitzhugh Lee, "Causes of Lee's Defeat at Gettysburg," *SHSP*, 4 (1877), 74-5.

41. *Ibid.*, 74-6.

42. Fitzhugh Lee to Henry B. McClellan, July 31, 1878, Henry B. McClellan Papers, Virginia Historical Society.

43. Fitzhugh Lee, *General Lee* (New York: D. Appleton and Co., 1894), 254.

44. Thomas L. Rosser, *Addresses of Gen'l T. L. Rosser, at the Seventh Annual Reunion of the Association of the Maryland Line, Academy of Music, Baltimore, Md., February 22, 1889 and on Memorial Day, Staunton, Va., June 8, 1889* (New York: The L. A. Williams Printing Co., 1889), 41-2.

45. Roger S. Keller, ed, *Riding With Rosser* (Shippensburg, Pa.: Burd Street Press, 1997), 22-3.

Chapter 10

1. Edward Porter Alexander, *Military Memoirs of a Confederate: A Critical Narrative*, (New York: Charles Scribner's Sons, 1907), 374 and 377.

2. Samuel P. Bates, *The Battle of Gettysburg* (Philadelphia: T. H. Davis & Co., 1875), 41-2.

3. Comte de Paris, *The Battle of Gettysburg: From the History of the Civil War in America* (Philadelphia: Porter & Coates, 1886).

4. *Ibid.*, 236-7.

5. Abner Doubleday, *Chancellorsville and Gettysburg* (New York: Charles Scribner's Sons, 1882).

6. *Ibid.*, 108-10.

7. Jesse Bowman Young, *The Battle of Gettysburg: A Comprehensive Narrative* (New York: Harper, 1913).

8. *Ibid.*, 374-5.

9. Francis Marshal, *The Battle of Gettysburg: The Crest-Wave of the American Civil War* (New York: The Neale Publishing Co., 1914).

10. *Ibid.*, 97-8.

11. *Ibid.*, 149.

12. *Ibid.*, 192.

13. James K. P. Scott, *The Story of the Battles at Gettysburg* (Harrisburg: The Telegraph Press, 1927).

14. *Ibid.*, 122.

15. *Ibid.*, 123.

16. Blackford, *War Years with Jeb Stuart*, 232.

17. *Ibid.*, 229.

18. *Ibid.*, 232.

19. McClellan, *Life and Campaigns*, 333.

20. *Ibid.*, 333-4.

21. *Ibid.*, 334.

22. *Ibid.*, 321.

23. *Ibid.*, 335-7.

24. Robert J. Trout, ed., *Riding With Stuart: Reminiscences of an Aide-de-Camp* (Shippensburg, Pa: White Mane Publishing Co, Inc., 1994), 73.

25. *Ibid.*, 101-102. According to editor Trout, the text of Garnett's speech was published in booklet form in 1907.

26. *Ibid.*, 103.

27. Mitchell, *The Letters of John S. Mosby*, 87.

28. "Col. John S. Mosby's Defense of the Great Cavalry Leader." *SHSP*, 23 (January-December, 1895), 348-353, and "Confederate Cavalry in the Gettysburg Campaign, pt. 1," in Robert U. Johnson and Clarence C. Buel, eds., *Battles and Leaders of the Civil War*, 4 vols. (New York: Century Publishing Co., 1884-1888), 3: 252.

29. Mitchell, *The Letters of John S. Mosby*, 88.

30. *Ibid.*, 79.

31. *The Richmond Dispatch,* February 16, 1896. Mosby's letter appeared two weeks after the second installment of Marshall's speech was printed.

32. *Ibid.*

33. *Ibid.*

34. Lee's order is located in *OR* 27, pt. 3, 923.

35. See Mitchell, *The Letters of John S. Mosby*, as well as the additional vast collection of letters in the John S. Mosby Collection, Eleanor S. Brockenbrough Library, Museum of the Confederacy, Richmond Va.

36. G. Moxley Sorrel, *Recollections of a Confederate Staff Officer* (New York: Neal Publishing Co., 1905).

37. *Ibid.*, 160-61.

38. *Ibid.*, 162.

39. *Ibid.*, 162-63.

40. In a 1915 letter to Flora Stuart, Mosby stated, "His book . . . does General Stuart great injustice." Mitchell, *The Letters of John S. Mosby,* 221.

41. Mosby, *Stuart's Cavalry in the Gettysburg Campaign,* 178.

42. *Ibid.*, 191.

43. *Ibid.*, 192.

44. *Ibid.*

45. *Ibid.*, 196 (emphasis in original).

46. *Ibid.*, 208-10.

47. *Ibid.*, 215.

48. *Ibid.*, 216.

49. *Ibid.*, 220-1.

50. John S. Mosby, *The Memoirs of Colonel John S. Mosby* (Boston, Ma: Little, Brown and Company, 1917).

51. *Ibid.,* 213-15, 219-20 and 229.

Chapter 11

1. John W. Thomason, Jr., *Jeb Stuart* (New York: Charles Scribner's Sons, 1929).

2. *Ibid.,* 423-24.

3. *Ibid.,* 427.

4. *Ibid.,* 440-41.

5. *Ibid.,* 446-47.

6. Douglas Southall Freeman, *R. E. Lee: A Biography,* 4 vols. (New York: Charles Scribner's Sons, 1935).

7. *Ibid.,* 3:147-48.

8. Douglas Southall Freeman, *Lee Lieutenants: A Study in Command,* 3 vols. (New York: Charles Scribner's Sons, 1944).

9. *Ibid.,* 3:71-2.

10. *Ibid.,* 3:140.

11. Edward J. Stackpole, *They Met at Gettysburg* (Harrisburg, Pa.: Eagle Books, 1956).

12. *Ibid.,* 59-60.

13. Clifford Dowdey, *Death of a Nation: The Story of Lee and His Men at Gettysburg* (New York: Alfred A. Knopf, 1958).

14. *Ibid.,* 51-2.

15. *Ibid.,* 60-61.

16. *Ibid.,* 338-39.

17. Glenn Tucker, *High Tide at Gettysburg* (Indianapolis: Bobbs-Merrill, 1958).

18. *Ibid.,* 87-88.

19. *Ibid.,* 390-91.

20. Wilbur Sturtevant Nye, *Here Come the Rebels!* (Baton Rouge: Louisiana State University Press, 1965).

21. *Ibid.,* 313-14.

22. See Edwin B. Coddington, *The Gettysburg Campaign: A Study in Command* (New York: Charles Scribner's Sons, 1968).

23. Coddington's statement that Meade was "just as surprised" as Lee of the confrontation at Gettysburg is not entirely accurate. Though uncertain as to the location of Lee's entire force, Meade was aware prior to July 1, due to several Federal cavalry reports, that some elements of the Confederate army were in the vicinity of Cashtown and Carlisle. Lee, conversely, did not know that the Union forces were so close to Gettysburg.

24. *Ibid.,* 205-8.

25. Emory M. Thomas, *Bold Dragoon.*

26. *Ibid.,* 255.

27. *Ibid.,* 255-56.

28. Edward G. Longacre, *The Cavalry at Gettysburg: A Tactical Study of Mounted Operations During the Civil War's Pivotal Campaign, 9 June-14 July 1863* (Rutherford, N. J.: Fairleigh-Dickinson University Press, 1986).

29. *Ibid.*, 202.

30. Edward G. Longacre, *Lee's Cavalrymen: A History of the Mounted Forces of the Army of Northern Virginia* (Mechanicsburg, Pa.: Stackpole, 2002).

31. Mark Nesbitt, *Saber and Scapegoat: J.E.B. Stuart and the Gettysburg Controversy* (Mechanicsburg, PA.: Stackpole Books, 1994).

32. *Ibid.*, xvi-xvii.

33. *Ibid.*, 193.

34. Scott E. Bowden and Bill Ward, *Last Chance for Victory: Robert E. Lee and the Gettysburg Campaign* (Conshohocken, Pa.: Savas Publishing Co., 2001).

35. *Ibid.*, 111.

36. *Ibid.*

37. *Ibid.*, 119-20.

38. *Ibid.*, 124-25.

39. *Ibid.*, 511-12.

40. Noah Andre Trudeau, *Gettysburg: A Testing of Courage* (New York: Harper Collins, 2002).

41. *Ibid.*, 65.

42. *Ibid.*, 69-70.

43. Steven E. Woodworth, *Beneath a Northern Sky: A Short History of the Gettysburg Campaign* (Wilmington, Del.: Scholarly Resources, 2003).

44. *Ibid.*, 40-1.

45. Stephen W. Sears, *Gettysburg* (Boston: Houghton Mifflin Co., 2003).

46. *Ibid.*, 105.

47. *Ibid.*, 502.

48. Pro-Stuart articles include, but are not limited to, Patrick Brennan, "It Wasn't Stuart's Fault," *North & South*, Vol. 6, No. 5 (July 2003): 22-39; David Powell, "Stuart's Ride: Lee, Stuart, and the Confederate Cavalry in the Gettysburg Campaign," *The Gettysburg Magazine* 20 (January 1999): 27-43; and Daniel Zimmerman, "J.E.B. Stuart: Gettysburg Scapegoat?" *America's Civil War* 11 (May 1998), 50-57.

49. Anti-Stuart articles include, but are not limited to: Paul R. Gorman, "J.E.B. Stuart and Gettysburg," *The Gettysburg Magazine* 1 (July 1989): 86-92; David L. Calihan, "Jeb Stuart's Fateful Ride," *The Gettysburg Magazine* 24 (January 2001): 6-18; and Douglas Craig Haines, "Jeb Stuart's Advance to Gettysburg," *The Gettysburg Magazine* 29 (July 2003): 26-61.

Chapter 12

1. The sole source for the existence of this report is the published diary of John Beauchamp Jones, a clerk at the Confederate War Department. Jones recounts the contents of Stuart's dispatch verbatim, but offers no explanation as to why this information was not passed to Lee. Jones, *A Confederate War Clerk's Diary*, vol. 1, 366. Unfortunately, the dispatch is not in the *Official Records*; if it was, much of the debate over Stuart's role in the campaign would have taken a significantly different turn.

2. Marshall, *An Aide-de-Camp of Lee*, 215.

3. *Ibid.*, 216. In his 1904 book, Stuart's scout Thomas Nelson Conrad claims he also notified Lee of Hooker's move north. Conrad wrote: "Scarcely had Chancellorsville been

fought and won when an order reached me from Stuart's headquarters to 'go at once to Washington and report to these headquarters as soon as possible.' . . . I learned from my allies in the War Department that a conflict of judgment between Hooker and Halleck—the former wishing to move on Richmond and the latter fearing to uncover Washington to Lee's advances—had resulted in the displacement of Hooker and the appointment of Meade. Knowing that Lee was cautiously moving northward, fearing that Hooker would move on Richmond, I at once prepared a dispatch and sent it on my 'doctor's line' to Fredericksburg to be telegraphed to the war department at Richmond, stating that Hooker had been overruled and that he was made to rush to the rescue of Washington with all of his available forces. This information being communicated to Lee, perhaps confirming advice he had received from his own scouts, relieved him from his watch over Richmond and caused him to press toward the Upper Potomac and cross into Pennsylvania and Maryland with all of his army." Conrad, *The Rebel Scout,* 82-83. Conrad's claims cannot be substantiated in any records or corroborated by ther sources.

4. Long, *Memoirs of Robert E. Lee,* 275.

5. James L. Morrison, ed., *The Memoirs of Henry Heth* (Westport, Conn.: Greenwood Press, 1974), 174.

6. Letter of William Allen, April 16, 1877, included in "Causes of Lee's Defeat at Gettysburg," *SHSP* (1877), 81.

7. Jones, *Campbell Brown's Civil War,* 204-205.

8. *OR* 27, pt. 2, 321.

9. *Ibid.*

10. Quoted in Nesbitt, *Saber and Scapegoat*, viii.

11. McClellan, *The Life and Campaigns,* 336-37.

12. Wade Hampton was only promoted to lieutenant general to make him senior to Maj. Gen. Joseph Wheeler, who outranked him. Hampton categorically refused to serve under Wheeler. The only way to make such an arrangement work was for Hampton to be promoted over Wheeler, and that is precisely what happened in February 1865.

13. Mitchell, *The Letters of Major General James E. B. Stuart*, 326-28.

14. *OR* 27, pt. 2, 321.

15. *Ibid.,* 707-08.

16. McClellan, *The Life and Campaigns,* 294.

17. Blackford, *War Years with Jeb Stuart,* 225.

18. Thomas, *Bold Dragoon,* 40.

19. Though it ranges beyond the scope of this volume, several works have addressed the wagon train of Lee's wounded during the retreat from Gettysburg. The most recent is *One Continuous Fight: The Retreat from Gettysburg and the Wagon Train of Wounded* (Columbus, Ohio: Ironclad Publishing, 2006) by Eric J. Wittenberg, J. David Petruzzi, and Michael F. Nugent. The reader may be interested in the chapter devoted specifically to the wagon train and the accompanying tour of the routes taken during the retreat. The work is part of Ironclad's "Discovering Civil War America" series.

20. John S. Mosby, "Stuart at Gettysburg," *Philadelphia Weekly Times,* December 19, 1877.

21. McClellan, *The Life and Campaigns,* 322.

22. G. N. Saussy, "Stuart's Men Were Weary When They Reached Lee," *Richmond Times-Dispatch,* March 20, 1910.

23. W. W. Goldsborough, *The Maryland Line in the Confederate Army, 1861-1865* (Baltimore: Press of Guggenheimer, Weil, & Co., 1900), 176; Robert J. Driver, *First and Second Maryland Cavalry*, *C.S.A.* (Charlottesville, Rockbridge Publishing, 1999), 50.

24. George W. Booth, *Personal Reminiscences of a Maryland Soldier in the War Between the States, 1861-1865* (Baltimore: Press of Fleet, McGinley & Co., 1898), 88.

25. C. W. Chick to Thomas T. Munford, April 15, 1886, in *The Bachelder Papers*, 3, 1,339-40.

26. *OR* 27, pt. 3, 421.

27. For more information on the July 3 fight on East Cavalry Field, please see Eric J. Wittenberg, *Protecting the Flank: The Battles for Brinkerhoff's Ridge and East Cavalry Field, Battle of Gettysburg, July 2-3, 1863* (Celina, OH: Ironclad Publishing, 2002), the inaugural volume of the "Discovering Civil War America" series.

28. For the most detailed discussion of the movements of both armies, see John W. Schildt, *Roads to Gettysburg* (Preston, W.V.: McClain Printing Co., 1984), which spells out the progress of the various corps of each of the armies as they made their way toward Gettysburg. See, also, Bradley M. Gottfried, *Roads to Gettysburg: Lee's Invasion of the North, 1863.* (Shippensburg, Pa.: White Mane Books, 2001).

29. Mosby, "Stuart at Gettysburg."

30. For an examination of the Confederate cavalry during the advance on Harrisburg, see Wilbur Sturtevant Nye, *Here Come the Rebels!* (Baton Rouge: Louisiana State University Press, 1965) and Scott Mingus, Sr., *Flames Beyond the Susquehanna: The Gordon Expedition, June 1863* (Columbus, Ohio: Ironclad Publishing, 2006).

31. George Morley Vickers, *Under Both Flags, A Panorama of the Great Civil War* (Philadelphia: People's Publishing Co., 1896), 80.

32. For a detailed examination of the role played by Jenkins and his command, see Paul M. Shevchuk, "The Wounding of Albert Jenkins, July 2, 1863," *The Gettysburg Magazine*, 3 (July 1990), 51-64.

33. J.E.B. Stuart to Flora Cooke Stuart, September 12, 1862, Thomas D. Perry Collection, Special Collections, Virginia Polytechnic University, Blacksburg, Virginia.

34. Warner, *Generals in Gray*, 259-60. Robertson was Stuart's principal rival for the hand of Flora Cooke, and many historians speculate that rivalry was the root of Stuart's animosity toward Robertson.

35. For more on Brandy Station, see Eric J. Wittenberg, *The Union Cavalry Comes of Age: Hartwood Church to Brandy Station, 1863* (Dulles, VA: Brassey's, 2003).

36. Busey and Martin, *Regimental Strengths and Losses*, 197.

37. J. E. Copeland, "The Fighting at Brandy Station," *Confederate Veteran*, 30 (1922), 451.

38. George Dallas Mosgrove, *Kentucky Cavaliers in Dixie: The Reminiscences of a Confederate Cavalryman* (Louisville, KY: Courier-Journal Job Printing Co., 1895), 85.

39. Thomas W. Colley, "Brigadier General William E. Jones," *Confederate Veteran*, 6 (1898), 267.

40. John D. Imboden, "Fire, Sword and the Halter," included in *The Annals of the War, Written by Leading Participants, North and South* (Philadelphia: Weekly Times Publishing Co., 1879), 173.

41. Mitchell, *The Letters of Major-General James E. B. Stuart*, 221.

42. J.E.B. Stuart to Samuel Cooper, October 24, 1862, J.E.B. Stuart Papers, Virginia Historical Society, Richmond, Virginia.

43. Quoted in Dobbie Edward Lambert, *Grumble: The W. E. Jones Brigade 1863-64* (Wahiawa, Hi.: Lambert Enterprises, Inc., 1992), 8.

44. *OR* 12, pt. 2, 727; Mosby, *Stuart's Cavalry*, 18.

45. Busey and Martin, *Regimental Strengths and Losses*, 198. The 35th Battalion Virginia Cavalry normally served with this brigade, but was with Ewell's Corps on detached duty. For the most recent scholarship on White's Battalion during the Gettysburg Campaign, see J. David Petruzzi, "He Rides Over Everything In Sight," *America's Civil War* 19 (March 2006), 42-49. When Jones finally received orders to come to Pennsylvania, the 12th Virginia Cavalry was left behind to guard river crossings.

46. Harold J. Woodward, Jr., *Defender of the Valley: Brigadier General John Daniel Imboden C.S.A.* (Berryville, Va.: Rockbridge Publishing, 1996), 10-17.

47. *Ibid.,* 50-1.

48. Busey and Martin, *Regimental Strengths and Losses*, 200.

49. Quoted in Mosby, *Stuart's Cavalry*, 200-01.

50. Patrick Bowmaster, ed., "Confederate Brig. Gen. B. H. 'Bev' Robertson Interviewed on the Gettysburg Campaign," *Gettysburg: Historical Articles of Lasting Interest*, 20 (January, 1999), 23. The questions asked indicate the correspondent did not fully understand the nature of Robertson's mission as envisioned and ordered by Stuart.

51. *Ibid.*

52. *Ibid.*, 23-24.

53. *Ibid.*, 24.

54. Beverly H. Robertson, "A Reply to Colonel Mosby by General Robertson," *Century Illustrated Magazine*, vol. 34, no. 4 (August, 1887), 618.

55. John S. Mosby, "A Rejoinder to General Robertson by Colonel Mosby," *Century Illustrated Magazine*, vol. 35, no. 2 (December, 1887), 322-323.

56. *OR* 27, pt. 3, 1006.

57. *Ibid,* 1007. Robertson spent the rest of the war holding minor commands in South Carolina. He died in 1910 in Washington D.C.

58. David Powell, "Stuart's Ride: Lee, Stuart, and the Confederate Cavalry in the Gettysburg Campaign," *The Gettysburg Magazine* 20 (January 1999), 38-9.

59. See Shevchuk, "The Wounding of Albert Jenkins, July 2, 1863," 51-64.

60. For a detailed discussion of the fight for Brinkerhoff's Ridge, see Wittenberg, *Protecting the Flank: The Battles for Brinkerhoff's Ridge and East Cavalry Field*, 21-40.

61. John S. Mosby, "General Stuart at Gettysburg," *Philadelphia Weekly Times*, December 15, 1877.

62. Mosby's command claimed 218 head of cattle, 15 horses, and 12 blacks as their bounty for their excursion into Pennsylvania. While the cattle undoubtedly helped to meet the army's commissary needs, Mosby would have been better served to link up with Stuart's column. See James J. Williamson, *Mosby's Rangers: A Record of the Operations of the Forty-Third Battalion Virginia Cavalry, From Its Organization to the Surrender, from the Diary of a Private, Supplemented and Verified with Official Reports of Federal Officers and also of Mosby* (New York: Ralph B. Kenyon, 1896), 79-80.

63. Smith, *The Story of a Cavalry Regiment*, 90.

64. Wilson, *Captain Charles Corbit's Charge*, 21, 31.

Bibliography

NEWSPAPERS

Alexandria Gazette
Alta California (San Francisco)
Baltimore American
Baltimore Evening Sun
Brooklyn Daily Eagle
Carlisle American
Carlisle Herald
Carlisle Sentinel
Carlisle Volunteer
Charleston Mercury
Daily Constitutional Union (Washington, D.C.)
Gettysburg Times
Hanover Record Herald
Hanover Spectator
Mobile, Alabama Daily Advertiser and Register
The National Intelligencer
The National Tribune
The News and Observer (Raleigh, N. C.)
New York Herald
New York Times
Philadelphia Evening Bulletin
Philadelphia Inquirer
Philadelphia Press
Philadelphia Record
Philadelphia Weekly Times
Richmond Dispatch
Richmond Times-Dispatch
Richmond Examiner
St. Mary's Beacon
Washington National Republican
Washington Star

MANUSCRIPT SOURCES

Cumberland County Historical Society, Carlisle, Pennsylvania:
    Civil War File Collection:
    Anthony Buchanan, "The Confederate Invasion of Carlisle and
        the Affects on the Community of Carlisle"
    Clark L. Dankle, "The Confederate Invasion of Carlisle, 1863"
    Josephine Donovan, "The Confederate Invasion of Carlisle"
    Letter of Fitzhugh Lee of August 25, 1882
    Margaret Fleming Murray Letter of July 3, 1863
    Mary Penny Murray Letter of July 25, 1863
    Personal Observations, Narratives, and Notes Taken Down by Charles F.
        Hines, During the Shelling of Carlisle
    Cynthia A. Pickel, "Carlisle and the Big Scare of 1863"
    John S. Revegnes, "The Confederate Occupation and Bombardment of
        Carlisle"
    James W. Sullivan, "Boyhood Memories of the Civil War, 1861-1865"

Dauphin County Historical Society, Harrisburg, Pennsylvania:
    Dull Family Collection
    Civil War Papers
    Papers of General Joseph F. Knipe

Delaware Public Archives, Hall of Records, Dover, Delaware:
    A. H. Huber, "Account of the 1st Del. Cavalry at Westminster, MD, 1863,"
        Governor's Correspondence, RG 1801, Box 55510
    A. H. Huber, "The Real Facts About the Fight at Westminster, Maryland,
        June 29, 1863," RG 1801.035, Box 390195

Special Collections, Boyd Lee Spahr Library, Dickinson College, Carlisle,
Pennsylvania:
    Thomas Griffith Letters
    Conway Hillman Letters
    Pamphlets Collection
    John K. Stayman Letters

Archives, Fredericksburg and Spotsylvania National Military Park, Fredericksburg,
Virginia:
    Jesse Speakman Diary

Archives, Georgia Historical Society, Savannah, Georgia:
    Joseph F. Waring Papers

Archives, Gettysburg National Military Park, Gettysburg, Pennsylvania:
    Atchinson Blinn diary for 1863
    William G. Delony letters of July 4 and 7, 1863

"History of Hunterstown"
Turney Holley letter of July 10, 1863
Thomas Herbert Shriver letter to his mother of August 11, 1863

Historical Society of Pennsylvania, Philadelphia, Pennsylvania:
John Gunmere diary for 1863

Eloise A. Haven Collection, Kentwood, Michigan, Allan D. Pease Papers

Manuscripts Division, Library of Congress, Washington, D. C.:
Jubal A. Early Papers
Louis T. Wigfall Papers

Mississippi Department of Archives and History, Jackson, Mississippi:
Diary of S. A. J. Creekmore for 1863

The National Archives, Washington, D. C.:
RG 94, Muster Rolls
RG 393, Department of the Susquehanna and Pennsylvania, 1862-1865, Collection No. 4612

North Carolina Department of Archives and History, Raleigh, North Carolina:
Media Evans Memoir

Southern Historical Collections, Wilson Library, University of North Carolina, Chapel Hill:
William Allen Papers
Munford Family Papers

University of Virginia, Alderman Library, Charlottesville, Virginia:
John W. Daniel Papers
Robert T. Hubard Memoir
Fitzhugh Lee Papers

Virginia Historical Society, Richmond, Virginia:
Henry B. McClellan Papers
David Gregg McIntosh Papers
J.E.B. Stuart Papers

Thomas D. Perry Collection, Ararat, Virginia:
J.E.B. Stuart Letters

Western Michigan University Archives and Regional History Center, Kalamazoo, Michigan:
William H. Rockwell Letters

York County Historical Society, York, Pennsylvania:
Rudisill Family Papers:
Lida Bowman Meckley Reminiscences of the Civil War

York Heritage Trust, York, Pennsylvania:
Cassandra Small Letters

PUBLISHED PRIMARY SOURCES

"A Monument at Hanover, Pa." *The National Tribune*, July 21, 1887.

Alexander, Edward Porter. *Fighting for the Confederacy: The Personal Recollections of General Edward Porter Alexander*. Edited by Gary W. Gallagher. Chapel Hill: University of North Carolina Press, 1989.

——. *Military Memoirs of a Confederate*. New York: Charles Scribner's Sons, 1907.

Allen, William. "The Strategy of the Gettysburg Campaign: Objects, Progress, Results." *The Gettysburg Papers*. Compiled by Ken Bandy and Florence Freeland. Dayton, Ohio: Morningside, 1986.

Allum, J. P. "The Fight at Hanover." *The National Tribune*, September 29, 1887.

Baylor, George. *Bull Run to Bull Run; or, Four Years in the Army of Northern Virginia*. Richmond: B.F. Johnson Publishing Co., 1900.

Beach, William H. *The First New York (Lincoln) Cavalry, From April 19, 1862 to July 7, 1865*. New York: The Lincoln Cavalry Assoc., 1902.

Beale, George W. *A Lieutenant of Cavalry in Lee's Army*. Boston: Gorham Press, 1918.

——. "A Soldier's Account of the Gettysburg Campaign." *Southern Historical Society Papers* 11 (July 1883): 320-327.

Beale, Richard L. T. *History of the Ninth Virginia Cavalry in the War Between the States*. Richmond, Va.: B. F. Johnson Publishing Co., 1899.

Beaudrye, Louis N. *Historic Records of the Fifth New York Cavalry*. Albany: S. R. Gray, 1865.

——. *War Journal of Louis N. Beaudrye, Fifth New York Cavalry*. Ed., Richard E. Beaudrye. Jefferson, N.C.: McFarland & Co., 1996.

Bigelow, John A. "Draw Saber, Charge!" *National Tribune*, May 27, 1886.

Blackford, Susan Leigh, ed. *Letters From Lee's Army: Memoirs of Life In and Out of the Army in Virginia During the War Between the States*. New York: Charles Scribner's Sons, 1947.

Blackford, William W. *War Years with Jeb Stuart*. New York: Charles Scribner's Sons, 1945.

Booth, George Wilson. *Personal Reminiscences of a Maryland Soldier in the War Between the States, 1861-1865*. Baltimore: Press of Fleet, McGinley & Co., 1898.

Bouldin, E. E. "In the Thick of the Fighting at Gettysburg: The Wounding of General Jenkins—How Confederates Held Their Own with Handful of Ammunition—The Terrible Scene. Locating the Lines Afterward." *The Richmond Dispatch*, March 26, 1911.

Bowmaster, Patrick, ed. "Confederate Brig. Gen. B. H. 'Bev' Robertson Interviewed on the Gettysburg Campaign." *Gettysburg: Historical Articles of Lasting Interest* 20 (January 1999): 19-26.

Bush, B. Conrad, comp. *Articles from Wyoming County Newspapers and Letters from Soldiers of the 5th New York Cavalry*. West Falls, N. Y.: Bush Research, 2000.

Buxton, J.A. "One of Stuart's Couriers." *Confederate Veteran* 30 (1922): 343-44.

Campbell, William J. "Stuart's Great Ride Around the Enemy." *Confederate Veteran* 9 (1901): 222.

Carter, William R. *Sabres, Saddles, and Spurs*. Edited by Walbrook D. Swank. Shippensburg, Pa.: Burd Street Press, 1998.

CEG. "The Hunterstown Fight." *The National Tribune*, October 10, 1901.

Clark, Stephen A. "Farnsworth's Death." *The National Tribune*, December 3, 1891.

————."Hanover, Pa." *The National Tribune*, February 23, 1888.

Colley, Thomas W. "Brigadier General William E. Jones." *Confederate Veteran* 6 (1898): 267.

Commonwealth of Pennsylvania. *Report of the Select Committee Relative to the Soldiers' National Cemetery*. Harrisburg, Pa.: Singerly & Myers, State Printers, 1865.

Conrad, Thomas Nelson. *The Rebel Scout: A Thrilling History of Scouting Life in the Southern Army*. Washington, D.C: The National Publishing Co., 1904.

Cooke, John Esten. *Wearing of the Gray, Being Personal Portraits, Scenes & Adventures of the War*. New York: E. B. Treat & Co., 1867.

Copeland, J. E. "The Fighting at Brandy Station." *Confederate Veteran* 30 (1922): 451.

Coski, John, ed. "Forgotten Warrior." *North & South*, Vol. 2, No. 7 (September, 1999): 76-89.

Doubleday, Abner. *Chancellorsville and Gettysburg*. New York: Charles Scribner's Sons, 1882.

Dowdey, Clifford, ed. *The Wartime Papers of R. E. Lee*. Boston: Little, Brown & Co., 1961.

Dunaway, Wayland Fuller. *Reminiscences of a Rebel*. New York: The Neale Publishing Co., 1913.

Early, Jubal A. "Causes of Lee's Defeat at Gettysburg." *Southern Historical Society Papers* IV (1877), 282-302.

Eckert, Edward K. and Nicholas J. Amato, eds. *Ten Years in the Saddle: The Memoir of William Woods Averell, 1851-1862*. San Rafael, Calif.: Presidio Press, 1978.

Eggleston, George Cary. *A Rebel's Recollections*. Baton Rouge: Louisiana State University Press, 1996.

Emerson, Edward W., ed. *Life and Letters of Charles Russell Lowell*. Boston: Houghton-Mifflin Co., 1907.

French, Marcellus. "Southern Scout Cavalry Alert at Gettysburg." *Richmond Times-Dispatch*, June 19, 1910.

Galloway, Tammy Harden, ed. *Dear Old Roswell: The Civil Letters of the King Family of Roswell, Georgia*. Macon, Ga.: Mercer University Press, 2004.

Garnett, Theodore Sanford. *Riding With Stuart: Reminiscences of an Aide-de-Camp*. Robert J. Trout, ed. Shippensburg, Pa.: White Mane, 1994.

"General Stuart's Expedition into Pennsylvania." *Southern Historical Society Papers* 14 (1886): 480-484.

"General J.E.B. Stuart's Report of Operations After Gettysburg." *Southern Historical Society Papers* 2 (1874): 65-78.

Gillespie, Samuel L. *A History of Company A, First Ohio Cavalry, 1861-1865.* Washington Court House, Ohio: Press of Ohio State Register, 1898.

Goldsborough, W. W. *The Maryland Line in the Confederate Army, 1861-1865.* Baltimore: Press of Guggenheimer, Weil, & Co., 1900

Graham, W. A. "From Brandy Station to The Heights of Gettysburg." *The News & Observer*, February 7, 1904.

Graham, William A. "Nineteenth Regiment (Second Cavalry)." Included in Walter Clark, ed. *Histories of the Several Regiments and Battalions from North Carolina in the Great War, 1861-1865.* Goldsboro, N.C.: Nash Bros., 1901. 2:79-98.

Green, N. H. "Cavalry Fight at Hunterstown." *The National Tribune*, May 31, 1923.

Haden, Benjamin J. *Reminiscences of J. E. B. Stuart's Cavalry.* Charlottesville, Va.: Progress Publishing Co., 1912.

Hard, Abner N. *History of the Eighth Cavalry Regiment, Illinois Volunteers During the Great Rebellion.* Aurora, Ill.: privately published, 1868.

Harris, Samuel. *The Personal Reminiscences of Samuel Harris.* Detroit: The Robinson Press, 1897.

Hassler, William W., ed. *The General to His Lady: The Civil War Letters of William Dorsey Pender to Fanny Pender.* Chapel Hill: University of North Carolina Press, 1965.

Heth, Henry. "Letter from Major-General Henry Heth, of A. P. Hill's Corps." *Southern Historical Society Papers* 4 (1898): 151-160.

——. "Why Lee Lost at Gettysburg." Included in Peter Cozzens, ed., *Battles and Leaders of the Civil War*, Vol. 5. Urbana: University of Illinois Press, 2001: 364-373.

Holcombe, Return I. *History of the First Regiment Minnesota Volunteer Infantry.* Stillwater, Minn.: Easton & Masterman Printers, 1916.

Howard, Wiley C. *Sketch of Cobb Legion Cavalry and Some Scenes and Incidents Remembered.* Atlanta: Atlanta Camp 159, S.C.V., 1901.

Hudgins, Garland C. and Richard B. Kleese, eds. *Recollections of an Old Dominion Dragoon: The Civil War Experiences of Sgt. Robert S. Hudgins II, Co. B, 3rd Virginia Cavalry.* Orange, Va.: Publisher's Press, Inc., 1993.

Hunter, Robert W. "An Address Delivered on Fitzhugh Lee Day at the Jamestown Exposition." *Southern Historical Society Papers* 35 (January-December 1907): 142-145.

Husby, Karla J. and Eric J. Wittenberg, eds. *Under Custer's Command: The Civil War Journal of James Henry Avery.* Dulles, Va.: Brassey's, Inc., 2000.

Ide, Horace K. *History of the 1st Vermont Cavalry Volunteers in the War of the Great Rebellion.* Ed., Elliot W. Hoffman. Baltimore, Md.: Butternut & Blue, 2000.

Imboden, John D. "Fire, Sword, and the Halter." Included in *Annals of the War: Written by Leading Participants, North and South, Originally Published in the Philadelphia Weekly Times.* Philadelphia: Weekly Times Publishing Co., 1879.

In Memoriam: John Hammond. Chicago: P. F. Pettibone & Co., 1890.

Isham, Asa B. *An Historical Sketch of the Seventh Regiment Michigan Volunteer Cavalry.* New York: Town Topics Publishing Company, 1893.

Jackson, Henry E. Untitled letter. *Confederate Veteran* 7 (1899): 415.

Jewell, James Robbins, ed. "Theodore Garnett Recalls Cavalry Service With General Stuart, June 16-28, 1863." *Gettysburg: Articles of Lasting Historical Interest* 20 (June 1999): 44-50.

Jones, John B. *A Rebel War Clerk's Diary at the Confederate States Capital.* 2 vols. Philadelphia: J. B. Lippincott, 1866.

Jones, Terry L., ed. *Campbell Brown's Civil War: With Ewell and the Army of Northern Virginia.* Baton Rouge: Louisiana State University Press, 2001.

Keller, Roger S., ed. *Riding With Rosser.* Shippensburg, Pa.: Burd Street Press, 1997.

Kidd, James H. *Personal Recollections of a Cavalryman with Custer's Michigan Brigade in the Civil War.* Ionia, Mich.: Sentinel Printing Co., 1908.

Kinkaid, Thomas H. C. "Thirty Days in the Militia." *The National Tribune*, April 25, 1895.

Klement, Frank L., ed. "Edwin B. Bigelow: A Michigan Sergeant in the Civil War." *Michigan History* 38 (September 1954): 193-252.

Ladd, David L. and Audrey J., eds. *The Bachelder Papers: Gettysburg in Their Own Words.* 3 vols. Dayton, Ohio: Morningside, 1995.

Lang, Theodore F. *Loyal West Virginia from 1861-1865.* Baltimore, Md.: The Deutsch Publishing Co., 1895.

Lee, Fitzhugh. "Causes of Lee's Defeat at Gettysburg." *Southern Historical Society Papers* IV (1877): 69-76.

——. *General Lee.* New York: D. Appleton and Co., 1894.

Lee, William O., comp. *Personal and Historical Sketches and Facial History of and by Members of the Seventh Regiment Michigan Volunteer Cavalry 1862-1865.* Detroit: 7th Michigan Cavalry Assoc., 1902.

Lochren, William. "The First Minnesota at Gettysburg." In *Glimpses of the Nation's Struggle: A Series of Papers Read before the Minnesota Commandery of the Military Order of the Loyal Legion of the United States.* 1893.

Long, Armistead L., ed. *Memoirs of Robert E. Lee: His Military and Personal History.* New York: J. M. Stoddart & Co., 1886.

Longstreet, James. *From Manassas to Appomattox: Memoirs of the Civil War in America.* Philadelphia: J. B. Lippincott Co., 1896.

——. "Lee in Pennsylvania." Included in *Annals of the War: Written by Leading Participants, North and South, Originally Published in the Philadelphia Weekly Times.* Philadelphia: Weekly Times Publishing Co., 1879.

——. "Lee's Invasion of Pennsylvania." Included in eds. Robert U. Johnson and Clarence C. Buel, eds. *Battles and Leaders of the Civil War.* 4 vols. New York: Century Publishing Co., 1884-1888. 3: 244-250.

Mackey, T. J. "Duel of General Wade Hampton on the Battle-Field at Gettysburg with a Federal Soldier," *Southern Historical Society Papers* 22 (1894): 122-26.

Mahan, Dennis Hart. *Advanced-Guard, Outpost, and Detachment Service of Troops, with the Essential Principles of Strategy, and Grand Tactics.* New York: John Wiley, 1863.

Mark, Penrose G. *Red, White and Blue Badge: A History of the 93rd Regiment Known as the "Lebanon Infantry" and One of the 300 Fighting Regiments from September 12th, 1861 to June 27th, 1865.* Harrisburg, Pa.: The Aughinbaugh Press, 1911.

Marshall, Charles. *An Aide-de-Camp of Lee*. Edited by Sir Frederick Maurice. Boston: Little, Brown & Co., 1927.

———. "Events Leading Up to the Battle of Gettysburg." *Southern Historical Society Papers* 23 (1895): 205-229.

Matthews, H. H. "The Pelham-Breathed Battery, Part XII: The Raid Into Maryland, Hanover and Carlisle, Pa., Up to and including Gettysburg." *St. Mary's Beacon*, April 20, 1905.

Mattoon, G. W. "Custer's Fight at Hunterstown." *The National Tribune*, November 21, 1901.

McCabe, W. Gordon. "Major Andrew Reid Venable, Jr." *Southern Historical Society Papers* 37 (January-December 1909): 60-73.

McClellan, Henry B. "A Soldier's Gallant Exploit." *Philadelphia Weekly Times*, August 17, 1878.

———. *The Life and Campaigns of Major General J. E. B. Stuart*. Boston: Houghton-Mifflin, 1895.

———. "Stuart at Gettysburg." *Philadelphia Weekly Times*, October 6, 1877.

McDonald, William M. *A History of the Laurel Brigade, Originally Ashby's Cavalry*. Baltimore: Sun Job Printing Office, 1907.

McKim, Randolph Harrison. "A Reply to Colonel John S. Mosby." *The Southern Historical Society Papers* 37 (January-December 1909): 210-231.

Merington, Marguerite, ed. *The Custer Story: The Life and Letters of General George A. Custer and His Wife Elizabeth*. New York: Devin-Adair Co., 1950.

Mitchell, Adele H., ed. *The Letters of Major General James E. B. Stuart*. Richmond, Va.: Stuart-Mosby Historical Society, 1990.

———. *The Letters of John S. Mosby*. 2nd ed. Richmond: Stuart-Mosby Historical Society, 1986.

Moore, James, M. D. *Kilpatrick and Our Cavalry*. New York: W. J. Widdleton, 1865.

Morrison, James L., ed. *The Memoirs of Henry Heth*. Westport, Conn.: Greenwood Press, 1974.

Mosby, John S. "A Rejoinder to General Robertson by Colonel Mosby." *Century Illustrated Magazine*, vol. 35, no. 2 (December, 1887): 322-323.

———. "Col. John S. Mosby's Defense of the Great Cavalry Leader." *Southern Historical Society Papers* 23 (January-December. 1895): 348-353.

———. "Confederate Cavalry in the Gettysburg Campaign, Part 1." Included in Robert U. Johnson and Clarence C. Buel, eds. *Battles and Leaders of the Civil War*. 4 vols. New York: Century Publishing Co., 1884-1888. 3:252.

———. "General Stuart at Gettysburg." *Philadelphia Weekly Times*, December 15, 1877.

———. *The Memoirs of Colonel John S. Mosby*. Edited by Charles Wells Russell. Boston: Little, Brown & Co., 1917.

———. "Stuart at Gettysburg." *Philadelphia Weekly Times*, December 29, 1877.

———. *Stuart's Cavalry in the Gettysburg Campaign*. New York: Moffatt, Yard & Co., 1908.

Mosgrove, George Dallas. *Kentucky Cavaliers in Dixie: The Reminiscences of a Confederate Cavalryman*. Louisville, Ky.: Courier-Journal Job Printing Co., 1895.

Motts, Sarah E. *Personal Experiences of a House That Stood on the Road*. Carlisle, Pa.: privately published, 1941.

Myers, Frank M. *The Comanches: A History of White's Battalion, Virginia Cavalry*. Baltimore: Kelly, Piet & Co., 1871.

Nicholson, John P., comp. *Pennsylvania at Gettysburg: Ceremonies at the Dedication of the Monuments Erected by the Commonwealth of Pennsylvania to Mark the Positions of the Pennsylvania Commands Engaged in the Battle*. 4 vols. Harrisburg: B. Singerly, 1893.

New York Monuments Commission. *New York at Gettysburg*. 3 vols. Albany, N. Y.: J. B. Lyon Co., 1902.

Overbey, James L. "War Record of James L. Overbey." *Confederate Reminiscences and Letters 1861-1865*. Vol. XI. Atlanta: Georgia Division, United Daughters of the Confederacy, 1999: 47-48.

Paris, Comte de. *The Battle of Gettysburg: From the History of the Civil War in America*. Philadelphia: Porter & Coates, 1886.

Parsons, Henry C. "Gettysburg: The Campaign was a Chapter of Accidents." *The National Tribune*, August 7, 1890.

Paul, E. A. "Operations of Our Cavalry – The Michigan Cavalry Brigade." *New York Times,* August 6, 1863.

Peake, John W. "Recollections of a Boy Cavalryman." *Confederate Veteran* 34 (1926): 260-262.

Peck, Rufus H. *Reminiscences of a Confederate Soldier of Co. C, 2nd Va. Cavalry*. Fincastle, Va.: privately published, 1913.

Penfield, James. *The 1863-1864 Civil War Diary, 5th New York Volunteer Cavalry*. Crown Point, N.Y.: Penfield Foundation, 1999.

Regimental Publication Committee. *History of the Eighteenth Regiment of Cavalry, Pennsylvania Volunteers, 1862-1865*. New York: privately published, 1909.

"Reunited at Gettysburg." *Confederate Veteran* 30 (1922): 445.

Robbins, D. H. "Kilpatrick's Cavalry: The Lively Saber Fight at Hanover, Pa." *National Tribune,* May 20, 1915.

———. "Stuart at Hanover." *The National Tribune*, July 30, 1908.

Robertson, Beverly H. "A Reply to Colonel Mosby by General Robertson," *Century Illustrated Magazine*, vol. 34, no. 4 (August 1887): 6-39.

———. "Confederate Cavalry in the Gettysburg Campaign, Part 2." Included in Robert U. Johnson and Clarence C. Buel, eds. *Battles and Leaders of the Civil War*. 4 vols. New York: Century Publishing Co., 1884-1888. 3:252.

Robertson, Frank S. "Reminiscences of the Years 1861-1865." *The Historical Society of Washington County, Virginia Bulletin*. Series 2. No. 23 (1986): ___.

Robertson, John, comp. *Michigan in the War*. Lansing, Mich.: W. S. George & Co., 1882.

Rosser, Thomas L. *Addresses of Gen'l T. L. Rosser, at the Seventh Annual Reunion of the Association of the Maryland Line, Academy of Music, Baltimore, Md., February 22, 1889 and on Memorial Day, Staunton, Va., June 8, 1889*. New York: The L. A. Williams Printing Co., 1889.

Saussy, G. N. "Color of His Uniform Misunderstood." *Confederate Veteran* 16 (1908): 262.

———. "Stuart's Men Were Weary When They Reached Lee," *Richmond Times-Dispatch,* March 20, 1910.

Scott, James K. P. *The Story of the Battles at Gettysburg.* Harrisburg: The Telegraph Press, 1927.

Scott, John. *Partisan Life with Col. John S. Mosby.* New York: Harper & Bros., 1867.

Selvage, Edwin. "Reunited at Gettysburg." *Confederate Veteran* 30 (1922): 445-46.

Shoemaker, John J. *Shoemaker's Battery, Stuart Horse Artillery, Pelham's Battalion, Army of Northern Virginia.* Memphis, Tenn.: privately published, n.d.

Smith, John Day. *The History of the Nineteenth Regiment of Maine Volunteer Infantry 1862-1865.* Minneapolis: Great Western Printing Co., 1909.

Smith, Thomas West. *The Story of a Cavalry Regiment: "Scott's 900", Eleventh New York Cavalry From the St. Lawrence River to the Gulf of Mexico, 1861-1865.* Chicago: Veteran Assoc. of the Regiment, 1897.

Sorrel, G. Moxley. *Recollections of a Confederate Staff Officer.* New York: Neal Pub. Co., 1905.

Stevenson, James H. *"Boots and Saddles": A History of the First Volunteer Cavalry of the War, Known as the First New York (Lincoln) Cavalry and also as the Sabre Regiment, Its Organization, Campaigns and Battles.* Harrisburg, Pa.: Patriot Publishing Co., 1879.

Styple, William B., ed. *Writing & Fighting the Confederate War: The Letters of Peter Wellington Alexander, Confederate War Correspondent.* Kearny, N. J.: Belle Grove Publishing Co., 2002.

Swallow, William. "From Fredericksburg to Gettysburg." *Gettysburg Sources.* Edited by James L. McLean, Jr. and Judy W. McLean. 3 vols. Baltimore: Butternut & Blue, 1897. 2:1-36.

T. H. M. "Letter from the Californians in the Massachusetts Contingent." *Alta California,* August 2, 1863.

Taylor, Walter H. *Four Years With General Lee.* New York: D. Appleton, 1877.

———. *General Lee: His Campaigns in Virginia 1861 to 1865 with Personal Reminiscences.* Norfolk, Va.: Nusbaum Book and News Co., 1906.

"Tenth Annual Reunion of the Virginia Division Army Northern Virginia Association. Address of Major H. B. McClellan, of Lexington, Ky., on the Life, Campaigns, and Character of Gen'l. J.E.B. Stuart." *Southern Historical Society Papers* 8 (1880): 448-449.

"The Thirteenth Regiment of Virginia Cavalry in Gen. J.E.B. Stuart's Raid into Pennsylvania." *The Southern Bivouac* 1 (1883): 203-207.

Tobie, Edward P. *A History of the First Maine Cavalry 1861-1865.* Boston: Press of Emery & Hughes, 1887.

Toms, George W. "Kilpatrick's Cavalry at the Battle of Gettysburg." *The National Tribune,* September 17, 1885.

———. "Hanover, Pa." *The National Tribune,* September 15, 1887.

Tower, R. Lockwood, ed. *Lee's Adjutant: The Wartime Letters of Colonel Walter Herron Taylor, 1862-1865.* Columbia: University of South Carolina Press, 1995.

Trout, Robert J., ed. *In the Saddle With Stuart: The Story of Frank Smith Robertson of Jeb Stuart's Staff.* Gettysburg, Pa.: Thomas Publications, 1998.

———. *Riding With Stuart: Reminiscences of an Aide-de-Camp*. Shippensburg, Pa: White Mane Publishing Co., 1994.

United States War Department. *The War of the Rebellion: A Compilation of the Official Records of the Union and Confederate Armies*. 70 vols. in 128 parts. Washington: Government Printing Office, 1880-1901.

Vaughn, Robert V. "The Pennsylvania Militia: They Rendered Important Service During the Gettysburg Campaign." *The National Tribune*, April 1, 1915.

Vickers, George Morley. *Under Both Flags, A Panorama of the Great Civil War*. Philadelphia: People's Publishing Co., 1896.

Walker, Francis Amasa. *History of the Second Army Corps in the Army of the Potomac*. New York: Charles Scribner's Sons, 1886.

Wittenberg, Eric J., ed. *At Custer's Side: The Civil War Writings of James Harvey Kidd*. Kent, Ohio: The Kent State University Press, 2000.

———. *One of Custer's Wolverines: The Civil War Letters of Bvt. Brig. Gen. James H. Kidd, Sixth Michigan Cavalry*. Kent, Ohio: The Kent State University Press, 1999.

Wolf, Hazel C., ed. "Campaigning with the First Minnesota: A Civil War Diary." *Minnesota History* 25, no. 4 (December 1944): 342-61.

Young, Jesse Bowman. *The Battle of Gettysburg: A Comprehensive Narrative*. New York: Harper, 1913.

SECONDARY SOURCES

Articles

Brennan, Patrick. "It Wasn't Stuart's Fault." *North & South*, Vol. 6, No. 5 (July 2003): 22-39.

Calihan, David L. "Jeb Stuart's Fateful Ride." *The Gettysburg Magazine* 24 (January 2001): 6-18.

Chapman, John M. "Comanches on the War Path: The 35th Battalion Virginia Cavalry in the Gettysburg Campaign." *Civil War Regiments*, Vol. 6, No. 3 (1999): 1-30.

Cunningham, Steve A. and Beth A. White. "'The Ground Trembled as They Came': The 1st West Virginia Cavalry in the Gettysburg Campaign." *Civil War Regiments* Vol. 6, No. 3 (1999): 59-88.

Flower, Milton E. "Wednesday, July 1, 1863." *Essays on the Confederate Invasion, Occupation, and Bombardment of Carlisle During the Gettysburg Campaign of 1863*. Carlisle, Pa.: Cumberland County Historical Society, 1963: 17-18.

Gorman, Paul R. "J.E.B. Stuart and Gettysburg." *The Gettysburg Magazine* 1 (July 1989): 86-92.

Haines, Douglas Craig. "Jeb Stuart's Advance to Gettysburg." *Gettysburg: Historical Articles of Lasting Interest* 29 (July 2003): 26-61.

———. "R. S. Ewell's Command June 29-July 1, 1863." *Gettysburg: Historical Articles of Lasting Interest* 9 (July 1993): 17-32.

Herbert, T. W. "In Occupied Pennsylvania." *The Georgia Review*, vol. 4, no. 2 (1950): 103-114.

King, G. Wayne. "General Judson Kilpatrick." *New Jersey History* 91 (Spring 1973): 35-52.

Klingensmith, Harold A. "A Cavalry Regiment's First Campaign: The 18th Pennsylvania at Gettysburg." *The Gettysburg Magazine* 20 (June 1999): 51-74.

Krepps, John. "Before and After Hanover: Tracing Stuart's Cavalry Movements of June 30, 1863." *Blue and Gray* Vol. XXI, No. 1 (2003): 47-51.

Krolick, Marshall D. "Lee vs. Stuart: The Gettysburg Altercation." *Virginia Country's Civil War* 2 (1984): 22-32 and 34.

Longacre, Edward G. "Judson Kilpatrick." *Civil War Times Illustrated* 10 (April 1971): 24-33.

Miller, William E. "Troops Occupying Carlisle, July 1863." *A Paper Read Before a Meeting of the Hamilton Library Association, Carlisle, Pa., November 27, 1902.* Carlisle, Pa.: Cumberland County Historical Society, 1902.

Nye, Wilbur Sturtevant. "The Affair at Hunterstown." *Civil War Times Illustrated* (February 1971): 29-30.

Petruzzi, J. David. "The Fleeting Fame of Alfred Pleasonton." *America's Civil War* Vol. 18, No. 1 (March 2005): 22-28.

Petruzzi, J. David. "He Rides Over Everything in Sight." *America's Civil War*, Vol. 19, No. 1 (March 2006), 42-49.

Powell, David. "Stuart's Ride: Lee, Stuart, and the Confederate Cavalry in the Gettysburg Campaign." *The Gettysburg Magazine* 20 (January 1999): 27-43.

Ryan, Thomas J. "A Battle of Wits: Intelligence Operations During the Gettysburg Campaign. Part 3: Searching for Lee." *The Gettysburg Magazine* 31 (July 2004): 6-38.

———. "A Battle of Wits: Intelligence Operations During the Gettysburg Campaign. Part 4: The Intelligence Factor at Gettysburg." *The Gettysburg Magazine* 32 (January 2005): 7-38.

———. "Kilpatrick Bars Stuart's Route to Gettysburg." *The Gettysburg Magazine* 27 (July 2002): 7-28.

Schultz, Fred L. "A Cavalry Fight Was On." *Civil War Times Illustrated.* Vol. 23, No. 10 (February, 1985): 14-17 and 44-47.

Shevchuk, Paul M. "The Battle of Hunterstown, Pennsylvania, July 2, 1863." *The Gettysburg Magazine* 1 (July 1989): 93-104.

———. "The Lost Hours of 'JEB' Stuart." *The Gettysburg Magazine* 4 (January 1991): 65-74.

———. "The Wounding of Albert Jenkins, July 2, 1863." *The Gettysburg Magazine* 3 (July 1990): 51-63.

Thompson, D. W. "Salute to Baldy Smith." *Essays on the Confederate Invasion, Occupation, and Bombardment of Carlisle During the Gettysburg Campaign of 1863.* Carlisle, Pa.: Cumberland County Historical Society, 1963: 33-35.

Tucker, Glenn. "The Cavalry Invasion of the North." *Civil War Times Illustrated*, Vol. 2, No. 2 (July 1963): 18-20.

Winschel, Terry. "The Jeff Davis Legion at Gettysburg." *The Gettysburg Magazine* 12 (July 1995): 68-82.

Zimmerman, Daniel. "J.E.B. Stuart: Gettysburg Scapegoat?" *America's Civil War* 11 (May 1998): 50-57.

BOOKS

Allardice, Bruce S. *More Generals in Gray*. Baton Rouge: Louisiana State University Press, 1995.

Anthony, William. *Anthony's History of the Battle of Hanover (York County, Pennsylvania), Tuesday, June 30, 1863*. Hanover, Pa.: privately published, 1945.

Balfour, Daniel T. *13th Virginia Cavalry*. Lynchburg, Va.: H. E. Howard Co., 1986.

Bates, Samuel P. *History of Cumberland County, Pennsylvania*. Chicago: Warner Beers & Co., 1886.

——. *The Battle of Gettysburg*. Philadelphia: T. H. Davis & Co., 1875.

Bowden, Scott E. and Bill Ward. *Last Chance for Victory: Robert E. Lee and the Gettysburg Campaign*. Conshohocken, Pa.: Savas Publishing Co., 2001.

Brennan, Patrick. *"To Die Game": James Ewell Brown "Jeb" Stuart*. Gettysburg, Pa.: Farnsworth House Military Impressions, 1998.

Brown, R. Shepard. *Stringfellow of the Fourth: The Amazing Career of the Most Successful Confederate Spy*. New York: Crown Publishers, 1960.

Bundy, Carol. *The Nature of Sacrifice: A Biography of Charles Russell Lowell, Jr., 1835-64*. New York: Farrar, Straus & Giroux, 2005.

Busey, John W. and David G. Martin. *Regimental Strengths and Losses at Gettysburg*. Hightstown, N.J.: Longstreet House, 1986.

Cisco, Walter Brian. *Wade Hampton: Confederate Warrior, Conservative Statesman*. Washington, D.C.: Brassey's, Inc., 2004.

Civic Club of Carlisle, Pennsylvania. *Carlisle Old and New*. Harrisburg, Pa.: J. Horace McFarland Co., 1907.

Clark, Walter, ed. *Histories of the Several Regiments and Battalions from North Carolina in the Great War, 1861-1865*. 5 vols. Goldsboro, N.C.: Nash Brothers, 1901.

Coddington, Edwin B. *The Gettysburg Campaign: A Study in Command*. New York: Charles Scribner's Sons, 1968.

Commonwealth of Pennsylvania. *Report of the Select Committee Relative to the Soldiers' National Cemetery*. Harrisburg, PA: Singerly & Myers, State Printers, 1865.

"Corbit's Charge": Civil War Self-Guided Tour in Westminster, Maryland. Westminster, MD: Carroll County, Vistory Center, n.d.

Daly, Louise Haskell. *Alexander Cheves Haskell: The Portrait of a Man*. Norwood, Mass.: Plimpton Press, 1934.

Davis, Burke. *Jeb Stuart: The Last Cavalier*. New York: Rinehart, 1957.

Diffendorfer, G. M. *Cumberland County's Bit in the Gettysburg Campaign, As It Might Have Been Viewed by an Eyewitness Almost a Century Ago*. Carlisle, Pa.: Cumberland Valley Savings & Loan Assoc., 1962.

Divine, John E. *35th Battalion Virginia Cavalry*. Lynchburg, Va.: H. E. Howard Co., 1985.

Dowdey, Clifford. *Death of a Nation: The Story of Lee and His Men at Gettysburg*. New York: Alfred A. Knopf, 1958.

Driver, Robert J., Jr. and Harold E. Howard. *2nd Virginia Cavalry*. Lynchburg, Va.: H. E. Howard Co., 1995.

Driver, Robert J., Jr. *1st Virginia Cavalry*. Lynchburg, Va.: H. E. Howard Co., 1991.

——. *5th Virginia Cavalry*. Lynchburg, Va.: H. E. Howard Co., 1997.

———. *10ᵗʰ Virginia Cavalry*. Lynchburg, Va.: H.E. Howard Co., 1992.

———. *39ᵗʰ Battalion Virginia Cavalry*. Lynchburg, Va: H.E. Howard, Co. 1996.

———. *First and Second Maryland Cavalry, C.S.A.* Charlottesville, Va.: Rockbridge Publishing, 1999.

Eicher, John H. and David J. Eicher. *Civil War High Commands*. Stanford, Ca.: Stanford University Press, 2001.

Freeman, Douglas Southall. *Lee's Lieutenants: A Study in Command*. 3 vols. New York: Charles Scribner's Sons, 1944.

———. *R. E. Lee: A Biography*. 4 vols. New York: Charles Scribner's Sons, 1935.

Furgurson, Ernest B. *Chancellorsville 1863: The Souls of the Brave*. New York: Alfred A. Knopf, 1992.

Gibson, John, ed. *History of York County, Pennsylvania, From the Earliest Period to the Present Time, Divided Into General, Special, Township and Borough Histories, With a Biographical Department Appended*. Chicago: F. A. Battey, 1886.

Gladfelter, Armand. *The Flowering of the Codorus Palatine: A History of North Codorus Township PA 1838-1988 York, PA*. York, Pa.: Sesquicentennial Commission, 1988.

Goodyear, Samuel M. *General Robert E. Lee's Invasion of Carlisle, 1863*. Carlisle, Pa.: Cumberland County Historical Society, 1942.

Gottfried, Bradley M. *Roads to Gettysburg: Lee's Invasion of the North, 1863*. Shippensburg, Pa.: White Mane Books, 2001.

Hackley, Woodford B. *The Little Fork Rangers: A Sketch of Company D Fourth Virginia Cavalry*. Richmond, Va.: Press of the Dietz Printing Co., 1927.

Hanover Area Historical Society. *History and Battle of Hanover*. Hanover, Pa.: privately published, 2002.

Harrell, Roger D. *The 2ⁿᵈ North Carolina Cavalry*. Jefferson, N. C.: McFarland, 2004.

Helm, Lewis Marshall. *Black Horse Cavalry: Defend Our Beloved Country*. Falls Church, Va.: Higher Education Publications, 2004.

Heitman, Francis B. *Historical Register and Dictionary of the United States Army*. 2 vols. Washington, D.C.: U.S. Government Printing Office, 1903.

The Historical Publication Committee of the Hanover Chamber of Commerce. *Prelude to Gettysburg: Encounter at Hanover*. Shippensburg, PA: Burd Street Press, 1962.

Holland, Lynwood M. *Pierce Young: The Warwick of the South*. Athens, Ga.: University of Georgia Press, 1964.

Hopkins, Donald A. *The Little Jeff: The Jeff Davis Legion, Cavalry, Army of Northern Virginia*. Shippensburg, Pa.: White Mane, 1999.

Keen, Hugh C. and Horace Mewborn. *43ʳᵈ Battalion Virginia Cavalry Mosby's Command*. Lynchburg, Va.: H. E. Howard, 1993.

King, Elanine, William L. Ziegler, and H. Alvin Jones. *History of New Oxford: Looking at the Past, 1874-1974, 100ᵗʰ Anniversary*. New Oxford, Pa.: privately published, 1974.

Kirshner, Ralph. *The Class of 1861: Custer, Ames, and Their Classmates after West Point*. Carbondale, Ill.: Southern Illinois University Press, 1999.

Klein, Frederic Shriver. *Just South of Gettysburg: Carroll County, Maryland in the Civil War*. Westminster, Md.: The Newman Press, 1963.

Krick, Robert E. L. *Staff Officers in Gray: A Biographical Register of the Staff Officers in the Army of Northern Virginia*. Chapel Hill: University of North Carolina Press, 2003.

Krick, Robert K. *Lee's Colonels: A Biographical Roster of the Field Officers of the Army of Northern Virginia*. 4th ed. Dayton, Ohio: Morningside, 1992.

——. *9th Virginia Cavalry*. Lynchburg, Va.: H. E. Howard Co., 1982.

——. *The Gettysburg Death Roster: The Confederate Dead at Gettysburg*. Dayton, OH: Morningside Press, 1985.

Lambert, Dobbie Edward. *Grumble: The W. E. Jones Brigade 1863-64*. Wahiawa, Hi.: Lambert Enterprises, Inc., 1992.

Longacre, Edward G. *The Cavalry at Gettysburg: A Tactical Study of Mounted Operations During the Civil War's Pivotal Campaign, 9 June-14 July 1863*. Rutherford, N. J.: Fairleigh-Dickinson University Press, 1986.

——. *Custer and His Wolverines: The Michigan Cavalry Brigade, 1861-1865*. Conshohocken, Pa.: Combined Publishing, 1997.

——. *Fitz Lee: A Military Biography of Major General Fitzhugh Lee, C.S.A.* New York: Da Capo Press, 2005.

——. *Gentleman and Soldier: A Biography of Wade Hampton III*. Nashville, Tenn.: Rutledge Hill, 2003.

——. *Lee's Cavalrymen: A History of the Mounted Forces of the Army of Northern Virginia*. Mechanicsburg, Pa.: Stackpole, 2002.

Lovelace, David Shriver. *The Shrivers: Under Two Flags*. Westminster, Md.: Willow Bend Books, 2003.

Marshal, Francis. *The Battle of Gettysburg: The Crest-Wave of the American Civil War*. New York: The Neale Publishing Co., 1914.

Martin, Samuel J. *Kill-Cavalry: The Life of Union General Hugh Judson Kilpatrick*. Mechanicsburg, Pa.: Stackpole Books, 2000.

McClure, James. *East of Gettysburg: A Gray Shadow Crosses York County, Pa.* York, Pa.: York Daily Record, 2003.

——. *Almost Forgotten: A Glimpse of Black History in York County, Pa.* York, Pa.: York Daily Record, 2002.

McPherson, James M. *Battle Cry of Freedom*. New York: Oxford University Press, 1988.

Michigan Monument Commission. *Michigan at Gettysburg: July 1, 2, 3, 1863*. Detroit, Mich.: Winn & Hammond, 1889.

Mingus, Scott, Sr. *Flames Beyond the Susquehanna: The Gordon Expedition, June 1863*. Columbus, Ohio: Ironclad Publishing, 2006.

Moore, Robert H., II. *The 1st and 2nd Stuart Horse Artillery*. Lynchburg, Va.: H. E. Howard Co., 1985.

Morgan, James A., III. *Always Ready, Always Willing: A History of Battery M, Second U.S. Artillery from its Organization Through the Civil War*. Gaithersburg, Md.: Olde Soldier Books, Inc., n.d.

Morgan, James Henry. *Dickinson College: The History of One Hundred and Fifty Years 1783-1933*. Carlisle, Pa.: Dickinson College, 1933.

Nanzig, Thomas P. *3rd Virginia Cavalry*. Lynchburg, Va.: H. E. Howard Co., 1989.

Nesbitt, Mark. *Saber and Scapegoat: J.E.B. Stuart and the Gettysburg Controversy.* Mechanicsburg, Pa.: Stackpole Books, 1994.

Nichols, James L. *General Fitzhugh Lee: A Biography*. Lynchburg, Va.: H. E. Howard Co., 1989.

Nye, Wilbur Sturtevant. *Here Come the Rebels!* Baton Rouge: Louisiana State University Press, 1965.

O'Neill, Robert F., Jr. *The Cavalry Battles of Aldie, Middleburg and Upperville, Small but Important Riots, June 10-27, 1863*. Lynchburg, Va.: H. E. Howard Co., 1993.

Pfanz, Harry W. *Gettysburg: Culp's Hill and Cemetery Hill*. Chapel Hill: University of North Carolina Press, 1993.

Phisterer, Frederick. *New York in the War of the Rebellion, 1861-1865*. Albany: J.B. Lyon Co., 1912.

Prowell, George Reeser. *History of York County, Pennsylvania*. Chicago: J. H. Beers & Co., 1907.

Raus, Edmund J., Jr. *A Generation on the March: The Union Army at Gettysburg*. Gettysburg, Pa.: Thomas Publications, 1998.

Robertson, John. *Michigan in the War*. Lansing, Mich.: W.S. George & Co., 1882.

Rummel, George A., III. *Cavalry on the Roads to Gettysburg: Kilpatrick at Hanover and Hunterstown*. Shippensburg, Pa.: White Mane, 2000.

Schildt, John W. *Roads to Gettysburg*. Parsons, W.V.: McClain Printing Co., 1978.

Sears, Stephen W. *Gettysburg*. Boston: Houghton Mifflin Co., 2003.

Soderberg, Susan Cooke. *A Guide to Civil War Sites in Maryland: Blue and Gray in a Border State*. Shippensburg, Pa: White Mane, 1986.

Stackpole, Edward J. *They Met at Gettysburg*. Harrisburg, Pa.: Eagle Books, 1956.

Starr, Stephen Z. *The Union Cavalry in the Civil War*. 3 vols. Baton Rouge: Louisiana State University Press, 1979.

Stiles, Kenneth L. *4th Virginia Cavalry*. Lynchburg, Va.: H. E. Howard, Co., 1985.

Thomas, Emory N. *Bold Dragoon: The Life of J.E.B. Stuart*. New York: Harper & Row, 1986.

Thomason, John W., Jr. *Jeb Stuart*. New York: Charles Scribner's Sons, 1929.

Thompson, D. W., ed. *Two Hundred Years in Cumberland County*. Carlisle, Pa.: Hamilton Library and Historical Assoc. of Cumberland County, 1951.

Tousey, Thomas G. *Military History of Carlisle and Carlisle Barracks*. Richmond: The Dietz Press, 1939.

Trout, Robert J. *Galloping Thunder: The Stuart Horse Artillery Battalion*. Mechanicsburg, Pa.: Stackpole Books, 2002.

——. *They Followed the Plume: The Story of J.E.B. Stuart and His Staff.* Mechanicsburg, Pa.: Stackpole Books, 1993.

Trudeau, Noah Andre. *Gettysburg: A Testing of Courage*. New York: Harper Collins, 2002.

Tucker, Glenn. *High Tide at Gettysburg*. Indianapolis: Bobbs-Merrill, 1958.

The Union Mills Homestead Foundation. *Union Mills Homestead: 200 Years of History*. Union Mills, Md.: privately published, 1997.

Urwin, Gregory J. W. *Custer Victorious: The Civil War Battles of General George Armstrong Custer*. East Brunswick, N. J.: Associated University Presses, 1983.

Warner, Ezra J. *Generals in Blue: The Lives of the Union Commanders*. Baton Rouge: Louisiana State University Press, 1964.

———. *Generals in Gray: The Lives of the Confederate Commanders*. Baton Rouge: Louisiana State University Press, 1959.

Wellman, Manly Wade. *Giant in Gray: A Biography of Wade Hampton of South Carolina*. New York: Charles Scribner's Sons, 1949.

———. *Gray Riders: Jeb Stuart and His Men*. New York: Aladdin/Macmillan, 1954.

Wert, Jeffry D. *Custer: The Controversial Life of George Armstrong Custer*. New York: Simon & Schuster, 1996.

Whittaker, Frederick. *A Popular Life of Gen. George A. Custer*. New York: Sheldon & Co., 1876.

Wilson, James Harrison. *Captain Charles Corbit's Charge at Westminster With a Squadron of the First Delaware Cavalry, June 29, 1863*. Wilmington: The Historical Society of Delaware, 1913.

———. *The Life and Services of Brevet Brigadier-General Andrew Jonathan Alexander, United States Army*. New York: privately published, 1887.

Wing, Conway P. *History of Cumberland County*. Carlisle, Pa.: Cumberland County Historical Society, 1982.

Wittenberg, Eric J. *Gettysburg's Forgotten Cavalry Actions*. Gettysburg, Pa.: Thomas Publications, 1998.

———. *Protecting the Flank: The Battles for Brinkerhoff's Ridge and East Cavalry Field, Gettysburg, Pennsylvania*. Celina, Ohio: Ironclad Publishing, 2002.

———. *The Union Cavalry Comes of Age: Hartwood Church to Brandy Station, 1863*. Dulles, Va.: Brassey's, 2003.

Women's Club of Mercersburg. *Old Mercersburg*. New York: Frank Allaben Genealogical Co., 1912.

Woodward, Harold J. Jr. *Defender of the Valley: Brigadier General John Daniel Imboden C.S.A.* Berryville, Va.: Rockbridge Publishing, 1996.

Woodworth, Steven E. *Beneath a Northern Sky: A Short History of the Gettysburg Campaign*. Wilmington, Del.: Scholarly Resources, 2003.

Young, Bennett. *Confederate Wizards of the Saddle*. Boston: Chapple Publishing Co., 1914.

Young, Ronald C. *Lancaster County, Pennsylvania in the Civil War*. Lancaster, Pa.: privately published, 2003.

Index